PRAISE FOR **WORLD CLASS**

"You can't talk about the history of U.S. soccer without including Grant Wahl. His legendary career and fearless advocacy for the LGBTQ+ community will be a legacy that lives on through this anthology and beyond."

—**MEGAN RAPINOE**

"For me, Grant Wahl's *Sports Illustrated* cover story was the moment everything started. The time that we shared when I was in high school for that story was pretty special for me and my family. Grant was always energetic, always had a smile on his face, and always wanted to do right by his interview subjects. I was a sixteen-year-old kid from Akron, Ohio, and hadn't done anything of that magnitude before. When that story dropped, and it was written by Grant Wahl, you knew we were going to be linked for the rest of our lives. That cover story will live long beyond all of us and our families. Grant was an unbelievable person and I know he's looking down on all of us in pure joy and happiness, seeing his friends, family, colleagues, and everyone giving him his flowers, because he deserves that. This collection of Grant's work is a great testament to not only what he did when he was here, but what he's still doing to impact others."

—**LEBRON JAMES**

"I hesitate to call this collection sportswriting at its best, because I think it is just writing at its best. To me, Grant was an anthropologist, and sports was his lens for studying humanity."

—**DAVID EPSTEIN**, *New York Times* bestselling author
of *Range* and *The Sports Gene*

"For American fans, it is not enough to love soccer; we are also duty-bound to promote the sport to our otherwise distracted countryfolk. No one exemplified this better than Grant Wahl. This lovingly curated treasury of Wahl's work is more than a collection of world-class sportswriting; it is a record of soccer's meteoric rise in America over the course of his career, an ascension that he fomented as much as anyone else by rendering this 'foreign' sport accessible to millions. To read this book is to connect with and better understand a titan of the American game."

—**BRENDAN HUNT**, aka Coach Beard, co-creator of *Ted Lasso*

"Grant Wahl's job was to write about sports, but his art was to reveal what matters most in life. This anthology is a collection of brilliant storytelling and timeless wisdom about excellence from a world-class professional. He was the best of us, and his work lives on to make us all better."

—**ADAM GRANT**, #1 *New York Times* bestselling author of *Hidden Potential* and *Think Again*

"The title says everything: Grant was absolutely world class in everything he did. He was a world-class writer. He was a world-class person. He was a world-class friend. Reading his work again reminds me just how much he loved telling stories and standing up for what he believed in. Every word in this book surges with his energy and enthusiasm and love. I was one of the luckiest people in the world to get to know Grant. I miss him. But he's here in this wonderful collection of his best work."

—**JOE POSNANSKI**, *New York Times* bestselling author of *Why We Love Baseball*

"Here, arrayed for all to enjoy, is a glimpse into Grant's wide-ranging interests and extravagant talents: a mix of classic sportswriting and this century's answer to New Journalism; meticulously reported pieces and informed opinion; men and women; soccer and beyond; American and international. And the title could not be more apt, as Grant was—

and his work and legacy remain—world class. Grant was all class and tops in his class, with few peers matching his quality, rigor, vigor, and unswerving honor. He also considered the entire planet his beat, going wherever the story took him. Damn, we miss him."

—**L. JON WERTHEIM**, *Sports Illustrated* writer
and *60 Minutes* correspondent

"Grant Wahl took the craft of writing seriously, and he took the sport soccer seriously. His dedication to each of them resulted in some of the best, most compelling sports writing I've ever read. When a new Grant Wahl article came out, I dropped everything and read it. When a new Grant Wahl podcast episode dropped, it immediately went to the top of the queue. I will miss him and I will miss his work. He made me a better writer. He made me a better fan."

—**CLINT SMITH**, *New York Times* bestselling author
of *How the Word Is Passed*

WORLD CLASS

WORLD CLASS

Purpose, Passion, and the Pursuit of Greatness On and Off the Field

GRANT WAHL

Foreword by Dr. Céline Gounder

Edited by **Mark Mravic** and **Alexander Wolff**

BALLANTINE BOOKS
NEW YORK

Published in the United States by Ballantine Books, an imprint of Random House, a division of Penguin Random House LLC, New York.

BALLANTINE BOOKS & colophon are registered trademarks of Penguin Random House LLC.

Grateful acknowledgment is made to the following for permission to reprint previously published material:
Authentic Brands Group: Articles by Grant Wahl which were originally published in *Sports Illustrated,* copyright © Authentic Brands Group. Reprinted by permission.
The Daily Princetonian: "Rethinking the Legacy of 'Legendary' Pete Carril" by Grant Wahl, copyright © 1996 by *The Daily Princetonian.*

Photography credits can be found on page 323.

LIBRARY OF CONGRESS CATALOGING-IN-PUBLICATION DATA
Names: Wahl, Grant, author. | Wolff, Alexander, 1957– editor. | Mravic, Mark, 1962– editor.
Title: World class : purpose, passion, and the pursuit of greatness on and off the field / Grant Wahl ; edited by Mark Mravic and Alexander Wolff.
Description: First edition. | New York : Ballantine Books, 2024. | Includes bibliographical references.
Identifiers: LCCN 2023056275 (print) | LCCN 2023056276 (ebook) | ISBN 9780593726761 (hardcover) | ISBN 9780593726778 (ebook)
Subjects: LCSH: Sports journalism—United States. | Sports—United States.
Classification: LCC PN4784.S6 W34 2024 (print) | LCC PN4784.S6 (ebook) | DDC 070.4/497960973—dc23/eng/20240117
LC record available at https://lccn.loc.gov/2023056275
LC ebook record available at https://lccn.loc.gov/2023056276

Printed in the United States of America on acid-free paper

randomhousebooks.com

9 8 7 6 5 4 3 2 1

FIRST EDITION

Book design by Simon M. Sullivan

For Helen Wahl and Gloria Emerson

M ORE THAN A MILLION SPECTATORS GATHERED IN AUSTRALIA and New Zealand for the 2023 Women's World Cup. My husband, Grant Wahl, was supposed to be one of them. He had been to every Men's and Women's World Cup, except one, since 1994—fourteen in all. But this one was special: Thirty-two teams played, showcasing the global expansion and competitiveness of women's soccer. It was an opportunity to promote gender equality in sports and inspire young girls to pursue their dreams on the football pitch. It was expected to set a new bar for women's achievement in sports on the world stage. It was that and, as is so often the case with sports, so much more.

The U.S. Women's National Team, the favorite to win the competition, would lose to Sweden in a penalty shootout in the first knockout round. After the loss, USWNT star forward Megan Rapinoe posted on social media: "This game is so beautiful, even in its cruelest moments. . . . We lay it all out on the line every single time. Fighting with everything that we have, for everything we deserve, for every person we possibly can." Even before the start of the tournament, the USWNT had been fighting both on and off the field: a gender discrimination lawsuit pressing for equity in pay and working conditions with the men's team; an onslaught of "discriminatory, abusive, or menacing messages" on social media; and right-wing attacks, which turned to celebration after their defeat.

Spain, not the United States, won the tournament, defeating England 1–0. But that victory was overshadowed by the scandal that ensued. Luis Rubiales, at the time the head of the Royal Spanish Football Federation, kissed the Spanish forward Jenni Hermoso on the lips without her consent during the awards ceremony. This attack was just one of many indignities and offenses suffered by Spanish women soccer players over the years. The players were subjected to Orwellian surveillance. The team's coach for almost three decades called the players *chavalitas,* slang for "young girls." The Women's World Cup kicked off with the Spanish team in a full-on rebellion against its own federation, which made their triumph all the more remarkable.

As riveting as the action on and off the field may have been, I couldn't bring myself to watch the 2023 Women's World Cup. I followed at a distance in print and on the radio. Each story left me feeling gutted, freshly conscious of Grant's absence—not only in World Cup coverage, but at the center of my life. I know he would have been covering the tournament as he had the 2022 Men's World Cup in Qatar: not just the beautiful game on the pitch, but also the fight for equity, social justice, and human rights. He would have been holding FIFA, the soccer federations, politicians, and pundits to account.

Still, I had the comfort of shared grief—friends and colleagues (Grant's and mine alike) reached out to me, wondering what Grant would make of this or that game or goal or gaffe. The sense that *Grant should be there* was shared, and even in the acuteness of his absence, it brought comfort. I dreaded a time when his absence might *not* be broadly felt—four or six or twelve years in the future, when Grant's writing might be a distant memory, when there'd no longer be an empty seat and framed portrait in the press box in his honor. And because the events Grant covered were rooted so firmly in time, I think I feared that as we moved away from those moments, the whole constellation of his existence might recede, the light of his life growing dimmer by the day.

"Grief is not an emotion to move on from," said writer and podcaster Nora McInerny in a 2018 TED Talk. "It's a reality to move forward with." Some of my work in mourning has been to understand Grant's absence as presence—not naively, not religiously, not even as consolation, but as simple acknowledgment of our interwoven lives, a transmutation of loss into a different form of life and love.

In the weeks following Grant's death, as those of us who loved him struggled to articulate what he'd meant to us, we longed to nail down his presence—to fix it in words, in time, in truth.

Yet if I've learned anything in the past twelve months, it's that my relationship with Grant could not *be* pinned down—not then, not now— and that it didn't end with his death. I carry Grant with me not as a fixed image in a locket or a butterfly pinned to a board, but as a dynamic presence—his mind and his wit still swift and agile, responding both to the world he knew and to the one shaped, in part, by his absence.

Grant covered sports like this, too—in a way that allowed his meaning, his sensibility, his understanding to extend beyond the present moment and the present game, to take up the past and move into the future. Over the course of his career, Grant was told that he should "stick to sports." But in his mind, this was a false mantra. To "stick to sports"—to limit a story to the scoreboard, to dissection of a play, to the dribbles and drills of practice—is to strip sports of their meaning, power, and soul. Grant had a profound respect for sports, which is why he took them so seriously, in their entirety. Sports aren't just an escape. Grant knew that sports change the world, just as the world changes sports. At the Women's World Cup in 2019—with Rapinoe accepting awards as a crowd chanted, "EQUAL PAY! EQUAL PAY!"—Grant felt that process in motion, a ball soaring in midair. So did Rapinoe. "I feel like this team is just in the midst of changing the world around us as we live," Rapinoe told Grant that summer, "and it's just an incredible feeling."

Rereading Grant's work is hard. As I remember him reporting the stories in this collection, I recall the broader context of our lives—shared dinners, piles of laundry, our travels in different directions, quarrels that seem petty in retrospect but were pressing at the time. I feel, too, Grant's nimble mind and invisible hand at work, weaving together voices and details in his jovial, kindhearted, voluble way. I hear his laughter, the undulating pitch and volume of his voice as he shares a story, hits upon a phrase he likes, tries out a new metaphor or idea. And as I reread his work and press on with my own, I feel myself tending *our* lives in a similar way—unspooling what he meant not only to me, but to soccer, and sports; tugging his sensibility forward, even as the games he covered stay pinned in the past.

I am not, as Grant well knew, a "sports person." Before his sudden death, the idea of me writing a foreword to *any* compendium of sportswriting—including his—would have been not just ill-advised, but ludicrous. I am here on the force of loss and love alone. Had I asked myself, before knowing Grant, *What is sports?*—I might have answered with a blank expression. *Sports is sports.* A field, a ball, a back-and-forth, a contest of skill or might or luck. Grant taught me that sports is so much more than athletics—that it draws on histories, class tensions, economics, politics, old grudges, stubborn hopes; that through sports, we revisit the past and recast the future; that we are shaped not only by our wins, but by our losses, and that both move with us through time.

Sports can be leadership, like that shown by Rapinoe and the USWNT. It can be about equity for women, people of color, and LGBTQ+ people. The rise of the USWNT paralleled the history of American feminism, a movement for equal rights, opportunities, and treatment for women *and* men. That history begins with Title IX and spans the 1985 Mundialito, or "little World Cup," in which women wore hand-me-down men's uniforms; the FIFA president Sepp Blatter's call for women's players to wear "tighter shorts" to increase their appeal; the days of getting paid ten dollar per diems while on the road; and, finally, a promise of equitable pay for players of the women's and men's national teams, an agreement reached in 2022.

For women like Grant's mother, Helen, born in 1932, the USWNT was about seeing women finally enjoying the opportunities to compete in sports that she was denied. "Mom's attachment to the USWNT was something deeper, something visceral, something that transcended sports and spoke to her about the life she had lived and the gains she had always wanted to see," Grant wrote. Foreshadowing the USWNT loss that would come four years after her death, Helen told Grant, "I love them so much." She added, "They don't even have to win it, and I'll still love them."

Sports can be politics, something Grant understood even before becoming a professional journalist. In his college senior thesis, "Playing the Political Game: Soccer Clubs in Argentine Civil Society," he argued that Argentine soccer clubs helped build social bonds across class and partisan affiliation, in much the same way that unions, service clubs, and the social gospel movement did in the United States throughout the twentieth century. Later he would write about the role of former Ivorian soccer player Didier Drogba in helping unite his nation and end civil war. "We've proved to you that the people of Ivory Coast can live together side by side, play together toward the same goal: qualifying for the World Cup," Drogba told Grant. In the aftermath of a controversial coup d'état in Honduras, interim president Roberto Micheletti told Grant that "without distinction among classes, political parties, religion or race, soccer brings everyone together." FC Barcelona's motto, *Més que un club*—Catalan for "More than a club"—"highlights Barcelona's place as a touchstone for Catalan identity," wrote Grant. The motto was as much about Barça's resistance to the rise of fascism and General Francisco Franco's dictatorship as it was about the romance of soccer.

Sports can be rivalry. Grant wrote about U.S. star Claudio Reyna's brutal introduction to the "Holy War" between Glasgow clubs Celtic (Catholic) and Rangers (Protestant), a rivalry over politics, class, and religion. In *Good Rivals,* a docuseries released on Prime Video shortly before Grant's death, Grant and his colleagues documented the social, political, and sports rivalry between the U.S. and Mexican men's national soccer teams. Grant's preferred title had been *Good Neighbors,* harking back to Franklin D. Roosevelt's "Good Neighbor Policy," to promote better relations between the United States and its Latin American neighbors. (The series's executive producer, John Skipper, was kind enough to give me a movie poster with the "correct" title.)

Sports can be solidarity in the worst and best of times. Bob Bradley, the soccer coach at Princeton when Grant was an undergrad there, would go on to coach the Egyptian national soccer team. Bradley and his wife lived near the center of Cairo to better understand his team's players at a turbulent time in the country. Just months into Bradley's tenure, a match between Egyptian soccer clubs Al Masry and Al Ahly turned deadly, the result of violent clashes among fans. Though Al Ahly wasn't directly involved in the political events of the Arab Spring, its passionate fan base, "the Ultras Ahlawy," played a significant role in the protests. Instead of leaving the country, Bradley told Grant, he and his wife stayed in solidarity with "his brothers," the players, joining thousands of Egyptians who converged on Sphinx Square to mourn the tragedy. There can be solidarity in grief and in joy. After host South Korea beat Italy in the 2022 Men's World Cup, "Koreans and non-Koreans alike danced on chairs to the music of Bryan Adams and Bon Jovi," Grant wrote from Seoul.

Sports can be geopolitics. After 9/11, fear of terrorism made it far more difficult for talented athletes like Kene Obi, a 7'1" Nigerian basketball player who was, as Grant wrote, "the most prized big man at the world's most remote big-man camp," to pursue his dream of moving abroad and playing in the NBA. A year after the U.S. invasion of Iraq, President George W. Bush featured the Iraqi Olympic team in campaign ads for his reelection. Iraqi players and their coach told Grant that those ads were offensive, sparking an international incident. "The American army has killed so many people in Iraq," the coach, Adnan Hamad, told Grant. "What is freedom when I go to the [national] stadium and there are shootings on the road?"

Sports can be corruption. FC Sheriff is the soccer team of Transnistria, a Russian-controlled region in Moldova and "a trial run for what [Russia] did with Crimea and Eastern Ukraine," as Grant put it. But Sheriff is much more than a soccer team. It's a "giant money-laundering front" for a weapons-trafficking business.

Sports can be accountability. Grant was a modern Nelly Bly, the muckraker who helped reform the treatment of mental illness through her undercover reporting from a New York City psychiatric institution, where she posed as a patient. Grant helped uncover the anti-democratic nature of FIFA by running for its presidency. He called for greater transparency, term limits for FIFA presidents, video replay technology, and a woman as FIFA's general secretary, "to change the old-boy network culture." Thousands of soccer fans from around the world "expressed their support on Twitter and Facebook . . . making clear that the simple message of cleaning up FIFA resonated around the globe," Grant wrote. But he discovered that "when it comes to the politics of the sport, the fans just don't matter. Not one bit. . . . The old men in the navy suits have all the power." Later, an investigation led by the U.S. Department of Justice resulted in corruption-related charges against dozens of FIFA officials and sports marketing executives, who were found to be involved in a complex web of racketeering, wire fraud, money laundering, and bribery involving the bidding processes and marketing and broadcast rights for the World Cup and other high-profile tournaments. In the wake of the scandal, Blatter stepped down as FIFA president. Even though Grant ultimately failed to persuade a member nation to nominate him for the role, some of his campaign pledges would come to pass under new leadership.

Sports can be cruelty. While as a student journalist Grant called former Princeton basketball coach Pete Carril a genius, he also called him out for the "chronic lack of respect" and "daily hell" he inflicted on his players. "Carril told [a] player to stop playing for his mother and think of the team. She had died; the player was still grieving," wrote Grant. A culture of fear deterred many from speaking up. Grant did so in their stead.

Sports can be human rights. While some sports journalists accepted free first-class travel to Qatar ahead of the 2022 World Cup, Grant went on his own dime to document the working conditions of migrant workers. Despite new labor laws, Grant found that employers were still confiscating workers' passports; agents were still charging them onerous recruitment fees; and workers in the country were still facing barriers to switching to better jobs. Worst of all, up to 70 percent of migrant worker deaths in Qatar were going uninvestigated. The head of the committee responsible for organizing the Qatar World Cup, Nasser Al-Khater, expressed irritation that journalists would cover the death of a Filipino migrant worker amid what he called a "successful World Cup." He told the BBC, "I mean, death is a natural part of life." But many migrant workers had given their lives in modern-day slavery. To Grant, the migrant workers' plight was "a human rights disaster." "They just don't care," he wrote.

Sports can be remembering, not just escaping, and *witnessing,* not just watching. Grant got an early lesson in bearing witness and remembering from his college mentor Gloria Emerson, a *New York Times* Vietnam correspondent. And it's perhaps why Grant would reread a paper he wrote in college, a profile of Emerson, before every big tournament, the last time weeks before his death—to remind himself of her guiding principles. "Morality is an activity, not a belief or a contemplative state," she told Grant. That activity was an exercise in what her Vietnamese translator Nguyen Ngoc Luong called "an acute lack of forgetfulness." Emerson told Grant that she sought "to find a new path and a way not just to write about Vietnam, but to teach Americans something about the war and ourselves." Grant sought to do the same through sports.

In perhaps the most enduring photo of Grant, and certainly one of the World Cup photos I cherish most, he's wearing a rainbow T-shirt at a pressroom workstation in Ahmad bin Ali Stadium in Qatar. I recognize the precise posture of his concentration—hands poised over his keyboard, shoulders tensed, brow slightly furrowed—the way I'd seen him at his laptop thousands of times, all of it conveying the alacrity and alertness of his mind. Shortly before the photo was taken, stadium guards had detained Grant for his show of LGBTQ+ allyship in a country that forbids same-sex relationships. Grant's brother, Eric, a gay man who'd experienced harassment while growing up in Kansas, had told Grant not to wear the shirt in Qatar. Grant wore it anyway. Eric regarded that gesture as a final, stubborn gift: the little brother standing up for the big one, half a world away. Grant understood that he could hold others accountable not only through his writing, but also through his actions, his questions, his provocations—through what he refused to look past or forget. On his blog that day, Grant asked, "What's it like for ordinary Qataris who might wear a rainbow shirt when the world isn't watching here?"

"FÚTBOL IS LIFE," says Dani Rojas, the exuberant goal-scoring import on the AFC Richmond team coached by Ted Lasso in the Apple TV series. To me it was fitting that *Ted Lasso* dedicated one of its last episodes to Grant. In many ways, Grant was a quiet revolutionary, much like Ted. Both were kindhearted, optimistic, humble midwestern guys. Both tried to mentor, inspire, and uplift those around them to do and be better. Both were beloved. And just as Ted's presence transcends the fictional show, Grant's writing transcends the game. I'll amend that quote on Grant's behalf to say, "Sports is life." Perhaps this lesson is Grant's greatest legacy.

DR. CÉLINE GOUNDER
December 2023

Contents

8. FAR AFIELD

9. TAKING A STAND

Introduction
Master of Modern Sportswriting
Alexander Wolff

Y OU MAY BE HOLDING THIS BOOK BECAUSE A FAN OF GRANT Wahl has pressed it into your hands. Or maybe you sought it out yourself because Grant helped you interpret a game you didn't entirely grasp but sensed that you should—that by better understanding soccer, you might better understand the world. Or perhaps you've come to this collection because you love soccer and Grant's artful, dedicated approach to the game matched your passion.

Or maybe you recognize Grant as having addressed the ugly side of the Beautiful Game, whether staking out worksites in Qatar to speak to migrant laborers to document the human cost of staging the 2022 World Cup, or finding himself detained at that competition for wearing a rainbow T-shirt in solidarity with persecuted LGBTQ+ Qataris and visiting fans who might be targeted.

Regardless of how you found your way into these pages, take a moment to recognize that you're part of a community, an uncountable number of connections among people and places, a welter of lines back and forth across continents and through press boxes and off satellite dishes that encompasses Grant's impact. Like the game with which he became most closely identified, he projected himself far and wide, making a difference with his life and work.

That life ended on the evening of Friday, December 9, 2022, in Lusail Stadium on the outskirts of Doha as Grant watched a spellbinding match between Argentina and the Netherlands move through extra time toward its endgame. He had only just turned forty-nine. The cause of death, determined by the New York City medical examiner after Grant's body had been repatriated to where he lived with his wife, Dr. Céline Gounder, was the rupture of an undetected, slow-growing aneurysm in the ascending aorta. That wasn't the work of Covid-19. It wasn't retaliation by a repressive regime that Grant had criticized. It certainly wasn't—as online trolls of Dr. Gounder, an infectious disease specialist and leading Covid mitigationist, had it—an adverse reaction to some vaccine. Try though they did, paramedics on the scene could not have saved Grant with CPR or electric shocks.*

Having come to this book, welcome. Or, as Grant would say, "Hey there"—the guileless signature with which he opened his podcast, delivered in a voice redolent of the Kansas City suburbs where he grew up.

Now that you have it, how might you use it? You can read it from front to back and absorb in one gulp the breadth of Grant's curiosity, talent, and dedication to readers, whether through iconic *Sports Illustrated* cover stories or bootleg classics from his college days. You can pick up with any of the nine thematic chapters, each featuring examples of a type of piece that Grant made his own, and treat yourself to a kind of master class in the craft of sportswriting, Grant Wahl 101. Or you can dip in randomly—Grant on shuffle—and be reminded each time how he could deliver an engaging, enlightening, relevant story.

Grant was the multitool modern sports journalist—quick to post, clear and direct, worldly, socially aware, able to write long or short or in between. He never talked down to the reader. He was keen to shed light and unafraid of the heat his work might give off. He brought old-school reportorial ethics into the twenty-first century, making sure to show his face after criticizing someone, because just as he stood by his words, he also never forgot that there was a human being at the other end of them. "He was one of those rare sportswriters you'd love to read a column from, a match report from, a profile, a podcast, a TV report," says sports media critic Bryan Curtis. "He really was built for the modern age of sportswriting."

Grant's career tracked with the evolution of the craft over the three decades he practiced it. He embraced any medium that could help him

* To learn more about why he died and help protect others, Grant's family is supporting research into the genetics of thoracic aortic aneurysms led by the John Ritter Foundation for Aortic Health. Grant didn't have Marfan's syndrome, but the autopsy revealed that he did have a previously undetected mutation in the FBN1 gene, the same gene that is mutated in Marfan's. The John Ritter Foundation, founded by Ritter's widow and fellow actor Amy Yasbeck shortly after her husband's sudden death in 2003, underwrites research, education, and advocacy.

reach more people. His features for *Sports Illustrated*, many of them cover stories, reflected the weeks of reporting and far-flung travel he invested in each. He wrote books, reaching the *New York Times* best-seller list with his first, *The Beckham Experiment: How the World's Most Famous Athlete Tried to Conquer America.* He launched a podcast that became the audio watering hole for the burgeoning tribe of stateside soccer fans, and he turned up regularly on AM sports talk radio and Sirius XM FC. He ventured into TV and video with a regular studio show, sideline reporting, and analysis for major networks and delivered pioneering long-form packages that explored soccer's global reach. And he engaged avidly in social media, relishing the direct and immediate back-and-forth, sharing information and perspectives, and not shrinking when a discussion became contentious. His was the ideal voice to speak to both longtime soccer insiders and the much larger pool of new-comers and potential converts. The sport in the United States benefited as a result of Grant's passion, but not because he hyped the game or proselytized for it. He simply took soccer seriously.

Sports Illustrated still set the agenda for American sports coverage when Grant arrived there in the midnineties and soccer was only beginning to consolidate the interest sparked by the 1994 World Cup, which the United States had hosted several years before he joined the staff. So for Grant's first dozen years as a writer at *SI*, the sport remained his side hustle. College basketball assignments would keep him busy through the winter, offering prominent editorial play and the best opportunities to land a cover. But he kept a hand in with soccer, and each summer he seized any chance to turn to the game. He secured the sport a foothold in the magazine's pages by covering tournaments such as the World Cup and the Olympics, where U.S. teams, especially the women, made more and more noise, and reported on the burgeoning rivalry between the United States and Mexico. He used those stories as a proof of concept, a foundation for building out his ambitions. If this collection includes more of his soccer stories than his college basketball work, it's partly because his most memorable soccer stories appeared later in his career, when he was in greatest command of his craft. But there was also a sparkle to his soccer writing. Grant wrote about the sport with a sense of discovery and the conscientiousness that came with knowing that the largest American readership for coverage of the sport was his.

Behind the scenes, Grant began to lobby for coverage of Major League Soccer and the top European competitions and, on occasion, a place on the cover. Given the game's global footprint, soccer fans had begun to seek out stories on the web, precisely where *SI* was trying to raise its profile. Grant marshaled surveys and stats to make the case to editors that younger, more ethnically diverse Americans—not incidentally, tomorrow's *Sports Illustrated* readers—*did* follow soccer and that it would be bad business to blow them off. From former youth players who once piled into minivans and as adults now expected proper coverage of the game, to urban hipsters huddled around big screens at sports bars for European derbies on Saturday mornings, to Mexican American Gen Zers toggling back and forth between their two favorite national teams, something was happening in the culture, and TV coverage began to reflect it.

Grant had little patience for the reflexive anti-soccer cheap shots so common among sportswriters of a certain generation. The worst cranks—New York *Daily News* columnist Dick Young once called soccer players "commie pansies" and proudly heckled Pelé at the press conference where the Brazilian legend was introduced as a member of the old North American Soccer League's New York Cosmos—had long since passed from the scene. But in the early 2000s, Frank Deford, *SI*'s oldest lion and a hidebound soccerphobe, submitted yet another opinion piece denigrating the sport. Pained to read one of his original heroes trolling the game to which he would dedicate so much of his professional life, Grant marched into the offices of his superiors to ask, "Why exactly are we running this?"

As logical as he was tenacious, Grant steadily wore down skeptics and won converts in-house—and it hardly hurt that editors quickly realized that approving a soccer assignment was more than just the path of least resistance. They'd get Grant off their back, to be sure, and that was no small thing. But they'd also collect the payoff of a clean, smart, richly contextualized story that, oh by the way, captured the currency and excitement of the game for 17 million readers. And so the sport in the United States and Grant's own career wound up tracing parallel paths. "Right place, right time—sure," says Mary Reynics, who edited both of Grant's books for Crown and commissioned this volume. "But also, right person."

More than half the pieces included here feature individuals. Some are legends such as David Beckham, Didier Drogba, and Diego Maradona. Others are personalities like Luis Suárez and Jay DeMerit, coaches such as José Mourinho and Roy Williams, and prodigies captured at the dawn of their careers like LeBron James. Many stories lift up the women to whom Grant paid early and consistent attention—stars such as Abby Wambach and Megan Rapinoe—yet in this collection they occupy no separate section, for Grant believed that they should be regarded simply as elite athletes, deserving of coverage for that reason alone. Still others are anonymous sporting visionaries, out-of-the-box thinkers looking to squeeze any advantage from an offensive possession or a set piece. And some pieces feature not notable people but exotic places, whether the Nigerian upcountry (where Grant found a camp for aspiring NBA big men), the badlands of Transnistria (where in the shadow of Vladimir Putin he reported on the unlikeliest powerhouse soccer club), or the streets of Seoul (where Grant's love note to the cohosts of the 2002 World Cup landed him a guest spot on South Korea's answer to *Oprah*). Whenever he filed from such datelines, the man who had been sent to France to cover the 1998 World Cup as a twenty-four-year-old made sure to activate his sense of wonder, even as he became more and more willing to register his indignation.

Grant's craftsmanship came from years of devotedly reading first-rate magazine journalism as well as his classical training in the form. He swore by the dictum, championed by legendary *New Yorker* writer John McPhee, that your opening paragraph should "shine like a light through the story"—a feature of Grant's best work. His lede on LeBron James (page 3) made sure to place the young James in a frame with Michael Jordan, whereas Freddy Adu (page 13) keeps the company of stray dogs. His openers paint vivid scenes: from the hurly-burly of downtown Cairo into which Bob Bradley was dropped to rescue Egypt's World Cup hopes (page 72) to a guy in crocodile boots in Nacogdoches, Texas, trying to get down a bet on the fifteen-year-old Clint Dempsey (page 206).

Grant knew, too, that the most evocative writing engages the senses. In his dispatch after France's 1998 World Cup victory (page 22), his descriptions of Zinedine Zidane's exploits on the pitch stand alongside a postmatch pratfall: Zidane's stumble as he navigated the interview area, caught vividly by the camera of Grant's eye. And in the lede of his profile of Didier Drogba (page 199), Grant evoked the smell of the rainy season in Drogba's native Ivory Coast. It's a subtle touch, Proustian in its specificity, that helps the reader better understand why even a multimillionaire star of the Premier League is drawn so powerfully back home.

Most of all, Grant had curiosity, the essential implement in a reporter's toolkit. His activated antennae helped make him the first to introduce readers to such prospects as James and Adu and to persuade editors to let him pursue explanatory pieces about innovative tactics in both basketball (page 85) and soccer (page 106). And it propelled him—compelled him, even—to hit the road. In some exotic locale for a scheduled event, he would poke around for further story subjects, to which he might later return for a feature or video. "The older I get, the more I realize I don't know," he mused at the end of one episode of his video series *Exploring Planet Fútbol*. "But I like going to places where I can learn those things, and also they're willing to let me in."

Journalists aren't supposed to become a part of the story, but sometimes Grant decided that he had to. With his Beckham book, his campaign for the presidency of FIFA, and his efforts to expose Qatari government policies during the months before he died, he unavoidably found himself in the spotlight. Once there, he drew courage from the examples of a procession of public-facing, idealistic role models, including three women—his mother, Helen; his wife, Céline; and an unforgettable professor, the journalist Gloria Emerson. None shrank from important issues, controversy, or hard truths.

Once a story was filed, Grant set himself up as its great protector and champion. He cared about every phrase, word, and comma. He monitored each layer of editing, sometimes torturing himself by following edits in real time. He once described a shot as tracing "an angry parabola," only to have the phrase cut by an editor less enamored of it. After that, he hunted for ways to slip it into his stories, succeeding in his 2014 profile of Luis Suárez (page 122). Whenever he can, ESPN soccer writer Gabriele Marcotti drops that phrase into his own pieces in homage to his colleague.

That combination of scrupulousness and idealism marked Grant's work from his salad days as a campus reporter through his long ride as *SI*'s man on the beat, until he realized his dream of complete editorial independence with his own soccer site on Substack. The highlights captured in this volume gather up the full range of his remit, from trophy lifts to base corruption, from the stirring to the shameful.

—————

THE STORY OF Grant David Wahl begins with details that would have kindled the curiosity of the reporter he became. His paternal grandfather, Edward Wahl, had grown up with seven surviving siblings in the central Kansas town of Saxman, in a cabin with a hand pump for water and an outhouse in the back. Edward's parents were German immigrants, and from a small shop behind their home August Wahl worked as a gunsmith, the trade he had learned back in East Prussia. Edward's mother, Olga, helped support the family by baking and cooking for others.

Edward made his way out despite the Great Depression. He earned a law degree from the University of Kansas, then returned home to serve as city attorney in nearby Lyons, the county seat, and married a local music teacher with Bavarian roots, Vera Volkmann. The man people in Rice County came to know as Big Ed eventually went into private practice, specializing in trusts and estates, whereupon Edward and Vera left the little Lutheran church outside Saxman, which still held services in German, and began attending Lyons's First Methodist Church, where Vera's family had long been members. According to family lore, Edward calculated that among the larger, prevailing Methodist congregation he had better prospects for finding clients, including many who could pay him only in goods and services. Today Saxman is a ghost town. But immigrants such as August and Olga Wahl passed down through the generations an ethic of making do and empathy for those who tried to live by that creed.

The first of Edward and Vera's two children, Grant's father, David, learned those lessons well. At Washington High School in Kansas City, Kansas, where he would teach government, sociology, and civics for nearly three decades, David met Helen Grace Smith, a phys ed teacher turned school counselor six years his senior. Active and competitive, Helen was a native of the Kansas City suburb of Independence, Missouri, Harry S. Truman's hometown, with political convictions to match. She had been reluctant to rush into marriage and children. But on a snow-swept day in December 1968, with school on break, she and Dave married in a small chapel on the KU campus. After their two sons, Eric and Grant, came along, she chose to stay home in their simple ranch house in Mission, Kansas, to raise them through their early childhood. Living on one salary often made for tough kitchen table choices—yes to magazine subscriptions, no to cable TV—that would shape how the Wahl boys perceived the world. On regular trips to visit Grandma Vera in Lyons, the family would cultivate an appreciation for how good they nonetheless had it and why a simple piece of fruit found its way into Christmas stockings.

For Christmas in 1982, Helen and Dave also gave the then ten-year-old Grant a subscription to *Sports Illustrated*. Each week he turned every page. "That was my way into this world," he recalled years later. "I knew I wasn't going to be an athlete. I felt like I got to know the writers—guys like Frank Deford became these mythical heroes to me."

Still in elementary school, he wrote the editors to tell them he intended someday to join the writing staff. His parents and older brother were floored when someone in New York wrote back. "It said something like 'Dear Grant, thanks for your letter. That's cute. Keep writing,'" Eric remembers. "But coming from where we did, you can't imagine what that gesture meant to him."

Grant had grown up comfortable in his own somewhat dorky skin. He was the kid who memorized every county in Kansas and, when homework loomed, would tie his shoelaces to a chair in the basement until he got it done. By the end of his senior year at Shawnee Mission East High in 1992, Grant was an Eagle Scout and a stalwart of the cross-country team but no less goofy. He and his buddies might drive around town in hockey masks or stage a golf tournament among themselves, the Minor Masters, with the prize a green thrift-shop blazer. But he had also let others know he was serious about his dream to write for *SI*. When financial aid to attend Princeton came through, he chose the school that had produced Deford as well as the Pulitzer Prize winner and *New Yorker* editor David Remnick. In the late twentieth century, if you wanted to be a quarterback, you went to Miami; if you wanted to be a magazine writer, you went to Princeton.

Grant spent part of his freshman year working in the dining hall. And then, shortly after Big Ed's death in 1993, the Wahls inherited a parcel of family farmland in Rice County. Grant no longer had to wash dishes—

which meant more time to write for *The Daily Princetonian,* even if the family's modest change of fortune hardly placed him on an equal footing with the prep school crowd. The "Hey there" that would later open his podcast rang true. "It was easy for people from cushier backgrounds to take Grant's earnestness for an angle or a ploy," Eric says, "until they discovered they were getting the real Grant."

From the courses he chose to how he spent extracurricular time, Grant tried to "do things that would help me work at *Sports Illustrated* someday," he would say. His resident adviser, Joel Samuels, served on the sports staff of *The Daily Princetonian* and took Grant under his wing. "That lasted about two weeks," Samuels recalls. "Grant eclipsed me very, very quickly." If some duty at the *Prince* beckoned, coursework could wait. On Mondays that first fall, the paper ran longer stories about cross-country than football because the freshman on the beat reported and wrote with such depth and grace.

After Grant inevitably ascended to the sports editorship, he made sure to sustain staff morale. Closing nights might end with pizza and beer, and a departmental intramural hockey team featured Grant in goal in boots. But he also expected the section to uphold strict journalistic standards. When Grant found out that several men's rugby players had misled one of his staffers, trying to get a fantastical version of a team trip in print as a practical joke, he vowed to team leadership that the *Prince* would no longer cover the offending sport as long as he was editor. When top editors asked how much space sports could fill beyond its customary back page, Grant & Co. would reply, "Whatever you can give us." Several times during the fall of 1995, sports actually crept past the editorials.

Grant had watched some soccer while growing up, primarily the Kansas City Comets of the Major Indoor Soccer League, who used laser lights and loud music to attract fans. And he had caught the 1990 World Cup—on an over-the-air Spanish-language channel because English-language coverage was limited to a cable package the family still couldn't afford. But watching the exploits of such nations as Cameroon, Colombia, and Ireland on a TV set with wires sprouting from its top only intensified the romance. That first fall on campus, covering the Princeton men's soccer team as it reached the NCAA Final Four, he peppered coach Bob Bradley with questions about strategy and tactics. During sophomore year, when he landed in the infirmary with mononucleosis, he befriended a varsity soccer player with intestinal flu named Jesse Marsch, who would go on to play in Major League Soccer and coach in Austria, Germany, and England's Premier League. As the two undergraduates convalesced, watching the Winter Olympics together, Marsch fielded Grant's questions about the game, and not for the last time.

As it happened, two favorite authors of Grant's youth would serve as visiting faculty during his time at Princeton. When Deford turned up to teach a seminar, more than two hundred students applied for a handful of spots, forcing the department to restrict enrollment to American Studies concentrators. Grant had declared for Politics and pleaded with Deford to make an exception, to no avail. "I turned into a bit of a stalker," he later admitted. "He took pity on me and took me to lunch." Grant thanked him with the gift of a wheel of cheese. He had better luck with Remnick, who stood in for John McPhee for a semester to teach The Literature of Fact, the school's renowned nonfiction writing course. Upon finding out that McPhee, too, literally strapped himself into a chair when on deadline, Grant must have had a redoubled sense of his destiny.

But before landing in Remnick's class, Grant took the course he credited with securing his commitment to journalism. Politics and the Press was taught by Gloria Emerson, the former *New York Times* reporter whose 1977 book, *Winners and Losers,* about Vietnam's haunting place in American life, won the National Book Award. Her reporting paid particular attention to the war's effect on grunt GIs and Vietnamese civilians, and she famously called out John Lennon and Yoko Ono, whose style of protest she found inane. Grant would proudly point out that, of all the courses he had taken, his grade in that class had invited the most improvement. Emerson, by then in her midsixties, became "this semi-best friend of mine," Grant would later say. "[She was] just an amazing, tough New Yorker who started out in fashion writing and ended up becoming a war correspondent and a legendary one at that. You can call her my mentor."

On Sundays through much of 1994 and into '95, as Emerson recovered from a broken leg, Grant would swing by her apartment to deliver cigarettes and jelly donuts. She eventually gave him a key to her place, which included a spare room that Grant turned into his private writing studio. "She was exactly the kind of person he needed to be around—to experience that generational hauteur, that intellect from a different age," Eric says. "I think what she liked most about Grant was his earnest streak. She had an outward gruffness that scared people in some ways, but if you put your chips in and made a good-faith effort to take part in her game of intellectual repartee, she took you in."

As a capstone piece for The Literature of Fact, Grant had the richest possible subject. After reading his profile of Emerson (page 131), Remnick called it "among the very best student papers I've ever seen."

In 1994, Grant won a fellowship for Princeton undergraduates to fund summer travel for research. He split his time between Boston and Buenos Aires to compare Red Sox fan culture with its *fútbol* counterpart in Argentina. Bob Bradley shared the name of a contact at the storied club Boca Juniors, and Grant talked his way onto a bus filled with fans bound for an away match at Rosario Central. Traveling at night to avoid police patrols, with the *hinchada* anointing him "our good luck charm from the north," Grant experienced a special kind of exhilaration. "Fists clenched, they pound on the walls, the windows, the cushions in front of them," he wrote in an account of that journey for a student publication, *The Vigil*. "Each man belts out the words, their meanings overshadowed by the sheer force of the delivery. *'Boooo-ca, Boca de mi viiiiii-da, vos sos la alegriiiiii-a de mi corazoooon!'* They do not sing the verses; they expel them, so forcefully that I can feel the passion coursing through the hard, bouncing seats."

Even the Boston stopover of that summer nudged him further toward soccer. The United States served as host of the 1994 World Cup, and Argentina contested two group stage matches in Foxboro, Massachusetts, where Grant sat in the stands, enthralled. "The trip confirmed for me that I really did want to become a sports journalist writing high-level magazine stories," he later reported to the foundation that had underwritten his travels. "It also showed me that I could take on ambitious projects and do them well."

The following summer he returned to Argentina with an even more challenging brief—a senior thesis topic on the role of the soccer club as civic association in Argentine life. Invoking Alexis de Tocqueville and the social theorist Robert Putnam, "Playing the Political Game: Soccer Clubs in Argentine Civil Society" analyzed how the country's more than three thousand *fútbol* clubs built social capital that could help Argentina transition to a more functional democracy. Grant collected data and spoke to soccer officials, journalists, academics, and politicians. He spent time with characters like Quique Ocampo, aka El Carnicero, or the Butcher, founder of Boca's most prominent fan group. And he turned up regularly in the terraces of stadiums across Buenos Aires, precincts that respectable *porteños* avoided for their violence, because he wanted to better understand "the emotions felt by the participants" and avoid "becoming trapped in an academic cocoon." He argued that the Argentine soccer club is "a central gathering place, one of the few venues in a stratified, hierarchical society where all social classes came together, whether it was at a table in the club's cafeteria, on a club's tennis court, or in the giant theater-in-the-round known as the soccer stadium."

Yet his thesis was no gauzy manifesto of football-conquers-all. Grant delved into the pathologies—fan violence, sexism, huge disparities in wealth—that kept the culture of Argentine soccer from more fully fostering democracy in a country shaped by Peronism, military rule, and hyperinflation. In one chapter he explained how directors of *fútbol* clubs forged alliances across the divides of political party so long as both sides derived some financial benefit. "Here," he quoted one Argentine, "it is said that among firemen no one steps on the firehose." Even as a college student, Grant had a nose for the game's blazer-wrapped con men and the grifts they engaged in. It remained for him simply to ascend to a platform from which to hold them to account.

Back at Princeton for his senior year, sporting the black shearling aviator jacket he had picked up in Buenos Aires, Grant probably came off as more of a sophisticate than he actually was. He soon turned the head of a junior molecular biology major in his eating club. Grant's courtship of Céline Gounder featured him capering about in a fresh snowfall, wearing nothing but a bathrobe and hiking boots—whatever got his fired-with-purpose, doctor-to-be girlfriend to unleash the breadth of her smile. When he took her to meet Gloria Emerson, Céline knew that things were serious. "Thank God she liked me," Céline says. "It was love at first sight. Not me and Grant—me and Gloria."

Grant would write his thesis in the room Emerson had set aside for him—as he called it, "the most scenic study carrel in all of Princeton." In an author's note, Grant made sure to point out that, even as Emerson had encouraged him, one professor dismissed his proposed topic as "a silly idea." That "silly idea" wound up winning senior thesis prizes in both Politics and Latin American Studies. The defiance in Grant's author's note foreshadowed a professional career in which he would relish a fight with deskbound second-guessers who might deter him from chasing a story he believed in.

The summer after graduation, Grant landed an internship in the sports department of the *Miami Herald.* He impressed enough that editors offered him a staff position for the fall. Instead, he took a job as a fact-checker at *SI,* with only a vague promise of a chance to write. But by now he was accustomed to placing bets on himself. Céline herself graduated the following spring and completed a master's in epidemiology at Johns Hopkins. With a place now awaiting her at med school in Seattle, she believed it fell to her to propose if Grant were to follow her across the country. Her plans to do so over a romantic dinner at Commune, a fancy Manhattan restaurant, got scuppered when her would-be fiancé accidentally set his menu on fire. She proposed the next morning, this time while wedged alongside Grant in the Ikea love seat of his tiny studio apartment.

Jon Wertheim, another middle-class public school kid from the Midwest, had also begun at *SI* in 1996, and the two shared an office. He remembers Grant making light of his own Eagle Scout pedigree. "It was sort of 'That's my nerdy self,'" Wertheim remembers. "But I think that helped inform his approach to the job. He always had this great curiosity. He wanted to know about everything and everyone."

Grant attached himself immediately to college basketball, a major beat where many writers up the masthead had distinguished themselves. If soccer was a learned subject, college hoops had come down as an heirloom from his family's ties to the University of Kansas. He would turn his relocation to the Pacific Northwest into a virtue, cultivating sources and finding stories at schools such as Gonzaga and Arizona, helping to drain East Coast bias from the magazine's basketball coverage. But his first bylined piece was a soccer story, examining a controversy surrounding Howard University's powerful teams of the 1970s (page 146). The following summer, after landing a promotion to writer in less than a year on staff, he joined a team of three in France for the World Cup. Wertheim remembers Grant returning from Paris abuzz, already plotting ways to persuade editors to cover the Women's World Cup a year later. "One of his talents was that he saw around corners," Wertheim says. "He understood that soccer was the growth stock. He understood the richness of the stories, the women as well as the men—the internationalism.

"He had a lot of old-school sensibilities. He didn't cut corners, he didn't go for cheap yucks, he didn't do hot takes or clickbait. But in other ways Grant was a visionary. He once wrote of Lionel Messi, 'He has the ability to see shapes and patterns before anybody else does.' Grant could have been describing himself. The LeBron [cover] story [when James was still a junior in high school] was a great bit of foresight. And he saw early that sports and social justice would have this huge intersection."

In a 2003 piece, he introduced the English superstar David Beckham to SI's readers and, four years later, revisited him for a cover story after Beckham joined the Los Angeles Galaxy of MLS. Grant realized that the groundbreaking signing offered a chance to tell a book-length story of glamour and substance that would blend Old World football with the new frontier of the American game. For more than a year Grant filled his notebook and, with Céline bound for South Africa to study ways to diagnose and prevent tuberculosis, took a leave from SI to follow her there. He wrote most of The Beckham Experiment in a Johannesburg coffee shop. The story he wound up telling was consummately Grant, a kind of soccer Upstairs, Downstairs that made sure to celebrate the grafters on MLS minimums as they labored in Beckham's gilded shadow.

The Beckham book's appearance on the bestseller list gave Grant another proof point to persuade SI to let him cover soccer full-time. Already a prominent figure on the SI website who foresaw the media industry's digital future and how demographic change would shape Americans' habits, he made a further case: a commitment to soccer could help SI cultivate the younger, more online readership that his bosses claimed to want to reach. He was detailed to the sport full-time late in 2009, with the first World Cup on African soil set for the following summer. He called it "winning the career lottery." As he would later reflect, "I never expected to do soccer full-time. I'd like to say this was all planned and inevitable, but it wasn't."

Grant and Céline's marriage was one of mutual support as much as mutual devotion. But it took some coordination. Grant wore his work life portably, flying his latest college hoops or soccer sortie out of whichever airport was nearest the site of his wife's calling of the moment. The two seized what time they could between the last epidemic or soccer scandal and the next, literally: Céline spent two months volunteering in West Africa during the Ebola outbreak; for Grant, the oily scene in a hotel lobby in Zurich prompted him to run for the presidency of FIFA, the sport's world governing body (page 280). He would write much of his second book, *Masters of Modern Soccer,* on the White Mountain Apache reservation in Arizona, where Céline was treating Indigenous patients.

Their respective life's work may have differed in particulars but not in kind. Both devoted themselves to understanding as best they could, sharing that understanding as widely as possible, and urging that others act on the facts to bring about a better, more just world—to demonstrate that good journalism and good science alike demand that we not look away. "We couldn't always be what the other one wanted or needed," Céline says. "But I think we also understood that we were each and together part of something bigger."

Céline deserves some credit for transforming someone who used to lug a grease-soaked bag of Wendy's back to his desk into a foodie who could flush out the best sushi in dozens of cities around the world. But at heart Grant was still that goofball from Shawnee Mission East. He became notorious among the press corps as the guy who, over the length of a Cup or Copa or Euro, would "launder" his jeans by stashing them in a freezer.

He defended that practice with the same stubborn, contrarian streak his editors would sometimes see. Asked by a colleague how to cope with editing, Grant once advised, "Hire a therapist." "You can't be 'more unique' or 'less unique,'" Grant once muttered as a story of his went through the *SI* editorial gauntlet. "There's no modifying 'unique.'" Those editorial clashes were never born of a desire to lord it over a coworker but in service of the highest ideal, what he believed to be the best possible story. "Grant had a really low threshold for moral outrage," Wertheim said, "whether it was a comma in his copy or the mistreatment of migrant workers or LGBTQ+ people."

That devotion to principle helped account for the end of his run at *SI* during the early weeks of the Covid-19 pandemic. In 2019, a Canadian marketing firm, Authentic Brands Group, had bought *Sports Illustrated* and hired a media company called Maven to run *SI*'s journalistic operations. When Maven took a scythe to salaries across the board, Grant objected loudly and publicly, insisting that management commit to restoring the old pay scale as soon as the pandemic had passed. Just like that, after nearly a quarter century of prizewinning work, dozens of covers, and nothing but stellar evaluations, he was shown the door.*

As his wife played a high-profile role advocating for vigilance and vaccination during the Covid-19 pandemic, eventually joining the pandemic advisory board for the Biden administration's transition team, Grant worked to reboot his career. In August 2021, he launched his Substack, Fútbol with Grant Wahl, turning down offers from legacy brands so he could have editorial freedom. No overlord would veto a story idea with some tossed-off "Nobody cares" or "Who's gonna read it?" Grant was going to make people care, compel them to read. He sustained a manic travel schedule, delivering a stream of high-quality, magazine-style content to thousands of paid subscribers and many more unpaid, while continuing to amplify his written voice with podcasting, video storytelling, and his usual social media presence. Sprinkled through this volume are highlights from the fifteen months when Grant served as his own assignment editor, including an excerpt from a story of which he was especially proud, about the laborers who had toiled under Qatar's onerous *kafala* system as the country prepared to host the World Cup (page 293).

As hard as they both were working, Grant and Céline had found a groove in their life together now that Grant could control his schedule. For someone who was always having his passport stamped, he had nonetheless circumscribed his life in Manhattan. A half block in Chelsea included all he really needed: a desk in a coworking space; a table at Smithfield, the tavern where he'd meet friends to watch Champions League matches; and the apartment he shared with Céline, where their dogs, Coco and Zizou, would wait expectantly for him to come through the door.

In early November 2022, just before heading to the airport to fly to

---

* After filing a complaint with the union over his dismissal, Grant reached a settlement that provided for his writing three further stories for *SI*.

Qatar, Grant performed a rite that was partly an act of devotion and partly a renewal of vows. He pulled out his profile of Gloria Emerson and reread it.

———

ON THAT DEVASTATING December night, after learning of Grant's death on the other side of the world, Mark Mravic, a longtime friend and collaborator and this collection's coeditor, posted two sentences to Twitter. "Life is random and meaningless," he wrote. "Anyone care to debate?"

Years before, Mravic had left a spot as a graduate student in philosophy to go into journalism, and at *Sports Illustrated,* in addition to duty as Grant's favorite editor, he served as unofficial staff philosophe. Now, as the hours ticked by, Mravic found himself fielding the counterargument on blast. The refutation that led him to "yield my point, humbly" about the purposelessness of life came, Mravic later put it, in the form of "Céline's grace and composure, Eric's strength, the coming together of family and friends and colleagues and fans." But it came first in a chorus from around the world, a balm out of the dark. No one, not even someone who had worked with Grant as long and as closely as anyone else, had known the extent of his good works.

"Grant wasn't a close friend," says Musa Okwonga, who cohosts the *Stadio* podcast for The Ringer. "He was a good friend." That distinction nods at how Grant assembled a kind of global family of soccer followers and at countless acts of kindness that people who had brushed up against him over the years recalled in the wake of his death. A round of layoffs in the business? There was Grant, working the phones, haranguing sports editors and soccer producers about the virtues of someone out on the street. A fresh entry-level hire on the video team or among the web producers at SI.com? There was Grant, making sure she was invited to one of the regular dinners he and Céline hosted, where former *SI* editor in chief Chris Stone remembers him as "a true middle-of-the-table guy," head on a swivel, lubricating conversation, *saloniste* of soccer and more—"out of noblesse oblige or a sense of mentorship," as Wertheim puts it, "but also because he honestly wanted to know who you were and where you came from and what you thought." A blind email from a random someone eager to make a life and living covering the game? There was Grant, lending an ear and sharing advice, as giants such as Emerson,

Deford, and Remnick had once done for him—or simply acknowledging the correspondent, as that clerk in the *SI* letters department had done when Grant was a grade-schooler. Some soccer writer with a first book out? There was Grant, not just inviting the author onto his podcast but eventually carving out a regular segment dedicated to writing about the game and conducting interviews with the respect that comes from having always, at the very least, actually read the book. A fellow journalist victimized by a crime far from home, as then freelancer Alexander Abnos was in Rio de Janeiro at the 2014 World Cup, where thieves robbed him at gunpoint of his wallet, laptop, and phone? There was Grant, who five years earlier had himself been mugged in Honduras (page 247), tracking Abnos down, letting him vent, and reassuring him with calmness and by example that life would go on. As Okwonga puts it, "Grant went the long way 'round. He helped everyone and still ascended to that level."

Grant thought of other reporters as teammates—a formulation that applied beyond the ranks of the outlet that cut his paycheck. As Wertheim notes, "If you were practicing acts of journalism, if you had that blank screen you were obligated to fill, if you got quotes and went places and tried to tell stories and truths while fighting jet lag, Grant thought of you as a kindred spirit."

Those responses to colleagues weren't in the least transactional. "Truly good people like this don't live their life needing their goodness rewarded," wrote *Indianapolis Star* columnist Gregg Doyel, a former Florida Marlins beat writer with whom Grant briefly overlapped at the *Herald* in Miami. "Their goodness is their reward. They get joy from it, and down deep, I suspect, they know how we feel about them."

As he sat in Lusail Stadium, two rows behind the spot where Grant had collapsed, Chris Jones of the Canadian Broadcasting Corporation couldn't help but think that his friend had become the latest itinerant worker to die in Qatar. But Jones, too, was lifted by memories of Grant's compassion and humanity and added his tribute to the mix. The outpouring left Céline overwhelmed. "It was hard at times sharing Grant with the rest of the world," she confessed at the celebration of his life in late December 2022. "Until this past week, I didn't realize just how much he shared himself with all of you. I know he struggled with sharing me, too. It's your shared love for me and for us that's keeping me going right now."

———

VIOLENCE AT A soccer match, Grant pointed out in that senior thesis long ago, "is easier to bring into vision than other violence because it occurs in places where journalists already congregate." Grant's death also took place almost literally as the world watched. Given the scope of his kindness and the impact of his work, his death would have likely touched off the same scale of grief had it come on a trip back to Rice County, Kansas, to collect family lore, as he and Eric had spoken of doing—if instead of half a world from home, he had died on the abandoned streets of Saxman. Yet on another level, Grant's death in Qatar chimed with the result of that competition, Argentina's World Cup triumph. He died only days before and in the very place where the country that had made a *fútbol* writer of him won the trophy that vindicated Lionel Messi, the player Grant had helped make a household name in the United States. The soccer world took note of the irony—that Grant had so narrowly missed a sight he had waited his entire adult life to see.

To Musa Okwonga—Uganda born, Eton educated, Berlin based, and so just the kind of third-culture cosmopolitan Grant befriended in pressrooms—the American sportswriter called to mind the poet William Blake, the bard of innocence and experience. Blake had a knack for capturing both the joy in the suspension of care and the despondency that can come with real life. "We want to get into the stadium and through the turnstiles, and nothing else matters except what is happening on the pitch," Okwonga said of his sportswriting colleagues. "But Grant's ability to say, 'Actually, these workers haven't been paid, these workers have died, and the organizers of this tournament don't respect them and their families' . . . that's extremely rare. His passion was so evident and his knowledge ran so deep, it gave him the authority to step back at any point in the tournament, even on the eve of the [World Cup] Final, and say, 'This is problematic.'

"If you truly love something, you engage with the worst aspects. I think that's why he was so universally admired—even by the people he went after."

The Blakean phrase is "contrary states." "Just an incredible designed set piece by the Dutch," Grant's final tweet read. The lede of his penultimate Substack post, calling out the Qataris once more, was "They just don't care" (page 310). There he was, hailing a match that showcased the country that had touched off his love for soccer, yet refusing to overlook the ongoing exploitation of human beings in the name of that sport. He sat with that duality to the last.

But then that's where so many of us are eager to sit. We're fans, to be sure, yet there's more to us than tribal attachments and unthinking enthusiasms. When a tribune like Grant comes along, may we always look to see where he wants to lead us.

———

WITH THE SUPPORT of his family, friends, and fans, proceeds from this collection will help establish a journalism award at Princeton in Grant Wahl's name to fund the work of promising writers whose ambition shouldn't be limited by the means of their families. You hold this book in your hands. In the spirit of the man whose work fills it, please consider pressing it into the hands of someone else.

1
PRODIGIES

SCIENTISTS CALL IT THE OBSERVER EFFECT—WHEN THE ACT OF observing influences the phenomenon being observed. And when a national media outlet trains its attention on a young sports prodigy, that change often takes the form of heightened expectations, which can touch off a downward spiral if the athlete isn't prepared to metabolize them. LeBron James, the subject of Wahl's most famous up-and-coming-star story, had no problem processing the hype. But another subject, the thirteen-year-old soccer player Freddy Adu, encountered all sorts of problems. Indeed, *Sports Illustrated* editors were still smarting from a 1994 piece about Schea Cotton, a high school basketball player from southern California who had just finished his freshman year. "Swelling the egos of young, immature players could actually impede their development," says former *SI* senior editor Greg Kelly. "And when Cotton's development stalled, it seemed like we shared some of the blame." Kelly took on the role of reasonable skeptic when he and Wahl collaborated on the James cover story. In covering a young athlete with seemingly boundless potential, Wahl would later tell an interviewer, the writer should take care to include "the obligatory two paragraphs where you throw in the caveats. But there's a reason you're writing the story. You try to find people you trust who see the talent, who can tell you where the potential is and where the pitfalls might be. You try to strike a balance."

The Chosen One

FROM *Sports Illustrated*, FEBRUARY 18, 2002

In 2002, Wahl wasn't the only person predicting stardom for a seventeen-year-old from Akron, Ohio, named LeBron James. But to land a spot in *SI*'s feature well, much less on the cover, for a story on a high school junior required a persuasive in-house sales job. Wahl had an ally in senior editor Greg Kelly, who came up with the cover billing THE CHOSEN ONE, words that James wound up having tattooed on his arm. "We piled into my rental car and drove to Cleveland to an NBA game," Wahl would recall. "Michael Jordan hits a buzzer-beater. After the game, Jordan comes out to meet him"—not for the first time, it became instantly clear. Wahl was struck by James's talent and potential, to be sure. But the ease with which James interacted with Jordan that night, effortlessly assuming his place alongside someone from whom great things were routinely expected, confirmed for Wahl that he was indeed witnessing the beginning of something big. "He wrote the LeBron piece as if he'd been doing journalism for thirty years," remembers the soccer journalist and podcaster Musa Okwonga. In fact, Wahl had then been doing it for six.

RESPLENDENT IN A SLEEK NAVY BLUE SUIT, HIS BURNISHED DOME gleaming in the light, Michael Jordan steps into the tunnel of Cleveland's Gund Arena, flashes a million-watt smile, and gives LeBron James, the top high school player in the country, a warm, we're-old-pals handshake. "Where's Mama?" Jordan asks.

"She's in New Orleans," LeBron says, grinning at the memory of how well his mother, Gloria, had gotten on with Jordan when they met in Chicago last summer.

It's 10:00 P.M. on the last night of January, and the moment feels charged, even a little historic. Remember that photograph of a teenaged

Bill Clinton meeting JFK? Same vibe. Here, together, are His Airness and King James, the thirty-eight-year-old master and the seventeen-year-old prodigy, the best of all time and the high school junior whom some people—from drooling NBA general managers to warring shoe company execs to awestruck fans—believe could be the Air Apparent.

Jordan has just hit another buzzer-beater to sink the Cavaliers, but another game is afoot. A spectacularly gifted 6'7", 225-pound guard who averages 29.6 points, 8.3 rebounds, and 5.9 assists for St. Vincent–St. Mary High in Akron, LeBron is thought to possess all the elements necessary to do for some apparel company what Jordan did for Nike. Not only does he have the requisite high-flying game and an Iversonian street cred that Jordan himself lacked, but he can also turn on the charm when necessary. It's why LeBron is a year from signing what's expected to be the most lucrative shoe deal in history for an NBA rookie, estimated at $20 million over five years, and why Jordan, who represents his own division of Nike athletic wear, would want LeBron in the Swoosh family.

Tonight, however, LeBron is wearing a black coat and stocking cap bearing the logo of Adidas, his high school team's sponsor, which Jordan can't help but notice yet chooses to ignore. They schmooze for a few minutes, bantering about LeBron's upcoming game, until Jordan leaves, offering this piece of advice: "One dribble, stop and pull up. That's what I want to see."

LeBron nods and smiles. "That's my guy," he says. All things considered, it's hard to decide what's more impressive—that LeBron could be hailed as the best high school player even though he's only a junior, or that many NBA scouts believe he would be the first pick in this year's draft (if league rules didn't forbid his entering it), or that he can get an audience with Jordan as easily as a haircut appointment.

Then again, the world behind the velvet rope is nothing new to LeBron. Last summer he was the only schoolboy invited to play in Jordan's top-secret workouts in Chicago. LeBron speaks regularly with Boston Celtics star Antoine Walker, who is his best friend among NBA players. Those floor tickets to the Cavaliers game? LeBron's surrogate father, Eddie Jackson, simply made a call to Cleveland coach John Lucas. Already LeBron has hung out with Michael Finley, Tracy McGrady, and Jerry Stackhouse, to say nothing of his favorite rapper, Jay-Z. "He's a cool guy, too," LeBron says. "We went to his hotel first, and then I had back-stage passes."

Did we say LeBron just turned seventeen?

"At this age LeBron is better than anybody I've seen in thirty-seven years in this business, including Kevin [Garnett] and Kobe [Bryant] and Tracy," says Sonny Vaccaro, the Adidas rep who signed the first shoe deals with Jordan (for Nike), Bryant, and McGrady.

Says Germantown (Pa.) Academy coach Jim Fenerty, who watched LeBron pile up 38 points and seventeen rebounds in a 70–64 defeat of his Patriots in December, "We played Kobe when Kobe was a senior, and LeBron is the best player we've ever played against. LeBron is physically stronger than Kobe was as a senior, and we've never had anybody shoot better against us."

If that sounds like enough hot air to pump up all the tires in Akron, check out LeBron's résumé. Last season, while leading St. Vincent–St. Mary to its second straight Division III state title, he became the first sophomore to win Ohio's Mr. Basketball award. His stock skyrocketed last July at the Adidas ABCD Camp, where he won MVP honors, and it threatened to soar off the charts after he totaled 36 points, nine re-bounds, and four assists to almost single-handedly keep the Irish close in a 72–66 loss to national powerhouse Oak Hill Academy in Trenton, N.J., on Sunday. Must have been the shoes: LeBron was wearing special American flag–themed Adidases given to him last Friday by Bryant, who was in nearby Philadelphia for the NBA All-Star Game.

"A lot of players know how to play the game," LeBron says, "but they really don't know how to play the game, if you know what I mean. They can put the ball in the hoop, but I see things before they even happen. You know how a guy can make his team so much better? That's one thing I learned from watching Jordan."

Indeed, while NBA scouts are universal in their praise of LeBron's all-around package—his shooting range, his fluid handle, his disarming explosiveness—their most common comparison is with another breath-taking passer, Magic Johnson. "The most surprising thing is that a guy who could dominate offensively is so unselfish," says one scout. "Most of these young guys don't know how to play, but he looks to make the pass first, and he's great at it."

"If I were a general manager, there are only four or five NBA players that I wouldn't trade to get him right now," says former Phoenix Suns coach Danny Ainge, who was in Trenton to see LeBron play for the second time. "I love Jason Williams at Duke, and I've heard of the Chinese guy [7'6" Yao Ming], but if LeBron came out this year, I wouldn't even have to think about it. I'd take him number one."

It's a moot point, though. After causing a stir last summer by saying that he might become the first high school junior to declare for the draft—and challenge the NBA rule that prevents players in this country from being selected until their high school class graduates—LeBron vows he'll stick around to get his diploma from St. Vincent–St. Mary in the spring of 2003. "The rule's not fair, but that's life," says LeBron, who has a 2.8 GPA. "I'll stay another year because my friends are here. The only thing I think is bad, they let that seventeen-year-old golfer [Ty Tryon] on the PGA Tour. You've got tennis players competing professionally when they're fourteen. Why not basketball players?"

With LeBron staying at St. Vincent–St. Mary another year, the buzz around him should rise to an unprecedented level for a high school athlete. "This is like a mid–major college environment right now," says Frank Jessie, the school's athletic director. This year the Fighting Irish moved their home games to the University of Akron's 5,100-seat James A. Rhodes Arena. Some 1,750 season tickets were sold (at $100 to $120 a pop), and St. Vincent–St. Mary is drawing 4,075 fans, almost double the attendance of the university's men's team.

LeBron may be the reason for the hysteria, but he isn't your typical high school hoops phenom. For the last two years, in fact, he has risked career-threatening injury as an all-state wide receiver on the St. Vincent–St. Mary football team. At first Gloria refused to let LeBron play last fall, but after the twenty-two-year-old singer Aaliyah died in a plane crash last August, he persuaded her to let him play. "You're not promised tomorrow," LeBron says. "I had to be out on the field with my team." Though LeBron did break the index finger of his left (nonshooting) hand, he helped lead the Irish to the state semifinals.

Gloria knows she can protect LeBron for just so long. She gave birth to him at sixteen, and after her mother died two years later, she and LeBron drifted from apartment to apartment around Akron. (On one occasion their building was condemned and bulldozed by the city.) "I saw drugs, guns, killings; it was crazy," LeBron says. "But my mom kept food in my mouth and clothes on my back."

The Jameses' nomadic existence and unsettled home life took a toll, however. In the fourth grade, LeBron says, he missed more than a hundred days of school. Nor did it help that Jackson, who has been in a relationship with Gloria since LeBron was two, spent three years in jail after pleading guilty to a 1991 charge of aggravated cocaine trafficking.

Late in the fourth grade LeBron moved in with the family of Frankie Walker, his youth basketball coach. "It changed my life," LeBron says. "The next year I had perfect attendance and a B average." By the sixth grade LeBron was splitting time between the Walkers' home and Gloria's, and soon Jackson reentered the picture, providing financial support, Gloria says, from his work as a concert promoter and a full-time drug counselor at an Akron outreach program. LeBron, who has never met his biological father, refers to Jackson as "Dad."

LeBron has been Akron's rising star ever since he led his eighth-grade team to the finals of a national AAU tournament. Though he says he's considering Duke, North Carolina, Florida, Ohio State, and Louisville, no one believes he'll go to college. Meanwhile Gloria, thirty-four, and Eddie, thirty-five, are busy crisscrossing the country, "listening to folks, letting them give their sales pitch, weighing the options," as Gloria puts it. They attended the Super Bowl in New Orleans after having met with "some representatives there in regards to some marketing" for LeBron, which is all Gloria will say.

Adidas already has a relationship with LeBron through its sponsorship, now in its second year, of the St. Vincent–St. Mary team (LeBron even got to help design the Irish's uniforms) and of an Oakland AAU team that he has played on the last two years. Gloria and Eddie have visited the suburban Los Angeles home of Vaccaro, and LeBron has attended Vaccaro's ABCD Camp in Teaneck, N.J. Nike has gone to a full-court press as well, hosting Gloria and Eddie in Oregon for a meeting with company chairman Phil Knight. "Why go through the middleman when you can go straight to the top?" Gloria says. "Nike's very interested."

Jordan could play a role, too. "This is going to be like a Shakespearean drama," Vaccaro predicts. "Basically, only two people are involved: me or Michael? Adidas or Nike? Whoever it is, LeBron's going to translate far and wide. I believe that."

"A lot of NBA players who wear Nike have never gotten to meet Phil Knight, but it's also an honor to meet the Adidas people like Sonny Vaccaro," Jackson says with perfect politesse. Either way, Jackson knows LeBron's in the driver's seat, yet he also knows firsthand that the distance from jail to the office of a multinational's chairman is shorter than you'd think. Not long before his meeting with Knight, Jackson pleaded no contest to a disorderly conduct charge and received a suspended thirty-day sentence for his role in an altercation last July at an Akron bar.

For now LeBron exists in a weird netherworld between high school student and multimillionaire, between dependent child and made man. He's both, of course. At Gund Arena during the Cavaliers game, middle-aged fathers and mothers asked him to pose for pictures; LeBron dutifully complied. Later, an eleven-year-old boy in a Jordan jersey collared him for an autograph, one of dozens he signed during the evening. Even Cleveland Browns coach Butch Davis chatted up LeBron after the game. "Hey, LeBron! How you doing?" Davis said, slapping him on the back. "Want to be a wide receiver for us? Just for the red zone, how about that?"

It's heady stuff, but in so many other ways LeBron remains a kid. During a Cavaliers time-out, he frantically waved his arms as the rally crew shot plastic miniballs into the crowd. (He eventually snagged one, which he was still clutching when he met Jordan after the game.) On the ride back to Akron in a reporter's car, LeBron simultaneously blasted Jay-Z over the stereo, gabbed on his cellphone, and checked his two-way pager for messages from pals like Sebastian Telfair, the Brooklyn whiz kid who's regarded as the nation's best sophomore.

He's almost there, but not yet. Only one more year—with no injuries, no complications—and he'll make it. Then he can worry about the next step. Above the television in the Jameses' modest west Akron apartment, LeBron keeps an ersatz *SI* cover featuring his photograph and the cover line IS HE THE NEXT MICHAEL JORDAN? It's preposterously too early to answer, of course, yet judging from young LeBron's unprecedented rise, it's a question that is at least worth asking.

Modern Maturity

FROM *Sports Illustrated,* OCTOBER 29, 2001

When Wahl got the rare chance early on to write about soccer in the pages of *Sports Illustrated,* he often massaged the assignment to tell the story he wanted to—as in this case, when he turned what was ostensibly a gamer on the 2001 MLS Cup (which ran only in select issues to certain subscribers) into a miniprofile of budding star Landon Donovan. Wahl had been covering Donovan since the 2000 Olympics, where his performance as an eighteen-year-old had established his status as American soccer's next big thing (and left Wahl baffled as to why coach Clive Charles hadn't played him more). Over the ensuing two decades, the pair—close in age, following similar career trajectories—developed a strong, mutually supportive relationship. Wahl found Donovan unusually curious, introspective, and candid for a star athlete—and a valued, reliable source. When David Beckham declined one-on-one interviews for Wahl's book *The Beckham Experiment: How the World's Most Famous Athlete Tried to Conquer America,* Donovan, the LA Galaxy's other major name, became the go-to voice for insights into the strange dynamics that marked Beckham's arrival in Major League Soccer.

For his part, Donovan came to trust Wahl, often confiding in him his ambivalence about the trappings of stardom, his sometimes flagging passion for the sport, and the psychological demands he faced as a modern athlete. But it was more than a writer-subject relationship; the two shared interests outside of sports, bonding over food, trading travel tips, and shooting the breeze. "We live in a world where we're all digital and on our phones and tweeting and texting," Donovan told the soccer writer Michael Lewis, recalling his relationship with Wahl. "We would just sit and have good long conversations, and I really valued that."

Eventually the two would become colleagues as well. In September 2021, Wahl and Donovan teamed up on a podcast project, *Road to Qatar,* providing postgame analysis after every USMNT World Cup qualifier. Donovan was also a centerpiece of *Good Rivals,* the 2022 Prime Video documentary series Wahl coproduced on the United States–Mexico soccer rivalry.

IN HIS PRIME, JOHN MCENROE NEVER HIT A TRUER HALF-VOLLEY. Late in the first half of MLS Cup 2001 on Sunday in Columbus, Ohio, nineteen-year-old San Jose Earthquakes forward Landon Donovan met a wicked short-hopped cross precisely on the sweet spot of his right foot. Suddenly the ball was in the back of the Los Angeles Galaxy net. "It took a glorious bounce," Donovan said after his brilliant play had set San Jose on course for a 2–1 come-from-behind victory in overtime. "It was one of those times when you know you've hit it well." Said Earthquakes coach Frank Yallop, "The last four goals Landon has scored have all been world class."

The Earthquakes had a lot of heroes in their remarkable jump from league doormats in 2000 to champions in '01. There was MLS Defender of the Year Jeff Agoos, the only player in league history to win four titles. There was defender Troy Dayak, who returned from a career-threatening neck injury this season and scored the walk-off header in a semifinal upset of the Miami Fusion. Then there was substitute forward Dwayne De Rosario, whose swerving golden goal on Sunday gave the championship to MLS's most historically inept franchise.

Most of all, though, the 2001 MLS playoffs will be remembered as the coming of age for Donovan. As recently as a year ago, Donovan was carrying a teddy bear on road trips, and he didn't even start on the U.S. under-23 team at the 2000 Olympics. After joining MLS last March, however, he ditched the bear, earned a starting spot on the senior national team, and established himself as the MVP of the MLS postseason, scoring five goals in six games for the Earthquakes.

Did we mention that he's only nineteen? Or that he's American? "This has been the best year of my life," Donovan said last week. "I have grown so much from playing day in and day out."

Donovan is Exhibit A for MLS's value when it comes to developing young U.S. players. In 1999, he signed a four-year, $400,000 contract with German Bundesliga club Bayer Leverkusen, only to be stuck playing on its reserve team in the fourth division. Homesick and disillusioned by the German emphasis on toughness over creativity, Donovan asked for a loan to MLS last spring. "I wanted to get out of Germany so bad," Donovan says. "If I weren't playing in MLS, I wouldn't be with the national team."

In the Americans' must-win World Cup qualifier against Jamaica on October 7, Donovan's penetrating run drew the berth-clinching penalty kick during the waning moments of the game. Nobody has observed his rapid ascent more closely than U.S. coach Bruce Arena. "Going from eighteen to nineteen years old, you're going to change," Arena says. "Landon already had a terrific first touch and was a good finisher, but what surprised me is how well he holds the ball. He's stronger and wiser, and he's an outstanding passer. He's dangerous every time he touches the ball."

Arena had a different impression of Donovan when he first saw him play three years ago. During a scrimmage in Bradenton, Florida, between Donovan's U.S. under-17 team and Arena's D.C. United, Donovan taunted the United players, who were in the process of winning three of the first four MLS titles. "He was a punk," Arena recalls. "That was my first contact with him, so you say, 'Holy s——, the kid has some balls.' But he has matured. Now he knows he can get his leg broken, too."

That hasn't happened yet, though not from a lack of physical play by opponents. Donovan absorbed twenty-five fouls in the playoffs, more than any other player, and in the semis he turned the top-seeded Fusion, the league's most skillful team, into a band of Laimbeer-worthy hack artists. Miami drew one red card and three yellows by systematically scything down Donovan. Then there was the off-the-ball headbutt he took from Ian Woan and the blatant kick in the shins from Ian Bishop. "I'd never seen guys be that cheap and dirty before," Donovan says. "Everybody plays harder in the postseason."

In other words, Donovan is learning, and growing up—fast. Not many nineteen-year-olds have their own car, their own apartment, and the pressure of being called the savior of American soccer. The responsibility is exhilarating, but there's fear that Donovan might become the oldest twenty-year-old in the world. (In this respect dying his hair an unfortunate shade of yellow seems to have been a good thing.) Donovan's mother, Donna Kenney-Cash, has noticed the differences between Landon and his twin sister, Tristan, who still lives at the family's Redlands, California, house. "Landon's more like a twenty-five- or thirty-year-old," his mother says, "while Tristan acts like any other kid her age. Sometimes I wish he could have been naive just a little bit longer."

So much was going through Donovan's mind after the game on Sunday. He was thinking of his brother Josh, twenty-two, who was set to leave for South Carolina on Monday to enlist, hoping to become an Army paratrooper. As Landon savored the MLS title in the back corner of the Earthquakes' locker room, he couldn't help but look forward to next June when, in all likelihood, he'll appear on the biggest stage, a World Cup stadium in Japan or South Korea. "I'm sure I'll dream about it in the off-season," he said. "That's what I'll be working for."

Didn't You Used to Be the Future?

From *Sports Illustrated*, April 19, 2010

Wahl had trained his reportorial eye on Freddy Adu since the Ghana-born player had been setting soccer message boards ablaze as he tore up the Maryland youth circuit as a preteen, sparking whispers that here at last might be the great American player the world had been waiting for. Wahl first wrote about thirteen-year-old Freddy for a 2003 *SI* package on potential future stars ("Chosen One, II," Adu's piece was forebodingly headlined) and followed up with another feature the next year after Freddy signed with Major League Soccer and DC United, at age fourteen for $1 million, making him, absurdly in retrospect, the highest-paid player in the league. Examining the pressures Freddy was under, Wahl concluded that first piece by asking "Are we ready for Freddy? And more to the point, is Freddy ready for us?"

Freddy was not. For this story—which ran in advance of the 2010 World Cup that so many had anticipated to be Adu's grand stage—Wahl found the player, now twenty, toiling in Greece, his promise long dissipated and with it the spotlight. A decade later, Wahl again caught up with Adu, wiser and more candid but still genial, for an eight-part podcast series, *American Prodigy,* that looked back on the Freddy phenomenon, including Wahl's own role in it. At one point during their interview, he asked Adu, "Do I owe you an apology?" While Adu brushed the question aside with a laugh, Wahl remained conflicted. "Did I do enough to temper everyone's expectations?" he wondered in that podcast. "Was I blinded by our obsession with sports prodigies? These questions still hit me when we mark the anniversary of my LeBron James cover story. People congratulate me for it. And sometimes I'll tell them, 'Thanks, but I did our Freddy Adu stories, too.'"

S TRAY DOGS. FREDDY ADU SEES THEM EVERYWHERE IN THESSA-loníki. Scavenging trash in the vacant lot by his practice field. Wandering in packs outside the hotel he called home for two months. Shadowing pedestrians with enough menace to spark visions of giant-needled rabies shots. Greece's second largest city is beautiful in many respects: the seaside beaches, the bustling restaurants, the sigh-inducing women. But no matter how hard Adu tries, he can't avoid the stray dogs.

They are a constant backdrop to Adu's own fight for survival in the Darwinian world of European soccer. Six years after making his professional debut at age fourteen with MLS's D.C. United, Adu is still trying to find consistent playing time with the Greek club Aris, his fourth European team in three years. He lives a dual existence. To mainstream U.S. sports fans he remains one of this country's best-known soccer players. Adu has nearly 350,000 Twitter followers (more than any other soccer star in the world except Brazil's Kaká). He has sat on David Letterman's couch, been the subject of a *60 Minutes* profile, and gotten a shout-out in a Jay-Z lyric.

Yet barring a major surprise, Adu, now twenty, will not be on the U.S.'s twenty-three-man World Cup roster in South Africa. With unproductive stops in Portugal and France before Greece, he has strayed from the path that he and so many others had envisioned when he signed a $1 million Nike deal in 2003 and became the highest-paid player in MLS before he had ever kicked a ball in the league. As a rookie Adu appeared with Pelé in a national ad campaign for Sierra Mist and had a sponsorship deal with Campbell's Soup. In '03 former MLS deputy commissioner Ivan Gazidis (who now runs England's Arsenal) called Adu "probably the best young player in the world."

There are so many questions: What happened? Why has Adu shown promise in major competitions at the youth level but failed to establish himself professionally in Europe? Does he have a future with the national team? And how many more opportunities will Adu get overseas? "I believe in him. That's why we signed him," says Antonio Calzado, Aris's international general manager. "But is this the last chance for Freddy to get to the top? Probably it is."

Yet if this sounds like a sad story, then why does U.S. goalkeeper Tim Howard maintain that Adu "has skills with the ball that not many—if any—American players possess"? And why is Adu so upbeat? "I'm only twenty," he says, flashing his magnetic smile. "People panic sometimes when things don't go right. I don't. I've still got a long way to go, but I'm on the right track now. I'm finally, *finally* on the right track."

———

GAME TIME IN Thessaloníki. It's a glorious spring night, perfect weather for the crosstown rivalry between Aris and PAOK, and Aris's Super 3 fan club is leaving nothing to chance. As the players march onto the field, the hard cores in the east stands ignite a fireworks display that makes it look as though the entire section has been napalmed. Nothing in the U.S.—or in the rest of Europe, for that matter—is quite like it. "It's crazy here, man," says Adu. No kidding. Since Adu and fellow American Eddie Johnson joined Aris in January, they've been sprayed by shards of glass after opposing fans shattered the roof over their bench and scurried for cover in the players' tunnel during a battle royal between bottle-throwing supporters.

Aris, in fifth place in the Greek league, defeats PAOK 2–0, sending the Super 3 into flare-burning, rocket-launching ecstasy. But for the third straight game Adu stays rooted to the bench. After starting four times on the left wing and scoring two goals in February, Adu has played twice in the last eight games through Sunday. The prevailing view among Greek journalists and fans is that Adu has good technical skills, especially with his favored left foot, but he plays "too young," with an underdeveloped awareness for tactics, defensive duties, and knowing when less is more on offense.

The scouting report among coaches is that Adu is capable of a dangerous pass or shot but that he's not fast and doesn't have much of an engine for the modern game. The Aris coach, Héctor Cúper, argues that Adu also needs to be tougher mentally. "I think Adu is paying a little bit for the acceleration he had to professional soccer," says Cúper, who has coached Italy's Inter Milan and led Spain's Valencia to two Champions League finals. He notes that in European clubs' youth programs, "you are allowed to be more free, to prepare more technically," but at the senior level "you have to *win*. When someone jumps directly to this level, you must be a phenomenon from your head to your feet. If you aren't, it's very difficult. He has to be very strong psychologically."

Adu showed promise for U.S. youth teams, notably during the U20 World Cup in 2007 (where he captained the team and led an upset of Brazil) and the '08 Olympics (particularly in a 2–2 tie against the Netherlands). So the question persists: Why hasn't that success carried over to his pro career? "I watch video of me playing well in the Under-20 World Cup or the Olympics, and I'm like, 'Man, how can I not be playing here?'" Adu says. "It's taken me the last year and a half to figure it out. I was always satisfied with making one or two plays during training and thinking I had a good practice. There's so much more to it than that. Coaches see the times you cut off passing lanes or got behind the ball. Those are things that tell them they can count on you for ninety minutes."

Until Adu finds regular playing time at the club level, it's hard to envision that he'll get called back to the national team. He was on the U.S. roster for last year's Confederations Cup but didn't see the field, and he hasn't been in a U.S. camp since struggling with the B team at last July's Gold Cup and barely playing at the club level last fall. "It's a case of a young player who has aspirations but still hasn't been able to establish himself," says U.S. coach Bob Bradley. "When you go to Europe, nothing is ever going to just get handed to you. It's that ability to establish yourself within the team, with the coaches. He's in the midst of all that, and when you add on the pressure of the early recognition and the hype, that makes it in some ways harder."

Now that he's twenty, it's easier for Adu to interact with his teammates off the field, and Aris players say they enjoy sharing a coffee or going to dinner with him. It was more challenging for Adu as a fourteen-year-old at D.C. United, where, he says, he "only felt comfortable with a couple of people. There were some guys who never warmed up to you because of everything you had." Adu showed only flashes of his potential in MLS, scoring twelve goals in three and a half seasons with D.C. United and Real Salt Lake, and he joined Portugal's Benfica on a $2 million transfer in 2007. At first he saw occasional action there, scoring two goals in eleven appearances, but Benfica went through three coaches in 2007–08, and the last of them (Fernando Chalana) did not play Adu at all after he returned from the Olympic qualifying tournament.

Things really went downhill when Benfica loaned Adu to Monaco of the French league for 2008–09. Jérôme de Bontin, a French-American member of the U.S. Soccer Federation's board of trustees, had taken over as president at Monaco, and he wanted to add Americans to the team. "Maybe the highlight of his stay was the first day of practice," says de Bontin. "Freddy scored three beautiful goals. Everybody in the academy was excited about him, not to mention the fact that he was a riot in the locker room." But Monaco's coach, a Brazilian named Ricardo Carvalho, started Adu only once that season. Says de Bontin, "Everybody had the same analysis. He had incredible talent, yet he was lacking standard tactical knowledge that most players his age had. It was tied to the fact that he became professional at fourteen and in some ways stopped learning at fifteen."

While Adu was not an automatic starter during his MLS days, the league's small rosters could never replicate the constant battle for playing time on European teams with no roster limits. As U.S. under-20 coach Thomas Rongen says, "Our creative players have a tough time sometimes adjusting to the day-to-day of competing in Europe, which is different from our youth national teams or MLS." Rongen adds that while Adu at his best can change a game in the attacking end, "a lot of coaches say he is still to a certain extent a luxury player." The modern game values athleticism and requires even the best players to have some defensive responsibilities, and, Rongen says, "that was an area where Freddy really needed to grow and become better." Nor has Adu proved himself to be such a phenomenon offensively that a team in Europe (or, for that matter, MLS) would choose to build around him.

Last fall Adu went out on loan again from Benfica, this time to Belenenses, a team at the bottom of the Portuguese first division. It was a hastily arranged deal that came together on the last day before the transfer deadline. "I didn't even have a chance to talk to the coach before I went there," says Adu, who started just once and soon began seeking a way out. In January, he joined Aris on an eighteen-month loan. Adu now has until the end of the 2010–11 season, when his contract runs out, to prove himself in European soccer. "It's like they gave you a lifeline," Adu says. "I started four games in a row, which is the most I have since MLS. I feel like a new person, and I'm happy again." It wasn't the only change Adu made; he also dumped his agent, IMG's Max Eisenbud, and rehired his previous one, Richard Motzkin.

If Adu can't make an impact as a pro in Europe over the next year, he will most likely return to MLS. The question these days is how to view him: as a sixth-year pro who hasn't lived up to the hype or as a twenty-year-old who still has potential? De Bontin hopes Adu can be another Franck Ribéry, the late-blooming French midfielder who played for several midlevel teams before rising to the top of the soccer world, starting for France in the 2006 World Cup final and starring for German powerhouse Bayern Munich. ("Freddy has enough talent to succeed," de Bontin says.) Adu certainly thinks such a track is possible. "I want to be one of the best players to play this sport one day," he says. "I still have the chance to do that, and I want to work hard to get there."

It is an odd twist, the hope that an athlete who turned pro at thirteen could become, in the end, a late bloomer. But if Freddy Adu is going to make it, that's how it will have to be.

2

TROPHY LIFTS

To countless soccer-loving Americans, a World Cup or Olympic or Champions League final wasn't truly over until Wahl had weighed in from Paris or Johannesburg or Rio. Whether delivered in print or uploaded to SI.com, Wahl's game reports—on title matches involving clubs and countries, men and women—featured the same hallmarks of color and context. Yet as larger forces led *Sports Illustrated* to publish its print magazine less and less frequently, the brand began to move fast-closing news stories to its website. Even then Wahl couldn't shake the habits he had learned over more than a decade as a deadline artist for a sports newsweekly, including filing valedictory dispatches from the NCAA men's basketball Final Four. And when he moved on to Substack, he promised subscribers what he nostalgically referred to as the "magazine-style feature"—by which he meant the kind of sweeping account that read like the first rough draft of history, even if it had been pulled together in a frenzy after the final whistle or buzzer. A Wahl gamer had all the elements of a definitive piece, from a featurized retelling of the twists and turns that had brought a team to the cusp of a title to a peek behind the curtain before, during, and after the climactic game. And if some drama had unspooled during the course of the match, you could count on Wahl to both contextualize it and tease out the most salient reactions from the babel of the press conference and the mosh pit of the mixed zone. "He had the best postgame in journalism," says soccer podcaster and reporter Musa Okwonga. "He always asked the right questions."

Coup de Grâce

FROM *Sports Illustrated*, JULY 20, 1998

For the four decades after its launch in 1954, *Sports Illustrated* treated soccer as an afterthought, though the sport did begin to find more space in the magazine after the United States hosted the World Cup in 1994. When Wahl arrived as a reporter two years later, he made clear his passion for *fútbol*. (The Argentina scarf hanging on his office wall was but one giveaway.) Because his deep knowledge of the game was apparent as well, *SI* dispatched him as one of three correspondents to France for World Cup '98—a plum gig for someone only twenty-four years old. Toward the end of the five-week tournament the two senior writers had other assignments beckoning, leaving editors with a tough call: Could they trust Wahl to cover the World Cup final on Sunday and file a two-thousand-word story first thing Monday morning New York time, knowing that, if he missed the mark, there would be little time to make changes before the magazine closed that night? One of the biggest arguments in his favor was Wahl himself: He badly wanted the job and was sure he could deliver. Any doubts evaporated when the editors read the first few sentences he filed, which demonstrate a polish and command worthy of the staff's most seasoned pros. Only later did Wahl reveal that he had made a rookie mistake and left his laptop at the hotel; unflustered, he composed the story in his head as he walked from the Stade de France among a jubilant throng after Les Bleus's 3–0 upset of Brazil. The piece established Wahl as *SI*'s soccer writer, though it also served as a reminder of where the sport stood in the pecking order: Despite Wahl's fierce lobbying from across the Atlantic that Monday, the cover of the issue wasn't Zinedine Zidane displaying his brilliance in a story of global resonance but New Orleans Saints coach Mike Ditka smoking a cigar during the NFL offseason.

I N SAINT-DENIS, THE PARIS SUBURB WHERE THE FRENCH ONCE buried their kings, a new one ascended last week. Zinedine Zidane certainly doesn't look the part. He's quiet, usually gazing down at the ground. He's going prematurely bald. He can appear slow and sometimes clumsy. At one point on his way through the interview room at the Stade de France after the World Cup final on Sunday, he stumbled on the carpet like a young girl wearing her first high heels. Give Zidane a ball and put him on a soccer field, though, and he becomes the Baryshnikov of the midfield, deftly toe-poking a pass in one direction, gamely looping a long ball in the other, holding his head regally erect all the while. It should be noted that Zizou, as he is known, never trips on grass.

He also scores, but not very often and almost never with his noggin. Which made the two goals he netted with his ever-expanding forehead against Brazil on Sunday nearly as shocking as the game's outcome: a 3–0 victory that gave France its first world championship after sixty-eight years of futility. Not since the 1978 World Cup in Argentina had the host country won the eleven-pound gold trophy. Never had mighty Brazil, the defending and four-time champion, suffered a more lopsided defeat in eighty World Cup games dating to 1930.

That Zidane is the son of Algerian immigrants was appropriate. The increasing number of immigrants in France is a hot political topic there, and the team that dethroned Brazil included players who were born or had roots in lands ranging from Armenia to Ghana, Guadeloupe to New Caledonia. Two years ago, the leader of France's right-wing National Front party, Jean-Marie Le Pen, had complained that it was "artificial to bring players from abroad and call it the French team," even though every member of the World Cup squad had been a French citizen for years. As Les Bleus marched to the final, however, the racial and cultural diversity of the team became a point of Gallic pride. Wrote a columnist for the newsmagazine Le Nouvel Observateur, "They can be blacks, whites and all shades of beige, but that doesn't prevent them from singing their national anthem with conviction, even if that irritates Mr. Le Pen."

The twenty-six-year-old Zidane, who grew up in a rough section of Marseilles called La Castellane, was by Sunday night receiving hugs from French president Jacques Chirac and being toasted in the wildest celebration Paris has seen since the liberation. Zizou was also savoring a measure of redemption. Ever since he had burst onto the French soccer scene with Bordeaux three years ago, he had been compared to Michel Platini, the greatest of French playmakers, who guided Les Bleus to the World Cup semifinals in 1982 and '86—but until Sunday those comparisons had been a curse. Although Zidane had come to be recognized as one of the world's best playmakers while with his club in Italy's Serie A, Juventus, he had been dubbed *le chat noir* (the black cat) by the French media because he seemed jinxed in the big games, performing dismally in the 1996 European Championships and the '97 and '98 Champions League finals.

Early in this Cup, Zidane created his own bad luck. He was ejected from France's second game for foolishly raking his cleats over the back of a fallen Saudi Arabian player. After serving a two-game suspension, he returned for his team's quarterfinal victory over Italy, and though he flashed moments of passing brilliance (not to mention brilliant passing), he provided nothing memorable until Sunday. "It's true that I wanted to score a goal, but two you can hardly imagine," Zidane said after the win over Brazil.

"He scored with his head," marveled French coach Aimé Jacquet. "Who could have predicted that?"

For that matter, hardly anyone predicted a victory by France, a team that had never before reached the Cup final. Even after Les Bleus advanced with a 2–1 semifinal triumph over Croatia, there was something of a pretender's air about them. Although they had scored more goals than any other country in the first round (nine to Brazil's six), they had then found the back of the net only three times (compared with Brazil's eight) from the second round through the semis. Worse yet, all three of those goals had been scored by defenders. So it wasn't surprising last week that Romário, the injured Brazilian forward, predicted a 4–0 win for his team, or that Brazil coach Mário Zagallo assured reporters that he had never been more confident of a victory. "France only has Zidane," Zagallo said. "Brazil has several like him." The consensus was that Brazil was an even more skilled and entertaining outfit than it had been in '94. "At this moment," defender Roberto Carlos said two days before the final, "our team has no weaknesses." This wasn't necessarily true. In fact, Brazil's twenty-one-year-old star striker, Ronaldo, was suffering from a mysterious ailment. The two-time world player of the year sat out two practices after supposedly injuring his left ankle in Brazil's semifinal victory over the Netherlands five days before the final. Then, in the hours leading up to Sunday's 9:00 P.M. game, word spread that Ronaldo would not start. His girlfriend, Susana Werner (aka Ronaldinha), told *SI* that the medicine he was taking for his ankle had made him sick. When FIFA, soccer's international governing body, issued the starting lineups at 8:15, Ronaldo's name was not on the list. Then, just before kickoff, FIFA announced that he would start after all. Ronaldo played all ninety minutes, seemingly at full speed and certainly without a limp. The next day he revealed that he had experienced convulsions for a half minute hours before the match. The Brazil team doctor said Ronaldo was feeling "emotional stress."

Whatever the reason for Ronaldo's brief withdrawal from the lineup, France held him and the rest of the Brazilian offense in check. The only time Ronaldo got free with the ball was early in the second half, when he had ten feet of open space between him and French keeper Fabien Barthez. Ronaldo wound up and fired; Barthez smothered the shot like a circus performer catching a cannonball. "Ronaldo was not fit to play, and this was a major psychological blow," Zagallo said after the game. "Everyone was very upset, and so the team played to less than its full potential." Considering the vague nature of Ronaldo's injury, Zagallo's plaint sounded a lot like a whine. In the end, the makers of the bronzed Ronaldo likenesses being sold for $300 at Brazil's training camp might have had it right: Ronaldo was a bust.

Part of the credit for stopping him should have gone to Laurent Blanc, the veteran French defender who missed the final because of a dubious red card against Croatia. A former teammate of Ronaldo's on the Spanish club Barcelona, Blanc briefed his replacement, Frank Leboeuf, before the final. "He told me that when Ronaldo dribbles, he takes the left side every time," Leboeuf explained later. "So once I was in front of him, it was easy to tackle him."

No World Cup champion has owed more to its back line than France. These four Musketeers—Blanc, Marcel Desailly, Bixente Lizarazu, and Lilian Thuram—allowed only one goal (by Croatia) in the run of play for the tournament, even though two of the defenders were playing out of position. The graceful central defender Desailly, a native of Ghana, usually plays defensive midfield for his club, AC Milan. Thuram, a native of Guadeloupe and Les Bleus's unparalleled right back, normally roams the middle of the defense for his Italian club, Parma. "If you approach the game with the right attitude," said Thuram, "you can play any position."

Or, like Thuram, seemingly *every* position. In the win over Croatia, Thuram became a national hero by scoring both of his team's goals. His skill as a defender had never been questioned—Thuram was named foreign player of the year in Serie A last season—but he had not scored in thirty-six previous games for the national team. After his second goal, Thuram fell to the Stade de France turf and struck the pose of Rodin's *The Thinker,* which made sense, for he is an avid reader of philosophy whose favorite book is Antoine de Saint-Exupéry's *The Little Prince.* Thuram's two-way play was so breathtaking that it made one wonder: Could the best player in the world be a defender? "You write and write about me and Ronaldo," Zidane said last week, "but you don't even see that the greatest footballer of all is right in front of you: Lilian Thuram."

One sequence that involved Thuram midway through the first half on Sunday neatly summed up the contrasts of the game. With the final scoreless, Thuram lunged to steal a pass on the right sideline, then kept the ball alive by lifting it over two onrushing Brazilian defenders as though he were flipping a pancake. The ball traced the sideline chalk until it came to French midfielder Christian Karembeu, a New Caledonian, who hustled down the right side into Brazil's defensive third. Just when it appeared Karembeu had lost the ball, Roberto Carlos muffed the easy clearance, and suddenly France had a corner kick.

Zidane outleaped Brazilian midfielder Leonardo to the ball and drilled in his first goal. Just before intermission, Zizou worked the same magic on another corner, this one from the left side. Then midway through the second half, after Desailly was ejected for his second yellow card, France braced for Brazil's final assault. None came. Midfielder Emmanuel Petit insulted Brazil with a shorthanded goal in injury time. Had its bumbling forwards, Stéphane Guivarc'h and Christophe Dugarry, not botched wide-open shots, France might have won 6–0.

Afterward, Chirac and other pols scurried to attach themselves to the new champions of *le foot,* a sport that had been viewed with typical French disdain before the tournament. It was as if Thuram had opened *The Little Prince* and read a passage to the nation: "It is only with the heart that one can see rightly. What is essential is invisible to the eye." How else could one explain the public outpouring that took place on the day of the final, when thousands of French citizens lined the streets of Paris to cheer the team bus? "It was like after the war in 1945," said Leboeuf.

After the game on Sunday, a million revelers flocked to the Arc de Triomphe, waving what seemed to be a million tricolors. Elderly women with wide smiles chanted *"On est le champion!"* (We are the champion!) Teenagers with ZIZOU painted on their chests kicked crushed Coke cans and screamed as if they had just scored in the Cup final. Firecrackers popped. Whistles blew. Klaxons blared. It was 3:00 A.M. on the Champs-Elysées, and the celebration had only just begun.

Out of This World

FROM *Sports Illustrated*, JULY 19, 1999

Scarcely a year earlier, an NFL coach chomping on a cigar had beaten out Wahl's story from the men's World Cup for a spot on *Sports Illustrated*'s cover. That this piece on the U.S. women's national team's 1999 World Cup title did claim that iconic real estate was more a result of jingoism, historic TV ratings, and a sleepy summer sports calendar than any spasm of soccer boosterism or feminist consciousness in the corridors of *SI*. But Wahl understood the trophy's importance, and he activated all his talents to convey it, delivering everything readers expected in a fast-closing newsmagazine story: an opener informed by thorough reporting; a billboard or "nut" paragraph summarizing what had happened and contextualizing what it meant; and a catalog of the many subplots in the U.S. team's victory, from a sidelined superstar hooked up to an IV to a headed clearance off the goal line in extra time to a goalkeeper who fudged the rules to make a crucial penalty save. In the heat of deadline Wahl even came up with a bumper sticker–worthy coinage—KEPT HER COOL, LOST HER SHIRT—to describe Brandi Chastain's winning penalty kick and its celebratory aftermath. The cover image of the exultant Chastain in a sports bra surmounting the word *Yes!* would touch off a round of complaints from prudish readers. But it became symbolic, helping to fix fast the moment. What the 1958 NFL title game between the Colts and the Giants was to pro football and the 1979 NCAA final between Magic Johnson's Michigan State and Larry Bird's Indiana State was to college basketball, that match was to women's soccer in the United States. And from the sense of occasion suffusing his account, you can tell that Wahl knew it.

S HE WASN'T EVEN SUPPOSED TO TAKE THE KICK. NOT WHEN THE list of U.S. shooters was first drawn up, anyway. In the waning moments of extra time during last Saturday's scoreless Women's World Cup final in Pasadena, U.S. coach Tony DiCicco asked assistant Lauren Gregg to write down the players who could convert their shots with the weight of a nation on their shoulders in a penalty-kick shoot-out. Only five would be guaranteed a chance, and defender Brandi Chastain was not among Gregg's choices. She was sixth on the assistant's list, a reserve to be used only if the U.S. and China were still tied after five rounds.

Until four months ago Chastain had been among DiCicco's top picks to take a penalty kick—but then she banged a right-footed shot off the crossbar in a 2–1 exhibition loss to China. Still, DiCicco didn't feel comfortable leaving her off the list. He had watched his team practice PKs in training all week, had watched Chastain work on blasting shots with her less dominant left foot, and had liked what he'd seen. He also knew that penalty kicks, like free throws, have almost nothing to do with physical skills. In a city park on a summer day, most semiathletic citizens—Americans, even—could poke the ball twelve yards past a well-trained goalkeeper. But as a method of deciding a World Cup final, penalties are without a doubt sports' most diabolical invention, requiring a Zen-like concentration. As DiCicco would say later, "Brandi always wants to take penalty kicks. Not many players do."

So he played a hunch, sending Gregg over to Chastain for a short talk. "Brandi, do you think you can make it?" Gregg asked.

"Yeah, I do," Chastain replied.

"You'll have to use your left foot."

Chastain nodded. Ten harrowing minutes later, taking the shot that could break a 4–4 tie and give the U.S. the Cup, she sent a laser past Chinese goalkeeper Gao Hong. With one swift kick Chastain coronated the U.S. women as Queens of the World, which seemed like the next logical step for a team that had gone from near obscurity to a national conversation piece in just three weeks. With an estimated 40 million U.S. viewers, the Cup final was the most watched soccer match in the history of network television, and the turnout of 90,185 at the Rose Bowl was the largest ever at a women's sporting event.

A media throng of 2,100 attended the tournament as well—or 2,099 more than greeted the U.S. team in 1991, when it returned from China carrying the first Women's World Cup trophy. Entering this year's event, the favored Americans faced a doubly daunting task: win the tournament and make a case for the start-up of a women's pro league in the U.S. Their victory was a seminal moment in women's sports and will no doubt engender years of debate over who was the biggest hero of this Cup. Was it goalkeeper Briana Scurry, whose diving save on China's third-round penalty kick set the stage for the game-winner? Or forward Mia Hamm, who keyed the U.S. attack without scoring a goal in the last four Cup games, then overcame her self-doubt during the shoot-out? Or Kristine Lilly, the midfielder who robbed China of victory in extra time by heading a ball out of the goalmouth? Or was it Chastain, who kept her cool before her climactic boot and lost her shirt afterward?

All those Americans are worthy, but none more than the one who wasn't even on the field during those last nerve-racking moments. Instead, midfielder Michelle Akers was on a gurney in the U.S. locker room, wearing an oxygen mask and with an IV in each arm. At the end of regulation, Akers had smacked into Scurry on a Chinese corner kick and slumped woozily to the turf. After being led off the field, she was surrounded by doctors trying to decide whether her concussion and dehydration merited a trip to the emergency room.

"I was loony," Akers said late Saturday night, after absorbing four liters of fluid intravenously, twice the postgame dosage she normally receives to combat chronic fatigue syndrome. Akers was so loony, in fact, that during extra time she kept asking for the score, even though a TV in the room was tuned to the game. She struggled to even follow the shoot-out, but when it came time for Chastain's kick, she pulled herself up to watch. As soon as Chastain scored, Akers ripped out her IV lines, tossed aside the oxygen mask, and walked—haltingly, but under her own power—to the field for the awards ceremony.

The team's oldest player at thirty-three, Akers was also its most important—just as she had been in '91 when she scored a Cup-high ten goals. Because of chronic fatigue, she has since been forced to move from forward to defensive midfield, yet she's still dominant. On defense Akers retreated time and again to make crucial clears. On offense she played the most pressure-packed position, receiving the ball in the midfield and making split-second decisions before defenders converged on her. "She'll keep nine out of ten balls when she's under pressure," says Jim Rudy, Akers's coach at Central Florida. "That gives the midfield great confidence to go forward immediately, which forces the other team to defend in numbers. It changes the whole psychology of the game. It's like, Here they come again."

So go ahead, lionize Akers. Her teammates do. They call her Mufasa, after the gallant feline in *The Lion King*, ostensibly for her long mane of curly hair but just as much for her unsurpassed strength. Though a devout Christian, she plays with a vengeance, and it was no coincidence that she was the only U.S. player to get a yellow card (two, in fact) in the tournament. "It's not like I go out there and think I'm the Terminator," she says. "I play hard, and people just bounce off me, or I go through them. I don't notice it until after I get hit in the face."

The KO of Akers nearly revived the Chinese, who had entered the final with the tournament's most potent offense. For almost the entire game the Americans had harried China with their version of a full-court press—the 100 defense—which prevented the Chinese midfielders from giving quick support to their forwards. But with Akers off the field during extra time, the Chinese began attacking with greater abandon. After taking just two shots on goal in the game's regulation ninety minutes, they fired three in the thirty-minute extra time, including one that should have been decisive: defender Fan Yunjie's header off a corner kick. "I was like, Uh-oh, the ball's behind me," Scurry said later. But so, too, was Lilly. Stationed at her usual spot on the near post, she headed the ball off the goal line. "Just doing my job," Lilly said.

The Americans recovered to force the game into penalty kicks, which were knotted at two when midfielder Liu Ying faced Scurry. "I saw her body language when she was walking up to the penalty spot," Scurry said. "She didn't look like she really wanted to be there. Her shoulders were slumped, and she looked tired. I thought, This is the one."

Just as Liu approached the ball, Scurry sprang forward from her haunches and immediately leaped to her left, where she parried Liu's strong but poorly placed shot with ease. Though Scurry had violated the rules—goalkeepers are allowed to move laterally before the shot but forbidden from advancing toward the shooter—she was willing to take the risk. "If I jump out and save it but the referee calls it back, they have to do it again," she said. "Now I know where they're shooting, and it's even more pressure on them."

Did somebody say pressure? After Lilly nailed her PK to give the U.S. a 3–2 lead and China drew even again to open the fourth round, no player had more pressure on her than Hamm, whose ensuing shot was a fascinating character study. When asked earlier in the tournament why she wasn't the team's top choice for taking penalty kicks, Hamm, the greatest goal scorer in soccer history, admitted that it was due to a short-age of confidence. Sure enough, in the last anxiety-filled minutes before the World Cup shoot-out, Hamm asked Gregg if forward Shannon Mac-Millan could take the shot instead. She couldn't, because DiCicco had already submitted the list—with Hamm's name on it—to the referee.

None of it mattered. Hamm, who went goalless after scoring twice in the first two games, banished her demons and buried her kick. After China's last kicker, star striker Sun Wen, converted to tie it at 4–all, up stepped Chastain, who had blamed herself for the loss to the Chinese in March. "I thought I had let my team down," she said on Saturday night. "In this environment everyone works so hard and puts themselves on the line. They didn't look at me and say, 'God, you let us down,' but I felt like that inside."

At the start of the Cup, DiCicco had made an odd request of the thirty-year-old Chastain: Switch to your left foot when practicing pen-alty kicks. "Whenever Brandi kicked with her right foot, she would al-ways shoot to the goalkeeper's left," he explained. "It got to the point where the keeper knew where she was going." But Chastain is the U.S. player who is most adept with both feet, and she didn't flinch, just as she didn't when DiCicco moved her ahead of midfielder Julie Foudy on Gregg's list. Upon beating Gao—to the keeper's left, no less—Chastain fell to her knees like Björn Borg after winning Wimbledon and ripped off her jersey, waving it above her head to the thundering crowd.

It was the second time that a World Cup final at the Rose Bowl had ended on penalty kicks after a scoreless tie, though this was an entirely different game than the 1994 men's final, in which Brazil beat Italy. The main reason, of course, was that American fans were following their own team, suffering with it, waiting for that one tiny advantage that fi-nally came in the shoot-out.

Whether the U.S. team accomplished its other mission—to generate a fan base and corporate support for a women's pro league—remains to be seen. Mark Abbott, the former CEO of Major League Soccer, is expected to present a business plan to the U.S. Soccer Federation by the end of the year for a proposed league that would begin play in 2001. The international soccer community, however, is circumspect. "There's a huge difference between the short focus of the World Cup, where all the stars are concentrated, and week-in and week-out games at a lower level," says FIFA spokesman Keith Cooper. "There are thirty outstanding, hard-core female players in the world. If you want a national league, say ten teams, you only have three per team. There's a rapid falloff in talent from the top."

Crowds and TV viewers haven't exactly flocked to MLS, despite the commercial success here of the '94 Cup and a broader talent base of male players. Still, it's conceivable that a U.S. women's league would cater to more women and more suburban households than MLS. The U.S. team will also have another chance to drum up national support next summer, when it defends its Olympic title in Sydney.

While the U.S. squad should remain largely intact, Akers hasn't decided whether she will retire or play for one more gold medal, and she wasn't inclined to think about it last Saturday night as she shuffled onto the veranda of the Pasadena Ritz-Carlton for the team's celebration party. She looked typically drained. Her face was wan and discolored with pale blotches, and she wore a butterfly bandage on the crook of each arm where the IVs had left their marks. She was smiling, though, cradling a nonalcoholic beer and speaking with her parents, Bob and Sue, and with 1991 World Cup teammate Carin Gabarra. As if on cue, Gloria Gaynor's "I Will Survive" came over the loudspeakers.

Then Akers, whom DiCicco calls the best woman player ever, couldn't resist repeating what President Clinton had told her when he visited the U.S. locker room after the game: "From someone who knows how to take a hit, I really admire you."

Rock Chalk, Champions

FROM *Sports Illustrated*, APRIL 14, 2008

During its heyday as a newsweekly, each issue of *Sports Illustrated* came together in a rush, with a typical closing story filed over Saturday night, wrestled into publishable shape on Sunday, and shipped to the printer by Monday evening. Editors made one huge exception: They held open the cover and six to eight pages for Monday night's NCAA men's basketball championship game. From the final buzzer around midnight, until 4:00 A.M. or so, the writer on assignment faced the magazine's toughest deadline. To ease that burden, editors assigned *two* writers to the Final Four. On Sunday each sent in a prefile focused on one winner of Saturday's semifinals; whichever team were to win on Monday night, that writer would need to add only a top, bottom, and a few feathered-in paragraphs. In 2003, Wahl had followed Kansas, the school both his parents attended, into the title game, only to watch the Jayhawks lose to Syracuse and his prefile die on the pressroom floor. Subsequent prefiles in 2004 and '05 met a similar fate. And then his fortunes turned. Beginning with Florida's title in 2006, continuing with the Gators again in '07, and ultimately in this account of a memorable overtime victory for Wahl University, he scored a three-peat.

THE BALL FLOATED THROUGH THE AIR, ITS PEBBLED SURFACE spinning softly, as serene and peaceful as a space capsule in a low-earth orbit. At 10:29 P.M. CDT on Monday at the Alamodome in San Antonio, the fate of a college basketball season rested on Kansas guard Mario Chalmers—or, to be more precise, on his last-ditch three-pointer, a make-or-break heave with 2.1 seconds left that would either send the NCAA title game into overtime or give Memphis, clinging to a 63–60 lead, its first championship in school history.

In his mind's eye Chalmers had been here before. As a four-year-old in Anchorage he and his father, Ronnie, would set up a makeshift basketball arena in their family room, complete with two Nerf basketball goals, couches for team benches and even space for Mario's mother, Almarie, to perform "The Star-Spangled Banner." Mario would often skip to the finish and (*three, two, one!*) launch a bomb with the championship on the line. In those days, as on Monday night, Super Mario was *money.* "As soon as it left my hand it felt good, and I knew it was going in," Chalmers said after his miraculous trey from the top of the key had completed KU's rise from a nine-point abyss with 2:12 left in regulation. "I just waited for it to hit the net."

The Jayhawks' 75–68 overtime victory was a rare fantastic finish in college basketball's crown jewel, the most riveting final since Connecticut upset Duke 77–74 in 1999, and it showcased the remarkable balance of Kansas, the only Final Four team not to have an All-America. If the hero wasn't Chalmers, the Final Four's Most Outstanding Player, it was forward Darrell Arthur, who overpowered Tigers forward Joey Dorsey with 20 points and ten rebounds. Or swingman Brandon Rush, whose two overtime buckets crushed Memphis's hopes. Or maybe the entire Kansas defense, which slowed the Tigers' dribble-drive motion attack and held them to just 40.3 percent shooting.

But Memphis had a hand in its own demise. All season long the Tigers had claimed that their woeful 60.7 percent free throw shooting wouldn't be their undoing when the games counted most, and sure enough, the Tigers had made fifty of their last fifty-nine foul shots entering Monday's final. But against Kansas their confidence finally failed them at the worst possible moment. Guards Chris Douglas-Roberts and Derrick Rose, Memphis's two best players, sank only one of five from the line in the final 1:15 of regulation, opening the door for the Jayhawks' comeback. "I let them down by missing those free throws," said Douglas-Roberts, who apologized to the team in the locker room and blamed himself for the loss.

Rose hadn't acted like a freshman all night, scoring 18 points and leading a second-half charge, but with that 63–60 lead he cracked, failing to heed coach John Calipari's instructions to foul Kansas point guard Sherron Collins before he could dish to Chalmers for the equalizing three-pointer. Afterward Rose was inconsolable, crying outside the locker room as the Reverend Jesse Jackson, the team's unofficial spiritual adviser, held him up. "Don't look like a freshman crying. It looks pitiful," Jackson whispered into Rose's left ear. "Smile through your tears and speak above your pain."

On the other side the emotion was just as raw, courtesy of Chalmers's last-second lifeline. "It will probably be," said Jayhawks coach Bill Self, "the biggest shot ever made in Kansas history."

IN PRESENTING KANSAS with its third NCAA basketball championship, the forty-five-year-old Self laid to rest any remaining doubts that he couldn't win the Big One. But it was the Jayhawks' stomach-churning 59–57 defeat of tenth-seeded Davidson to reach San Antonio—Self's first Elite Eight victory in five tries at three schools—that liberated not just the coach but also his entire team from paralyzing self-doubt. "I believe in some weird way that the Elite Eight game was the best thing that could have happened for us," Self said last week during a quiet moment in his hotel aerie overlooking the Alamodome. "We had to play out of our comfort zone, and we didn't play great, but we found a way to win. It was a relief for our guys. Now they could just go have fun and play."

By the time Davidson guard Jason Richards's last-second shot that would have won the game caromed off the backboard, Self had fallen to his knees, bowled over by the weight of the moment. Survival, not celebration, was the prevailing sensation. But Self was a new man once he returned home that night with his wife, Cindy, and their children, Lauren, seventeen, and Tyler, fourteen. At 2:00 A.M. the family gathered on the sofa of the sprawling basement game room and watched the replay of the victory with a new outlook. "Our house had been full for weeks, and now it was just us," Cindy said later. "Everybody was so excited, but Bill was the only one awake at the end. The rest of us were zonked out. I think it was three thirty when he finally said, 'OK, everybody, go to bed.'"

As Kansas prepared for the Final Four, memories of their long journey to get there came flooding back for Bill and Cindy, sweethearts since their days as Oklahoma State students. At a tip-off event in San Antonio last Thursday night, Bill sat onstage with the other three head coaches and recalled how in 1984 he injured his knee before his senior season while working at the Kansas basketball camp run by then Jayhawks coach Larry Brown. "Coach Brown felt terrible," said Self, who was a four-year letterman at guard for OSU, "and the worse he felt, the more I limped." When Brown asked Self what he could do to repay him, Self's reply was direct: Hire me as your graduate assistant next year. And Brown did, tapping Self to replace a departing GA named John Calipari.

The most troublesome memory for Self was one from the end of his second season at Kansas, in 2005, after the Jayhawks had been upset in the first round of the NCAAs by Bucknell. A few weeks later he sat in a private room at a St. Louis restaurant watching the previous team he had coached, Illinois, lose in the national title game to North Carolina, which was coached by his predecessor at Kansas, Roy Williams. "I was happy that Illinois was there, but I was also, to be quite candid, jealous," Self says. "Because those were the guys my staff had put together. Then you had the Kansas contingent that was jealous because Roy was playing and we were not. It was the most frustrating time for me as a coach that didn't have anything to do with winning or losing."

There would be another first-round defeat, to Bradley, the next year followed by a loss in the Elite Eight last season, this time as a number one seed to UCLA. Says Cindy, "It was like 'Ugh, are we going to get over this hump?'"

IT SEEMED AS though Self had yet another high-talent, low-mettle team destined for an early March exit when the Jayhawks lost for the third time in seven games, on February 23 at 13–12 Oklahoma State. At a time when the coach had hoped his players would close ranks—in addition to the late-season stumble, both senior forward Darnell Jackson's cousin and senior guard Rodrick Stewart's adopted brother had died on February 20 after having been shot in unrelated incidents—they failed to do so. "When's the last time you had a players-only meeting?" Self asked his team after the game. "Have you talked about how you're going to rally Darnell and Rod?" The players shook their heads. "Well," Self replied, "I thought you guys cared."

The seniors organized a private team meal at Henry T's, Jackson's favorite restaurant, where they expressed support for their teammates and allowed each one to air his grievances. "We really laid down in that [Oklahoma State] game," guard Russell Robinson said last week, "and we were pointing the finger and not taking responsibility for our own mistakes." Thanks to the return of senior leadership, Self said in San Antonio, "this has been a totally different team."

Yet nobody would have predicted the no-that's-not-a-misprint score line with 6:48 left in the first half of last Saturday's second semifinal: *Kansas 40, North Carolina 12.* While the major theme heading into the game had been Williams's first game against Kansas since he had famously departed Lawrence in 2003, the story instead was the Jayhawks' suffocating defense, which nearly made the proud Tar Heels cry UNCle. "Good defense should beat good offense any day," Self said last Thursday, and Kansas provided plenty of evidence. The Jayhawks sent waves of double teams at national player of the year Tyler Hansbrough, forced point guard Ty Lawson into uncharacteristic mistakes, and slowed North Carolina's vaunted secondary break.

For all that defensive mastery—the Tar Heels shot only 35.8 percent from the field—it didn't hurt that Kansas hit 53.1 percent of its shots. And while UNC roared back, cutting the lead to 54–50 midway through the second half, KU finished with a 30–16 run for a comfortable 84–66 victory. The upset of the tournament's overall top seed was a powerful validation for the Jayhawks' contention that they play better on the rare occasions when they're underdogs. Whether that's an admirable trait in a champion is debatable, but Kansas clearly benefited from avoiding the favorite's tag in an unprecedented Final Four that had all the number one seeds. "There was so much pressure on us to get here, but now we've made it and all the pressure's off," Collins said after the North Carolina game.

In that case, no Jayhawk showed more grace under (no) pressure on Saturday than Rush, whose level of aggressiveness is monitored as closely back home as the winter wheat harvests. "Brandon can get comfortable, and I don't think that's the best way he needs to play," said Self. "I think he's the best wing in the country, but my message to him is the same all the time: attack, attack, attack." Asked before the semifinal if he was tired of the questions about his game intensity, Rush said that he didn't mind at all. "I love being questioned about it," he said, "because I think I've got a pretty good answer to it." He certainly did against the Tar Heels, scoring 10 points in the Jayhawks' 25–2 first-half run and finishing with a game-high 25.

WHILE KANSAS FANS were partying on the San Antonio Riverwalk at 1:00 A.M. on Sunday, the coaching staff (Self, assistants Joe Dooley, Danny Manning, and Kurtis Townsend, and Ronnie Chalmers, who is the team's director of basketball operations) was assembling in room 2124 at the downtown Hilton for a Memphis game-planning session. In a fitting nod to KU's last national title team, the scouting report for Memphis was prepared by Manning—the Sunflower State legend whose 31 points and eighteen rebounds against Oklahoma had led the squad known as Danny and the Miracles to the championship twenty years earlier. After a fifteen-year NBA career, Manning joined Self's staff in 2003, starting as the director of student-athlete development and working his way up to full-time assistant this season.

How many college basketball greats have had the humility to return to their alma mater and pay their dues under a new regime? Manning shied away from media requests all season, directing the spotlight to the players, but his impact on the team was undeniable. It was Manning's focus on footwork and positioning that helped turn Jackson into one of the nation's most improved frontcourt players this season. And it was Manning's embodiment of past glory that gave the Jayhawks added incentive. "He has a big influence because he has been here before, and he has won it all," said Rush last week. "He's always remembering the speeches he gave in the big games."

In the wee hours of Sunday morning, though, Manning was just another bleary-eyed assistant breaking down the Memphis tendencies as video clips from the Tigers' NCAA tournament games flashed on the plasma screen in front of the Kansas coaches. "Fast-break points, points in the paint—that's the bottom line," Manning said, noting his biggest concerns about Memphis's hard-driving attack. For his part, Self was floored by the Tigers' ascendant freshman point guard, Derrick Rose, marveling at his quick first step and the way he used his chiseled 6'3", 190-pound body to overwhelm UCLA's Darren Collison for 25 points in the first semifinal on Saturday. "When did he get to be such a good shooter?" Self asked, adding that the 5'11" Collins might have a hard time matching up against Memphis's taller guards despite his competitive desire to do so.

But the Kansas coaches also saw weaknesses they could exploit. Mississippi State had used an effective 2-3 zone to slow the pace and clog the driving lanes in Memphis's hard-fought 77–74 second-round victory. And while Rose and Douglas-Roberts would command plenty of help defense to stop their penetration, Memphis's outside shooters—guards Antonio Anderson, Willie Kemp, and Doneal Mack—had been inconsistent from three-point range all season. "We have to make them shoot [outside] shots, cut off the lanes, and make it look crowded [inside]," Self said, sounding a lot like Tennessee coach Bruce Pearl, whose willingness to let Memphis shoot (and miss) threes had led to the Tigers' only loss of the season before Monday night.

Yet the late-night session wasn't all about X's and O's. The defense-obsessed Self would occasionally stop and blurt out his continued astonishment over his team's takedown of the Tar Heels. ("We held Carolina nine minutes without a field goal!") The coaches also took a fifteen-minute break to welcome several former Jayhawks—Scot Pollard, Ryan Robertson, Greg Gurley, and T. J. Pugh—who gathered with their girlfriends and wives around Self, the coach holding court on the semifinal win while perched on the countertop of the room's bar. That the alums had all played for Roy Williams was one sign of how Self has won over the fan base.

Shortly after 2:00 A.M., Manning took a call on his cellphone. "I got him! I got Manning!" shouted the young caller to his friends before hanging up. After the guy dialed Manning's number two more times in the next five minutes, the other coaches chuckled. *"Danny Manning! Danny Manning!"* they teased.

ON MONDAY NIGHT, however, Self and his staff were all business, and their game plan accomplished something UCLA's couldn't two days earlier, obstructing the Tigers' fearsome drives with a sagging man-to-man defense. Although Kansas didn't shut down Rose and Douglas-Roberts (22 points), the Memphis backcourt couldn't match its usual efficiency, shooting a combined 14 for 33. "I think I did a pretty good job on

[Douglas-Roberts]," said Rush. "In the second half I tried to buckle down and sit down on his left hand. Then my team helped me out, too."

When it was over, as confetti cannons belched and chants of "Rock chalk, Jayhawk" echoed through the Alamodome, Rush and Manning, player and assistant coach, met at half-court for a long embrace. Talk about your college hoops flashbacks. On a glorious spring night twenty years ago in Kansas City, a transcendent number 25 in Kansas blue (Manning) led the Jayhawks to a national title. On Monday night in San Antonio, another number 25 in Kansas blue (Rush) helped take over a championship game that appeared lost and put KU back into the history books. The calendar may be different and the uniform shorts a little longer, but that championship feeling?

It's timeless.

Unflappable. Unapologetic. Unequaled.

FROM *Sports Illustrated*, JULY 8, 2019

It would be hard to find a more triumphant sporting performance under a more intense global spotlight than Megan Rapinoe's at the 2019 Women's World Cup in France. On her shoulders sat the weight of expectations for the defending champion U.S. team that she captained, the ongoing lawsuit with U.S. Soccer over equal pay that she spearheaded, and the open antagonism of a U.S. president and his millions of followers over her outspoken activism on LGBTQ+ and other social justice issues. The glare was brightest for the quarterfinal with the host, France, before which Donald Trump had called out Rapinoe for saying she had no interest in visiting the White House if the team won the title. Recalling the vibe in the stadium for that match, Wahl said later that year, "I've been covering this sport for a long time, and there are few moments I've ever had like that, where you're just like 'This feels like history.'"

Rapinoe would go on to win the FIFA Player of the Year Award and the Ballon d'Or and be named *SI*'s 2019 Sportsperson of the Year. Wahl sorely wanted to write that story—Sportsperson was perhaps the juiciest plum at *SI*—but the magazine's editors assigned it to senior writer Jenny Vrentas, whose main beat was the NFL. "I think we all wanted a woman's voice and a voice that could take a little more of a thirty-thousand-foot view," says Chris Stone, editor in chief at the time. Vrentas knew that Wahl would be frustrated, but his reaction was the kind of thing she and her colleagues had come to expect. "He pulled me into a conference room," Vrentas recalls, "and said, 'Of course I'm disappointed I didn't get the assignment, but that has nothing to do with you. I'm here to support you, I'm excited for you, and I want to help in any way I can.' That was really meaningful, because I don't think a lot of people at *Sports Illustrated* would have handled it that way."

WHICH MEGAN RAPINOE POSE DID YOU PREFER? WAS IT THE one with her arms outstretched like a marble statue in the Louvre, aka the Purple-Haired Lesbian Goddess, that we saw after her goals against France in the Women's World Cup quarterfinals and against the Netherlands in Sunday's final? Or was it the pose we saw on her Instagram, the one with her arms overflowing as she held a preposterous trio of Women's World Cup trophies for the tournament title, the Golden Boot (top scorer), and the Golden Ball (MVP)?

Or maybe *pose* isn't the right word? That would imply something artificial, which is the last way you'd describe Rapinoe's monthlong tour de force during the U.S.'s second straight Women's World Cup title run, the fourth in the team's glorious history. Rarely in the annals of sports have we seen an athlete at the highest level talk the talk—and did she ever, demanding equal pay for women's players, increased investment in the women's game, and greater respect for the LGBTQ, African American, and other minority communities—and then walk the walk, even with President Donald Trump calling her out on Twitter.

"Megan should WIN first before she TALKS! Finish the job!" Trump tweeted on June 26 after a months-old video of Rapinoe saying "I'm not going to the f——king White House" if the U.S. team was invited was published and went viral. Two days later, after standing her ground in a press conference, Rapinoe responded on the field by scoring both goals in the Americans' 2–1 victory over the host French, the defining win that made another trophy possible. Three times in the knockout rounds, Rapinoe faced the ultimate pressure of taking a penalty kick for her country in the World Cup. Three times she converted, including on the game-winning goal at the final in Lyon. By Sunday, even Trump backed off, tweeting "America is proud of you all!"

We'll go there. Muhammad Ali is a singular figure in American life. But there are elements of a modern-day Ali in Rapinoe's stance toward sports and social activism, to say nothing of her ability to turn the glare of publicity—much of it controversial—to her advantage. Who else would say with glee that she was looking forward to a "total s——tshow circus" in a World Cup quarterfinal and then make the most of it when it happened?

"I'm *made* for this," the thirty-four-year-old Rapinoe said after the final. "I mean, I love it. Obviously, getting to play at the highest level in a World Cup with a team like we have is just ridiculous. But to be able to couple that with everything off the field and to back up all those words with performances and back up all those performances with words, it's just incredible. I feel like this team is just in the midst of changing the world around us as we live, and it's just an incredible feeling."

The U.S. players are in the midst of suing the U.S. Soccer Federation for gender discrimination—though both sides have agreed to try mediation first—and in the heady moments after Sunday's final whistle, the American Outlaws supporters group engaged in a lusty chant of "EQUAL PAY! EQUAL PAY!" The chorus rang through the stadium as Rapinoe accepted her awards and shared conversations with FIFA president Gianni Infantino, French president Emmanuel Macron, and U.S. Soccer president Carlos Cordeiro.

Rapinoe knows her power, knows that she has to win to maximize it, and she isn't afraid to push the envelope deploying her influence.

"Everyone's asking what's next and what we want to come from all this," she said. "And it's to stop having the conversation about equal pay and 'Are we worth it?' and 'Should we?' and the investment piece. What are we going to do about it? Gianni, what are we going to do about it? Carlos, what are we going to do about it? Everyone. It's time to sit down with everyone and really get to work. This game has done so much for all of us. We've put so much into it. It's a testament to the quality on the field, and I don't think everything else is matching that. So how do we get everything to match up and continue to push this forward? Because I think at this point the argument that we have been having is totally null and void."

So thoroughly did Rapinoe back up her talk on the field that you half wondered if she was impervious to the cascading criticism she was receiving from one side of a divided country, whether it was over her 2016 decision to take a knee during the national anthem in support of Colin Kaepernick's protest over police treatment of black Americans (U.S. Soccer later passed a rule requiring standing) or over her continuing protest of refusing to sing the national anthem or put her hand over her heart. But no, she's human.

"Megan actually is very sensitive," her twin sister, Rachael, said last week when asked how Megan responded in private to Trump's tweet.

"But in regards to her profession she's very good at compartmentalizing, so she doesn't really get too rattled. I definitely gave her a lot of space. She wasn't talking about it a lot, so I could tell she was trying to process it and not be too affected by it. When everything went down in 2016, at the time we had a different president. But now she's not even protected by her own president. That's something that's almost surreal to me, that we have a president of the United States that's essentially going after my sister, but also kind of the team, too."

But what a team these 19ers were. One of the greatest sports teams of all time? Probably. The most meaningful team in history? Perhaps, considering all the things the 19ers have represented to different people. The greatest U.S. women's soccer team ever? *Oh yes, certainly.*

"I do think this is a team that across the board is the best we've seen," said no less an authority than two-time U.S. World Cup champion Julie Foudy of ESPN. This was the first USWNT to win back-to-back World Cup titles and reach three finals in a row. Until the last game, it had scored in the first twelve minutes of every World Cup match in France before it. The U.S. won every game in its romp to the trophy, outscored its opponents 26–3, led for 442 of 630 minutes, and never trailed. There was a raft of stories written during this tournament about the rest of the world catching up to the U.S., but that isn't entirely true. While Europe is certainly improving, the U.S. is getting better, too, maybe even at a faster rate.

─────────

IT WOULD BE easy to view the U.S.'s dominant run through this World Cup as an ass-kicking inevitability, a constant march onward and upward to back-to-back titles. *Here we go again.* But the journey over the past four years was anything but easy. In 2016, the U.S. suffered a quarterfinal elimination in the Olympics to Sweden—the U.S.'s earliest exit ever from a major tournament—in which Rapinoe, on the wrong side of thirty and not at full strength after a knee injury, looked like she might be finished on the international stage. Then in 2017, vowing to unlock more creativity in the attack, coach Jill Ellis launched a period of experimentation (with formations and new players) that proved an old adage: Real change can be an ugly and uncomfortable process long before it becomes glorious.

The grimmest night of all was March 8, 2017, at the SheBelieves Cup in Washington, D.C.'s RFK Stadium, when a thoroughly disjointed U.S. team went down 2–0 after nine minutes to France and ultimately lost 3–0. With Rapinoe not being called into the team in the wake of her taking a knee, Ellis tried a 3-4-3 formation, left several regulars on the bench—including Alex Morgan, Julie Ertz, Crystal Dunn, Lindsey Horan, and Kelley O'Hara—and produced a result that left U.S. fans and media howling after two home defeats in the three-game tournament.

"I remember thinking after that loss that we had a long way to go," O'Hara said last week. "But that's kind of a good thing, you know? You don't ever want to feel like it's easy all the time and there's no obstacles or need for growth. After 2016, [Ellis said,] 'I'm about to put this team through an evolution that I feel is necessary to win us a World Cup in 2019.' And as hard as that was—it was hectic and stressful and full of uncertainty for a lot of people—it was necessary. I respect her a lot for doing that and sticking to her guns, and I respect the individuals on this team and how we handled ourselves through that time."

Morgan added, "You have to give credit to Jill for looking at new things throughout the course of the last three years in order to see what the right direction was for us. . . . When you have a chance to coach a team for two World Cups in a row, you're able to learn a lot along the way, what worked and what didn't. For Jill, it was a little bit of experimenting, and she did it in a way that a lot of people criticized. But at the same time, when you get to where we are now, you can't help but applaud that."

Yet even the U.S. players bristled at times during Ellis's tinkering, and after a 1–0 home loss to Australia in July 2017 at the Tournament of Nations, several veterans went to then federation president Sunil Gulati and told him they had deep concerns about the direction of the team under Ellis—and that if those concerns weren't addressed, they wanted a new coach. The players had specific issues with what they felt was Ellis's lack of communication off the field and the team's declining performances on the field. At a meeting several months later, Gulati responded to the team (with Ellis in the room) that she wasn't going anywhere before World Cup 2019, and Gulati's replacement, Carlos Cordeiro, kept Ellis in charge.

Winning has a way of easing tensions, however, and in 2018 the U.S.

went undefeated as Ellis and assistant Tony Gustavsson, her offensive guru, landed on a 4-3-3 formation with an attacking style that was much more freewheeling than that of the 2015 World Cup–winning team. The linchpins were an explosive starting front line (Rapinoe, Morgan, and Tobin Heath), an indispensable role in the defensive midfield for Ertz, and a remarkable depth (Carli Lloyd, Christen Press, and Mallory Pugh as subs!) possessed by no other team on the planet. Concerns over the defense would continue into the World Cup, especially when it came to Hope Solo's untested goalkeeping replacement, Alyssa Naeher, but Naeher proved herself when it mattered most by making two giant saves (one of them on a late penalty) in a 2–1 semifinal win against England.

As painful as Ellis's experimenting was in 2017, it also unearthed some gems. One of the starters in the France debacle was a twenty-one-year-old midfielder from Cincinnati named Rose Lavelle, who was making her second appearance with the national team.

"I got subbed out at halftime because I was pretty awful," Lavelle said last week. "I remember thinking 'Wow, that's like the top of the top. I need to get better, and that's where I need to be in the next couple years if I want to compete for a spot on this team.' "

Now twenty-four, Lavelle was the World Cup's breakout star, the creative maestro on the U.S. team in both the semifinal and the final. Watching Lavelle in full flight on the ball is exhilarating, the kind of jolt that people will always pay real money to witness in person. In the sixty-ninth minute of Sunday's final, she found herself on the ball with a half acre of space in front of her and went to work, bamboozling Dutch defender Stefanie van der Gragt to create room for her left-footed knock-out punch.

"It's so surreal that I just won a World Cup with people I grew up idolizing," said Lavelle. "I can't put it into words. It's amazing."

Last week was a vindication for Ellis, the first coach to win back-to-back Women's World Cup titles. She used nearly all the capital she had won in 2015 to remake her U.S. team after the Olympic failure, and that sometimes excruciating process paid off in France.

"Coming out of the Olympics, it was a moment to kind of reflect and look at making sure we played competitive games and increased our roster in terms of finding players like Rose Lavelle," Ellis said last week. "Sometimes it's part of the growing pains when you want to shift something. But full credit to the players. You build the system around them. They're the gasoline that makes it work. That process was to get to this point with players in their right spots."

Over the last three years, Ellis was especially supportive of her most Promethean players, even through long periods of injuries, whether they were Lavelle (hamstring), Heath (back), or Rapinoe (knee). Without them, the U.S. wouldn't have won in France. As Foudy said, "Her most creative players, she has had a commitment to them to say, 'I'm going to have patience. You're going to get back.' As a player it's everything, especially at that level where it's so cutthroat, it's hard to feel confidence when you're injured and away from the group. And Jill was willing to tinker. Sometimes you would hammer her for it, but you have to live through those moments to learn and grow. I think she's been courageous in that way."

THE 19ERS, LIKE the 91ers, the 99ers, and the 15ers before them, will be known for far more than what they accomplished in ninety-minute segments on a soccer field.

"The fabric of this national team," Foudy said, "has always been 'It's more than soccer.' "

This World Cup produced record numbers of viewers for women's soccer in countries around the world, including Brazil (where 35 million people watched the France-Brazil Round of 16 game), China, France, England, Italy, the Netherlands, and Spain. The USWNT now has an impact there, too.

"In '99, we envisioned this as a catalyst that would spark a global movement, but the reality is I think it was a domestic one," said Foudy. "I see the 19ers as responsible for a *global* movement. We're seeing the numbers, but even beyond that, they set an example for women on standards of expectations. There are so many countries who are finally standing up and saying this isn't right, and they have the courage as a player to stand up in one of these countries and say, 'This needs to be better, not just for us but for the next generation.' I think a lot of that comes from them seeing this U.S. group do this at a level that's unprecedented."

Meanwhile, the public pressure on FIFA to invest more of its $2.7 billion in reserves in the women's game, particularly from Rapinoe, appeared to be having an effect. Infantino announced last week a proposal to expand the Women's World Cup from twenty-four to thirty-two teams, double the prize money to $60 million, double FIFA's grassroots global investment in the women's game to $1 billion, and start a FIFA World League for women's national teams and a FIFA Women's Club World Cup. Rapinoe said it was promising, but she noted that his prize money proposal would mean the gap in prize money between the women and the men is actually increasing, not closing. After Rapinoe called out the FIFA president on Saturday, they had a brief conversation at the awards podium following the final.

"There was a wry smile," Rapinoe said with a grin. "He did say he'd like to have a conversation, and I said I'd love to."

That's power. And after a World Cup that will put her in the canon of American athletic achievements, that's Pinoe.

3
SHAMANS OF THE SIDELINES

THE TWO SPORTS WAHL COVERED MOST EXTENSIVELY, BASKET-
ball and soccer, present coaches with a similar challenge. Each sport
is highly extemporaneous, and a coach's greatest impact is likely to
come in practice with drills and controlled scrimmages, or pregame
or at halftime with tactical guidance. Once the ball has been tipped
off or kicked, he can't really influence what's taking place between
the lines. But there's something fascinating about a control freak
who tries to impose order on chaos. Perhaps that's why currents of
mysticism and paradox run through Wahl's profiles of coaching figures. And why readers are so enduringly fascinated by these characters who try to control the uncontrollable and whom we're so ready
to credit with a team's victory. There's a reason coaches speak to reporters and so often sound like patients on a couch: Talk long
enough, and they might explain themselves; and in explaining themselves, they—and we—might better understand why they do what
they do.

What's So Special About José Mourinho?

FROM *Sports Illustrated*, MARCH 7, 2011

Even in 2011, the notion that a Portuguese soccer manager was the best coach in the world, in any sport, would have been a hard sell to an American readership. To back up the claim for José Mourinho, Wahl draws comparisons here to Phil Jackson, Bill Belichick, Mike Krzyzewski, and even Dick Vermeil. Indeed, Wahl was fascinated by foreign coaches' connections to American sports and America in general: Sir Alex Ferguson drawing inspiration from David Maraniss's Vince Lombardi biography; Gareth Southgate cribbing tactics from the NBA; Pep Guardiola living in anonymity in Manhattan during a year away from the game. This profile of Mourinho caught him at the pinnacle of his career, having taken over storied Real Madrid on the heels of his third Champions League title. The mercurial Mourinho remained a favorite subject for Wahl in the ensuing years. He gave Wahl an exclusive American interview after rejoining Chelsea in 2013, and he served as the centerpiece of Wahl's 2015 long-form video, *Under the Badge*, on the football culture at the London club. In 2018, as Mourinho's European career waned, Wahl called for him to make what he saw as the inevitable move to the United States. "MLS could use the entertainment that Mourinho brings," Wahl said in a video column on SI.com. "And I can't wait to hear him argue that MLS's salary cap and enforced parity make for the truest test in the world of who's *really* a good coach." As of 2023, Mourinho had yet to take up the challenge.

JOSÉ MOURINHO HAS A PROBLEM. WHEN FANS APPROACH THE world's most famous coach—and they do so in great numbers, from Madrid to London to Los Angeles—they are seldom satisfied with a typical autograph. They want something unique. Distinct. Dare it be said: *special.* "I'll sign JOSÉ MOURINHO," says the Real Madrid manager after a practice in the Spanish capital. "But most of the people say, 'No, no, no. You will sign THE SPECIAL ONE!'" Mourinho sighs, the edges of his trademark smirk curling into a faint smile. "Everybody wants me to be the Special One. But I don't worry. There could be a worse nickname."

Besides, it's his own creation. In 2004, during Mourinho's first press conference as Chelsea manager, he grew exasperated by the skepticism over his arrival from his native Portugal. "The English press was speaking to me like I was coming from the moon," he says. "'Who are you? Do you have the quality to work in England?' For God's sake, give me a chance. I won the Champions League with Porto. I'm a special one. Don't kill me on my first day!

"But they got it as if I was saying"—here he adopts the voice of the Almighty—"*I am the Special One.*"

And so it went. Such is the force of Mourinho's personality that more than three years after he left England, his puppet alter ego still stars in the popular BBC satire *Special 1 TV*. These days even Mourinho's critics—and there are many—would have to admit the accuracy of his audacious nickname. In January, FIFA named him the 2010 World Coach of the Year, the result of a remarkable trophy haul at Inter Milan that included winning the Italian Serie A, the Italian Cup, and the crown jewel of global club soccer, the UEFA Champions League. In seven full seasons as a manager with Porto, Chelsea, and Inter, Mourinho, forty-eight, has won fourteen major trophies, including two Champions League titles and six domestic league championships.

Where does Mourinho rank among the world's soccer coaches? "He's at the top, there's no doubt about that," says the legendary Manchester United coach Sir Alex Ferguson, Mourinho's friend and rival. "You have certain criteria in terms of top management, and that is longevity of success—which is very difficult today—and what you win. You have to regard his achievements as really first-class."

Now, nine months after taking over Real Madrid, Mourinho faces his most pressure-packed test yet: to return the most decorated club of all time to its past glory, not just in Spain (where archrival Barcelona has won four of the last six La Liga titles) but also in Europe (where Real Madrid has not advanced to the Champions League quarterfinals since 2004). "Real Madrid wants to be again the best—of the present and of the future," says Mourinho. "That's my challenge." If he can burnish his own résumé in the process, so much the better—no coach has won European crowns with three different teams. Real meets Lyon at Madrid's Bernabéu Stadium on March 16 in the second leg of their home-and-home Round of 16 series; the teams tied 1–1 at Lyon on February 22.

As Mourinho has risen to the summit, he has expanded his horizons, analyzing the management styles at Microsoft and Apple, reading Colin Powell's autobiography and Phil Jackson's books, studying John Wooden's Pyramid of Success. He wants to come to the U.S., both to observe NFL coaching staffs and, eventually, to manage the U.S. national team or an MLS club. "A football coach who only understands football is not a great coach," says Mourinho. "We have to be good in other things. I never forget: My players are men. Men with different personalities, different cultures. To deal with this is very important in building a team. I think I have, maybe, a gift."

Mourinho can't help himself. He is by turns smart, vain, funny, needy, tough and as thin-skinned as a pinot grape. But who's to argue with him? He has a gift. No coach today compares. Phil Jackson may have won eleven NBA titles, but he always had the best players. Mourinho conquered the Champions League with Porto and Inter Milan, teams with nowhere near the talent and payrolls of their top rivals. Joe Torre and Mike Krzyzewski may have reached the pinnacle four times, but they did not have to connect with their players in five languages. Mourinho speaks Portuguese, English, French, Italian, and Spanish fluently. Bill Belichick owns three Super Bowl rings as a head coach, but even he can't match Mourinho's most remarkable record: He has gone nine years without losing a league game at home, 148 matches with four different teams.

Nor do any American coaches face the crushing weekly pressure of European soccer, the only game that matters on the Continent. In the political tinderbox of Real Madrid, where a single defeat can spark a crisis, Mourinho might not even survive the season. But there is a reason his $12 million annual salary is the highest of any coach on the planet. He's the best in the world.

MILAN, MAY 2010. *The news is out: Mourinho is leaving Inter Milan for Real Madrid. Outside the Bernabéu after the Champions League final, an*

Italian TV camera captures Mourinho ducking into a luxury sedan. The car advances, then abruptly stops. Mourinho emerges from behind the smoked-glass windows and walks twenty yards to Inter defender Marco Materazzi, the hardman best known for absorbing Zinedine Zidane's headbutt in the 2006 World Cup final. Mourinho and Materazzi embrace for five, ten, twenty seconds. Both men's shoulders are heaving. Two of the toughest men in soccer are sobbing like Dick Vermeil.

Ask people what makes Mourinho unique, and one common response is this: His players almost universally adore him. Didier Drogba, the prolific Chelsea striker, says he felt "like an orphan" after Mourinho departed West London in 2007. "He's a great man," Drogba says. "You can see how close players are with him. He has a way of getting into players' minds as a manager—and as a man, the kind of man who's ready to give you all his confidence and trust because he expects that you'll give it back." Drogba, too, shed tears when Mourinho left, one of the few times, he says, that he has cried in his adult life.

Materazzi's native language is Italian. Drogba's is French. Mourinho has a rule: When he addresses his teams, he does so in the language of the team's country, the better to integrate the players into the club and the culture. (At Inter he spoke Italian even though only four of his twenty-four first-team players were Italian.) But in private meetings with individual players Mourinho communicates whenever possible in their native tongues. "By speaking five languages I can have a special relation with them," he says. "A player feels more comfortable explaining emotions in the language where he has no doubts. So he has no problem to open his heart, to criticize, to be criticized."

In other words, Mourinho's ability to connect is equal parts psychology and linguistics. To sit across from Mourinho and interview him is to be subject to a form of high-level seduction, though not in a sexual way. He'll lean close, elbows on knees, hands folded together, as though he's sharing a secret that nobody else knows. Is it a kind of performance art? Of course. But isn't most of sports? The details are in the delivery, and invariably Mourinho's players, to say nothing of the global media, buy what he is selling. If Ferguson is known for the scorching-hot diatribes of a drill sergeant, Mourinho is the sports world's version of a pickup artist.

MANCHESTER, ENGLAND, MARCH 2004. Who is this man? How dare he violate the sacred turf of Old Trafford? It's the second leg of the Champions League Round of 16, and tiny Porto has just stunned the soccer world, scoring in the ninetieth minute to eliminate mighty Manchester United. Now Mourinho is bursting from the coach's box, racing down the touchline—fists pumping like pistons, coattails flapping in his jet wash— all the way to his celebrating players at the corner flag. Who is this man? He's an attention magnet, that's what he is.

Unlike most managers, Mourinho broke into elite coaching not as a former star player—his brief career as a defender ended at age twenty-four—but as an interpreter. He translated for English manager Sir Bobby Robson for five seasons, first in Portugal and then in Spain, at Barcelona. When Robson left Barça in 1997, Mourinho stayed on as an assistant coach under Louis van Gaal, earning the Dutchman's trust for his tactical acumen, player relationships and famously detailed scouting reports. (Mourinho had started analyzing teams as a teenager for his father, Félix, a former player and coach in Portugal.) "He works like a crazy man," says Drogba. "At Chelsea he was doing the same [scouting reports] for fourth division teams in the FA Cup as he was for Manchester United. It shows you how serious he is."

By the time Mourinho took over at Porto in the Portuguese first division in 2002, he'd formed a guiding soccer philosophy. The decisive moments in most games, he argues, are *transitions,* the instants when teams spring from defense to attack (and vice versa) after a change of possession, when opponents can be off balance. "These are periods of three or four seconds," he says. "If the players are of high quality, the game sometimes is nonstop. You must have a great balance. That's why I believe in having players with the tactical culture to analyze the game. All of them have to think the same thing at the same time. It's not basketball, because in basketball there are five players. Here there are eleven."

If the game is about transitions, then so, too, is Mourinho's career, which saw him move from Porto to Chelsea to Inter Milan, never staying more than three full seasons at one club, all the while dominating the headlines more than any of his players.

"I had the luck of making history in those three clubs," he says. "At Porto it was winning the [2003–04] Champions League without money. We played Manchester United and Real Madrid, where the salary of one player was enough to pay the Porto team. Chelsea was also very special, because it was the first time Chelsea was champion [of England] in fifty years. In the [2009–10] Champions League with Inter, we were far from being the most powerful team. We had to play four times in the competition against the best team in the world last season, which was Barcelona."

Inter's stunning upset of Barça in the Champions League semifinals—a 3–2 aggregate win in which Inter held off Barcelona in the second leg despite going down to ten men inside a half hour—convinced everyone that Mourinho, more than any other coach alive, had the chops to win with inferior players. It also further polarized the world's soccer watchers into two camps: one that hailed Mourinho as a practical genius and another that derided him as a defensive-minded killjoy. And it drew the attention of Real Madrid president Florentino Pérez. In his previous term, from 2000 to 2006, Pérez had signed the so-called Galácticos, a Dream Team that included Zidane, Ronaldo, David Beckham, and Luís Figo. Pérez started his second term in '09 by buying two more former World Players of the Year, Cristiano Ronaldo and Kaká, but Real Madrid saw Barcelona sweep to victory in the Spanish league.

This season's new Galáctico was Mourinho himself, the miracle man who had vanquished Barça, Real Madrid's most bitter enemy. He didn't come cheaply. Real Madrid paid Inter a reported $10 million transfer fee and signed Mourinho to a four-year deal worth an estimated $48 million. Beyond the money, his hiring heralded a cultural transformation for the club. "What Mourinho brings is a newfound respect for the coach, a position that has always been criminally undervalued at Real Madrid," says Sid Lowe, the Madrid-based correspondent for *The Guardian*. "Now the coach is the most important guy at the club. Whether that will last, of course, is another issue."

Indeed, Real Madrid's fans and directors are accustomed to winning with panache, a word that has rarely described Mourinho's teams. Jorge Valdano, Real's director of soccer, once called the style of Mourinho's Chelsea "s—— on a stick," and the two men have jousted in the Spanish media this season. For his part the Special One points out that he now has more entertaining and possession-oriented players. "With Inter we had no qualities to control the game by having ball possession all the time," Mourinho says. "At Real Madrid, I am adapting to the qualities of the players. We have people that can control the game not by defending but by having possession of the ball."

None is more electrifying than Ronaldo, twenty-six, a whooshing force of speed, skill, and hair gel who's engaged in an epic battle with Barcelona's twenty-three-year-old Lionel Messi. Through Sunday, Ronaldo had scored thirty-four goals in thirty-nine games in all competitions; Messi, thirty-nine in thirty-five. Under Mourinho, his Portuguese countryman, Ronaldo has returned to the devastating form he showed two years ago with Manchester United. "I've always had great players, but I've never had a Cristiano Ronaldo," Mourinho says. "Last year Real relied too much on Cristiano to decide things. The best thing is not to make him feel responsible for the success or nonsuccess of the team. He's one more—with different qualities, of course. He can make the difference when things are very equalized, but behind him he has a structure. I think he's much more comfortable."

In many ways the season's first six months have been a prologue to the Spanish Armageddon that could erupt over the next three. Real Madrid and Barça may well be the world's two best teams, and so Mourinho will be judged on how his side performs in the big games: the Champions League and head-to-head against Barcelona. The Catalans won round one on their home turf in November, a 5–0 humiliation that was the worst loss of Mourinho's career. Yet it remains one of only two Real Madrid defeats in thirty-two league and Champions League games, and the two rivals could meet as many as four more times this season: in La Liga (April 17), in the Spanish cup final (April 20), and perhaps in a two-leg Champions League showdown.

The rivalry represents more than just two cities, tracing as it does to the days when Real Madrid was a symbol of the Franco regime, Barcelona of Catalan resistance. For now Barça has the advantage: a seven-point lead in La Liga. And yet it would be folly to dismiss Mourinho, who knows as well as anyone that the one time he beat Barcelona in four tries last season was in the game that mattered most.

LONDON, APRIL 2007. Talk about odd pairings. WWE Raw has come to England, and now Shane McMahon is interrupting his ring monologue: "Wait a minute, I know you! That's José Mourinho! The head coach, if you will, of the Chelsea football team!" A chorus of boos (and a few cheers) rains down on Mourinho, who's sitting between his two children in the front row. Mourinho smiles, wags a finger at McMahon. The coach is in on this. So maybe Shane-O-Mac butchered his name, pronouncing it HOE-zay instead of the correct joe-ZAY. Who cares? It's the Special One and pro wrestling! It's . . . a perfect match.

When Mourinho returns home from Real Madrid's Valdebebas training center, he's no longer the boss. That role falls to his wife of twenty-one years, Tami, and their kids: daughter Matilde, fourteen, and son José Jr., ten. "I have to do what they want," Mourinho says. "I have to watch the programs they want to see, the movies they want to go to. I have to go to the wrestling because they enjoy the wrestling."

Mourinho's children have attended the American schools in London, Milan, and Madrid. He expects they will go to college in the U.S. And therein lies an opportunity for soccer in America. "We want to be close to our kids the maximum we can," he says. "So in a few years when they go in that direction, me and my wife are going to go in the same direction. I see myself coaching a [club] team, coaching the national team or helping develop soccer in the U.S. When I'm tired of winning things in Europe, it's something I want to do. I want to coach the Portuguese national team, and I want to work in the United States."

Do the math: Matilde will be college age in four years, José Jr. in eight. The timing would set up well for Mourinho to take over the U.S. soon after, say, World Cup 2018. He already brings his teams to Los Angeles for preseason training every year. "I love it," Mourinho says of America. "The people have a very open mentality. Everybody is the same. Status doesn't count a lot. I like it very much in this way."

If Mourinho eventually crosses the Atlantic, it would be the perfect coda to his international high-wire act. In the ultimate global sport, he has become the ultimate global coach, crossing borders, switching languages, and winning championships wherever he goes. For the Special One, remember, the game is all about the transitions.

The Return of the Native

FROM *Sports Illustrated*, NOVEMBER 17, 2003

The opening paragraphs of this story, which appeared in *Sports Illustrated*'s 2003 college basketball preview issue, deftly use two epigraphs and an anecdote to establish the issue at hand: Roy Williams's lifelong entanglement with Dean Smith, the coach whose spirit still haunted a North Carolina program now suddenly on the rocks, and Williams's return to campus to set things right. Even more impressive is how Wahl got that native North Carolinian to open up about his insecurities and vulnerabilities, as well as his bond with Smith, the titanic figure who had launched Williams's career in Chapel Hill and still colored everything he did. By now Wahl had been on the college basketball beat for seven years and begun to forge relationships with the sport's most prominent figures. But he had connected especially with Williams, who had been coaching at Kansas when Wahl first met him. Between the lines you can sense the still agonized Williams trying to justify his decision to leave Lawrence, as if the young Kansas Citian sitting across from him were a proxy for all of Jayhawk Nation. Two years after this story ran, Williams would lead the Tar Heels to an NCAA title. And in 2009, moments after Carolina won another, Williams spotted Wahl in the bowels of Detroit's Ford Field. Knowing that *SI* had assigned Wahl to the Tar Heels' side of the bracket, he said, "Guess you'll be writing tonight!"

I could give a s—— about Carolina right now.

> —Kansas coach ROY WILLIAMS to CBS's Bonnie Bernstein after the
> Jayhawks' 81–78 loss to Syracuse in the 2003 NCAA final

All the junk that's been going on, it's been hard. . . . Thanks for not pursuing it any farther—further.

> —WILLIAMS, concluding his press conference twenty minutes later

FORGET THE SWEAR WORD. YES, ROY WILLIAMS DROPPED AN S bomb on national TV last April. Yes, he's sorry. Yes, it was out of character. (Anyone, coach or player, who curses even once during Williams's practices has to run wind sprints.) But what did his outburst reveal anyway? That badgering him with the same loaded question—"Are you going to Carolina? Are you going to Carolina?"—would make him angry? That he really didn't "give a s—" about North Carolina, the place closest to his heart? Please.

But Williams *did* expose his soul that night, did in fact answer that loaded question, and he did so with one simple word—the final word, it just so happens, of his 3,244-word postgame press conference.

Thanks for not pursuing it any farther—further.

Imagine that. Stuck in the white-hot center of a firestorm—from the unceasing Carolina queries, the pain of a crushing defeat, all those emotions tumbling out of him—Williams stopped and corrected himself. Dean Smith would have smiled. Years ago, whenever Smith used the terms *farther* or *further,* the old coach, Williams's mentor, would stop practice, turn to his team and explain the difference. "*Farther* pertains to distance," Smith would say, "but if we're going to discuss this, we can discuss it *further* as we walk."

The second that Williams unleashed that f word, anybody in the Carolina Family could have told you: He's coming. You can't change how you're wired, can't change your family roots, least of all when that family—the most storied clan in college basketball—is quaking at its very foundations. Roy Williams may have been speaking that night in New Orleans, but the last word? Dean Smith got the last word.

FIVE MONTHS LATER, on a gorgeous fall day in Chapel Hill, Williams is still deliberating, still chewing over the Decision.

"It's strange," he says. "I know I did the right thing. But if you had told me the feelings I was gonna have about myself standing up in front of my [Kansas] team and the feelings I would have calling our four recruits, I couldn't have come here. There's no doubt in my mind. And yet even saying that, I still think I did the right thing. I'm not looking back. But that is the lowest I have ever felt about myself. I've never felt like 'Gosh, Roy, you're hurting people.'"

During his seven days of self-torture, Williams would wake in the middle of the night and throw up. Shouldn't he just stay at Kansas, his adopted home? He'd had so much success there in fifteen years: nine regular-season conference titles, four Final Fours, a winning percentage (.805) so far beyond any other active coach's that he could lose every game this season and still be on top. The fans worshipped him. It was public knowledge that a KU donor was ready to name a building on campus after Ol' Roy. And what about those promises? Like the one he made after turning down Carolina in 2000, that his next big press conference would be to announce he was either "dying or retiring." Or the line he had for any prospect who asked if he'd ever leave Lawrence: "I've turned down eleven different NBA teams. I've said no to North Carolina, and that's the only place I would have ever left Kansas for."

Then he'd think of Carolina. Williams couldn't turn down Dean Smith again, could he? Who would have imagined he'd get a second chance? It must be fate. And he'd hear the voices of all those proud former Tar Heels: We need you, Coach. Nobody had begged him like that in 2000. But Carolina was still Carolina then, with four starters returning from a Final Four team, not the shell of a program it had become under Matt Doherty, the fiery young coach who'd lost his players, alienated the Carolina Family, and been forced to resign. Thirty-six losses in two years! No team in the country had fallen further—no, farther—than UNC.

Twice Williams resolved to call Dick Baddour, the Carolina athletic director, and turn down the job. Twice he stopped before dialing. In the end, he says, there were "a thousand reasons" why Carolina won by split decision, but one outstripped the others. In 2001, Kansas had forced out Bob Frederick, the athletic director who'd hired Williams, and replaced him with Fresno State's Al Bohl, a fast-talking football man who quickly earned a reputation as a blowhard. "The dissatisfaction I had for the last year and a half at Kansas was the biggest factor," Williams says. "Except for the time I was on the court, I wasn't real happy."

On April 14, a week after the championship game, Williams called Smith with some final questions: *Coach, do you think everyone there will be pleased with me coming back? Would I be their choice? Are you sure that you want me to take this job?* When Smith said yes to all three, Williams ended the misery—sort of. At the press conference announcing his arrival in Chapel Hill, he wore a tie festooned with Jayhawks.

The scene in Lawrence in the days surrounding Williams's departure was like one *Hoosiers* moment after another. After he was fired in a last-ditch attempt to keep Williams, Bohl lashed out in a bizarre press conference on his front lawn, charging that the coach was vindictive and hateful. ("My lawyer called and said this is bad," Williams says, "but in a way it shows people what you've been putting up with.") Locals churned out BENEDICT WILLIAMS T-shirts. At the team banquet senior Nick Collison's dad, Dave, shouted down a heckler who yelled "Traitor!" at Williams, and two dozen former Jayhawks lined up outside to shake the coach's hand. Roy and his wife, Wanda, broke down in tears. "I was still their coach," he says.

Williams laughs when asked if he's considered seeking therapy. "I've wondered," he says. "I think I'm gonna be fine, but my makeup is that I care what people think. That statement about dying or retiring, that really haunted me. Those BENEDICT WILLIAMS T-shirts, that hit me harder than anything has ever hit me."

There are lighter moments, of course, like the time in Lawrence last summer when one woman, spying Williams at a restaurant, theatrically stuck out her tongue and left the premises. But some topics aren't joking matters. For instance, don't ever expect Williams to put the Jayhawks on Carolina's schedule. And if the Tar Heels ever drew Kansas in the post-season? "You mean one of those 'miracles' that happen in the tournament?" Williams says. "I think I'd strangle everyone on the committee."

On the other hand, at least it would mean Carolina was back in the tournament.

All families are creepy in a way.

—Diane Arbus

When the fifty-three-year-old Williams led his first Tar Heels practice in the wee hours of October 18, at a raucous Dean Smith Center in Chapel Hill, he took the latest step in a daunting restoration project. See, his task isn't just to stop the losing, though that will be challenge enough, but to resuscitate the powder-blue empire that Smith built over thirty-six years and a record 879 victories. It's about nothing less than saving college basketball's first family. "We have to win or I'm not gonna be sitting here in four years," Williams says. "But if I cannot get everybody, particularly the former players, back on the same page with us, and supporting us, and not going to bed until they find out what Carolina did that night, then I will not have done the job I want to do. And that may be even more important to me than winning."

For his part Smith has never liked the term Carolina Family, favoring Carolina fraternity. But whatever you choose to call that brotherhood—from Michael Jordan to Phil Ford, James Worthy to Larry Brown, Vince Carter to Billy Cunningham—everyone agrees that it's special. "You ever see the movie *Soul Food*? That's it," says former Tar Heels point guard Kenny Smith. "I know Antawn Jamison's father as well as anyone's dad, and I never played with Antawn. I used to think all schools were like that until I got to the NBA and realized they weren't."

But as soon as Doherty, class of '84, took over for the retired Bill Guthridge three years ago, the Family began squabbling as it never had before. Many blamed Doherty, a former Williams assistant at Kansas, for what they saw as a willful desecration of Carolina tradition. The new coach not only brought his own staff from Notre Dame, forcing Ford—Guthridge's most popular assistant and UNC's all-time leading scorer—into athletic administration, but his brusque style also hastened the departures of three longtime basketball secretaries, including Angela Lee, the liaison to three decades of former players.

Yet Doherty wasn't the only lightning rod. Other Family members, most notably former Smith lieutenants Guthridge and Eddie Fogler, were still upset with Williams for leaving Carolina at the altar in 2000.

Still others fumed about what they thought was the unseemly manner in which Baddour and UNC chancellor James Moeser guillotined Doherty last spring, enlisting his players to turn state's evidence and then publicly questioning his leadership after he resigned. What had happened to the genteel Carolina way? "There's no way that eighteen- and nineteen-year-olds should be dictating the future of a coach," argued Jordan, Doherty's ex-teammate, who railed at anyone who would listen about the nerve of today's "new-jack players."

Over time the alums who once migrated from the NBA to Chapel Hill each summer slowly began withdrawing from a program they no longer recognized. "If you go to Thanksgiving dinner with your mom and dad every year and one year the turkey doesn't taste right, that's one thing, but we almost stopped having dinners," Kenny Smith says. "Everyone realizes now that all you need to do to get the Family back is continue what Coach Smith already established. It's hard for someone coming in with his own aspirations and ideas to understand sometimes. The biggest thing Coach Williams realizes is that you don't have to do anything."

Oh, but he is planning something for this season: the first full Carolina basketball reunion since the dedication of the Dean Dome in 1986. "It was the greatest thing I ever did at Kansas, bringing those players back and making sure they knew it was their program," Williams says. Already there are signs of a revival. More former Tar Heels appeared on campus for pickup games last summer than in recent years, and the Carolina Pros charity game, which was conspicuously held at North Carolina State's arena in 2002, switched to the Dean Dome this year.

Likewise, Williams pulled off the delicate operation of retaining his Kansas staff (Jerod Haase, Joe Holladay, and Steve Robinson) while keeping Ford in the fold. ("I understand," says Ford. "Even though I'm not on that staff, I am on that staff, if you know what I mean.") Along the way, Williams made peace with Guthridge and Fogler, his fellow assistants on UNC's 1982 national title team. "The only reason I was mad at him was because he hadn't come [in 2000]," Guthridge says. "But that was selfish on my part, because outside of my family I love North Carolina basketball more than anything and I knew he was the right person for the job."

And so the Family recovers. In perhaps the most striking example of its resilience, Doherty remains a card-carrying member as he takes the year off from coaching. He's living in Charlotte, prepping for a TV gig, enrolling in some graduate-level courses in leadership and takeover strategy. "I've made some mistakes, [things] I would handle differently if I had to do them over again," he says. "But here I am, I had to resign my position, and yet I was on the phone today with Larry Brown. I talked to Michael Jordan last week. Coach Williams called me today, and I talked to Coach Smith a week ago. It's a powerful group, and it's neat to be a part of it."

Says Williams, "I try to make sure people understand if I say anything about what happened here in the past, I'm not blaming Matt. I will do anything I can to help him. And if he's not back at the reunion this year, I'm gonna be really ticked."

NOONTIME IN CHAPEL HILL. Cars honk. Pedestrians gawk. Williams is taking his daily constitutional: up Manning Road, over to Franklin Street (where he starts jogging to avoid crowds), past the statue of Silent Sam ("Legend says he fires his gun every time a virgin walks by"), and back, eventually, to the Dean Dome. But not before the new coach, while jabbering away with his guest, crosses an intersection right . . . in the path . . . of a moving car!

The driver slams on his brakes.

"They'll stop as long as we aren't losing," Williams cracks.

Left unsaid is how Carolina fans will react if his team doesn't match the outlandish expectations of hoops mavens. Let's see if we've got this straight: UNC, without adding a single impact player to last year's NIT squad, appears in many preseason Top 10s? Sure, the Heels have three of the nation's best sophomores—guards Raymond Felton and Rashad McCants and center Sean May, who's now recovered from a broken left foot—but are they really a Final Four contender?

Perhaps it's just a case of pundits noticing the similarities to another talented but untried bunch with a cinch Hall of Fame coach and seeing the next Syracuse. Williams has a standard line for anyone who suggests that he alone makes the difference: Ol' Roy ain't that good. For starters, Carolina's personnel isn't really the same as it was last year. ("You and I both know if Sean May doesn't get hurt, we aren't walking on this street right now," Williams says.) But even if May is at full speed—just about every discussion in Chapel Hill contains the worried phrase "if they stay healthy"—an overnight return to the elite may be asking too much. "I'm not so sure they're going to be better just like that," Williams says. "We've got some major problems to overcome. The fact is, the depth here is worse than it was at Kansas last year. It's almost embarrassing to be at North Carolina and have one point guard and just one big guy who can consistently play at this level."

To be fair, the Doherty Era had its moments: a 21–2 start and national Coach of the Year honors his first season, a 67–56 upset of Williams's Jayhawks on the way to last year's preseason NIT title, and an 82–79 takedown of archrival Duke last spring. But Doherty's three-year reign was torpedoed, in the end, by an 8–20 record in 2001–02, the unscheduled departures from the team of six Tar Heels, and so much antagonism between him and his players last season that a half dozen were considering transferring after the 19–16 campaign.

"Coach Doherty was worried about his relationship with the players more than winning," says McCants, who bickered with the coach during the season. "That didn't work. It ain't about liking a coach; it's about getting the job done."

Adds Felton, "The situation with Coach Doherty shouldn't have gone down that way. Half the guys on the team don't take criticism real well, and Coach Doherty's the type of guy, he'd always tell you what you did wrong. Sometimes he took it overboard, but there's no fault in that. I wish him the best of luck."

To a man the players hope they can dispel the reputation they earned in some precincts last season as mutinous brats, a notion bolstered, fairly or unfairly, by images of them visiting Baddour's office the week before Doherty was forced out. "People put the blame on us like we got Coach Doherty fired," says May. "We didn't go to Dick Baddour. He came to us. We just told him stuff that happened during the year."

These days, the young Tar Heels say all the right things about how they appreciate "a clean slate" (McCants), how they're "so hungry" (Felton) for the new season, how "everything has been clicking so far" (May), but they acknowledge something else too: They don't know Williams very well at all. Not yet. Between June 27 and September 5 Williams spent only five days in Chapel Hill, splitting the rest of his time between the recruiting trail—he landed four crucial commitments for next year's freshman class, headed by 6'8" forward Marvin Williams of Bremerton, Washington—and the Olympic qualifying tournament, serving on the staff of U.S. coach Larry Brown.

In the short time they spent with Williams last spring, the young Heels got a taste of what they can expect. On the one hand, Williams reassured players like McCants in individual meetings. ("He told me he wasn't worried about me as a person, that he's expecting me to be a leader," McCants says.) At the same time, the new staff laid into the Tar Heels for their grades and their punctuality. Says May, "At our first team meeting a couple of guys thought they could roll in late. It was just two or three minutes, but they got on us. To them you're late if you're on time, so you'd better be early."

Yet even as the summer wore on, an apprehension lingered in some players' minds. After all, they reasoned, didn't Doherty shadow Williams for seven years? "A lot of guys think because Coach Doherty was at Kansas, Coach Williams is just gonna be a tougher Coach Doherty," May says. "Coach Williams is intense, but they're two different types of coaches. We hope he's not the same as Coach Doherty, but for some reason he wins, and I don't care as long as we're winning."

As part of their research over the summer, May and McCants eagerly pumped Kansas guard Keith Langford for the skinny on Williams at Jordan's camp in Santa Barbara, California. While Langford didn't sugar-coat things—"Expect to work your ass off all the time," he told them—he also explained how he had come to trust Williams after his initial wariness. "There were certain days I didn't really like him, but he's gonna get the best out of you," Langford says. "I told them personal stories about how humble he is, how he has a modest house and isn't just trying to impress recruits all the time. Over two years we really started to develop a relationship."

It certainly says something that despite Langford's anger over Williams's departure from Lawrence—he hinted to reporters that he might transfer—he called Williams the next day to apologize. "If I can respect him, I can also respect what he wanted to do," Langford says.

This year's Tar Heels should be reminiscent of Williams's Kansas teams, which employed a high-speed version of the secondary break Doherty learned from Williams. "We won't be stopping to set up so many plays because we're gonna push the ball upcourt and get a fast-break layup or an open three," Felton says with unvarnished glee. "It's not a big adjustment, but it's a challenge because we have to get into shape."

For his part, Williams says he hasn't watched a single tape of last season, the better to form his own impressions once practice started. "What happened last year may not be the style I'm gonna play," he says, "and emotionally, whether any of us like to admit it or not, these kids went through some turmoil last year. What was happening in their lives off the court had a great deal to do with how they played on the court."

As summer turned into fall, the vibe was undeniably optimistic. May was delighted to hear that the new staff, unlike Doherty's, would let him use a one-two jump stop on his half-hook. (Doherty's staff mandated the two-footed stop.) "As long as you make sixty percent of your shots, I don't care what you do," Holladay told May. And on the first day of conditioning in September, junior swingman Jawad Williams redlined to the point of throwing up. "I've never done that in my life," he told Haase, "but I'll trade that for a Final Four."

⸺

ULTIMATELY, DOHERTY'S DEMISE in Chapel Hill came down to this: Doherty, the Carolina guy, *wasn't Carolina enough.* Smith and Williams, by contrast, are bound more tightly than Smith & Wesson. It's an oft-told (though nonetheless poignant) story: As the son of an alcoholic father, a boy raised near his native Asheville by his saintly single mother, Mimmie, who worked yeoman's hours to make ends meet, Williams found the structure he craved in Smith's hermetic roundball universe. Williams absorbed every nuance of the Carolina philosophy, taking notes from the moment he joined the freshman team, in '68, to the day he reluctantly left Smith's side for Kansas twenty years later.

You can see Smith in the way Williams schedules every practice down to the minute, the way he always gives his team a Thought for the Day, the way his players dive on the floor, take charges, and point to their teammates in gratitude for assists. The resemblance is uncanny. As former Tar Heel Jeff Lebo, now the coach at Chattanooga, puts it, "When I saw Kansas the last three years, I saw North Carolina."

Even after Williams turned down Carolina in 2000, he and Smith (who upon retirement became a consultant to the athletic department) never missed a golf date, never stopped talking hoops over the phone. Williams still picks up his mentor's Final Four tickets so that Smith can avoid standing in line, and on one recent day Williams tiptoed into Smith's basement office "just to see if I felt like we'd put him in a dungeon where there's one light hanging from the ceiling and one table and one chair and it smells bad." A torture chamber it wasn't. ("I like it," says Smith, "I have two secretaries, and I'm out of the way, so nobody finds me.")

Truth be told, while Doherty strained to put his own stamp on the Tar Heels' program, Smith (Kansas, class of '53) became KU's de facto fourth assistant. It was Smith who suggested posting a picture of the Georgia Dome, site of the Final Four, in the lockers of every Jayhawk two years ago and Smith who gave Williams the idea of having his team sign a pledge last season: *If I truly want to win a national championship, I pledge that I will box out on every possession.*

Williams vows to continue consulting his old boss on X's and O's this season, and he holds out hope that Smith will start attending every home game, not just the rare ones that aren't televised. "People think part of the reason I didn't come three years ago was because it wasn't gonna be my program, which is far from the truth," Williams says. "Coach Smith and I will talk basketball, and we will talk quite a bit. Why would I not want to use such a great resource?"

Granted, Williams and Smith don't share the same DNA. Not exactly. "I'm not gonna wear a coat and tie to the office every day like Coach Smith did," Williams says. "If I curse at all, it's more than he ever does. And he's much more innovative. I copy people. I'm not the dumbest guy on the block, but he is more intelligent than 99.9 percent of basketball coaches." Williams notes that whereas he reads for entertainment (his recent favorites include Rick Reilly's *Missing Links*), Smith reads for intellectual enrichment, devouring such tomes as *Parables of Kierkegaard*.

In some ways, though, Williams interprets the Smith Gospels even more strictly than the man who created them. Consider: In the year 2003, Williams, a devout Southern Baptist, still requires all his recruits to attend church (or synagogue, mosque, etc.) during the first semester of their freshman year. It's an old Smith rule, but while Smith softened his stance in the 1960s, allowing players to abstain with a note from their parents, Williams has never relented.

Ever the puritan, Williams is possessed of a manic zeal for following rules. "He really goes by the book," Nick Collison says. "We'd have a barbecue at an assistant coach's house, and then three months later we'd each get a bill for $6.59." When Williams takes the NCAA's annual recruiting rules compliance test—a forty-question, open-book exam required of all coaches—he'll challenge himself by doing it closed book instead. "My record is nineteen minutes, and the most I've ever missed is two," he says proudly.

That sort of relentless and uncompromising virtue is precisely what Williams's supporters adore in him and what his detractors resent. Though he's among the most respected teachers in the game, the term rival coaches often use to describe Williams is sanctimonious. Five years ago Williams famously reported Florida for possible violations in its recruiting battle for Mike Miller (the NCAA turned up no evidence of wrongdoing), and he admits he has blown the whistle on coaches in his own conference. "I don't think coaches should say, 'Well, he's cheating,' but then do nothing," he says. "If somebody robs a bank, they should be called on the carpet for that."

It isn't complicated, really. Williams subscribes to a few sacred beliefs. No one will outwork him. No one will agonize more about doing "the right thing." No one will adhere more strictly to the rules, whether they're handed down by the NCAA or Smith or the Lord Almighty. He is not an innovator, remember, but a copier, one who clings to the Carolina blueprint as an article of faith.

So when the desperation rang in his ears last spring—*We need you, Coach*—there was only one thing to do. Three decades ago Dean Smith helped bring order and stability to Roy Williams's world. The least Williams can do now is to repay the favor.

The American Pharaoh

From *Sports Illustrated*, OCTOBER 14, 2013

Was it serendipity or something in the water at Nassau Hall that made Princeton in the early 1990s the proving ground for two figures who would go on to have such a profound influence on American soccer over the next three decades? Several times a week during soccer season, Wahl, a soccer beat writer for the college newspaper, would meet with Tigers coach Bob Bradley in his office. The scene would play out countless times over the ensuing years, as Wahl graduated to *Sports Illustrated* and Bradley, who had led Princeton to the NCAA Final Four in 1993, to managerial positions in Major League Soccer and then, in 2006, to the U.S. men's national team. Despite their long relationship, Wahl didn't hesitate when he felt he needed to be critical of Bradley, and Bradley expected nothing less. "There was a real level of respect between us," Bradley says. "We were both stubborn and proud. I knew that he would do everything to get to the bottom of things. To get it right. He knew that I would do everything to protect the team and keep certain things tight." Bradley remembers Wahl as being "fearless in pursuit of the truth. . . . His way of telling beautiful stories while also digging deep into the most difficult issues in the game around the world highlighted his integrity and values."

The two met up in Cairo for this 2013 piece, with Bradley coaching Egypt and on the cusp of qualifying the team for the 2014 World Cup, amid intense turmoil in that country. (The quest ultimately fell short: Egypt lost to Ghana on aggregate goals in the final-round two-match playoff.) Whenever the two had time to catch up, they covered plenty of ground: "Latest trends in the game, the challenges of journalism in the world of the internet and social media, the appreciation of the best books and stories," Bradley says. "I've been incredibly fortunate to coach some young players who went on to great things. I had the same pride watching Grant grow over the years."

*L*ook. There's Bob Bradley, the American coach of the Egyptian national soccer team. On a warm September night in Cairo, Bradley and his wife, Lindsay, arrive at the open-air El Prince restaurant in Imbaba, a vibrant working-class neighborhood in the Egyptian capital. Two years after a popular revolution, two months after a military takeover, one month after the mass killing of eight hundred protesters, the country remains on edge. A car bomb, the first in ages, went off the other day. Its intended target: the minister of the interior. Authorities just extended the state of emergency, including a curfew of 11:00 P.M. on most days and 7:00 P.M. on Fridays, the holy day, the day of demonstrations.

And yet in a divided country of 85 million, at least one unifying force has no opposition these days, and this bald fifty-five-year-old coach from Essex Fells, New Jersey—the most visible American in Egypt's daily public life—embodies that hope. As Bradley walks into the packed restaurant, diners rise from their tables and give him a standing ovation. Cellphone cameras go into overdrive. The waitstaff commences a chant, in English: "World Cup! World Cup! World Cup!"

Look. There's Bradley again. It's Sunday morning, and the coach and his wife are seated in the back of a Kia sedan inching through Cairo gridlock. Along the way they pass signposts of their two years in Egypt: the headquarters of the country's most famous club soccer team, Al Ahly, with murals along its walls depicting the seventy-four Al Ahly fans who died in last year's Port Said Stadium tragedy; the home base of the Egyptian soccer federation (including Bradley's old office), which was torched by angry ultras after the court ruling on the Port Said deaths; and, finally, the Children's Cancer Hospital, where the Bradleys have donated their time and money as they've become an unexpected and deeply valued part of the Cairo community.

Inside, meeting young cancer patients and their parents, Bradley kneels low, offering smiles, ready with hugs. He and his wife are naturals, connecting with kids who've lost their hair, kids on IV drips, kids half asleep in the arms of their tired-eyed parents. "Who's your favorite player?" Bradley asks one ailing boy.

"Aboutrika!" the child cries out, referring to the national team's star midfielder, Mohammed Aboutrika.

"Yeah," says Bradley. "Me, too."

In another room Bradley encounters a beaming father. "You're the American Superman!" he says. "You're going to take us to the World Cup!"

Look. It's the word Bradley uses most often to start sentences, an unvarnished Jersey Guy way of talking. Even his Egyptian friends have started using it. (These days Egyptians also see any bald white guy of a certain age and yell, "Bob!") But there's more to it than that.

Look. No, really. *Look.* Use your eyes. Observe. Think. Bob Bradley did not come to Egypt to blow a whistle and stick his head in the desert sand. "Wherever you live, this ability to look around you and be aware of others, this is what you try to do," he says. "We live here. We're aware of what's going on."

In August, one month after the Egyptian military overthrew the Muslim Brotherhood and President Mohamed Morsi, Bradley watched from his high-rise apartment on the bank of the Nile as protesters marched toward Ramses Square, only to encounter police forces. Black helicopters and smoke filled the air. Bradley heard gunfire pushing back the crowd: *POP! POP! POP!*

"Up until the last few weeks you always knew when and where things were heating up," he says. "Cairo's a huge city, and things just carry on. But for a few days it was more random and reckless." On August 15, the U.S. State Department advised all Americans living in Egypt to evacuate the country. Ninety-nine percent of foreign soccer coaches in his situation would have left long ago.

But the Bradleys stayed. "Look, as I've gotten to know these players, we're brothers," says Bradley. "We're in something together. If this is who you are, you challenge people to be in all the way, and you explain what that means. Then you have to show them that you're in all the way. That's just how it is."

And while he stayed, the most amazing thing happened: The Pharaohs kept winning, kept advancing toward this soccer-mad nation's third World Cup berth and its first since 1990. You could throw any obstacle at Bradley's team—a suspension of the domestic league, players who were earning no money, empty stadiums for home qualifiers, political divides within the squad, the uncertainty and turmoil that come with each day in Egypt. Before their last World Cup qualifier, against

Guinea last month, some Egyptian players had to use magic markers to write their numbers on their shorts. Still, nothing has stopped the Pharaohs.

Of the more than two hundred national teams that have chosen to participate in qualifying for World Cup 2014, the last one with a perfect record isn't Spain or Germany or Argentina. Only Egypt—*Egypt!*—has been spotless. Six games, six victories. And now comes the final test: a two-game home-and-away playoff starting on Tuesday at powerful Ghana. Only the winner will advance to Brazil next summer.

Mido, a former Egyptian star forward who now works as an analyst for Al Jazeera, says that his countrymen were skeptical at first of the American coach, imagining that Bradley would care only about fitness and the physical aspect of the sport. But he has won them over. "I think he has done great," says Mido. "He has been so strong mentally to stay in Egypt with all that's happened. The easy option was to leave, but he chose to fight."

The story of Bob Bradley and Egypt began transcending sports a long time ago. Now it's a symbol of hope for a nation. "It would be great for [the team] to qualify and experience with the Egyptian people the joy of caring about something together," says Jeffrey Stout, a Princeton religion professor and a Bradley confidant dating back to the coach's time at the school, from 1984 to '95. "That is what Bob could imagine ahead of time. What he couldn't imagine is how significant it would be for him and the team to behave well in public under circumstances where almost nobody else does. In a crisis situation for a country, there's this one place where people are doing the just thing in front of everyone, every day. And getting a group with differences to show what it's like to have relationships that don't involve dominating each other [and to hold] each other accountable—that's a thumbnail sketch of what democracy is.

"For them to do that? That's a big deal."

EGYPT IS HARDLY what Bradley imagined as a next destination after he was fired by the U.S. following a Gold Cup–final loss to Mexico in July 2011. He aspired to a job in Europe and believed (not unreasonably) that he'd built a worthy résumé during his nine seasons as an MLS coach and, especially, four years with the Americans. That history included taking the MLS Cup in 1998 with the Chicago Fire, beating Spain to reach the 2009 Confederations Cup final, and winning the U.S.'s 2010 World Cup group, ahead of England, before losing in the Round of 16 to Ghana. But European clubs didn't bite. "When you're an American, earning respect and getting your foot in the door is hard, whether you're a player or a coach," says Bradley. "I feel strongly that with everything I've done, if I were German, Dutch, Spanish, French, or Italian, I'd have had many opportunities in Europe."

Egypt came calling for several reasons: Bradley had impressed its federation by coaching the U.S. to a 3–0 victory over the Pharaohs in the 2009 Confederations Cup, and he had worked closely with an Egyptian American, Zak Abdel, his goalkeepers coach with the U.S. and in MLS.

Egypt had soccer talent—the team had won three straight African championships, in 2006, '08, and '10—but after a series of World Cup qualifying failures, Bradley saw the importance of breaking through and reaching Brazil in '14. For years Bradley had preached to his players and his children the value of embracing new challenges. Now he turned that expectation on himself. "When opportunities come along, you don't look back," he says. "Don't be afraid to put everything you have into something. If you're worried about the outcome, you don't get anywhere."

Bob and Lindsay went all in. With three children all in their twenties and out of the house—daughters Kerry and Ryan lived in LA; Michael, a U.S. midfielder, plays in Italy for Roma—the timing made sense. "I was like 'OK, let's try this adventure and see what happens,'" says Lindsay, a former lacrosse standout at Virginia. Instead of living outside Egypt or in a gated compound on the outskirts of Cairo, the couple chose an apartment in Zamalek, close to the city center. The idea: The new coach couldn't know his players unless he had a sense of life on the ground in the postrevolution metropolis.

For more than a century, Egyptians' soccer passions have been tied to politics. Al Ahly, founded in Cairo in 1907 by opponents of the British protectorate, served as a meeting point for the students who staged the 1919 revolution that gained Egypt independence. One of the team's first presidents, Saad Zaghloul, also acted as the head of the country's nationalist party; and Gamal Abdel Nasser would hold the Al Ahly post (despite not being known as a soccer fan) before serving as the nation's president from 1956 to '70. Meanwhile Al Ahly's archrival, Zamalek, was known as "the King's Club," for its British sympathizers.

During his twenty-nine years as head of state, starting in 1981, Hosni Mubarak fostered close ties with the national team, not least during the glory years of the Pharaohs' African three-peat. The national team's doctor still has a photo of himself and Mubarak on the wall of his office at a Cairo gym.

As Egyptian soccer expert James Dorsey points out, extreme fan groups, or ultras (especially those supporting Al Ahly), played a pivotal role in the Arab Spring as part of a street-savvy resistance that helped overthrow Mubarak's regime in February 2011. Depending on whom you listen to, that support may have led to the tragic events a year later, on February 1, 2012, when Al Ahly visited Al Masry, a team in Port Said whose fans had clashed in previous years with their Al Ahly counterparts.

"I'll remember it forever because I saw it on TV live, and I've seen it hundreds of times since," says Bradley, who was watching from the hospitality room at Cairo Stadium, where he was scouting a game alongside his wife and Abdel. "The final whistle blows and fans come running onto the field, and Ahly players are running for their lives. What immediately hits you is that there are police on the field, and they're not doing anything."

Someone shut off the Port Said Stadium lights. Someone bolted an exit gate, trapping the Al Ahly fans inside. It was a bloodbath. Al Ahly's players managed to escape to the safety of their locker room, which soon became a makeshift morgue. One young Al Ahly fan died in the arms of Aboutrika, a ten-year veteran of the team.

Back in Cairo, the Bradleys left the game with Abdel, who translated radio updates to their growing horror. "Ten people are dead. . . . It's up to twenty-five. . . . OK, now it's forty. . . . Fifty now. . . . They're saying seventy-four dead." "Lindsay was crying, and Bob wasn't saying anything," Abdel recalls. "I'd never seen him like that before."

But Bradley did have questions—lots of them. The coach reads about Egypt constantly (even on Twitter, though you'll never see him create his own account), and what he's learned from media and from his own experience applies as much to Port Said as it does to Egyptian life in general. "It's always easy to see what's on the surface," says Bradley.

"What is harder to understand—what's more complex—is what goes on *beneath* the surface."

It's unlikely that anyone will ever know exactly what transpired in Port Said, but Bradley felt it was his duty as a leader to show the Egyptian people that he understood what they were going through. That included risking the wrath of authorities by saying on Al Jazeera English that he believed Port Said had been a massacre (implying premeditation), as opposed to spontaneous fan violence. "Exactly what went on, how it went down—I still don't know," he says. "Nobody does. But look, this was a massacre."

At the time of Port Said, Bradley was only four months (and one game) into his national-team tenure. He and Lindsay could have taken the first plane out of Cairo. Instead they did something that astonished Egyptians: One day after the tragedy, they joined thousands of marchers at Sphinx Square in support of the victims and their families. The next day, they attended a memorial at Al Ahly headquarters. "I hugged each player and looked into his eyes," says Bradley. "I knew what they had seen in that locker room. I could read it on their faces."

From that moment on, nothing would be the same in Egyptian soccer. The domestic league was suspended. Several players, including Aboutrika, announced they were retiring from the sport. A year later, in March, angry Al Ahly fans would set fire to the Egyptian federation building after a court acquitted seven of nine police officials from the Port Said case.

But in those searing days of February 2012, Egyptians noticed something in their new American coach, who quietly donated money to the victims' families. He was one of them now. When the Bradleys met with the families of the deceased, mothers gave Lindsay photographs of their children, young people in their teens and twenties who'd gone to a game and had never come home. Mother to mother, they knew she would understand.

"How many of you have heard of Bruce Springsteen?"

New Jersey to his core, a fan of the Boss for life, Bradley thought at least one of his players would raise a hand when he asked this at one of his first team meetings. To his dismay, nobody did.

"Who is he?" asked midfielder Hossam Ghaly.

"Come on, friend, and sit with me," said Bradley, who started playing "Land of Hope and Dreams" on his iPhone. The lyrics applied to Egypt, too, Bradley thought, and so he had Abdel translate some for the room: "Leave behind your sorrows / Let this day be the last / Tomorrow there'll be sunshine / And all this darkness past."

In many ways Bradley has approached the Pharaohs the same way that he did the U.S. team: Keep practices relatively short, high energy, and organized to the minute; demand teamwide accountability and the willingness to say constructive things that others (including the coach) might not want to hear; and preach the purity of the team, the need to rely on the inner circle of players and coaches, shutting out all distractions, all excuses for failure.

But, recognizing that he's in a new environment, Bradley has also summoned all of his powers to connect not just with his players but also with the Egyptian people. In long conversations between Bradley and Stout, the Princeton professor, they spoke about respect as a concept that resonates with Mediterranean cultures. The two friends have talked about what it means to Egyptians for Bradley to identify as a family member more than as a U.S. citizen. Bradley, for example, often refers to his players, publicly and privately, as "my brothers." And yet there was always the understanding that those players would believe in Bradley only if they saw him back it up with his actions every day.

In his meetings with players, Bradley addresses challenges that he never faced as the U.S. coach. After Port Said, Al Masry goalkeeper Amir Abdelhamid—a reserve for Egypt—expressed concern about driving to the national team camp in Cairo because his car's license plates identified him as being from Port Said. Meanwhile, with domestic players not being paid while the league is suspended, the strain is palpable.

Not every player has bought in. Before a friendly against Chile in February, Bradley informed Egypt's veteran first-choice goalkeeper, Essam El-Hadary, that he wasn't going to start. At halftime El-Hadary told a journalist that he was retiring from the Pharaohs, which became the big postgame story. El-Hadary believed he could force Bradley to recall him, but instead the coach thanked him the next morning for his services. Bradley hasn't brought him back since.

The coach has pushed back on a few Egyptian traditions, too, notably the use of the term *captain*. In Egypt, not only does the player with the most seniority wear the captain's armband during games—a practice that Bradley accepts as something he can't change—but the term *captain* is used frequently as an honorific for anyone who's seen as a leader, even (in Bradley's opinion) blowhards who don't deserve it. After hearing "Captain Bradley" a few too many times at a recent practice, Bradley called one of his equipment managers, Abdullah Mohamed, and asked him to stand with him in front of the team. "Listen," Bradley told them, "every other word here is *captain-captain-captain*. We have media who used to play on the national team who rip us, and then they come here and you guys show them this phony respect and call them *captain*. And they're trying to destroy our team. Meanwhile, here's Abdullah. He's a good man. He works hard. He will do anything for us. Look, I've been here for two years. How long have you been here, Abdullah? Twenty years. I'm not captain. *He's captain!*"

It's a running theme with Bradley. When the Egyptian league was still operating, a television broadcast showed him sitting in the stands next to Abdel and, one seat down, Bradley's driver, Hany Abdel Wadood. When a federation board member angrily demanded that the driver be told to wait in his car outside the stadium, Bradley asked Wadood to move into the seat next to him.

The coach has kept his inner circle small, limiting it to his players and assistants. No relationship has grown stronger than the one between Bradley and Aboutrika, one of the most fascinating figures in world soccer. A few years ago, when Egypt and Al Ahly were the champions of Africa, the midfield wizard was regarded as the world's best player not plying his trade in Europe or South America. He could have moved to a top international club had he wished; though not particularly fast or smooth, Aboutrika is blessed with a vision for making passes that nobody else could have visualized. But he loved Egypt and made good money, so he stayed, earning the devotion of Egyptian fans. Aboutrika was different in other ways, too. Devoutly religious and the owner of a university degree in philosophy, he didn't lack the courage to speak his mind. After scoring a goal at the 2008 Africa Cup of Nations, he revealed a T-shirt that read SYMPATHIZE WITH GAZA, only increasing his stature throughout the Middle East.

By the time Bradley took over in late 2011, however, there were whispers that Aboutrika, at thirty-three, was too old. In the days before Bradley's first game, against Brazil, Aboutrika wasn't even starting for Al Ahly, so the coach left him off his squad. The decision caused an uproar (NEW COACH DROPS STAR MIDFIELDER!), and Aboutrika's dream of making his first World Cup appeared in jeopardy. Yet Bradley took notice: Aboutrika never lashed out to the media in the way that many players would have; instead he said it was on him to earn back a spot in the national team. As Bradley kept an eye on Al Ahly games, the old Aboutrika reemerged.

Then Port Said happened, and everything stopped. After waiting several weeks to respect the dead, Bradley arranged a meeting with Aboutrika in Cairo. The start of World Cup qualifying was three months away; the player had thought about it and he didn't want to retire after all, he told Bradley. His message was clear: *Whatever you need from me, I'll do it. I would love to have one more chance to reach the World Cup.*

"I got a sense with him," says Bradley. "When you talk about having a blood brother in this, where you bleed for him and he'll bleed for you—this was a really good man."

Aboutrika's reemergence has been crucial for the Pharaohs. In his first game back, a March 2012 friendly against Uganda, he scored the game winner in stoppage time. During Egypt's rampage through its World Cup qualifying group, he started all six matches and scored five goals, including two in the key victory, a 3–2 come-from-behind win at Guinea. What's more, at thirty-four he's mentoring Egypt's promising young forward, twenty-one-year-old Mohamed Salah. It's no coincidence that at his club team, FC Basel, Salah wears number 22. Aboutrika's number.

Stout hears these stories about Aboutrika from his old friend and shakes his head with wonder. "Here's somebody who gets up every day and asks, 'How do I do the just thing concretely to other people?'" the professor says in Princeton, where he first coached youth teams with Bradley in the 1980s. "Now you have a coach and a player who are both like that? It's unusual to have either of those things in any team, anywhere. The players are gathering around it. It's like Red Auerbach and Bill Russell—that level of human beings, coming from these different worlds. What remarkable athletic thing can happen because of the way they deal with their business every day and with each other?"

"You meet a lot of people in Egypt who have two faces," says Tomasz Kaczmarek, the Pharaohs' conditioning coach. "They're one way in the media and another way when the camera is off. Aboutrika has one face."

Only sometimes, in today's polarized Egyptian political climate, that honesty comes with a price.

EGYPT IS SO close to the World Cup. Just two games away. Yet it's impossible to separate the Egyptian players from what's happening around them. The military takeover in June removed the Muslim Brotherhood and the democratically elected (but plainly faltering) Morsi from power. The majority of Egyptians now support the military leaders, who cracked down violently in July on massed Brotherhood protesters, a handful of them armed, before outlawing the Brotherhood altogether.

But demonstrations continue. The divide in Egypt persists. "Now, in this country, if you disagree with me, you're my enemy—that's the mentality," says Abdel. "My older sister here, she thinks [the military takeover] was a revolution. My brother in the States thinks it's a coup. Now they don't talk to each other. Can you imagine? Brother and sister? It's crazy."

As Bradley prepares his team for the winner-take-all, aggregate-goal playoff against Ghana (Egypt will host the second leg in Cairo on November 19), he faces the ongoing challenge of keeping his players together. "At a time when the country is divided, you want to make sure the national team stands together in a strong way," he says.

But that's tough. These days many of his players support the military rulers. Aboutrika, however, backs the Muslim Brotherhood. Occasionally, he and Bradley talk about political stories they've both read. Bradley has always encouraged debate and give-and-take on his teams, but he has never led in the midst of a political crisis. During the turmoil of July and August, Aboutrika was active on his Twitter feed, writing: "I supported Dr. Morsi out of complete conviction . . . in light of the success of the January 25 revolution and the freedoms and expression of opinion that followed. . . . I think there will be a real democracy and respect for other opinions, but unfortunately this hasn't happened. So I decided not to talk politics. . . . But when it has to do with reputation and dignity I will not be quiet."

Aboutrika's pro-Brotherhood statements have caused tension with some teammates, but there has of yet been no noticeable toll on the Pharaohs' on-field chemistry. For his part, Bradley has walked a fine line. "Look," he says, "Trika has had the strength to always stand behind his beliefs and say what he thinks, and that doesn't always work here. But I will defend that part of him forever, because he is a good man and cares about Egypt. In order to focus on doing everything to get to the World Cup, he's picked up on the need to not be high profile at the moment."

It would be easy to wrap a bow around the Pharaohs' World Cup qualifying success, to view the team as an oasis of harmony sealed off from the rest of society. But life isn't like that. The truth: Much of Bradley's finest coaching has taken place in that spot he so often talks about, beneath the surface. Coaxing a group with conflicting opinions into behaving in public? Holding each other accountable? Finding a way to reach a common goal in the face of so many challenges? For them to do that? That's a big deal.

Aboutrika hasn't tweeted since late August, but one of his final posts struck a note of hope for all Egyptians: "Loving your country doesn't mean advertising. It means actions and feelings that translate this love. This love is among the ways that we get closer to God. I love you, Egypt."

Next Tuesday, on a soccer field in Ghana, those actions will recommence.

4
UNDER THE HOOD

WAHL WAS A CONSUMER OF THE WORK OF MICHAEL LEWIS AND Malcolm Gladwell, two compulsively readable writers dedicated to explanatory journalism who both wrote often about sports. During his days on the college basketball beat, Wahl found himself likening what coach Billy Donovan had achieved at Florida to a Silicon Valley start-up and fit the particulars of the spread of the Princeton Offense to the definition of a social epidemic as popularized in Gladwell's book *The Tipping Point: How Little Things Can Make a Big Difference.* (In the first piece that follows, about the birth of the dribble drive motion offense that helped teams at the University of Memphis achieve unprecedented success during the late 2000s, Wahl actually used the Michael Lewis term "the new new thing.") But Wahl brought his own tactics to explaining various phenomena. Sometimes he proceeded with a straight-ahead, fine-grained breakdown, methodically unpacking foundational elements. On other occasions he constructed just the right metaphorical frame. Occasionally he deployed stats and analytics, but he always paired them with lively writing to keep eyes from glazing over. More than anything, amid the *why* and *how,* Wahl had a nose for the most engaging *who:* finding and showcasing the obscure innovator or prophet without honor.

Fast and Furious

FROM *Sports Illustrated*, FEBRUARY 18, 2008

In 2008, with the Memphis Tigers unbeaten and ranked number one, Wahl dug into the offense that coach John Calipari called dribble drive motion, or DDM. Unlike a piece he had written five years earlier about the Princeton Offense, which centered on longtime Tigers coach and Hall of Famer Pete Carril, this story highlights an obscure underdog, Vance Walberg, a California high school and junior college coach who had Calipari's ear. As with his Princeton piece, Wahl found teams from high school to the NBA using an attack in which skill and smarts trumped physicality. And you can see the tracery of the Princeton story in this one: anecdote blended with vivid description. Inside a tour de force of explanatory journalism, Wahl has nested a poignant portrait of a basketball lifer who has just left Pepperdine, his first Division I head coaching job, after only two seasons. But there would be a happy ending. Walberg hooked on as an assistant coach at UMass; served as an NBA assistant in Denver, Philadelphia, and Sacramento; and finally, in 2016, fetched up in Fresno for a satisfying second stint at Clovis West High School, where he had spent thirteen seasons before going into college and pro coaching. All told, Walberg has led the Golden Eagles to more than five hundred victories—and watched with pride as his daughter Heather Long had a successful, eight-year run as coach of the girls' team at rival Clovis North.

WHEN HOOPS HISTORIANS LOOK BACK ON THE 2007–08 college basketball season, they may conclude that its most significant moment came on an Indian summer evening in October '03. At the head of a heavy oak table in his Memphis steak house sat Tigers coach John Calipari, who has led teams to both the Final Four and the NBA playoffs. Next to him was an obscure junior college coach from

Fresno named Vance Walberg. For six days Walberg had observed Cali-pari's practices, continuing an annual pilgrimage that had given him deeper insight into the work of two dozen elite college coaches, from Bob Knight to Dean Smith to Billy Donovan.

But now, after the appetizers and the porterhouses had been cleared from the table, Calipari asked Walberg something that no other coach had bothered to ask him. "So tell me, Vance," he said, "what do you run?"

Walberg laughed. "You don't want to know," he replied. "It's a little bit off the wall."

"No, really," Calipari said. "Show me."

And so, using a pepper shaker as the basket, white sugar packets as offensive players, and pink Sweet'N Low packets as defenders, Walberg explained his quirky creation, a high-scoring scheme featuring four pe-rimeter players and a host of innovations. Unlike Knight's classic mo-tion offense (which is based on screens) or Pete Carril's Princeton-style offense (which is based on cuts), Walberg's attack was founded on drib-ble penetration. To Calipari, at least, it embodied two wholly unconven-tional notions. One, there were no screens, the better to create spacing for drives. Two, the post man ran to the *weak* side of the lane (instead of the ball side), leaving the ball handler an open driving path to the bas-ket.

But there was plenty more. As Walberg pushed the packets through the phases of his offense, Calipari experienced a new kind of sugar rush. Walberg's scheme was madness. It was genius.

And it was unlike anything Calipari, an old-school motion and play-calling acolyte, had ever run. "The players are unleashed when they play this way," he says, "because every player has the green light to take his man on every play." When Calipari junked his playbook and switched to Walberg's offense, his mentors thought he had lost his mind. "You've won hundreds of games playing a certain way, and now you're going to change?" Hall of Famer Larry Brown asked him. "And it's a junior col-lege coach from California? What are you, crazy?"

Now look. Through Sunday, Calipari's Tigers were 23–0, ranked number one in the nation and aiming to become the first team to enter the NCAA tournament undefeated since UNLV in 1991. But Memphis is only the tip of the Walberg iceberg, a spreading mass of teams using the

WORLD CLASS • 87

dribble drive motion offense—Calipari's felicitous term—at every level of the game.

In Jersey City legendary coach Bob Hurley, who adopted DDM two seasons ago, has taken St. Anthony (19–0) to number one in *USA Today*'s national high school rankings. Likewise, Omaha Central High has won the last two Nebraska Class A state championships while running DDM, and Grand Valley High in Parachute, Colorado, rode the attack to last year's Class 2A state title.

In California's Central Valley, where Walberg, fifty-one, coached for thirteen seasons at Clovis West High and four at Fresno City College, his high-pressure offense and defense have changed the way an entire region plays basketball. "It totally blew up here," says Fresno Central High coach Loren LeBeau, one of Walberg's former assistants. "We're in the top league in Fresno, and four of the six teams are running this style." Under coach Tom Gonsalves, the girls' team at St. Mary's High in Stockton has gone 25–0 and risen to number nine in the nation using DDM. Another practitioner, junior college coach Jeff Klein at Chaffey College in Rancho Cucamonga, describes the system this way: "It's almost like Vance invented a new language."

The Denver Nuggets are running elements of DDM, and so are the Boston Celtics. "[Calipari] and I fax each other," says Celtics coach Doc Rivers. Meanwhile, one vocal DDM skeptic has changed his mind. "If I were fortunate enough to get back into coaching, I'd seek Vance's help in a minute," says Brown, who joined Calipari and Walberg last September at a clinic in Mississippi attended by more than four hundred high school coaches. "When I was coaching UCLA, everybody ran the high-post offense and the 2-2-1 press because of Coach [John] Wooden. He won ten national titles, so you could understand that. But to see all these people who are incorporating what Vance does is mind-boggling."

It's enough to make you wonder: Who the hell is Vance Walberg? How is his offense spreading around the nation? And if his brainchild is the hottest thing in U.S. basketball, why is he out of a job?

———

WHERE DO INNOVATORS come from? An original idea—the new new thing—can be sparked anywhere, but the majority of college basketball's greatest innovators share a common trajectory: Unlike most of today's top coaches, who rose through the college ranks as assistants, they became head coaches early, often in anonymous hoops outposts. Carril was twenty-four when he became the jayvee coach at Easton (Pa.) High, the same age Knight was when he took over his first team, Army. Two of today's most respected innovators are Wisconsin's Bo Ryan, exponent of the Swing offense, who became the coach at Sun Valley High in Aston, Pennsylvania, at twenty-six, and Michigan's John Beilein, who won the top job at Newfane (N.Y.) Central High at twenty and later came up with the five-out offense.

No matter how obscure the team, "when you're a head coach you get to tinkering with what you want," says Walberg, who was twenty-two when he took over at Mountain View (Calif.) High. As a high school grinder over the years—he even coached badminton at one point—Walberg dabbled in variations of the flex offense and Knight's motion, among other schemes, but his real break came in 1997, when he had his Clovis West team use a cutting-edge four-out offense (i.e., four perimeter players) of the kind now favored by Saint Louis coach Rick Majerus.

"It was pure luck," Walberg says, despite all evidence to the contrary. His best player, a heady, relentless point guard named Chris Hernandez (who would later star at Stanford), was such a skilled dribble penetrator that Walberg moved his post man to the weakside block, clearing two bodies from Hernandez's path to the basket. When Hernandez broke down his defender he had several options: (1) shoot an open layup, (2) pass to the post man (if his defender left him to stop Hernandez), or (3) kick the ball out to an open teammate on the perimeter (if his defender had sagged to help out on Hernandez). The open player could shoot a three-pointer, but if one wasn't available, the team would attack again.

Because there were no screens and attackers were spaced so far apart, the formation opened yawning gaps for penetrators, as long as they had the talent to beat their defenders and the smarts to read defenses on the fly. "I wish I had chosen a fancier name than AASAA, but I wanted kids to understand that it was attack-attack-skip-attack-attack," says Walberg. "What am I trying to say? Get to the rim. It's basically *here we come.*" All of Walberg's teams hear the same slogan (We like three-pointers, but we love layups), and shot charts reveal that the teams take almost no midrange jumpers.

Walberg's invention shares some elements with European-style drive-and-kick formations and the fast-paced spread offense of Phoenix Suns coach Mike D'Antoni, parts of which are being used by Duke, Texas, and UMass. But Walberg is sui generis. Since '97 he has added myriad phases, wrinkles, and—perhaps most important—an elaborate set of competitive practice drills (with names such as Blood, Cardinal, and Scramble) that hone the fundamentals necessary for the offense. "Have you seen Vance at practice? Oh, man," says Brown. "His drills are all building blocks to his offense and defense, which is the key to coaching."

In fact, Calipari says he now does far more coaching in practice than during games, when he used to bark out play calls nearly every trip down the court. "The biggest strength of this offense," Walberg says, "is I feel we're teaching kids how to play basketball instead of how to run plays."

Dribble drive is tailor-made for today's high school and college teams, which favor speed in the absence of classic back-to-the-basket big men, but it isn't for everyone. It requires quick, smart, and talented guards who have a feel for the game. (See: Memphis point guard Derrick Rose.) It requires agile big men who can shoot from the perimeter and race downcourt. It requires deep benches and three-point shooters who can punish sagging man-to-man defenses and the inevitable zones. Not least, it requires complete commitment from coaches, who have to give up the control that comes with offensive play calling and conventional half-court defenses.

Indeed, Walberg is so committed that he might need to be committed. He's still disappointed that Memphis's swarming defense—the nation's best, holding opponents to 0.83 point per possession—hasn't adopted his gambling full-court press, which Walberg's California converts contend is even more Promethean than his offense. "Vance believes so much in what he does," says Brown, a disciple of Dean Smith and Henry Iba. "The first time I met him we were talking about defensive principles, and everything I said, he'd say, 'No, no, no, you can't do it that way.' I'd say, 'Well, Coach Smith and Mr. Iba taught me this.' And he'd still say, 'No, no, no.' Is he not a character?"

Walberg may have been a mad scientist, but he won games at an astonishing rate, usually with less talent than his opponents had. In the five years after it adopted his offense, Clovis West went 159–18, and during Walberg's four seasons at Fresno City College (2002–06) the Rams went 133–11, winning the '05 state juco title and regularly averaging more than 100 points a game. Nuggets assistant John Welch constantly observed Clovis West practices during his days at Fresno State under Jerry Tarkanian. He recalls, "People used to think it was funny: Why is a college assistant always over there with a high school coach? But I've been around some unbelievable coaches—Tark, Hubie Brown, Mike Fratello, now George Karl and Tim Grgurich—and I've learned as much from Vance as from anybody else."

By the summer of 2003, Welch had joined Hubie Brown's Memphis Grizzlies staff. One day he called his friend Calipari. "I've always respected Johnny Welch," says Calipari. "He's a basketball Benny, knows coaches, studies the game. He says, 'Look, I've got a guy coming in here, and I want him to spend some time with you. You ought to look at his offense.'"

WHY CHANGE? IT may seem obvious now that they're coaching the nation's top-ranked teams in college and high school basketball, but Calipari and Hurley didn't need to overhaul their systems. Calipari, forty-nine, had won 336 games in college and the NBA and had reached three Sweet 16s, two Elite Eights, and a Final Four when he and Walberg sat down for dinner that night at Cal's Championship Steakhouse. During his first three seasons at Memphis, however, Calipari had coached in only one NCAA tournament game. "It's like you're a teacher, and you're teaching for fifteen years, and your lesson plan never changed," he says. "This has been invigorating for me because it's gotten me to think, to study the game again."

Hurley, sixty, had won twenty-two state championships, nearly nine hundred games, and two mythical national titles as head coach at St. Anthony when he adopted dribble drive in the fall of 2005. "I've had very few original thoughts in my life," Hurley says, "but I'm smart enough to take from people who are successful and seem to have a greater view of the game. We got to a point where kids spent more time in the weight room than out on the court working on skills. [Dribble drive] gets you working on skills. You can move your center around. It doesn't have to be mud wrestling where just the stronger, more physical, more athletic kids win."

Both coaches have added their own elements to Walberg's framework. Hurley uses what he calls "a European-style pick-and-roll," while Calipari departs from Walberg orthodoxy in several ways. Instead of going straight into the offense, Memphis sometimes swings the ball around the perimeter or springs the point guard with (*gasp!*) a ball screen. And instead of sending his post man straight to the lane's weak side, Calipari allows him to go on what Memphis calls a "rim run," in which the penetrating guard throws a lob in the vicinity of the basket for an alley-oop dunk.

A born promoter, Calipari also came up with the name dribble drive motion for the offense. "It's just easier to understand," he says. "AASAA? Come on, what are you talking about?" Owing to the offense's continuous patterns, reads, and backdoor cuts, he also branded it "Princeton on steroids."

Whatever you call it, Calipari's team is smitten. "It turned out to be great for us," says swingman Chris Douglas-Roberts, one of the nation's most gifted penetrators. "It's about spacing and players making plays. A lot of players who are in conventional styles get bored sometimes because they feel like they can't show what they can do, but this offense lets a player show his strengths."

Although Calipari didn't adopt Walberg's scrambling full-court defense (he's convinced that winning at the highest level requires stopping opponents in the half-court), he did transform his defense in one major way. He says that during his days at UMass, from 1988 to '96, he wanted his teams to be *last* in the league in steals. "Why last? Because [gambling for] steals gets you out of position," he explains. "I wanted to give teams one tough shot, and that's it. Now we want to be *first* in steals—in the country. Because the way we play now, if the other team holds the ball, we're going to be on offense thirty percent of the time and on defense seventy percent. Now who's going to control the game? But if we're going after steals, we make them play faster." At week's end the Tigers had 8.7 thefts per game.

Opposing teams can play their own defensive trump cards, of course, and the most common gambit against Memphis's DDM attack has been to ditch man-to-man for zones and hybrid junk defenses, which clog the Tigers' driving lanes. Memphis has seen them all: 2-3 zones (Gonzaga), 3-2 zones (East Carolina), 1-3-1 zones (SMU), the triangle-and-two (USC). Arizona tried a two-man zone, with its post defenders stationed on the blocks. During its victory over Memphis in the 2006 NCAA West Regional final, UCLA used a one-man zone, keeping a big man in the lane.

The most successful defense against the Tigers this season was USC's triangle-and-two, which helped the Trojans take Memphis to overtime on December 4 before losing 62–58. "We got tentative against USC," says Calipari, who calls more set plays against zones and says he has installed countermeasures for the triangle-and-two. (When Middle Tennessee State brought it out later in December, Memphis won by 24.) Besides, he adds, "if your primary defense is man but you're playing us zone, how will you be any good at it? And if you do stay in the game, what are you thinking with four minutes to go? 'We can't beat these guys.'"

Perhaps, but it's also true that zones are more likely to expose the Tigers' potential Achilles' heel. Memphis shoots only 34.2 percent from three-point range. "John's got just about all the pieces," says Walberg, "with the exception of a knockdown shooter." Then again, a bad shooting night may not be enough to stop a team with perhaps five future NBA players. "Whatever you're running, you'd better have guys who can play," says Calipari. "If you forget that, you don't have to worry about being innovative."

The same could be said for Hurley's team, which includes six seniors (five of them guards) who have accepted Division I scholarships. Yet Hurley points out that talented players can always improve their skills, and he swears by Walberg's high-intensity practice drills. In fact, some coaches think Walberg's drills are his crowning achievement. "It's like a franchise for McDonald's," says Welch. "Not only are you getting a system, you're getting built-in drills to teach your system."

For all their success using DDM, Calipari and Hurley have one major difference. Calipari made three trips to visit Walberg in Fresno, studied his game tapes, and spent hundreds of hours speaking to Walberg about his offense. But Hurley and Walberg have never sat down and talked. One day last year they finally connected over the phone. "I love your Blood drills," Hurley told Walberg. "They're really great."

For a moment there was silence on the other end of the line. Walberg didn't know whether to be proud that Hurley had fallen for his creation or horrified that one of his most closely held secrets had crossed the continent. "Blood drills?" he said at last. "Bob, how do you know about Blood drills?"

HERB WELLING DOESN'T look like one of the most wired social connectors in U.S. basketball. By day he's a security guard at Omaha Central High, where he moonlights as an assistant coach for the boys' basketball team. A short, pear-shaped man, Welling, forty-five, wears tight purple Omaha Central T-shirts that make him look like a smaller cousin of the McDonald's character Grimace.

But underestimate Welling at your peril. He's the tactical brains behind Omaha Central, which has used DDM to win the last two Nebraska state titles and draw sellout crowds of rabid fans (including the Sage of Omaha, investor Warren Buffett, who knows a good product when he sees one). For years Welling was the right-hand man to Howard Garfinkel at his famed Five-Star Camps, where Welling met the top college and high school coaches in the country. "Herb and I talk once a week," says Hurley. "He originally called me, and we started talking about [DDM]." Before long, Welling had sent Hurley more than two hundred pages of notes on the offense.

But how had Welling "cracked the code," as he puts it? DDM wasn't something you could master from a phone call or a few game tapes or even from attending a clinic, which reveals no more than 10 percent of the scheme's secrets, according to Calipari. Welling had never visited one of Walberg's or Calipari's practices, but he remained undaunted. "I'm kind of psychotic for finding out stuff," he says. "At school they call me the Minister of Information."

Basketball coaches are a secretive lot. Indeed, for Walberg, sharing has always been a double-edged proposition. "I want to help people because a lot of people helped me," he says, "but [DDM] is kind of my ace in the hole." Before dribble drive broke nationally, Walberg would host dinners at his home for interested coaches from Fresno-area high schools and junior colleges, often sharing information liberally—perhaps too liberally. "Vance is too unselfish with his offense," says his friend Brad Felder, the Hanford (Calif.) High coach. "In the long run it will hurt him because the longer [the offense] is out there, the more others will adapt."

These days Walberg and Calipari have a policy: They'll let coaches observe their practices; they'll send them game tapes; they'll answer questions and host clinics. But Walberg and Calipari won't give out their playbooks, and they refuse to make instructional videos. "I want to wait a few years," says Walberg, who estimates he gets more than three hundred calls a year from coaches seeking info about his offense. "I talked with John, and we didn't really want it out."

Adds Calipari, "If I wanted to do these tapes, I could make a ton of dough. But that's Vance's money. That's not my money."

Perhaps, but the two coaches didn't account for Welling, whose pursuit of the prize was relentless. In 2005, after first hearing about Walberg's offense at Pete Newell's Big Man Camp in Las Vegas (where his stepson was a camper), Welling started breaking down game tapes that Walberg had sent him. Then Welling met Duane Silver, a retired high school coach in Waco, Texas, who had written a booklet on the drive-and-kick offense and maintained a coaching website. Silver introduced Welling to John Jordan, the coach at St. Francis High in La Cañada, California, who attended Walberg's clinics and drove six hours nearly every week to scout his games and practices in Fresno.

Jordan sent Welling a 100-page dossier on Walberg's offense and defense, which landed, in turn, on Hurley's desk in New Jersey. "Then I got various materials that they don't even know I have," says Welling. "We had about every clinic that Walberg's ever done. We had his practice booklet and a lot more. It would blow you away, but then I'd have to shoot you."

The Minister of Information also has Walberg's lingo down cold, from "drop zones" to "Blood drills." And that's only the start. Last summer Welling made two DDM instructional videos—one with the offense and one with practice drills—that sell for $39.95 each or $71.95 together (plus shipping and handling) through Sysko's Sports Productions, the basketball video retailer. "It's the number one seller out of our catalog over the last year," says Sysko's executive Jim Blaine, "and it's only been out for seven of those twelve months."

That's right: Herb Welling, a security guard from Omaha, is outselling videos by Wooden, Carril, Duke's Mike Krzyzewski, and North Carolina's Roy Williams. Told of Welling's success with his invention, Walberg—who turned down a Sysko's offer—manages only a thin smile. "Well," he finally says, "I guess that's America."

The way Walberg sees it, though, that's the least of his concerns at this point.

From: Ray West
Subj: Why?
Date: Sat., Jan. 19, 2008, 11:28 p.m.
To: Vance Walberg

Dear Mr. Walberg,

I am very sorry to hear of your resignation. I am just a small-school high school coach that studies the game more than most. I know you are an unbelievable innovator in a time of no innovations in basket-ball. You are brilliant! You can tell me to go to hell, but I must know the real reason you resigned. You didn't give it much time to recruit your style of players. I am 12–1 using your offense! I hope you coach again, you have been very nice to me with your help. You can e-mail me or just leave me wondering. Best of luck in the future. I hope you coach again. Thank you.

Respectfully,
Ray West

IN DIAGRAMS THE dribble drive is represented by what coaches call a squiggle: a zigzag line with an arrow at the end. It's an apt symbol as well for Walberg, who's trying to move forward while whipsawing from one emotional extreme to the other. On the one hand, he's enjoying the ulti-mate in mainstream professional respect. The top teams in the NBA (the Celtics), college (Memphis), and high school (St. Anthony) are running his stuff, and it's spreading like a benign virus through the sport he loves. Yet at the same time this is the most excruciating moment of his thirty-year career. On January 18, midway through his second season at Pep-perdine, Walberg abruptly resigned.

Both he and Pepperdine athletic director John Watson insist that he wasn't forced out, but Walberg says his dream job on the majestic shores of Malibu had become untenable. After he won 92 percent of his games at Fresno City College, his rebuilding Waves teams had gone 14–35. But it wasn't just about the losing. Since the summer of 2006, Walberg had lost six players through transfers and one through expulsion, erasing the depth that his attacking style demands. Meanwhile, at least one parent— Terry Tucker, the father of two Pepperdine players—was unhappy about things Walberg had done in practice: making one player suck his thumb for acting like "a baby," calling another player "a p——y" and labeling another "a turnover midget."

Though Walberg apologized to the last player and Watson took no disciplinary action—he ruled that Walberg's actions were "inappropriate" but not abusive—the tension and the losses were a volatile mix. During the three weeks before his resignation, Walberg says, he slept no more than two and a half hours on any night. Why wouldn't his players commit all the way like he had? "It just became really tough," Walberg says, struggling for words. "My wife and kids, we talked and talked. It was like a big part of my life was being taken out of me. I love coaching so much. You can't imagine not getting your players to buy in. They weren't bad kids, but I just couldn't get 'em over the line."

Those squiggles on the page are worth only so much, after all. Whatever you're running, you'd better have guys who can play. "If you believe in God, there's a reason for me to go through this," Walberg says. "What it is, I don't understand right now."

Walberg doesn't know what comes next. His friends say he was happiest at the high school and juco levels, where his teams won and the gyms were always filled. But he could also end up as an NBA assistant or perhaps join the Memphis staff. Walberg won't have trouble finding work. And for now, when he despairs, he can always flip on the TV and watch Calipari's team run the offense that he laid out in sugar packets on a restaurant table five seasons ago.

"No matter what, I'm super happy for John," Walberg says. "At least I know it works."

Forward Progress

ADAPTED FROM *Masters of Modern Soccer,*
EXCERPTED IN *Sports Illustrated,* MAY 30, 2016

When Wahl reached an agreement with Crown in 2007 to write *The Beckham Experiment,* he struck a two-book deal, leaving the second project undetermined. It took several years before he settled on a topic, which turned out to be one both borrowed and new. Inspired by George Will's 1990 baseball book *Men at Work: The Craft of Baseball,* in which the *Washington Post* columnist chose thoughtful major-league practitioners to illuminate each of a range of the game's skills, Wahl proposed doing the same for soccer. The U.S. fan base was now sophisticated enough to want to hear from Germany's Manuel Neuer on how he kept goal, from Belgium's Vincent Kompany on how he held a backline, and from Spain's Xabi Alonso on how he bossed the midfield. *Masters of Modern Soccer: How the World's Best Play the Twenty-first-Century Game* argued that what was once picturesquely called "the Beautiful Game" had evolved into something altogether modern. "Every single aspect of the game has improved," Kompany told Wahl, who prevailed on the players' clubs to assemble video packages that he would then watch with each of his chosen interpreters. The book, which showed how the game had become faster, more physical, and demanding of greater technical mastery, included a fascinating chapter about Mexico's Javier "Chicharito" Hernández and the craft of the striker, from which this is adapted.

ENGLISH IS NOT THE FIRST LANGUAGE OF JAVIER HERNÁNDEZ, the golden boy of Mexican soccer, and yet his command of it—largely from his four years at Manchester United—is such that he enjoys transporting evocative expressions from Spanish into his newer tongue. Flashing a language maven's smile that brightens a rainy day in the German Rhineland, North America's greatest modern striker explains his knack for being in the right place at the right time in the penalty box.

"If you're inside the box and a cross is coming," he says, his hair freshly gelled after training at Bay Arena, "sometimes you need, as we say in Spanish, to *smell the intuition*, to smell where the cross is going."

Chicharito ("Little Pea" in Spanish) is twenty-eight. He grew up absorbing the culture of the game from his father, Javier, and grandfather Tomás Balcázar, both of whom also represented Mexico in a World Cup. He has played in the Champions League for Man United, Real Madrid, and, this past winter, Leverkusen. He is constantly tinkering on the practice field, constantly studying his opponents, his teammates, himself. Like a master sommelier drawing on years of learning to sniff a glass of wine and identify it—South Australia, Clare Valley, 2009 Riesling—the 5'8", 156-pound Chicharito uses the sum of his experiences to smell an impending cross and decide in an instant which run to make.

What does intuition smell like?

"Press play," he says.

On the video screen in front of him, he's running down the left side of a four-on-four break, left to right, against archrival Cologne. Leverkusen midfielder Kevin Kampl is advancing with the ball down the right channel and passes it even wider right toward an onrushing Admir Mehmedi. Entering the box at speed in the left channel, Hernández looks to his right, sees all seven players involved—three of his own, four of Cologne's—and processes what he likes to call "the panoramic." Teammate Karim Bellarabi makes a near-post run, pulling centerback Dominic Maroh with him and opening space in front of the goal. Chicharito knows a cross is coming—there's no pressure on Mehmedi out wide—and now he has to decide: Should I continue my run to the far post? Or turn and cut hard to the open space in the middle?

Either way he will have to beat his marker, right back Marcel Risse.

"You play this sport in the mind, not only on the field," Chicharito says. "If [your opponent] is more clever than you, you can be faster and stronger, but probably you are not going to beat him. He's one step in front of you in the mind. On crosses, sometimes I make my move one or two seconds before the ball is coming because I'm trying to guess that the ball is coming there. It's intuition. So I run. Sometimes the ball comes . . . sometimes not. But that intuition is working."

Chicharito cuts hard to his right in the box—into the open space in front of the goal—even before Mehmedi hits a cross first-time toward that expanse. Here, Risse proves an easy mark, ball watching. In fact, you half expect Chicharito to reach around and tap Risse's far shoulder as he flies behind the defender's back, like a schoolboy pulling off a classroom prank. That split-second jump gives Hernández the advantage he needs, and the rest is execution: His snap-down header bounces off the turf and past goalkeeper Timo Horn, into the net.

Intuition. Anticipation. The scent of a goal scorer. Everything about Chicharito's craftsmanship is cool, save for perhaps the mariachi music that blares on the PA after each one of his strikes.

All four Leverkusen players involved in the break contributed, notes Chicharito, whose twenty-six total club goals this past season all have a story in the details. On this one his early recognition and decisive change of direction doomed Risse, who committed the cardinal sin of what Hernández calls "standing up"—losing focus, remaining flat-footed.

"Do you see how I run?" Chicharito asks, rewinding and watching the play in slow motion. "Just two or three steps, and then I beat him because he is standing up. He has no idea. Too late."

SOME PEOPLE IN this world—many of them elite athletes—are possessed of a laser focus, a preternatural ability to remain calm under any circumstance. Chicharito, by his own admission, is not one of them. When the topic is soccer, he's as animated as a Pixar film. Out of his seat, crouched low and looking you straight in the eyes, both hands waving, he jump-cuts from thought to thought as it enters and leaves his racing mind. Ask him to explain his idea of a modern forward, and his response takes nearly eight minutes.

"I like to breathe, eat, and talk about football," he says. Completing a forty-minute interview without him leaping atop his seat, like Tom Cruise on *Oprah,* feels like a minor victory.

This nonstop movement is precisely what serves Hernández best on the field. "I'm a person who cannot be doing nothing," he says. "I have a deficit. In Mexico we say *hiperactivo*—hyperactive. I am hyperactive! I cannot be standing here like this in my life. I need to keep walking with my phone, speaking. I can't be calm. On the pitch you can probably see that. I'm always *moving-moving-moving*. And I'm a cheeky player. I try to be there and there and there. And if you're standing up, I'll make it look like I'm moving this way—and then I move *that* way."

Yet there are times when Chicharito is in razor-sharp form, his mobility creating chance after chance, and the goals just don't come. On other occasions, even the chances run dry. Scoring, after all, remains the hardest thing to do in soccer. Why? For starters, the sport is more defensive minded than it used to be, the result of a century-long evolution in tactics. If you watch a match from any World Cup in the 1970s or '80s, for example, it's like viewing a different game. There are more attacking players on the field; the play is more open, with fewer crunching tackles. These days defenders are deployed in greater numbers, but they're also more physically robust, often ruthless, using extralegal means to short-circuit a dangerous forward.

"Defenders kick you without the ball," Hernández says. "They try to get you out of your focus and concentration, either physically or with verbal stuff."

The tangible barriers to goal scoring are severe enough, but they're compounded by the whims of the soccer gods.

"You have periods when, even if you close your eyes, you can score a goal," he says. "And then other periods when, even if the goal is open, you put the ball off the crossbar. Why? I don't know. It's a mystery."

The key when he misses a scoring chance, he says, is to follow the lead of former Mexico and U.S. coach Bora Milutinović, who always quizzed his players: What's the most important play? The next one.

"We are human beings," says Hernández. "When you miss a clear chance, obviously that hits you. What I want is to get focused on the *next* one. The one that I missed, I cannot do anything [about that]. The next one is the one I can change."

———

WHAT'S THE MOST frustrating thing about Chicharito's job? Failing to convert chances is tough, he argues, but even worse is not having any scoring opportunities at all.

"If I have six chances and I miss [all] six, of course I'm not going to be happy—but I'm calm because I had the chances," he says. "When you don't even have chances, *that's* the difficult thing."

Given his hyperactivity, this is a rare occurrence for Chicharito, who takes over the laptop and cues up another scene. The opponent, Hannover, from earlier this past season, is playing a high back line (its deepest defenders closer to midfield), a staple of the modern game for teams that want to keep possession in the attacking end of the field. But soccer is a game of space. If the field is a king-sized bed, a team can be only a queen-sized blanket. Move the blanket up, and it creates a void in the back. Hernández can exploit those high lines with his movement, especially during the early unbalanced moments of a counterattack.

"That's what I love most: to run into the channel [the space between an opposing fullback and his closest centerback] and get coordinated with my teammates," he says. "Some forwards are tall and big; we say those are more objective players"—target forwards—"because you can play long balls to them and they can hold the ball [while others catch up and join the attack]. I am not the tallest, not the strongest, not the quickest. But I am quick enough. I am strong enough. And I prefer to move more than be static. I prefer to run into space and receive balls at my feet."

On the screen Kampl is advancing the ball, right to left, just past midfield in the first stages of a counter. Hannover's high back line has forty yards of open space behind it, and Chicharito is walking a tightrope: He starts his run into the left channel, making eye contact with Kampl and trusting that his teammate will release a pass while Hernández is still *just* onside with the line of two retreating centerbacks.

Kampl nails the timing, rifling a diagonal pass that Chicharito meets twenty-five yards from the goal. Now the striker is one-on-one with the centerback Marcelo.

If Hernández had a dominant foot, Marcelo could cheat toward one direction in marking him. But Hernández is equally dangerous with either one—another hallmark of the modern forward—and so he dips into his bag of tricks. To many people, a "bicycle" in soccer is a dramatic overhead scissors kick. But Spanish speakers call that move a *chilena*, and Chicharito has a different one that he calls "the bicycle." At speed, he steps over the ball with his right foot and slows down just barely, causing Marcelo to lean to his left for a split second. Then Chicharito explodes to his left, blowing past the hapless defender.

"Now I'm looking at the ball," Hernández says, "but I can see in the panoramic that the keeper is coming." Here the forward is raising the wine glass to his nose once again. If the goalkeeper, Ron-Robert Zieler, stays on his line, Chicharito will take a hard shot. But Zieler is advancing, trying to cut down the angle. Chicharito knows the keeper has to guess one way, so he jabs a perfectly placed left-footed dagger—it's more like a pass than a shot—to the keeper's left and into the far right corner of the net.

In a sport where goals are as precious as pearls, the ensuing sensations can verge on the metaphysical.

"When you see the ball going into the net"—he snaps his fingers—"I don't think of anything at first," says Hernández, who has scored a combined 130 goals for club and country. "Then I celebrate and say thank you to God, and I dedicate my goals. But when the ball goes into the net, sometimes I don't remember that. You cannot explain exactly those moments. You need to *live* them."

WHAT IS A modern forward? For Chicharito, the best ones have to be complete players on and off the field.

"I prefer to have a little of everything," he says. "I can move with the ball and without it. I can jump. I can protect the ball. I can finish with my left and with my right. I can cross a ball. I can give an assist to another player. I can defend. And there are always things I want to improve. In the best leagues in the world you play three or four tournaments per year. So training, recovery, staying healthy—that's even more important now. Europe isn't like Mexico or MLS. Here, you don't stop."

Over the years people have called Hernández a goal poacher, a tag that suggests he's lacking in skill. But they couldn't be more wrong. Being in the right place at the right time *nearly all the time* to score goals is most definitely a talent. What's more, the poacher label ignores his ability to create space for himself in the box. Like a dominant post player in basketball, Chicharito has developed countermoves that apply his skill with both feet. And these days he's perfecting another wrinkle.

"I'm trying to improve on scoring goals from outside the box," he says. "If they try to stop me [in the box], I need a Plan B."

This time the foe is Borussia Mönchengladbach, earlier this past season. Attacking right to left on the screen, teammate Stefan Kießling is being defended closely on the ball at the top-left corner of the penalty box. Kießling sees Chicharito facing him, unmarked, eight yards away, just outside the top of the box, and lays off a short pass. Even before Hernández spins to his left, he has processed the scene. ("Panoramic!" he says with a smile.)

He has options: (1) pass the ball into the box; (2) dribble there himself and take on defenders; or (3) shoot from distance. On-screen, Chicharito's back is to the goal; off-screen, he's like Bill Bradley describing what it's like to have "a sense of where you are" in John McPhee's book of that name.

"I don't see the goal, but I *sense* it. I know the goal is there," he says. "When I was a kid, they taught me: You don't need to look at the goal sometimes; the goal is not going to move. But *you* are going to move, so you need to read where *you* are."

With the same decisiveness that he used to score with his left foot against Hannover, Chicharito now completes a spin move and powers a right-footed blast from outside the box. His defender, Håvard Nordtveit, is a split second late in jumping out at him—and even that action helps Hernández.

"He blocked the vision of the keeper," he notes, watching as the shot sails past Yann Sommer into the right side of the net, one of three Chicharito strikes in a 5–0 victory.

There may be mysteries when it comes to scoring goals, but improving as a player? That's more clear cut. It's why Chicharito watches so much video (scouting clips, live games from Germany, England, Mexico . . .)—"not just watching the ball and not just watching to enjoy the game," as he puts it. It's why he spends so many hours on the practice field, alone and with his team.

"You need to kick three hundred balls [a day] to perfect something," he says. "It's an education every day. You can always learn something new from football. If a player starts thinking they don't need to learn? They are dead."

Give Piece a Chance

FROM *Sports Illustrated,* JULY 16, 2018

No sport resists quantification quite like soccer, and no sports culture worships more fervently at the Altar of the Statistic than the one built up over more than a century in the United States, a country where the preeminent college of technology, MIT, hosts a huge annual conference on sports analytics. That paradox left Wahl in a curious position. As the leading American interpreter of the game, he wanted to consume soccer the way much of the world did, as balletic human drama. Yet his readership didn't mind if he plumbed soccer for the metrics that could shed light on the keys to success. Wahl somehow found his way through. Just as he had on the college basketball beat, he would seek out and hear out the numbers crunchers—he was a regular panelist at that MIT conference—and then convey what those numbers meant. In this story for *Sports Illustrated,* assigned and published in the midst of a World Cup in which nearly one in three goals was scored off free kicks, corners, or throw-ins, Wahl found a compelling personality to wrap the story around, a PhD program dropout with ties to sports gambling. Whether in web postings, podcasts, or news features like this one, Wahl would engage with such brave new soccer stats as XG, or expected goals, and the nerds who evangelized for them. He regarded every metric as a grappling hook that could help some new fan better grasp the game.

IN A WORLD CUP THAT HAS BEEN DEFINED BY SURPRISES AND DElightful attacks, it was one of the most creative moments of the tournament. And it started from a standstill. During a group-stage victory over Panama, England won a garden-variety free kick thirty-two yards from goal, dead center; but instead of shooting directly on net or curling the ball onto a player's head in the box, coach Gareth Southgate's team deployed something different. Starting from a line of six England players at the top of the penalty area (imagine that line as the base of a triangle, with the ball at the top), Jordan Henderson broke toward the free-kick taker, Kieran Trippier, met his pass on the ground and one-timed it into the air toward Harry Kane on the right edge of the six-yard box. Kane headed the ball down across the goalmouth to Raheem Sterling, whose own headed shot was saved, only for teammate John Stones—conveniently stationed at the back post—to head home the rebound.

The ensuing unfettered glee was earned. This was no accident, rather the result of a concerted effort by a coaching staff to maximize the scoring potential of dead-ball situations. England's players were quick to point out that they'd taken great pains to prepare for their set plays in the weeks leading up to the World Cup—and now the work had paid off. According to the data service Opta, England created a tournament-leading twenty-two goal-scoring chances on set pieces (defined as plays following a stoppage, such as free kicks, corner kicks, or throw-ins) through its first five games and converted them into five goals, tied for the tourney lead with Uruguay, which had scored as many times on twelve chances. For Uruguay, whose defense also had conceded just five set-piece scoring chances (sixth lowest in the tournament), it was clear that central-defense partners Diego Godín and José Giménez, club teammates at set-piece specialist Atlético Madrid, were making a difference.

Set pieces fueled deep World Cup runs for England and Uruguay, to say nothing of Russia 2018 itself. Through the quarterfinals, 30 percent of the tournament's goals had come on free kicks and corners, outpacing the previous high of 23 percent (in 2002 and '06) among the five most recent men's World Cups.

All of which has Fox Sports commentator and former U.S. defender Alexi Lalas proclaiming that soccer has turned into a "set-piece orgy." Says Lalas, "In a game that is often so random, [a set piece] is the one time where obviously it stops, and the players and the team and the coach can do something that alleviates some of the randomness. It's probably the closest thing we have to American football in a soccer game, and you ignore [set pieces] at your own peril. A set piece is to soccer what water is to life: You need it to survive."

Set pieces can help an underdog close the talent gap against a more powerful team. (See Iceland's quarterfinal run at Euro 2016, in which it shocked England with a long throw-in converted into a goal.) But a set piece can also make a heavyweight even more dangerous. When Germany won World Cup 2014, 27.8 percent of its goals came off set pieces. A given tournament produces a relatively small sample size, but that 30 percent of all goals that have been scored this summer on free kicks and corners is significantly higher than the rate last season in the top pro leagues of Germany (21.8 percent), England (20.2 percent), Italy (18.5 percent), Spain (16.9 percent), and France (15.6 percent).

To what do we attribute this rise of goals scored off of play stoppages? At least part of it comes down to this: Teams and analysts are (finally) taking set pieces more seriously than ever before.

IN THE SUMMER of 2014, Ted Knutson received what back then would have been considered a curious assignment. An American who graduated from Oklahoma, Knutson had fallen for soccer watching the 1998 World Cup. After school he went into the sports gambling business, where he met an Englishman named Matthew Benham, who himself was so successful employing data-driven algorithms in soccer betting that he eventually bought two clubs, England's Brentford and Denmark's Midtjylland. Benham's goal: Use his data analysis skills to exploit inefficiencies in the soccer world, allowing his clubs to compete at a level higher than their financial might indicated. Much of that data work involved identifying undervalued players who could be acquired to help his teams—but there were other aspects of the game to study, too, and this is how Benham came to hire Knutson, whom he asked to do a deep dive on set pieces.

"I thought I was going to work on stats," says Knutson, who now owns the data company StatsBomb, "but really it was more of a qualitative analysis so we could say, 'Hey, we think this is an area that's underexploited, and we think it really matters.' The thing about set pieces is: It's not 'the beautiful game,' and people kind of deride it as a very thuggish way to help score goals. But we took a more efficiency-based look, and we were like 'Well, helping to score goals when you're not scoring goals just seems like a positive—right?'"

Over a period of six hard-core weeks, Knutson researched everything he could about set pieces. He studied the work of Gianni Vio, a set-piece-specialist assistant at Fiorentina, in Italy, whose team had scored twenty-six set-piece goals in its previous thirty-eight-game season. Vio had written an entire book on set pieces, but it was published only in Italian, so Knutson hired a translator. "Vio was the pioneer here, in my mind, of how to systematize this stuff," Knutson says. In the book, Vio pointed out that the percentage of goals scored from set pieces was far greater than the percentage of time spent practicing them. "We'd go to different clubs and ask, 'How much time do you spend training set pieces?' And they'd be like 'Oh, I don't know—ten to fifteen minutes a week.' These inefficiencies really led us to think long and hard about it all."

Those studies also led Knutson to the English club Stoke City, which in the past years had found success capitalizing on deep throw-ins by an Irish midfielder named Rory Delap. Delap's long lobs had been the source of some snickering—but they were also effective. "Something like fifteen percent of Stoke's entire shot volume for the [2008–09] season was created off of long throws," says Knutson. "That's *insane*. We were like 'Wow, who's exploiting this?' And almost no one was."

He went back to 2011 and studied Sir Alex Ferguson's last two seasons at Manchester United, when his team started scoring far more goals off corners through headers by short players who could jump beyond expectation, like Patrice Evra. United, Knutson noticed, had its two best forwards, Wayne Rooney and Robin van Persie, serving up the corners rather than roaming the box. "The delivery—sort of a flat delivery to exactly the areas you want—is what matters," he says.

And he studied Atlético Madrid, which had seen a sustained uptick of set-piece goals under coach Diego Simeone. "They used to travel with their own crash pads and do diving-header practice for set pieces," Knutson says. "It was literally part of their road kit. [Their opponents] were like 'Man, this is so weird.'"

Once his research was done, Knutson reported back to Benham, and together they schemed. They eventually hired Vio as an assistant at Brentford, and for Midtjylland they hired an assistant, Brian Priske, who specialized in set pieces. Their objective: Create more chances on dead-ball plays, measured in a statistic they called "expected goals." The result: "Priske did very well with Midtjylland," Knutson says, "and then he went on to Copenhagen and also did very well there. Mads Buttgereit has continued the tradition at Midtjylland, and they've just won their second Danish title, scoring more than half a goal per game just from set pieces." (On Buttgereit's Twitter and LinkedIn profiles he identifies himself as a "set piece specialist.")

If that type of focused expertise sounds a lot like something you'd see in the NFL, it's by design. The soccer world is increasingly embracing specialization, and today's set-piece designs can appear to be straight off the gridiron. "The first thing we do when we analyze [a situation]," says Knutson, "is ask, 'What is the defense giving us? What do they want to do? And how do we break that?' There are tons of different types of plays. And like American football, you can build variations out of the same look—the same three-receiver set. Then you've got different plays that come out of that."

It's important to note here: Just because a team spends more time on set pieces doesn't necessarily mean it will spend less time on other aspects of the game. This isn't a zero-sum game, Knutson clarifies. "That's kind of how we looked at it. We asked, 'Can you take a good team and then add set pieces and long throws so that you're constantly dangerous? If there's a corner, instead of there being a 2.5 percent chance of scoring, can we make it into a 7 percent or 8 percent chance, which is what Atlético Madrid had for a couple years?' You're looking for places to constantly get little edges. If you can [do that] . . . you can go a lot deeper into a tournament."

Of course, it helps, too, to have a deadly free-kick specialist on the field who can change a game on his own, with one swing of his leg. In Russia, Cristiano Ronaldo set the tone early in the group stage with an eighty-eighth-minute free-kick goal that pulled Portugal even with Spain, 3–3, and through the quarterfinals there have been six direct free-kick goals, twice as many as there were four years ago in Brazil.

When it comes to the 2018 final, this Sunday in Moscow's Luzhniki Stadium, you can feel confident that at least one goal will come from a set piece. Even in a game built around near-constant movement, now more than ever the peak moments of drama and entertainment come when the ball is stopped.

5
PERSONS IN FULL

To flog soccer to an American sports audience, Wahl realized the value of colorful personalities who could transcend drab tactics and the preoccupations of insiders. He knew his editors at *Sports Illustrated* would be more willing to consider a feature on a striker with an appetite for opponents' ears or a goalkeeper with a scorpion kick. If Wahl had a knack for capturing characters, perhaps that's because he was an original himself, completely comfortable in his own skin. He was unfussy and open, to some almost suspiciously so. Catching sight of a tall, slim figure wrapped in monochromatic clothing, people could identify him at forty paces. As an undergraduate he had acknowledged his encroaching baldness with a disarmingly funny column in the student newspaper and never once thereafter considered a comb-over. On the road, he'd work out in a pair of basketball shorts and a gaudy headband that made him look as if he had stepped off the set of a Will Ferrell movie. And he never balked at putting himself outside his comfort zone. Whenever the opportunity arose, he accepted invitations to do TV commentary for Spanish-language outlets, in spite of what his Peruvian American colleague and friend Luis Miguel Echegaray called "a Gringo-Argentine accent." Wahl's World included much of the human pageant, beginning with the one-of-a-kind woman who raised him.

USWNT Inspires Older Fans, Too. One of Them Was My Mom

FROM SI.COM, JUNE 13, 2019

Helen Wahl left her job as a school counselor after the birth of her two boys. But once Eric and Grant had their school legs, she threw herself fully back into the world beyond the family's home in Mission, Kansas. She established the first mediation service in the state, which offered divorcing couples a way to resolve their differences outside the court system. And she cut a swath through Johnson County, serving on the library board, presiding over the local chapter of the National Women's Political Caucus, and teaching a college course called Living with Laughter. None of that went unnoticed by her sons. They quickly grasped the examples she shared with them from the No Comment section of her copies of *Ms.* magazine, and eventually came to vividly imagine the road not taken by their mother, a former phys ed teacher with a lifelong love of sports. "If the times had been different," Eric Wahl says, "Mom would have been a professional athlete." Several weeks after Helen's death, having been moved by the remembrance reprinted here, Megan Rapinoe pulled Grant aside after a press conference at the 2019 Women's World Cup to present him with a U.S. women's national team jersey, graced with Rapinoe's number 15 and the name HELEN WAHL on the back.

PARIS—WE TALK A LOT ABOUT HOW THE U.S. WOMEN'S NATIONAL team inspires millions of young girls (and boys), and that's obviously a fantastic thing. But it's only part of the story. The USWNT has a similar impact on American women (and men) who are a lot older than that, too, even people in their eighties.

One of them was my mother.

Helen Wahl grew up in the Midwest during the 1930s and '40s. She loved sports—playing them, watching them—and one of her first jobs was as a physical education teacher at a school. But she grew frustrated by the lack of opportunities for women to compete in sports (both recreationally and professionally), to say nothing of the way men talked to her about sports, as if she couldn't know anything because of her gender.

In 1957, she was in the stands at Kansas City's Municipal Auditorium for perhaps the greatest game in college basketball history, North Carolina's three-overtime defeat of her beloved Kansas Jayhawks in the NCAA championship game. And in the 1970s, as she and my dad, Dave, raised two young sons, Mom was one of the most enthusiastic supporters of Billie Jean King during her Battle of the Sexes tennis triumph over Bobby Riggs.

Mom was a fiercely proud feminist. An active member of the National Women's Political Caucus, she gave me and my brother, Eric, copies of *Ms.* magazine to read when we were kids. She explained to us the meaning of the proposed Equal Rights Amendment, and she told us the stories of Gloria Steinem and other activists. Years later, Mom couldn't have been happier that my mentor was Gloria Emerson, the former *New York Times* Vietnam War correspondent, one of the few women who covered that conflict.

So perhaps it shouldn't have been surprising that Mom became a devoted fan of the U.S. women's national team. It started in 1999, when she watched every game of the U.S.'s historic run to the World Cup title. I covered that tournament for *Sports Illustrated,* and she peppered me with questions about the players and their stories and the challenges they'd had to overcome as female athletes.

She loved everything about that U.S. team: the players' skill, their band-of-sisters chemistry, and the unabashed exuberance of Mia Hamm after scoring a goal and Brandi Chastain ripping her jersey off to celebrate the title-clinching penalty kick. My *SI* story that week—with Robert Beck's classic image of Chastain on the cover—was always Mom's favorite magazine story that I ever wrote.

Mom would religiously watch every USWNT game, even the friendlies, always calling the players by their first names, as if they were her friends, which is how she viewed them. And so she'd wonder aloud if Alex was getting her scoring form back or why Carli wasn't starting or if Megan's knee was going to get better. (It did.)

Both my parents fell in love with watching soccer late in life—the

Premier League, the Champions League, the U.S. men's national team—but Mom's attachment to the USWNT was something deeper, something visceral, something that transcended sports and spoke to her about the life she had lived and the gains she had always wanted to see.

Mom's favorite player? Easy: Megan Rapinoe. She was entranced by Rapinoe's game: her probing passes, her subtle technical mastery, her creative vision, even her occasional Technicolor hair. She admired Rapinoe for her fearlessness in taking stands for her beliefs, and when I told Mom that Rapinoe said her muse was the actress Tilda Swinton, one of Mom's favorites, she got a giant smile on her face.

Two weeks ago, on May 29, my wife, Céline, who's a doctor, called me and said we needed to visit Mom in Arizona immediately. She had been sick, and her weight and blood pressure had fallen extremely low. We flew across the country that day and spent all of a Thursday together with my dad and my brother, and thankfully Mom was able to speak. A lot of what she wanted to talk about with me was the USWNT and the World Cup.

"I love them so much," she said. "They don't even have to win it, and I'll still love them."

There are few things more difficult than saying goodbye to your mother when you know it's the last time you'll see her, but I was glad we got the opportunity. On Monday, the day before USA-Thailand, I got a call in Reims. My mother had passed away at age eighty-seven. I was having a coffee next to the beautiful cathedral there, and I spent the next hour sitting inside, thinking about Mom and my family, trying (and failing) to keep it together. The next night, inside the stadium, I thought about her the whole time, knowing how happy she was that I got to cover her favorite team.

I know that Helen Wahl wasn't alone, that there are countless other American women who have become USWNT fans late in their lives, not just because they enjoy watching sports but because this team represents something they always wanted to see for decades. And so, as I wrote Mom's obituary on Wednesday, I made sure to include this in the second paragraph, high up, where you put some of the most important stuff: "She enjoyed being a fan of Kansas basketball and the U.S. women's national soccer team."

London Calling

FROM *Sports Illustrated*, OCTOBER 16, 2006

The tiered structure of English football and the system of promotion and relegation were alien to most Americans in the mid-2000s, which would make the task of telling the underdog story of Jay DeMerit both compelling and challenging. How to convey to an audience that had yet to watch *Welcome to Wrexham* DeMerit's rise through the ranks from pub soccer to the peak of the pro game and the momentousness of his multimillion-dollar goal (as a defender, no less) to send Watford up to the Premier League? To make sense of the sheer improbability for an American readership, Wahl drew on cross-sport references and pop culture touchpoints, as well as simply letting the down-home DeMerit and his circle convey their own joyful bemusement. DeMerit's story didn't stop with Watford, either. Five months after this piece ran, the Wisconsin native earned his first call-up to the U.S. national team; he would reach a career highpoint in 2010 when he started all four games for the United States at the 2010 World Cup in South Africa. In 2011, DeMerit moved to MLS to join the newly instated Vancouver Whitecaps, for which he played three seasons before retiring, having lived a real-life football fairy tale.

THREE YEARS AGO, IN JAY DeMERIT'S PREVIOUS LIFE, SIR ELTON John didn't ask to shake his hand. Three years ago, before he scored one of the most lucrative goals in soccer history, yellow-clad Englishmen didn't chant his name, didn't wear his jersey, didn't burst into tears of joy over his flying header into a rippling net. Three years ago Jay DeMerit, late of Green Bay, was a soccer vagabond in a foreign land, an MLS reject plying the fields of London's city parks, a Sunday pub leaguer sharing a friend's attic bedroom in a dodgy part of town and subsisting on $70 a week and a steady diet of beans on toast.

Now, of all places, he's here: on the emerald grass of sold-out Vicarage Road, the cozy stadium of the English Premier League's Watford FC, a small-market outfit like DeMerit's beloved Green Bay Packers. It's an early-autumn afternoon fifteen miles north of London, and this time DeMerit's foes aren't a bunch of hungover blokes from the pub but rather the superstars of Manchester United, the world's most famous team. The sight of the Red Devils should intimidate the Hornets defender (*Welcome to the Premiership, Yank*), but not today. Not after his journey from the sport's lowest levels to a league with a global audience of 600 million.

When DeMerit dispossesses Man U forward Ryan Giggs early in the first half, the stand behind Watford's goal erupts: *U-S-A! U-S-A! U-S-A!* Later, after DeMerit swipes Cristiano Ronaldo's sneaky back-heel pass, the Watford hard cores launch into another favorite (also seen on yellow-and-black T-shirts):

Jaaaaaaaaay . . . Jay DeMerit!
Jay-Jay-Jay from the USA!

Man United ends up winning 2–1 on a second-half goal, but the Wisconsin cheesehead with Matt Damon's mug and David Beckham's old rooster-tail haircut has played a nearly flawless match, organizing Watford's back line while using his speed, smarts, and aerial prowess to help keep the game close. "I like the challenge of going up against some of the best players in the world each week," the twenty-six-year-old DeMerit says afterward. "If I can hold my own, it's only going to make me better. It's just another level I can get to."

Rare these days is the foreign crowd that embraces a U.S. athlete with such fervor. Even rarer is the still unfolding fable of DeMerit, the unlikeliest of the record thirteen American imports in the Premiership this season. How many Yanks go from mid–major college soccer to starting in the Premier League? From not being drafted by MLS to scoring a historic goal in front of 65,000 fans last May? From toiling in obscurity—DeMerit has never played for a U.S. team at any level—to staring down renowned strikers such as Thierry Henry, Wayne Rooney, and Andriy Shevchenko?

"Jay DeMerit came from nothing and made a decision to be something," says Aidy Boothroyd, the Watford manager. "He's the Rocky Balboa of English football."

For five months the good folks of Wisconsin have had a hard time grasping the magnitude of DeMerit's finest hour: scoring the goal that clinched Watford's promotion to the Premier League. "Some do, some don't," DeMerit says over coffee in Camden Town, the hip North London neighborhood where he recently bought the flat he shares with his girlfriend, Katherine Carter. "I had some friends in Green Bay go, 'I heard you played in a game?' Yeah. I did. 'I heard you scored?' Yeah. I did. They don't really get the implications, and that's OK. It's hard for people to understand sometimes."

Not that hard, though. The beauty of the Premiership—indeed, of most overseas leagues—is its meritocracy. Not only can players rise (and fall) through the ranks, but so can teams. After each season the worst three Premier League sides drop down a level, to be replaced by the three big winners of the second tier. Promotion and relegation, as the process is known, is a staple of England's four-division professional pyramid, and the stakes are enormous. These days each team that makes the jump to the Premiership is rewarded with television and sponsorship riches of up to $45 million.

In England the second tier's top two finishers receive automatic promotions, but the third Golden Ticket goes to the winner of a playoff among the next four teams. Which brings us to the scene of DeMerit moving upfield at Millennium Stadium in Cardiff, Wales, to receive the corner kick that would change his life. His Hornets, defying forecasts of relegation to England's third tier, had soared to third and had already upset Crystal Palace in the playoffs. Now, with promotion on the line, they were facing favored Leeds United, winner take all, in a sold-out three-tiered stadium so large that Boothroyd, channeling Norman Dale in *Hoosiers,* had taken his lads to see the field earlier that week—just to show that it was the same size as any other. "We came in with our mouths open," says DeMerit, "but everyone would tell you we weren't as intimidated when we walked out the tunnel for the game."

In the Watford fan shop you can still buy the DVD of the nationally televised broadcast, including the goose-bump moment in the first half when Ashley Young sent a corner kick into the box and DeMerit crashed through for the game's first goal. "Young delivers . . . [deafening roar] . . .

and JAY DEMERIT! . . . puts WATFORD in front! . . . The AMERI-CAN! . . . makes his MARK! . . . in the playoff FINAL!"

"A miracle," says Jay's mother, Karen, who was in the stands that day with his father, John, and brother, Todd. A wall of Watford fans rose as one, danced little jigs and unleashed their chant: "Yel-low Ar-MY! Yel-low Ar-MY!" At sports bars in Milwaukee and Chicago, friends of DeMerit watching on satellite TV roared. By day's end, the Hornets had won 3–0 and DeMerit had been interviewed on TV as the Man of the Match. Up in the stadium's Watford section, Kieren Keane turned to his mates and let out a war whoop. For two years DeMerit's dream had been Keane's dream. They wore the same ratty clothes, played on the same crappy pub-league fields, attended the same fruitless tryouts with bottom-feeder clubs such as Oxford United and Bristol Rovers.

Now one of them was going to the Premier League. "I knew he would score!" Keane screamed, half in ecstasy and half in anger that he hadn't taken the 22-to-1 wager offered by William Hill on number 6 to bag a goal. "It was in the stars!"

IT STARTED, LIKE any good buddy movie, with two friends seeking an adventure. *C'mon, Jay, let's go to Europe and give it a crack.* The year was 2003, and the more DeMerit listened to Keane, his Irish American team-mate on the Chicago Fire Reserves, a nonpaying MLS minor league af-filiate, the more it made sense. DeMerit's Danish ancestry meant he could acquire a coveted European Union work permit. What's more, DeMerit was convinced that he could hang with anyone after a solid col-lege career at Illinois-Chicago, even though no MLS team had drafted him or made a contract offer. "If someone had, I probably would have stayed," he says, "but no one did. So I said, 'Screw it, I'll go.'"

With little more than their backpacks, their soccer cleats, and enough dollars to cover overnight buses and youth hostels, they toured Europe for six weeks in search of a tryout. In the Netherlands they rented old bicycles and doorstepped the manager of Sparta Rotterdam. (All they got were free tickets to that night's game.) In Belgium they waited half an hour to speak with the coach at Royal Antwerp before giving up. (They left a note—*Your loss!*—under his door and skedaddled.) Only when their money ran out did they return, suitably chastened, to the cramped house they shared with Keane's mother, three brothers, and a sister in London's hardscrabble Wembley neighborhood.

That summer DeMerit returned to the U.S. and saved $1,000 working as a bouncer and bartender in Chicago. He went back to London in the fall looking for more tryouts—and any way to stay fit in the interim. "I knew I'd have to play in whatever park I could find," says DeMerit, who earned $70 a week playing with Keane for a ninth-division team called Southall Town on Saturdays and not a cent for their pub-league games on Sundays. "We'd bring the nets and set 'em up and play," DeMerit recalls. "Some of the guys would be drinking on the sidelines at eleven in the morning." At one point when their financial situation looked particularly grim, DeMerit and Keane took temporary jobs painting houses.

Yet after nearly two years of grinding, the big break came with astonishing swiftness. In July 2004, an old coach from Southall Town invited DeMerit and Keane to play a couple of preseason games with his new team, seventh-division Northwood FC. In one game both players impressed then Watford manager Ray Lewington enough that he offered them two-week trials. Pro sports can be cruel indeed—Keane couldn't crack Watford's roster and has since bounced around clubs in England, Scotland, and Spain—but DeMerit thrived with the reserve squad, and Lewington told him to suit up for the senior team's preseason finale against Spain's Real Zaragoza (which had beaten Real Madrid the previous season). "I thought maybe I'd get five minutes at the end," DeMerit says, "but I got to the stadium and I was in the starting lineup. I'd never even trained with the first team, so I was s—— myself."

DeMerit kept his composure for ninety minutes, and the next day Watford offered him a one-year, $45,000 contract. "I would have done it for free," says DeMerit, who recently signed his fourth contract in two years, a three-year deal that pays him $465,000 this season.

"Jay's got total respect from all the players here," says Watford defender Malky Mackay, a Scottish international. "He's always had the physical attributes, but his development has come in deciding when to challenge, when to drop off, and when to play the pass. He's certainly good enough to play in the Premiership and get into his national team." Second-year Watford manager Boothroyd goes one step further, predicting that DeMerit will someday become the U.S. captain.

The 6'1", 185-pound DeMerit would settle for receiving his first national-team call-up (he'll have to wait until the U.S. hires a new coach), but he has enough on his plate in a Premier League season that will test him like no other. Success for Watford, which has the Premiership's lowest payroll, will mean finishing no worse than seventeenth out of the twenty teams; the fight to avoid relegation could be just as thrilling as the race at the top of the standings. Two months into a thirty-eight-game season, Watford stood in nineteenth place through Sunday on four draws and three one-goal defeats. But like his Hornets, DeMerit had held his own in nearly every match—despite playing out of position in recent weeks at right back. "My goal is to keep progressing," he says, "whether that means being on the national team, continuing to move higher with Watford, or, if not, then moving somewhere else. There's no reason I can't continue to set higher goals and get to the pinnacle of my profession."

And if that means turning pop icons into his starstruck fans, hey, no problem. Before last spring's regular-season finale, a small man in a blue suit and pink glasses bustled into the Hornets' locker room. Sir Elton John, Watford's lifetime president, had a question: Where's the American? "It was kind of surreal," DeMerit says of their meeting. "We talked about Brett Favre, of all things."

These days, in fact, it's getting harder to tell which one's the rock star, Sir Elton or DeMerit. During his trip home over the summer, DeMerit spent a day in the recording studio with some old friends who own an indie music label in Minneapolis. The resulting track, a guitar-screeching ode to Watford called "Soccer Rocks," celebrates the fairy-tale story of an Everyman and his underdog team who somehow make it to the Premier League:

Let me bring your dream to you / Show you all what you could do / Soccer rocks!

The singer, like the player, is still a work in progress, but you can't fault his effort. Besides, you never know where the smallest opportunity might lead if the right people take notice. Boothroyd says he's sending the demo to Sir Elton.

Villainy or Victory?

FROM *Sports Illustrated*, JUNE 9, 2014

Wahl's fluency in Spanish and intimate familiarity with Latin American culture were invaluable tools in his journalism kit, allowing him to engage with some of the biggest names in international sports on their cultural terms, without the barrier of a translator. (Crucially, he would note, it also saved him precious interviewing time.) This would give him an edge as important as his *SI* calling card in landing interviews with the likes of Argentina's Lionel Messi—who, Wahl noted, appreciated Wahl's slightly Argentine-tinged accent—and, for this *SI* cover story, Uruguay's Luis Suárez, the most notorious and complex player in all of *fútbol* in the run-up to the 2014 World Cup. As for Wahl's wondering in the piece whether Suárez would carve his name in glory or infamy at Brazil '14, it would be the latter: To the shock of a global audience, *garra* got the better of Suárez during the first-round match between Italy and Uruguay, when he inexplicably dug his teeth into the shoulder of defender Giorgio Chiellini during a Uruguay attack, the third time in his career he had bitten an opponent on the field. Suárez would be booted from the tournament and serve a lengthy ban. Yet, perhaps finally finding the balance in *garra*, the Uruguayan concept that so informs this piece, Suárez emerged stronger from the incident. That fall he joined Messi at fabled Barcelona, where he would go on to score 142 goals in 191 appearances over six seasons. He also starred for Uruguay in the 2018 World Cup—and indeed, having avoided further incidents of infamy, was welcomed back into the *fútbol* fold.

IN URUGUAY, WHICH HAS SOMEHOW WON TWO WORLD CUPS WITH a population the size of Connecticut's, there is a word associated with passion for soccer: *garra*. The term has various definitions, but for most

Uruguayans *garra* represents the unyielding grit and determination that lie deep within the national psyche.

The embodiment of *garra*, the world's best soccer player over the past six months, has been talking for an hour now, pausing at times to sip yerba maté tea from the silver straw and wooden gourd that accompany him everywhere around Liverpool. Over the course of a lengthy conversation on the Big Themes—love, sacrifice, morality in sports—Luis Suárez has not attempted to bite anyone. He has not made like a *fútbol* Chevy Chase, tumbling to draw an imaginary penalty. He has not uttered anything that could be construed as incendiary. In fact, Suárez has been a perfect gentleman, hardly resembling the man demonized in tabloid headlines: CANNIBAL OF ANFIELD (*The Daily Telegraph*), YOU CHEAT! (*The Sun*), and RACIST (*The Mirror*).

In soccer terms Suárez has been clean for a year, which is to say he's had no new suspensions to add to his eighteen games in Premier League bans. And his transcendent season with Liverpool (thirty-one goals in thirty-three league matches, tying a league scoring record) has tiny Uruguay (population 3.5 million) dreaming of repeating its World Cup triumphs of 1930 and '50 with a run to glory in Brazil. But the fallout from previous incidents—biting two opponents; diving to earn penalties; insulting an African-born player with references to his skin color—has had a deep impact on Suárez. Ask the guy who has every motivation to stick to safe talking points a soccer question—What do you hope to achieve in your career?—and you expect something about leading La Celeste further in the World Cup than their semifinal finish four years ago, or winning the Premier League title (Liverpool fell an agonizing two points short this season), or adding another domestic Player of the Year award to go with his trophy from 2013–14.

Instead, Suárez, twenty-seven, pauses, takes a pull on his straw, and says in Spanish, "I want to change the bad-boy image that has stuck for a bit because I don't think I am at all how I have been portrayed. I would like that to change because it's awful to hear and read what is said of you."

Absolution is a tricky thing. Can it be achieved with one year of suspension-free behavior and utter brilliance on the field? Three years? Five? John Henry, the American owner of Liverpool and the Boston Red

Sox, thinks Suárez has served his time in PR purgatory. "All of us at the club, including every player, know that one, Luis is a good person and a great teammate, and two, he is hypercompetitive and can overreact," Henry told *SI* in an email. "He is a good person 99 percent of the time, and 1 percent of the time his desire to win overcomes everything else. So he had moments where he made very high-profile mistakes. But those mistakes were always in the heat of competition. [They have] caused him problems, but [they're] also a reason he is one of the best players we've ever seen."

Suárez is blessed with talent, the Promethean ability to create scoring chances out of nothing. His 0.94 goals-per-game average in the Premier League this season was the highest for a leading scorer in the English top flight since 1960–61, and it came without the aid of a single penalty kick. But to watch him battle for possession near the corner flag—burrowing into his defender, using a swim move as if he were an NFL defensive lineman—is to witness a player overflowing with *garra*.

Suárez himself employs the word in a variety of ways. "It defines me in the sense that I will fight for every ball, want to win every game, and get upset when I lose," he says, "because it gives you a *garra*, a bad sensation, simply because you hate to lose. Not only for me, but I think for a lot of Uruguayans." Last month, when Liverpool gave up three late goals to tie Crystal Palace 3–3 and squandered its shot at the league title, the searing image was of Suárez crouched on the field with his head under his jersey, the better to hide his uncontrollable weeping. "I couldn't stop," he told reporters afterward.

Over the past year, at least, Suárez has maintained a healthier balance on the *garra* precipice. "On the field, sometimes passion overwhelms you and you do things you regret afterward," he says. "At the same time, you have a chance to learn from those things. I think I [have] been a role model since last summer; I have been professional, and I have the desire to forge ahead and play well regardless of what is said to me."

Yet Henry's point—that Suárez's *garra* is part of what makes him great—raises a question that applies to sports as a whole. Do some athletes at times need to push the limits of acceptable conduct, of the rules even, to be dangerous on the field?

Suárez considers the question. More thought. More yerba maté.

"Players are always exposed to risk," he finally says. "Every soccer player can be on the edge, at the limit, be the bad guy. We have to get used to it." He smiles. "Sometimes I am one of those."

⸻

IF YOU'RE PLACING bets on the player who will etch his name in the history books at this World Cup, Suárez is at the top of the list, as long as he recovers as expected from a minor pretournament knee procedure. The tough part is knowing whether he will land in fame or in infamy.

No player today embodies soccer's fundamental humanity, its darkness and light, quite like Suárez, often on the same day in the same tournament. There's a fine line between genius and madness; to demonstrate we've come up with a measure for the more memorable moments involving soccer's most polarizing player. Call it the Suárez Spectrum.

The Curler That Killed South Korea

"I've scored many goals that I've liked," Suárez says, "but I think the best memory I have is the one against Korea in the 2010 World Cup." It came in a Round of 16 game, tied 1–1. After his opponents failed to clear an eightieth-minute corner kick, Uruguay's Nicolàs Lodeiro headed the ball onto the feet of Suárez. Draped in the penalty box by two defenders, Suárez instantly started breaking ankles, cutting away from the net and across the goal. With his momentum moving back upfield, he spun an angry parabola with his right foot off the far post and in. Game over.

Suárez Spectrum value: Pure soccer genius

Sleight of Hand

One round later in South Africa, Suárez found a creative (and controversial) way to carry his team past the quarterfinal match against Ghana. With the game tied 1–1 in the final seconds of extra time, the Ghanaians capped a wild goalmouth scramble at Uruguay's end with a close-range header that appeared certain to find the net. The only man standing in the way? Suárez, who spiked the ball on the goal line with his right hand like a volleyball player. *Penalty! Red card!* But then Ghana's Asamoah

Gyan slammed his spot kick off the crossbar, and Uruguay prevailed in the subsequent shoot-out.

Pundits the world over flamed Suárez as a cynical cheater, but what exactly was his mistake? This wasn't Diego Maradona scoring a goal with his fist at World Cup 1986, acting as if he'd used his head and escaping punishment. (Maradona later admitted he'd intentionally used his fist.) Suárez got caught and paid the price: ejection, a one-game suspension and a penalty kick for Ghana. "For me, I didn't do anything wrong," he says. "I sacrificed playing in a World Cup semifinal for my teammates to have a chance to."

Suárez didn't cheat; he saved Uruguay's World Cup, again. Teammates called him a hero and carried him off on their shoulders. Anyone who has a problem with what happened should blame the rule book, not the player.

Suárez Spectrum value: Game-theory brilliance

Falling Out of Favor

In England, diving and embellishing contact to draw penalties are viewed as cheating, more so than in Italy or Spain, for example, where such antics are part of the game. Like other top forwards imported into the Premier League, Suárez says he has adjusted his game to remain upright more often. ("I have changed," he says. "You can tell.") But he's also adamant that he has never deserved a rep as a diver. "How many yellow cards do I have for diving?" he asks. "I have a lot of yellow cards in my career, but most are for arguing, for fighting, for giving a kicking— not for diving. Sometimes I fall, but it's to get a penalty because I have been kicked."

There's some truth and some fiction here. Fact: Only two of Suárez's twenty-three Premier League yellow cards have been for diving or embellishment. But even Henry admits Suárez could have remained upright more in previous seasons. "Last year he often wasn't allowed to play his game," says the owner. "He was shoved, kicked and harassed continually. He has adjusted. Probably the biggest difference [in 2013– 14] is that he does everything he can now to stay on his feet, and that has made him even more dangerous."

Suárez Spectrum value: Pragmatism with a dose of Eddie Haskell

Like Mike (Tyson)

When Suárez sank his teeth into Chelsea fullback Branislav Ivanovic in April 2013, earning a ten-game suspension, the question wasn't just: Why? It was: How could Suárez—who'd already been suspended seven games for biting an opponent while playing for Ajax in the Netherlands three years earlier—let this happen a second time?

He knows *garra* is no excuse. "First, it was a matter of frustration in the heat of the play," he explains. "You feel frustrated because the play didn't go well. [He was bodied off the ball in front of the goal.] Second, you react in a fraction of a second. Something that may not seem like a big deal suddenly is, and you aren't conscious of your reaction or the repercussions." On this one Suárez is entirely apologetic.

Suárez Spectrum value: Pure madness

The Race Episode

Following a game between Liverpool and bitter rival Manchester United in October 2011, defender Patrice Evra charged that Suárez had insulted him racially during the match. While Suárez and his team argued that the Spanish noun *negro* doesn't necessarily have a negative connotation in Uruguay, an independent panel ruled in a 115-page report that Suárez was indeed at fault. After an extensive investigation Suárez was handed an eight-game suspension and a fine of $63,000. "The use by a footballer of insulting words, which include reference to another player's colour, is wholly unacceptable," the report concluded.

Here the player continues to defend himself. "My conscience is very clean," says Suárez, whose grandfather was black. "First, I am not racist. There are a lot of people who could testify to that. Second, there are conversations that happen on the field where a lot gets said. I am at peace. Of all the video that was available, there was not one piece of evidence to prove I had said something racist."

Suárez Spectrum value: A damaging episode for which he served a stiff penalty

Suárez hadn't suffered any negative incidents involving race before Evra, nor has he in the thirty-two months since. In April, he tweeted a photograph that showed him smiling and eating a banana with Liverpool teammate Philippe Coutinho. It was a gesture of support for a viral antiracism campaign started by Brazilian forward Neymar (hashtag: #weareallmonkeys) after one of his Barcelona teammates was targeted by a banana-throwing fan in Spain. Some jeered Suárez for the post. Many cheered. Such is the state of tribalism in global soccer.

THE COINCIDENCE IS almost too much to believe: Two of the top ten forwards in world soccer—a duo whose combined transfer-market value is north of $150 million—were born twenty-one days apart in the same town in a sleepy corner of Uruguay. The World Cup's most feared strike tandem pairs Luis Suárez and Edinson Cavani, late of Salto, a city of 100,000 located three hundred miles northwest of the capital, Montevideo. During South America's sixteen-game World Cup qualifying tournament, the duo combined for sixteen goals (eleven for Suárez, five for Cavani). "It's incredible," says Suárez of their common origin. "We actually never played as kids together; we met for the first time when we were twenty."

Cavani, who plays for Paris Saint-Germain, was a late bloomer, while Suárez moved with his family to Montevideo at age seven. In a period of economic turmoil for their country, Suárez's parents found work in the capital, Sandra on a cleaning crew at a shopping center and Rodolfo in a variety of jobs, including one as a security guard. "In Salto we were used to playing in the street and we were all friends," says Suárez. "Suddenly landing in Montevideo, we had to watch when crossing the road. People laughed at your accent in school. Everything was a bit different."

Suárez's parents divorced when Luis was nine, a jarring blow for a family of five brothers and two sisters. He remembers having to meet his mother at noon each day to pick up the money she'd made cleaning and then deliver it to his older sisters, who would buy food and cook for the kids before school the next day. "My mom couldn't join us because she had to work," he says. "It was a way of growing, fighting adversity, getting ahead. I think [my] hunger comes from all the suffering since childhood." As an eleven-year-old, Suárez would walk forty minutes by himself to practice, where he sometimes had to play in borrowed, ill-fitting cleats.

When he ponders the notion of sacrifice, Suárez thinks less of his goal-line hand ball against Ghana than he does of his mother toiling away with a mop or of his wife, Sofía, dropping everything at age sixteen to start a new life with him in the Dutch city of Groningen, home of Suárez's first European club. The couple met in Uruguay—he was fifteen, she was thirteen—and, to hear Luis tell the story, Sofía saved his future by persuading him to stop partying when officials at the Uruguayan club Nacional wanted to drop him from the youth team. Sofía and her family moved to Spain during an economic crisis, but Luis scraped together enough money to visit her twice. When he made the move from Nacional to the Dutch league in 2006, at nineteen, she rejoined him.

"She sacrificed herself at sixteen to live with me and move to a city like Groningen [the seventh largest in the Netherlands]," he says. "To leave her studies, leave her family, leave everything—just to be with me. . . . She didn't imagine then that I would get to the level where I am now."

The couple married in 2009 and have two children: Delfina, who's nearly four, and eight-month-old Benjamín. When Liverpool purchased Suárez for $31.5 million in January 2011, just seven months after his first child arrived, it was almost as if the family's move to northwest England was preordained. Delfina is an anagram of Liverpool's legendary stadium, Anfield.

LUIS SUÁREZ IS not an NBA fan, and as such he's unfamiliar with the oeuvre of Charles Barkley. But when told of Barkley's famous line about athletes not being role models, Suárez swats it down with the urgency of that goal-line hand ball in South Africa. "Of course they should be," he says. "Many times, [athletes'] attitudes are reflected in their performance on the field. I've had some attitudes on the field that weren't very good for my image. But those weren't really me—outside the field, I'm very shy. I realized I had to adjust my attitude on the field, to continue to play well but without the bad attitude."

That much he has done for the past year, lighting up the Premier League, spearheading Liverpool's return to the Champions League for the first time in five seasons, rarely causing a stir.

Now comes a new challenge: managing his emotions while steering Uruguay through a stacked World Cup group that includes two other previous world champions, Italy and England (whose media will not hesitate to pounce on another Suárez misstep). Who knows? Barkley, too, once drew near-universal wrath—for spitting on one fan and throwing another through a plate-glass window, among other indiscretions—and now he's viewed as a public treasure.

Is there a chance Suárez could do the same? Some World Cup *garra*—and a trophy on July 13 in Rio de Janeiro—just might do the trick.

The Most Passionate Prodigal

Previously unpublished, written for Humanities 440,
April 26, 1995

Wahl came under the spell of former *New York Times* Vietnam correspondent Gloria Emerson at Princeton during the fall of 1993, as a
student in her Politics and the Press seminar. A year later he wrote
this never-before-published profile of Emerson for The Literature of
Fact, the nonfiction writing course taught that semester by *New
Yorker* editor David Remnick. Pointillist in its observed details and
fearlessly mature in where it probes, the piece earned a scrawled
"Bravo" from Remnick on its first page. It stands as a kind of Rosetta
Stone to the practitioner Wahl aspired to be—a reporter who inter-
nalized Emerson's standards of curiosity and conviction. His mentor
challenged him, but he learned to regard every test of hers as a badge
of honor. "She'd take a shot at him, try to land a different viewpoint,
and he'd bounce back up at her like one of those bolo dolls," Wahl's
brother, Eric, remembers. "It was that kind of give-and-take that influenced how he interviewed people." Wahl was bereft when Emerson died by suicide in 2004, after Parkinson's disease left her unable
to write. From that point on, if Wahl sensed that anyone in his circle
was suffering from depression, he made every effort to intervene.

[Professor David Remnick's comment at the top: "Grant, This is splen-
did, among the very best student papers I've ever seen. Bravo. D."]

GLORIA EMERSON DOES NOT KEEP HER PURPLE HEART FRAMED
in the den or pinned to a uniform or encased in some quartzite
paperweight. Instead, she maintains it as she received it—in the ribbon
form, attached to a rectangle of yellowing tagboard. A veteran from
Saratoga Springs, New York, sent it to Emerson after he read *Winners
and Losers,* her rage-filled chronicle/memoir based on three years of in-

terviewing American families and two as a Vietnam correspondent for *The New York Times.* "He thought I had been wounded also," she says.

A view of Emerson's two-floor Princeton apartment suggests that those wounds have not healed. The first thing you see, right at the top of the stairs, is the photograph of a lone American GI, lying on the back of an armored personnel carrier in the middle of a treeless, puddled field. He is not wounded, nor is it an action shot at all. He is just lying there, smoking a joint, face up to a sky so gray it seems eerie, even on black-and-white film.

Then there is the picture of the Vietnamese girl whose parents had been killed. Emerson gave her a doll, a Raggedy Ann doll, and the children made fun of its red hair. The photographer said it took twenty minutes to coax the child into a half smile, but the look is more of a stare.

The books, all about the Vietnam War, take up an entire wall of the back room and overflow into a closet. Emerson arranges them alphabetically, by author—all but a few are inscribed.

The only non-Vietnam-related article is the photograph of Jacqueline Kennedy Onassis, circa 1962. Jackie watches over the kitchen. Products of New York high society, the two women met in Maine when Emerson was nineteen; Jackie invited Gloria to her wedding a few years later. "If I hadn't married, I might have had a life very much like Gloria Emerson's," Kennedy Onassis once said, a bit too wondrously.

"I don't think she quite understood what I did," Emerson says, shaking her head. "She had her own Vietnam that day in Dallas, though."

Emerson's association is explicit, and it relates even Jackie to Vietnam. Kennedy Onassis equals Dallas. Emerson equals Vietnam. Both tragedies are, at a personal level, all-encompassing and irreversible. And yet, amid Jackie and the pictures and posters and Indochinese artwork, Emerson no longer posts her Purple Heart anywhere in the apartment. She has in the past—the twenty-five pinholes in the tagboard suggest many comings and goings from the bulletin board in her office, right above the Royal typewriter. But yesterday, when she tried to look for it, it was so hidden among the photographs, letters, and telegrams strewn about her file cabinets that she found it only after a ninety-minute ordeal.

And so I ask the question: What makes her Purple Heart so important to find but so seemingly unimportant that it's been tossed haphazardly into a file cabinet?

No reply is forthcoming. Instead she rummages through her desk, in search of the award for the second time in two days. After two minutes she pulls it out. Creases run through the tagboard like thin veins. She makes me recite the inscription, printed in blue ballpoint; she wants to hear a man's voice read it.

The Purple Heart is awarded to Gloria Emerson for service set forth in the following citation: For "wounds" received in Southeast Asia in service to conscience and country. In the face of extreme danger, and with complete disregard for her own safety and sanity, she performed magnificently and selflessly, never allowing the truth to similarly become a casualty. She emerged sane, but touched, recording that which was so that it never again shall be. "All we remember is your living face, and that we loved you for being of our clay and spirit."

The last line comes from British veteran Guy Chapman's World War I memoir, *A Passionate Prodigality*. "And I can remember weeping when I got to that part," Emerson says. "I recognized it immediately, and thought it *astonishing* that this veteran had read this memoir." She exhales hard on "astonishing," in a voice so dignified, so Eastern, that it sounds like John Houseman's in the old Smith Barney commercials.

This is the woman who understood the grunts. Emerson still retains the soldier's spirit, as Chapman described it. "She is one of the great compassionate, empathetic souls of the world," says Wayne Karlin, a novelist and veteran of the war. "It's the way she operates, the way she writes. The way she does everything is completely and openly." In her post-*Times* career (she quit in 1972), Emerson has taken that approach to other cultures at war—Rhodesia, Nicaragua, El Salvador, Gaza, Algeria—and produced literary journalism that speaks for the people, whether you agree with it or not. Truth is paramount, of course, but for Emerson the delivery makes the difference. "Most journalists nail together the boards of the fence," she has said more than once. "I prefer to paint them."

But the problem is not the spirit to which Chapman refers; the problem is the clay. Only a few Vietnam correspondents were of the soldiers' clay; they molded their *being* to the rigors of war. "I had a kind of pure concentration," Emerson says, using her hands to illustrate blinders. "I didn't go to parties. I didn't smoke dope. I didn't listen to Aretha Franklin. I knew the only way I was going to get through it was to lead a life of extraordinary discipline. For a very nervous, impulsive, jumpy person, I became very calm, which was a bad sign. Because it's not in my nature to be deadly calm and quiet."

When the war was over, most of Emerson's colleagues wrote an account of Vietnam and moved on—their clay remained malleable. Many of them think that Emerson's did not. "A few reporters wrote brilliant books about Vietnam and then branched in to other subjects, such as [David] Halberstam and [Neil] Sheehan and Frances FitzGerald," Peter Arnett writes in *Live from the Battlefield.* "There were some, like Gloria Emerson, who never let go of Vietnam."

It is as if, for Emerson, Vietnam were a giant, fiery kiln that seared her body and soul, hardened her form, and at the same time, paradoxically, made her dangerously brittle.

———

THE TOUR OF duty for *Times* correspondents in Vietnam usually lasted eighteen months. Emerson completed it, asked for six more months, and received them. She did not fear an ambush in the jungle or the South Vietnamese, about whom she wrote most of her dispatches. She feared returning to the United States. "I was so terrified," she says of those last months in Vietnam. "Terrified to come back to this country, where I had not lived for twelve years, and find out what kind of people we were that we had permitted this appalling war to happen."

Curiosity finally won out—Emerson came back in the summer of 1972. Soon after, the *Times* sent her on a feature assignment to cover an Army parade in Social Circle, Georgia. She watched the children clapping and the soldiers saluting. The music from the band resonated in her head. Everyone was smiling, it seemed. Emerson began to waver—the blinders were still attached. Fifteen inches of text could never contain what she wanted to say, and so she did not complete the article. "I didn't know how to write," she explains. "Here I was, writing about Vietnamese villages, and I couldn't even write about our own villages. It was over for me, the career I wanted so desperately. But I had something more important to do."

She wanted to venture into the country, into the homes of the Americans who let the war happen, who allowed their children to die. The decision played in her mind. Emerson teetered at the edge of a nervous breakdown. She feared a country that would reelect Richard Nixon, "the prosecutor of the war," as she always calls him. On election night, as the returns came in, Emerson withdrew, deeper and deeper, into the couch of her Manhattan apartment. Could she love her country again? The question—and her uncertain inner response—were what drew her out. Emerson's approach to *Winners and Losers* was well documented: "the wanderings of a woman trying to love her country, asking simple-minded questions, and her memories of the war," as she now describes it. For two years she traveled the United States, stopping in small towns and large cities to interview veterans, who were never hard to find. Two decades later, she [still can] recite all of the places, in the exact order that she visited them.

There was more to her agenda than the interviews, however. Emerson assumed the role of educator and organized meetings of veterans nearly everywhere she visited. "I thought the only way to save myself was to live differently," she says. "To find a new path and a way not just to write about Vietnam, but to teach Americans something about the war and ourselves."

The meetings—at least three hundred—took place in dusty church basements, community centers, even prisons. Her delivery was part encyclopedia, part invective. Speaking without notes, Emerson stood, her six-foot-tall stature commanding the room, and explained that the Gulf of Tonkin Resolution was a mandate for war. She detailed the French role in Indochina and how Ho's Viet Minh troops defeated them. She brought up Ho's aid to Allied airmen who were shot down in World War II, as well as his earnest letters to President Truman seeking Vietnamese independence.

Pushing forward, Emerson—still standing, and feeling a fear that did not show—asked the men to write down some of their Vietnam memories, which they shared with each other in the group. "One hope was to make them see they had been badly used without further demoralizing them," she says. "It was important to tell Americans that no man *gave* his life, his life *was taken*. No one chose to die in Vietnam."

At the end, she would read a poem, usually "Dulce et Decorum Est" by World War I poet Wilfred Owen:

> *If in some smothering dreams you too could pace*
> *Behind the wagon that we flung him in,*
> *And watch the white eyes writhing in his face,*
> *His hanging face, like a devil's sick of sin;*
> *If you could hear, at every jolt, the blood*
> *Come gargling from the froth-corrupted lungs,*
> *Obscene as cancer, bitter as the cud*
> *Of vile, incurable sores on innocent tongues,—*
> *My friend, you would not tell with such high zest*
> *To children ardent for some desperate glory,*
> *The old Lie:* Dulce et decorum est
> Pro patria mori.

Often Emerson would ask a veteran to recite the poem instead. As they spoke, many of the veterans cried. The ones who entered the meetings as skeptics cried the most.

The gatherings, especially the first ones, helped Emerson as much as the veterans. They created a sense of understanding that she had found lacking in the old guard families of her upbringing and the conservative World War II veterans she interviewed. "Meeting with the groups of veterans, something became clear: that morality is an *activity*, not a belief or a contemplative state," she says. "I could not just walk away from Vietnam and move on to the next story. It was too huge, too murderous, too evil, and I could not put it aside."

The "activity"—the meetings and the writing workshops—would continue through the '80s. But her friends could see it coming from a distance, like a thunderstorm on the plains. With Emerson, the signal was so strong you could tell from half a world away. Not long before the end of the war, she received a letter from the interpreter she had worked with in Vietnam, Nguyen Ngoc Luong. He has spoken with other correspondents about Emerson after she left Saigon, and his message bore an uncanny resemblance to the one Peter Arnett would communicate twenty years later. "All have this remark about you: You are the only one who cannot overcome your Vietnam experience," Nguyen wrote. "There is an acute lack of forgetfulness in you about Vietnam."

"They saw I was still in that trench," she says. "They think I'm in too deep. Poor Gloria." She uses the past and present tenses interchangeably. Enunciating every word, Emerson pauses at the end of each sentence, purses her lips, then continues. "Tom Morgan [who profiled her for *Esquire*] said to me, 'You were at the top. You could have had anything you wanted.' But I didn't want anything. I didn't want to be at the top, *their* top.'"

IN 1977, AT a bookstore in Beverly Hills, Emerson saw several copies of *Winners and Losers* on display. Stopping, she looked in one direction and then the other, like a twelve-year-old up to mischief. No one was watching. She reached for the books and turned the covers face down. Beverly Hills did not need to read her story. "I wanted something so much bigger than a book," she says. "I didn't want it in a bookstore window. I wanted all the dead to rise from their graves."

Emerson's moment of happiness—the only one, she says—occurred seven years later while she was reading Graham Greene's *Getting to Know the General.* In it, Greene cited a brief description of General Bunker from *Winners and Losers.* In a five-word reference, he called Emerson's book "admirable." Emerson was overjoyed. She had interviewed Greene in 1978; his books sit atop the shelves of her office bookcase, facing outward, separate from the rest. An eight-by-ten photo of Greene rests, framed, on her desk. "I admired him beyond belief," she says. "He was one of the three or four most important people in my life." When Emerson read her name in Greene's book, she had to share the news. "I was lying in bed at two o'clock in the morning, and I read that magical sentence from Graham's book. I began calling people in France and England to say, 'Are you up? It's Gloria!'" As Emerson speaks, her eyes widen, and her hands seize the armrests of her chair. She is smiling for the first time in hours.

And yet *Winners and Losers* never satisfied her drive for absolution; Emerson's "lack of forgetfulness" became more acute. She saw the young soldiers, dead, in her dreams at night, the blood and the vacant stares. In her most frequent nightmare, she saw the boy on the helicopter whose hand she held. He died before they landed, but she refused to loosen her grip; finally, a soldier pried their hands apart. Afterward, Emerson did not hold hands in helicopters. The nightmare persisted for ten years.

Seeing it in the subconscious compounded her guilt. "I felt shame and grief at being a witness," she says. "I never hurt anyone. I never committed a single brutal act. But I saw so many I felt contaminated, by the brutality and the uselessness of it." There is more to it, though. "My own feeling was that war correspondents are in a sense war profiteers, that I got a salary and I got the prizes, and I got the lovely hero-grams. But the draftee didn't. And the Vietnamese didn't. And maybe I'm ashamed of that."

She said she would write nothing more about Vietnam. There were talented veterans who could do it, who *were* doing it. But when the editors wanted a story about Vietnam, they called Gloria. When the Vietnam War Memorial was unveiled in 1982, three national magazines asked Emerson to write a reaction. She redirected them to writers who had fought in Vietnam. The implication of the requests was clear, however: Emerson in some way represented the veterans; in a sense, she had become one of them.

The notion followed her. In 1985, journalists, military officials and veterans gathered at a conference in California called Vietnam Reconsidered. The organizers asked Emerson to represent the veterans, not the journalists. When it was time to speak, she called the veterans, all of them, to the podium. Security, she noticed, was tighter than it was for the rest of the conference, and she responded by asking a local veteran to lock the doors to the auditorium—the audience listened to every one of them, waiting by the dozens onstage. They would all be heard. Only then did Emerson authorize the doors to be unlocked.

Even though she never graduated from college—she spent only a month there—Emerson always felt most comfortable at the universities. Beginning in the mid-'70s, she took teaching stints at several schools— Harvard, Michigan, Vassar, Berkeley, Princeton. She likes to point out that they were courses about politics, not the war as such. "You'll notice," she argues, "that I never taught a course about Vietnam." To teach students about the war, year after year, would have pushed her to the edge again, she says.

And yet they were indeed courses about Vietnam. In her 1993 seminar at Princeton, called Politics and the Press: Women Covering the News, she opened our first class not with an introduction, not with a welcome, but with a simple declaration: "I have now put Vietnam behind me."

That was her goal, perhaps, but she could not fulfill it. Absolution is a tricky thing. Midway through the semester she gathered us for a special viewing of *Hearts and Minds,* the 1974 documentary film of the war. She wanted us to understand, the nineteen- and twenty-year-olds who would have been sergeants and corporals on the screen. Emerson had tried this before, nineteen years earlier, and the audience—three *New York Times* editors—failed to grasp the meaning. On that night in 1974, when she organized the New York screening of *Hearts and Minds,* she had invited four guests to her apartment: the three editors and Bobby Muller, the paraplegic who founded Vietnam Veterans of America.

"They had never seen anyone injured in the war, never known anyone who had fought in the war," she says. "And when Bobby came in, they were so awkward. They kind of stood up and looked embarrassed because he was paralyzed and in a wheelchair. I'll never forget that. How could you work for *The New York Times* and you don't know someone in Vietnam?"

The editors did not learn in 1974. Then again, neither did the Princeton students in 1993. Several nodded off during the documentary, and when Emerson called for discussion at the end, only one question was asked. She remembers the apathy with bitterness. "Why did I even show the film?" she asks, and it is hard to tell if she is referring to the first showing or the second or both.

The students are not unique, however. Few people ask Emerson questions anymore, except for the Swedish anthropologist and the Japanese journalist who visited her in the last year. The Americans don't care, it seems. After the mid-'80s, the meetings with the veterans slowed to a trickle. "They either know by now everything I can tell them," Emerson says, "or they don't know and don't want to hear it." She wrote two books in Reagan's decade: *Some American Men,* a psychological profile of men that she calls her "response to the clatter and roar of feminism," and *Gaza: A Year in the Intifada,* a pro-Palestinian work that enraged much of the American political community. Neither book was received well by the public or the critics; both are now out of print.

"She's gotten a little sadder," Wayne Karlin says, comparing the Gloria Emerson of the '90s to the woman of the '70s. "What we were doing— while it was in a period of great upheaval and death and destruction— I think there was some hope that ideas could be changed. A lot of that has . . . what can I say? . . . a lot of that has gone."

"For a while, I was deluded into thinking I had an effect," Emerson says of the meetings with the veterans and the letters she received for *Winners and Losers.* "But deep down I knew I would never see any proof of a success. I knew I would have nothing to show for twenty years. And I don't have anything to show for it."

———

FOR OVER A year, Gloria Emerson has been, in effect, crippled. The accident happened on February 7, 1994, on the sidewalk in front of her neighbor's apartment. A cold spell had taken over the East Coast, and the ice had reinforced itself three inches thick. No shovel could bash it away; no salt could melt it away. Emerson planned to walk to Nassau Street for some cigarettes, but when she stepped on an extra-slick spot in the ice, she fell. The impact shattered her right leg.

Emerson spent the next two weeks at Columbia Presbyterian Hospital in New York City. Despite being confined to a wheelchair, by the end of the week she had encountered men of three different nationalities from the war and attended a meeting of Vietnam veterans. "I was in bed, and a Vietnamese came into my room," Emerson says. "He was on staff at the hospital. I said 'Hello' in Vietnamese, and he was so surprised that this American lady in a wheelchair was talking to him. Right behind him was this tall man who was an electrician, and I knew immediately he was a veteran. And the man who took my X-rays, Leroy Lim, was a veteran—we had a wonderful time talking. He worked with a Cambodian, so I said 'Hello' in Khmer to him." Emerson laughs at the irony. "Not many people can be in a hospital for eleven days and find two Vietnam veterans and a Cambodian and a Vietnamese boat person."

The electrician, named Manfried, invited Emerson to a veterans' meeting in the hospital. "I don't know what Manfried had in mind, but it seemed right to show up," Emerson says. "He hadn't organized it well, but he was trying. Leroy came down from the X-ray room, and we argued about class. We had the old class talk."

After two weeks in the hospital, Emerson returned to her apartment in Princeton. The recovery process was supposed to last between eight months and a year. But in August, as she attempted to descend the stairs to the ground floor, Emerson fell forward. Steve Parasho, the man she hired to drive her to therapy sessions, was standing five steps below, too far to catch her. The tumble rebroke the leg. Emerson spent the next forty-two days in a full-length cast; she complained that it was too hot, that the sharp edges jabbed into her thighs, which had atrophied and taken on a sickly blue shade. She was unable to leave her bed.

Aside from losing one's sight or hearing, the stiffest punishment for a reporter is a lack of mobility. Fourteen months after the slip on the ice, Emerson still uses a walker. On the rare occasions when she leaves the apartment—to go to therapy or the Princeton Diner—she needs someone to inch along with her, the person's hand placed on the small of her back for support. Emerson had planned to write a book on Algeria before the accident and had spent two months there with French priests. But now she would not return—no reporter could enter the country, and even if she did, she could not walk.

And so Emerson sat in her office, faced the Royal typewriter, and wrote about Vietnam. Wayne Karlin had collected a series of short stories written by Vietnamese (North and South) and Americans on the war. They had been translated for his upcoming anthology, called *The Other Side of Heaven.* Emerson read them, and she began to have nightmares again, the same ones of the dead pilot and the bloody bodies. Despite them, or because of them—she is not sure—she agreed to write her own piece of fiction for the collection. "It was about a woman remembering some of the appalling things the American soldiers had done to the Vietnamese," she says. Emerson had last written fiction in her early twenties, two novels that were never published. No one would read this story, either. "I tore it up. Destroyed it," she says. She does not want to talk about it. "It was full of hatred."

She wrote an epilogue instead, three pages that took her a week to construct. After reading the stories from the anthology, however, Emerson says resolutely that she will write no more about the war and focus instead on raising money for a hospital in Hue. American veterans will aid in its construction. "I'm raising money," Emerson says, "and I'm not at all interested in writing another word about Vietnam. I have *nothing* left to say." A wry laugh escapes from her mouth. "Or perhaps I do, but I don't."

The ambiguity is warranted. *The Other Side of Heaven,* with Emerson's epilogue, will be released in September. Another article, about a veteran suffering from his guilt, appears in this month's *Washington Spectator.* And at the end of the month, Emerson will travel to Atlanta for a CNN conference to commemorate the twentieth anniversary of the end of the war.

FOR AN HOUR, the copier in Emerson's office has not stopped running. The day before, the *Times* ran an editorial chastising Robert McNamara for his new book, in which he admits U.S. policy in Vietnam was wrong. "I'm sending copies to everyone I know," Emerson says. She takes a sheet from the stack of one hundred and hands it to me. "Read it, out loud." She wants to hear the words in a man's voice. The reading takes ten minutes. At various times Emerson grabs my arm and repeats her favorite phrases from the page: McNamara's "stale tears," "the ghosts of those unlived lives" that "circle close around Mr. McNamara." Finally I reach the concluding paragraph:

> Mr. McNamara says he weeps easily and has strong feelings when he visits the Vietnam Memorial. But he says he will not speak of those feelings. Yet someone must, for that black wall is wide with the names of people who died in a war that he did not, at first, carefully research or, in the end, believe to be necessary.

When I finish, Emerson looks at me as if she has won a long-standing argument. With both hands, she holds the page in front of her. "Do you know what this means?" she asks from her wheelchair, her round eyes narrowing. "At last. I think the war is finally behind us."

6

CLUB AND COUNTRY

WAHL'S DELIGHT IN SERVING AS LEAD WRITER ON THE SOCCER beat at *Sports Illustrated* might have had its purest expression when he wrote about some variation of "the crest"—the teams that the most accomplished footballers regard as allegiances 1 and 1A, "club and country." By exploring the fan culture of a soccer club or the cultural distinctiveness expressed by a national side in how it plays the game, Wahl knew he could mine rich veins and deliver revelations to the American reader. He had experienced firsthand both kinds of crest in 1994 as a twenty-year-old, after his sophomore year in college, when he had attended matches of the Argentine club Boca Juniors as well as the group stage of the World Cup, featuring Argentina's national team, La Albiceleste, in Foxboro, Massachusetts. At *SI* he would find himself writing about soccer teams of every sort and at every level, from an obscure college side to the U.S. women's national team to FC Barcelona, as well as the rivalries touched off when opposing fan bases grind up against each other along a common border. "By our games you shall know us," a wise man once said. But by our teams you shall know us that much better.

Men on a Mission

FROM *Sports Illustrated*, FEBRUARY 24, 1997

Given his upbringing and what was to come, it should be no surprise that Wahl's first feature story for *Sports Illustrated* centered on a group of athletes whose achievements had been inspired by a sense of injustice. Shining a light on the dark corners of sports and celebrating those who fight to correct wrongs would be a powerful thread throughout his journalism, as would be his deftness in tackling complex stories—this one involving academic standards, charges of racism, and the obscure nuances of the NCAA rulebook, all viewed through the lens of twenty years' hindsight and treated with thoughtfulness and balance. But Wahl's debut feature, published three months after he joined the staff as a reporter, didn't appear in the issue that went to most subscribers. On certain weeks, *SI* would run what was known in-house as Advance Text—an extra section of the magazine sent only to higher-income zip codes, to appeal to certain advertisers. This secret section—most subscribers were unaware that it existed—was often the place for young reporters such as Wahl to pitch feature-length pieces close to their hearts, as well as for editors to evaluate those young reporters' chops and potential. Wahl did, however, get a main-magazine byline in the February 24, 1997, issue, writing a front-of-the-book "Catching Up with . . . ," the weekly column about figures who had appeared on the magazine's cover, on Jill Kinmont, the American skier who made *SI*'s cover at the age of eighteen in 1955 but had suffered a devastating crash three days after the issue came out, leaving her wheelchair bound for the rest of her life and contributing to the legend of the "*Sports Illustrated* jinx."

THE WAY IAN BAIN SEES IT, THE FORTUNES OF THE HOWARD University soccer team changed on a West Virginia highway one night in October 1973, when everything, it seemed, had broken down. Not just the team bus, which four hours earlier had sputtered to the roadside. And not just the Howard defense, which had scored on its own goal that day to seal what was only the Bison's third defeat in four years.

The sharpest blow of all, in fact, had come the previous January, when the NCAA had stripped Howard of its 1971 national soccer championship and placed the program on probation for the '73 season for having used four ineligible players. The title had been the first Division I championship in any sport ever won by a predominantly black college, and Bain had been a freshman midfielder on the victorious team. The day after the announcement, he clipped a newspaper article about it, as he had clipped other articles about the team, but this time he used pinking shears. The jagged edges reflected his mood. "We felt we had been wronged," he says.

Other reactions at Howard were less subtle. "We feel that it is simply because we are a black institution that the NCAA was requested to investigate," university president Dr. James E. Cheek said in an official statement at the time.

"It's pretty evident that a black school is not supposed to win," Howard coach Lincoln Phillips said after the 1972 semifinal, a 2–1 loss to St. Louis University in which Howard held out seven players accused by the NCAA of eligibility violations. (The NCAA later shortened the list to four.) The NCAA, Phillips went on, was "guilty of practicing racism."

The starting eleven on Howard's 1971 soccer team all hailed from Caribbean and African countries. The NCAA charged that two of the players had previously exhausted their eligibility by playing amateur soccer in Trinidad and two others had not taken NCAA-mandated entrance exams to predict a 1.6 grade point average. Howard argued that the four players had GPAs over 3.0 and that the violated rules were vague and discriminated against foreigners. The school eventually challenged the NCAA in court and won a partial ruling that an NCAA regulation regarding foreign students' eligibility was discriminatory but failed to have the national title restored.

The NCAA maintained throughout that it was only enforcing its rules, and it would later strip San Francisco of a national title in 1978 for using an ineligible foreign player who was white. David Berst, head of enforcement for the NCAA, denies racism played any part in the decision against Howard.

But feelings were running high that night on the broken-down bus. "We had no postseason to go to in '73, because of the probation, so people started talking about winning the championship in '74," says Bain, a native of Trinidad who was the Bison captain both of those seasons. He looked at his teammates and issued a declaration: "There will be no more losses like this next year."

And there weren't. In 1974, Howard achieved perfection. The Bison, playing under the slogan "Truth crushed to earth shall rise again," completed a 19–0 season with a 2–1, quadruple-overtime defeat of St. Louis in the national championship game. After three years of turmoil Howard had accomplished its famous first—for the second time.

IN THE LIVING room of his northern Virginia home, Bain reaches for a small Lucite block bearing the inscription 1971 NCAA SOCCER CHAMPIONSHIP. "I remember when the NCAA sent a letter demanding that we return all the prizes," he says. "We gave them the team plaque. But this one, they'll have to come to my house and get it."

Thirty miles to the north, in Columbia, Maryland, Phillips displays an identical block of Lucite in his trophy case. Now fifty-five and a staff coach for the U.S. Soccer Federation, Phillips speaks slowly, with a melodic Trinidadian lilt. Time has softened his stance on the NCAA. "I wouldn't say now that they were racist," he states. His understanding of the NCAA has been deepened by twelve years of working with its YES program, which puts on youth sports clinics in cities that are hosting national championship tournaments. "But they were insensitive. Very insensitive."

Soccer at Howard has always been tied to race and multinationalism. A coach named Ted Chambers organized a soccer club at the university in 1947, but local, predominantly white colleges refused to put Howard on their schedules. With no opponents, Howard played for the next three years against embassy teams in Washington.

From the start, the university soccer squad was composed mostly of students from outside the U.S., but the student body at large was also international. Out of 10,152 students in 1971, there were 1,700 foreign students from seventy-two nations. The foreigners who came to Howard entered the cultural maelstrom of the era, and the soccer players, as much as anyone, got a crash course in U.S. race relations.

"In Trinidad we had [social] divisions, but they were based more on class than race," says Keith Tulloch, a midfielder on the '74 team. "When I came here, it was the first time someone had ever called me nigger, the first time a player had ever spat in my face."

During road games the insults were legion. "They'd say, 'Go back, banana boat. Go back, monkey. Go back to the jungle,'" Phillips recalls. "I had to tell my players that anytime that is done, it's fine to get angry, but you have to know how to get angry: Put the balls in the back of the net."

Here Phillips smiles. "They did that with amazing regularity, you know."

At the start of the '74 season, Phillips asked Dom Basil Matthews, a professor at the university, to speak to the team one day before practice. The players listened as Matthews described their role in what he called a triangle of blackness.

"He told them if you look back at the slave trade, you see people taken away from Africa to the West Indies and the United States," Phillips says. "The farther they came away, the more they were stripped out of their culture. The only thing missing was that line back to Africa, an acceptance of one's self. That's where Howard University is positioned—within the middle of that triangle, bringing the cultures together. And soccer was a big part of that."

When Matthews finished, the team was silent. "That was the first time that all of us as a group related to the idea of race in the environment we were now living in," says Bain. "But it was beyond race. It was like [Nelson] Mandela speaking, someone who is in a situation of race but seems above the race issue. Matthews wanted the season to be not so much a blow against white America or the NCAA but to bring pride to all of the different African groups, so that people all over the black world would notice our team."

Inasmuch as Howard was a microcosm of that world, the professor's wish was granted. "It just grew and grew," says Winston Yallery-Arthur, a former Howard player and volunteer assistant coach. "People who had never been to a soccer game started coming to watch the team play." As word spread of the team's success, professors began canceling their two o'clock classes on game days. The school band learned to play a samba beat and kept it going for the duration of matches.

"We weren't just playing soccer," says Phillips. "We were representing the game, our school and blackness. We felt black people needed to tell themselves they could succeed just like anybody else. So we had to be good."

Howard rolled through the regular season, outscoring its opponents 63–6. In the NCAA tournament, the Bison dispatched George Washington and Clemson before edging past Philadelphia Textile, 5–3, to reach the Final Four.

On a rainy December weekend at St. Louis's Busch Stadium, Howard slipped by Hartwick 2–1 to set up a rematch of the 1971 title game against the home team, all-white, all-American St. Louis University.

St. Louis dominated the first half, taking a 1–0 lead, while Howard equalized in the second. As the match went into overtime, the Bison took control. One Howard shot glanced off the Billikens' crossbar; another popped off the left post.

Finally, in the fourth overtime, Kenneth Ilodigwe, a Nigerian, took a crossing pass from Richard Davy, a Jamaican, and poked the ball into the goal for the 2–1 victory.

TWENTY-TWO YEARS LATER, Bain sits in his basement combing through two scrapbooks of articles and photographs. These days he teaches high school Spanish, and sometimes his students show him pictures from his playing career that they have found in the school library.

"Do you know what my fondest memory is?" he says. "Seeing Lincoln in the locker room after the game." In Busch Stadium that night Phillips was crying tears of joy.

"They had taken something away that was very special," Phillips says. "And when we got it back, the burden we had been carrying was gone. There was relief."

Says Bain, "Had we lost that tournament, it would have affected the rest of our lives. We had to put something right that we felt was wrong."

Yes, Hard Feelings

FROM *Sports Illustrated*, MARCH 28, 2005

One measure of soccer's growing standing stateside as Wahl's career blossomed was the richness of the developing rivalry between the United States and Mexico. The dynamic is a distinctive one. The Mexican team's massive following in the United States among those of Mexican heritage guarantees a large and passionate crowd for games on U.S. soil—indeed, the Mexican federation regularly stages lucrative friendlies in cities such as Dallas, Houston, and Los Angeles—and for years, crowds at U.S. "home" games against Mexico would overwhelmingly be cheering on El Tri. In response, U.S. Soccer hosted a February 2001 World Cup qualifier against Mexico in Columbus, Ohio. The result was a historic 2–0 win for the Americans, which was followed by an even more significant 2–0 victory over Mexico in the Round of 16 at the 2002 World Cup. (The United States would defeat Mexico four times in a row in World Cup qualifiers in Columbus, each time by the now-legendary *dos a cero* score line.) As the United States began to get the upper hand in the once lopsided rivalry, Wahl reported on the social, cultural, and historical impulses underlying the United States–Mexico soccer dynamic. As comfortable working in Spanish as in English and with a wealth of contacts in Mexican *fútbol,* Wahl revisited the impassioned rivalry time and again over the years to explore its evolving narratives. In 2022, working with Meadowlark Media, he coproduced *Good Rivals,* a three-part documentary on the rivalry that debuted on Prime Video two weeks before his death.

LANDON DONOVAN DOESN'T KNOW WHAT'S COMING THIS SUNday. He can't know. Not until you've played for the U.S. at Estadio Azteca in Mexico City can you understand what it's like to face your nation's most bitter soccer rival in that 115,000-seat cauldron, a place where the Americans have never won a game. U.S. veterans of the Azteca speak in evocative terms about sensory overload. The sound of the hostile fans? "Like playing inside a beehive," says midfielder Cobi Jones. The towering, almost vertical grandstands? "Like Mad Max's Thunderdome," says retired defender Alexi Lalas. The choking smog and 7,200-foot altitude? "I once saw Cobi cough up something that looked like a brownie," says former forward Eric Wynalda. "It's like never smoking your whole life, then being told to smoke a pack of cigarettes and try to function normally. You get sick."

The Yanks will get another taste of the Azteca—site of Pelé's exploits in the 1970 World Cup and Diego Maradona's in '86—when they face Mexico during the final stage of World Cup qualifying. Each side won its first of ten qualifiers, placing them at the top of the six-team group from North and Central America and the Caribbean. Only three of those teams are assured a berth next year in Germany. Donovan, the twenty-three-year-old U.S. captain, is preparing for the worst. "I've never played in front of a hundred thousand," he says. "From what I hear, every condition you can imagine is as bad as it gets: the crowd, the noise, the altitude, the smog, the field, the heat. That's what Mexico counts on, and you have to take it out of play."

So debilitating are conditions at the Azteca, says U.S. Soccer Federation executive vice president Sunil Gulati, that the USSF has tried to strike a deal with its Mexican counterpart on the sites for their home-and-home World Cup qualifiers: If you host your game in some other city—say, low-altitude Monterrey—we'll stage ours in heavily Hispanic Los Angeles, where Mexico's supporters normally outnumber U.S. fans by a factor of ten. The Tricolores have never accepted, prompting the USSF to schedule two straight qualifiers with Mexico during frigid weather in Columbus, Ohio. Mexican journos dubbed the most recent one, a 2–0 U.S. victory on a 29°F day in February 2001, *La Guerra Fría.* The Cold War.

That's typical for the most heated international rivalry in North American sports. Since 1934, the U.S. and Mexico have clashed forty-nine times on the soccer pitch, and though the Mexicans have dominated the series, 28–11–10, the Yanks have gained the upper hand in recent years with six wins in the last eight matches. Their most stunning victory came at the 2002 World Cup in Jeonju, South Korea: With the stakes the highest and the stage the largest, the U.S. eliminated Mexico 2–0 in the second round. For Mexican Americans whose *fútbol* loyalty lies with their native land, the agony of that loss remains vividly painful. "I have cried three times in my life," said Regelio Ruiz, a thirty-six-year-old used-car salesman from Las Vegas, while attending a Mexico-Argentina game in LA this month. "That day was one of them."

As with any worthwhile rivalry, U.S.-Mexico has had its excruciating moments. Like the time in 1997 when Mexico's Ramón Ramírez karate-kicked Lalas in the groin ("a full-frontal assault on my manhood," as the recipient put it). Or the manifold occasions on which Wynalda lashed out at Mexico fans in the U.S. ("The more people I had rooting against me," he says, "the more people I flipped off.") Or the 2004 Olympic qualifying tournament in Guadalajara, when the crowd chanted "Osama, Osama." Or that epic '02 World Cup match, during which, Donovan says, Mexican forward Luis Hernández turned to him after an on-field tangle and snarled, "I will find your mother and kill her."

"To say things like that is pretty evil," Donovan says. "I'm sure it's something he's forgotten, but I never will."

Though the Tricolores don't deny the intensity of the competition, not all of them take it personally. "The U.S. has grown so much in its soccer, because it has a league now and many players in Europe," says longtime Mexico goalkeeper Jorge Campos, now a national team assistant coach. "But that doesn't mean we hate the Americans. Cobi Jones is a very good friend of mine."

Yet much more than soccer fuels many Mexican fans' animus toward the U.S. team, says Rodolfo de la Garza, a Columbia professor who specializes in immigration studies. "There are very few instances in the history of the two countries where Mexico has either been dealt with fairly or has won when there were differences," he explains. "Central to Mexican nationalism is anti-Americanism. The U.S. invaded Mexico on various occasions, and by their judgment the Mexicans lost half their land. There's a built-in structure of resentment, a built-in rivalry.

"Mexicans have one big sport. They invest completely in it, and it is deeply resented that the U.S. beat them at the World Cup. That sticks in their craw. It should be their game. But the power and the money of the U.S. has denied them even that."

Maybe so, but if you're an American soccer player, it's hard to see yourself as the hegemonic power when the whistling and booing is directed at you in, for instance, LA. Says Lalas, "There were times I'd get off the field and think, The thousands of people who just cheered against their national team have reaped the incredible benefits of coming to the U.S., and yet they don't recognize that the team in red, white, and blue is much more representative of their lives than the team they're cheering for. We've had players from all different ethnicities, so we really represent what this country is about."

The U.S.'s recent domination has led to extensive soul-searching in the Mexican soccer community—as well as numerous theories to explain the change in fortunes. "For me it's easy," says Javier Aguirre, who coached Mexico's 2002 World Cup team and now runs Osasuna in Spain's La Liga. "In the last ten years the Americans have had thirty to forty players in Europe. We have two or three players in Europe, and that is the great difference. Mexico doesn't have that type of competition." In other words, the comfort of staying at home and playing in the relatively lucrative (but insular) Mexican Football League might be stunting the Tricolores' development as soccer players. (Though that doesn't account for the fact that three of the four U.S. goal scorers in World Cup 2002 represented the supposedly inferior MLS.)

Martín Vásquez, a Mexican American and the only player ever to compete for both countries, says the rise of U.S. soccer is tied to the type of players being drawn to the sport these days, ones who might once have chosen baseball, basketball, or football. "In Mexico maybe some of the players are more gifted," says Vásquez, who's now an assistant for the MLS team Chivas USA, "but I think the American players are catching up because they have something the Mexican players don't have: athleticism."

Yet perhaps the most fascinating explanation is that the Tricolores have somehow lost the confidence they once had when facing their northern neighbor. Rare is the discussion that doesn't included the word *mentalidad*. "I think it's a psychological game now," says Guillermo Cantú, a former player for Mexico who now directs its national teams. "The mentality is on the American side, and we have to steal it."

Rafael Ramos, who covers the Mexican team for the Spanish-language newspaper *La Opinión* in Los Angeles, takes the notion a step further. "The Mexican writer Octavio Paz once said, Mexicans have more fear of victory than of defeat," he explains. "The fans are the same way. Just watch this next game against the U.S. No matter how much confidence they have in their team—in the altitude, in the smog, in the pressure they'll bring against the U.S.—they will grow worried. There will be total euphoria the first ten to fifteen minutes, but if a goal doesn't come, there will be complete silence. The doubt kills you. It's a very Mexican idiosyncrasy."

The U.S. players' explanations for their recent success aren't so complex. "When it comes down to soccer, we're the better team," says Donovan. "But if we want to get to the next level, we need to win World Cup qualifiers on the road. For too long we've had this mindset that a tie on the road is good. I don't care if you throw all the [Azteca] factors in. We're a better team, and we should beat Mexico."

More than any other U.S. player, Donovan inspires mixed emotions from the Mexican fans. On the one hand, they appreciate his fluency in Spanish and his fast-but-precise playing style, which some observers consider vaguely Mexican. Not for nothing did Donovan receive a third-place vote from the Mexican federation in the 2002 FIFA World Player of the Year balloting. On the other hand, Donovan offended his hosts at the '04 Olympic qualifying tournament in Guadalajara, where he was caught relieving himself discreetly on a training-field shrub. Caught on video, the incident got huge play in the Mexican media. "To me it was never a big deal," he says. "I would say chanting 'Osama, Osama' carries a lot more weight than me going to the bathroom on the side of their field."

Ultimately, Donovan's best response might be the one that translates into any language: Scoreboard, baby. "If you're a Mexican soccer fan, it must be incredibly disheartening at this point," says Lalas. "Because that one thing that you could pin your hopes on was 'At least we're going to kick your ass on the soccer field.' When that's taken away, it must be depressing. But I'll tell you what: We've taken it away, and we're not giving it back. It's up to them to come and get it. And I hope that we keep kicking their ass, time and time again."

But it's one thing for that to happen in a U.S. stadium, quite another if it took place in the vaunted Azteca. "If Mexico loses at home against the United States," says Ramos, "only God can say what might happen."

On Sunday he may find out.

A Pacific Passion Play

FROM *Sports Illustrated*, MAY 23, 2011

Wahl's vision was for soccer to be covered in the United States like any another sport—without a need to explain the game to readers or justify its coverage to editors. He found a place to do that on *Sports Illustrated*'s website, where he approached soccer, both domestic and international, in much the same way *SI*'s NFL or NBA writers covered their beats. Wahl was a workhorse on the web, writing multiple times a week—gamers, profiles, power rankings, interviews, mailbags, dispatches from reporting outposts, opinion columns, and more. But he knew that to make the main magazine, a soccer piece—especially one on Major League Soccer, which lacked the glamour and global names of European football, the power of the World Cup, and the social relevance of the women's game—needed a strong cultural hook to persuade editors to devote precious (and dwindling) print pages to it. He landed a rare MLS magazine feature with this story about the burgeoning three-way rivalry in the Pacific Northwest that was nurturing a fan culture to equal anything in Europe or South America. Wahl had grown familiar with the distinctive culture of Cascadia from having lived in Seattle while his wife, Céline, attended medical school at the University of Washington during the early '00s.

Please: Don't make it like Seattle.

—Portland's mayor (played by KYLE MACLACHLAN) on
commissioning the city's new theme song in the IFC series *Portlandia*

T HE MOMENT WHEN THE PACIFIC NORTHWEST SUCCUMBED TO
soccer nirvana came during—what else?—a steady downpour at
8:03 P.M. last Saturday at Qwest Field in Seattle. On the night the Seattle
Sounders and the Portland Timbers resumed the fiercest rivalry in
American club soccer, a sellout crowd of 36,593 watched in awe as the
Emerald City Supporters unveiled a 23,000-square-foot display of nine
green-and-blue banners telling the pictorial story of the Sounders'
DECADES OF DOMINANCE over their Oregon neighbors—like cave
paintings of a modern-day sports culture.

Over in the stadium's northeast corner more than five hundred members of the Timbers Army had their own defiant banners proclaiming
themselves KINGS OF CASCADIA and announcing WE'RE THE TIMBERS
ARMY. WHO ARE YOU? And if the visuals weren't enough, well, there
were the songs. Like the one Portland fans sing to the tune of "Oh My
Darling, Clementine":

Build a bonfire, build a bonfire,
Put Seattle on the top,
Put Vancouver in the middle,
And we'll burn the bloody lot!

Or this serenade from Seattle fans:

Port-scum, Port-scum,
Seedy little city on a river of piss,
We'll drink your beer and shag your sis!

Last week's showdown, which ended in a 1–1 tie, was just the latest
evidence that the Cascadia region has become the hotbed of Major
League Soccer. Two years after the Sounders joined the league, their average attendance (36,350) is far and away the highest in MLS—which
has a leaguewide average of 17,150—and would have ranked ninth in the

English Premier League, sixth in Spain's La Liga, second in France's Ligue 1, and fourth in Italy's Serie A. In Portland the expansion Timbers are the new darlings of MLS, winning their first four home games while boasting regular sellouts at Jeld-Wen Field (capacity 18,627), as well as a chain saw–wielding human mascot who saws a slab off a giant log for every Portland goal and clean sheet. Meanwhile, the Vancouver White-caps have joined the Timbers as another expansion heavyweight, averaging 19,970 fans, nearing the top of MLS in sponsorships and generating celebrity buzz north of the border. (NBA star Steve Nash, a native son and lifelong soccer fanatic, is one of the owners.)

MLS is growing up in its sixteenth season, and while the Pacific Northwest teams have no desire to foster a violent hooligan culture—beefed-up security kept the Portland supporters apart from Seattle fans on Saturday—they aren't aiming for a G-rated atmosphere, either. "It's not a Disney movie in that way," says Joe Roth, the Sounders' majority owner, who knows whereof he speaks, having run Disney Studios from 1994 to 2000. Roth believes Sounders-Timbers has the chance to become one of the best rivalries in American sports.

The game capped a fevered week of anticipation from the Emerald City to the Rose City and all the way to Los Angeles, where Roth laid down the smack to Timbers owner Merritt Paulson at a league owners meeting three days before. "We're going to kick your ass this weekend," said Roth, playfully cuffing Paulson, the son of former U.S. Treasury secretary Henry Paulson. "Take your best shot," replied Paulson, who (like most Oregonians) chafes at the notion of Portland as Seattle's little brother. "It's correct if you're talking about the size of the cities," he says, "but I have a lot of friends who've got two boys, and the elder boy is a little soft and the little one kicks his ass repeatedly."

WHILE LAST WEEK'S game was the first Seattle-Portland meeting in MLS, the rivalry dates to 1975, when the North American Soccer League's Sounders and Timbers had some legendary battles. Seattle, Portland, and Vancouver all competed in the NASL with the same franchise names, leaving a mark with fans who are still around. "When you tie in that history, it creates a sense of community and it adds a sense of richness to your club," says Keith Hodo, the copresident of Emerald City

Supporters, the Sounders' leading fan club. After the NASL folded in 1985, the enmity between the Sounders and the Timbers only continued as the teams competed against each other in minor leagues and in the U.S. Open Cup, a knockout tournament like England's FA Cup. "Any other rivalry in this league has sort of been a created rivalry," says Seattle coach Sigi Schmid. "This rivalry has history. It's been there the last thirty-plus years, and that makes it the best rivalry in the league."

Sounders goalkeeper Kasey Keller played for England's Millwall FC in its notoriously bitter rivalry with West Ham United and says he now sees some similarities in Seattle-Portland. "It's turning into that kind of rivalry here, and that's a cool thing to be in," Keller says, adding that he has no desire for there to be any Millwall-style fan violence. "It shows the healthiness of the sport and where it's moving." As if to prove the point, Keller was booed not long ago by Portland fans while attending a Trail Blazers game (even though he attended the University of Portland and briefly played for a semipro incarnation of the Timbers in 1989).

Fans on both sides of the divide can recall the rivalry's memorable moments. There was the time in 1975 when Portland beat Seattle on a sudden-death goal in the NASL playoffs and Timbers fans stormed the field like a college basketball crowd rushing the court after a huge upset. Or the time when the Timbers Army created a twenty-foot-high banner display of Timber Jim, the team's mascot, taking a chain saw to the Space Needle. Or the time in 2009 when forward Roger Levesque scored for Seattle against Portland and celebrated by impersonating a falling tree, with teammate Nate Jaqua taking simulated ax swipes at his feet. (So despised is Levesque by Timbers fans that when he joined Portland for one game as a guest player in '07 they still booed him every time he touched the ball.)

The fans never forget. Over pints of Cascade Autumn Gose and Lucky Lab No Pity last week at Bailey's Taproom in Portland, a half-dozen Timbers Army leaders described their fan group—which fills more than 3,600 seats in a designated section at all home games—and told their side of the grudgefest. "It's fair to say there's genuine malice toward each other," said Dave Hoyt, the group's president, a thirty-three-year-old hospital administrator. "We have put a lot of time into cultivating the hate over the years."

"And a lot of the malice goes beyond soccer," added Garrett Dittfurth,

thirty-two, an analyst at a public relations firm. "Seattle was like the pinnacle of American coolness in the '90s, right? Now things have changed
a little bit if you want to talk about creativity, arts, and music.

"Then there's that big-city mentality they have in Seattle, and down
here we're like 'You've gotta be kidding me,'" Dittfurth continued. "They
have a lot more of an East Coast mentality than we do, and that kind of
pervades on the field. You feel that air of superiority."

If the Emerald City Supporters group felt threatened by Portland's
rise, they certainly didn't show it on Friday night at a warehouse party in
Seattle's Capitol Hill neighborhood. As techno music thumped and a
three-on-three soccer tournament took place on an indoor field, the
youthful leaders of the ECS sipped from cups of Brougham Bitter (the
fan group's official craft beer) and explained how they had set a new
standard among MLS fans by leading stadium-wide chants, building a
membership of 1,200 hard-core members, and organizing group road
trips to games around North and Central America. They laughed when
reminded of the billboard the Timbers paid to put up last year near Seattle's Qwest Field:

PORTLAND, OREGON
SOCCER CITY USA 2011

"It was like shooting a tank with a pellet," said Hodo, a twenty-eight-
year-old programmer, who was wearing a Mohawk and a black T-shirt
for the punk band Rancid.

"We're at thirty-two thousand season tickets, and they sold like thirteen thousand," said copresident Greg Mockos, twenty-eight, an engi-
neering consultant. "On their opening night you could argue that maybe
they did exceed our passion, but tomorrow we'll remind them where
they stand. And the same with Vancouver."

How did soccer get so big in the Pacific Northwest? While the area's
NASL history certainly played a role, so did geography. "We're pretty
isolated up here, the only three cities until you get to California," says
Adrian Hanauer, the Sounders' general manager and a minority owner.
"There's nobody else for us to hate and battle with."

That said, the relationship with Vancouver is slightly different. Yes,
the Whitecaps have a history with Portland and Seattle, and the team

that's most successful in games involving the trio each season wins a traveling trophy called the Cascadia Cup. But Vancouver has its own Canadian rivalry with Toronto FC and the Montreal Impact, who will move up next year from the second tier to become MLS's nineteenth team. Vancouver's fans also seem to be lacking in vitriol. "It's hard to dislike them because they're so nice," says Timbers Army member Scott Van Swearingen. As the ECS's Mockos says, "They're like the nice cousin that's never going to offend anyone at a party."

The Sounders made their MLS debut in 2009, filling the void left by the departure of the NBA's SuperSonics. As comedian Drew Carey puts it, "We were like 'Hey, does your man treat you bad? Come out with us!'" Carey joined the ownership group as a minority partner in 2007 over a lunch in Los Angeles with Roth, during which he persuaded the Sounders' principal owner to embrace two unusual ideas: having a marching band for the team and allowing the fans to vote every four years on whether to keep the general manager. As an NFL fan, Carey had felt badly for supporters of the Detroit Lions, whose owners had kept Matt Millen in charge of the team for seven years despite his abject failures. "If they had the system the Sounders use in Detroit," Carey says, "the fans could have risen up and fired Matt Millen and made them hire somebody new."

Carey's populist idea (which he took from the elections for team presidents at clubs like Barcelona) was only part of an inaugural season in '09 that could not have gone any better. Seattle won the first of back-to-back U.S. Open Cups, qualified for the MLS playoffs, and led the league in attendance by a wide margin. "I tell people, 'If you are a soccer fan, you've got to come to a game here,'" says Schmid, a two-time MLS champion coach, "because it's everything we'd always hoped it would be."

The same could be said for the Timbers' debut this year. Portland's renovated stadium isn't as big as Seattle's, but the Timbers Army is right on top of the field and sings throughout the game. Before the club won its home opener 4–2 against Chicago last month, the Army delivered a moving a cappella version of the national anthem. "I don't think you'll ever see an atmosphere better than this," says the Timbers' Scottish coach, John Spencer.

One of Portland's distinctive aspects is Timber Joey, aka logger Joey

Webber, who (like his predecessor, Timber Jim) chain saws a slab of log in front of the fans whenever the team scores a goal. At the end of each home game, the Timbers players are presented their slabs and share in the celebration with the fans. Webber can tell you the exact day Timber Jim retired—January 24, 2008—and from that moment he wanted to take the legend's place at the log. "It was such a piece of home to me to see these logging skills used in Portland that I didn't want it to go away," says Webber. "It's a great tradition," says forward Kenny Cooper. "I haven't seen anything like it before."

Security prevented Timber Joey from bringing his chain saw into the Qwest Field stands on Saturday, but you'd better believe he'll have it with him on July 10 when it's Portland's turn to host Seattle. The 1–1 tie last week was a positive result for the Timbers, who were tied for fifth with the Sounders in the Western Conference (with 14 points) but had played two fewer games. Afterward, Spencer could barely contain his glee over producing one of the most rewarding ties he had ever experienced. "I can't wait to get 'em down to Portland and let them see our superfans at home," the Timbers' coach said. "Let's see if they can control the game the way we did up here tonight."

And with that, the war of words started for the next installment of the best rivalry in American soccer.

The World's Team

FROM *Sports Illustrated*, OCTOBER 8, 2012

This feature on the most popular and admired club in the world was slated for the cover of *SI*—a landmark for Wahl's budding career as a writer dedicated solely to soccer—before being bumped for a piece on the 2012 NFL referee lockout, which had come to a head with a series of disastrous incidents the previous Sunday in games being called by replacement refs. In fact, it was the second time Barcelona had been bumped from the *SI* cover in the span of a year. The previous December, in an effort to boost its social media following, the magazine had decided to let fans vote on Facebook for the "Moment of the Year," with the winner earning the cover for the 2011 year-end double issue. Lionel Messi's performance in Barcelona's Champions League final victory—"soccer's most thrilling display of the past twenty-five years," Wahl dubbed it in this story—was among the nominees, and when he tweeted out Messi's candidacy, it mobilized Barça fan clubs and the team itself. That global fan base vaulted Messi and Co. into the lead in the balloting, to the dismay of certain decision makers at the magazine who blanched at the thought of a foreign soccer player on the cover of an issue that would sit on newsstands for two weeks over the holidays. Thankfully for them (and suspiciously to others), the return of paralyzed Rutgers football player Eric LeGrand received a late push in the polling and surpassed Messi and Barcelona on the final day of the vote. Messi would have to wait until 2014 for his first *SI* cover, one of four alternates for that year's World Cup preview issue.

THE HOGWARTS OF SPORTS IS A SPARKLING STEEL-AND-GLASS building in Sant Joan Despí, a sleepy suburb not far from the Gaudí-bejeweled center of Barcelona. On a starlit night with breezes blowing in off the Mediterranean, the teams of FC Barcelona's youth academy descend in waves of yellow onto a manicured practice field. They march down from La Masia (the Farmhouse), the name given to the three-hundred-year-old residence that housed Barça's first academy and now adorning the decidedly less bucolic school at the club's new $87 million training headquarters.

It's a special evening, a chance for Barça to shoot team photographs under the floodlights and present its best and brightest to a gathering of proud parents in the stands. A phalanx of taxis waits in the parking lot, meters running, ready to ferry teen and preteen prospects from Catalonian towns back to their homes, as they do every night at the club's expense. Most of the remaining two-thirds of the academy's players—boarders from other Spanish regions and a dozen countries—live on-site in an educational and sporting laboratory that is both nurturing and fiercely competitive.

The children draw closer. You study their faces and can't help but wonder: Which of these eight- and twelve- and fourteen-year-olds might turn into the planet's best soccer player, the closest thing in sports to King of the World? Which ones will help add to Barça's Champions League titles, three in the last seven seasons? Usually such questions are preposterous. Most top European clubs—Manchester United, Real Madrid, Chelsea—are lucky to have even one homegrown player in their starting lineups. But La Masia's track record of developing champions is unprecedented, the evidence visible every time FC Barcelona takes the field.

In Barça's Champions League game against Spartak Moscow on September 19, eight of the team's eleven starters—including Lionel Messi, the world's preeminent player—were products of the club's youth academy. On Barça's first goal, forward Cristian Tello (who joined the club at age thirteen) cut inside on a dime and blasted a shot from distance into the right corner. Later, with Barça down 2–1, Tello slalomed past a defender and fed Messi (who also joined at thirteen) for the tap-in equalizer. Finally, as Spartak desperately crowded all eleven players behind the ball, Barça unspooled a majestic sequence from its own half: eighteen passes, short and long, on the ground and in the air, using the full width of the field.

There's a tantric rhythm to Barcelona's scoring buildups that Sting would love: Pass and move, pass and move. Each man on the ball has at least two options, creating triangles large and small, a blend of movement and geometry that calls to mind the turning wheel of a kaleidoscope as the attack proceeds inexorably downfield. Spartak was powerless. Barça's passing sequence involved nine players in fifty-five seconds, including academy products Xavi (from age eleven), Cesc Fàbregas (from ten), Pedro (from seventeen), Sergio Busquets (from seventeen) and, as ever, Messi. The twenty-five-year-old Argentine is capable of astonishing individual pyrotechnics—see his snaking sixty-yard scoring run to beat six Getafe defenders in 2007—but his game-winning header against Spartak off Alexis Sánchez's cross was something else, a true team goal, the difference between a cobra strike and a python's slow asphyxiation. Both, in the end, are lethal.

Today's Barça academy members know all of Messi's greatest hits. Only a few of these boys will survive the club's ruthless cuts and join him on the first team someday, but by the time they do they will feel FC Barcelona—the history, the identity, the style—in their blood and in their bones.

Barça's president, Sandro Rosell, knows this. On a hope-filled night with soccer's school of wizardry looming behind him, Rosell addresses the future Messis and Xavis and their parents in Catalan, waxing philosophical about the role of La Masia. "This is the essence of the club," he concludes, his hands outstretched, before leading everyone in a thunderous chant:

Visca Barça!
Visca Catalunya!

———

HISTORY MATTERS. AND SO, after Barcelona won the Champions League final in May 2011, pounding Manchester United 3–1 in soccer's most thrilling display of the past twenty-five years, defender Gerard Piqué did something no one else had tried at the sport's marquee annual event: He cut down the net. All 452 square feet of it. As he strode across the field, piles of nylon billowing over his shoulders, Piqué resembled a Catalonian fisherman bringing in a prize catch. "When I see a basketball team win, they cut down the net," explains Piqué, twenty-five, a Barça academy product. "So I said, 'Why not us?'"

Part of the net now hangs on a wall in Piqué's home, a tangible reminder of the day Barcelona reached a new pinnacle. It wasn't just that it had outclassed England's most storied team or that it claimed another coveted winner's trophy, one of a remarkable fourteen in twenty competitions over the past five seasons. (No other team has come close.) The spectacle also hailed the triumph of an idea: that beautiful, intricate soccer can be winning soccer, and that it can be homegrown. Two years ago all three finalists for the FIFA Ballon d'Or, given to the world's best player, had developed as children at FC Barcelona: Messi, the winner, and midfield string pullers Xavi and Andrés Iniesta. It was as though three people from the same middle school had won Nobel Prizes.

Imagine that nearly all the members of the New York Yankees lineup had played baseball in the organization since their early to mid-teens, and you'd have Barcelona, which meets Real Madrid this Sunday in the latest edition of the sports world's fiercest rivalry. "I've played with some of my teammates since I was twelve," says Fàbregas, now twenty-five. "When Messi first came, we were both thirteen. He was so tiny! We're all more like friends, and we fight for each other. I could go with this team to the end of the world."

Experts have scrambled to put Barcelona's feats in historical context. "In my time as manager, it's the best team we have played," said Sir Alex Ferguson, Man United's coach since 1986, after the 2011 defeat. Where does the Barcelona of the past five years rank among the top soccer teams of all time? "The short answer is by far the best," says Ray Hudson, the poet laureate of Spanish soccer for beIN Sports television, launching into a six-minute ode that is anything but a short answer. "I can't imagine anybody going beyond this purest example of football. They have spoiled the game for me. When I try to watch other teams and other leagues, it's like I've just read a wonderful novel and gone back to nursery-rhyme books."

As Barcelona aims for its third Champions League title in five seasons, its popularity, like Piqué's clever net removal, transcends soccer itself. In 1992, the Dream Team swaggered into the Barcelona Olympics with the signature basketball players of a generation—Michael Jordan, Magic Johnson, Larry Bird—and changed the face of global sports. Now, twenty years later, it's as though Barcelona is returning the favor, mesmerizing hard-core *fútbol* followers while winning new hearts and minds for the Beautiful Game. When *SI* conducted a Facebook survey asking users to name their top sports moment of 2011, Messi's Champions League final performance received more first-place votes from the U.S. than the champions of the NFL, NBA, and NHL. In New York City's Times Square, chances are you'll see as many Messi Barcelona jerseys on people as the shirt of any other athlete. Barça's Facebook page has 35 million subscribers, more than any other sports team.

There have been other international sports dynasties—Jordan's six-time NBA champion Bulls, for example—but at least one authority on soccer and the NBA thinks Barcelona has left those teams behind. "To win in Spain and around Europe and the world club competition the way they have, it's unprecedented in the modern era," says two-time NBA MVP Steve Nash, an ardent *culé* (Barça fan) who dragged his girlfriend to watch Messi's Marauders on a pub TV during a Jamaican vacation last year. "And to do it with the style and beauty they've done it with, you've got to give them extra credit. Not that the Bulls weren't fun to watch, but this is something else."

In an era in which supporting the Yankees and the Heat feels like cheering for Microsoft, you can root for FC Barcelona and feel good about it on every level. Barça is the paragon of a championship sports team: exciting, homegrown, tied to the community, with an inspiring social mission and the world's most magical player. What's more, Barcelona players are the core of Spain's national team, the first to hold the World Cup and two European crowns at the same time.

History matters. Barcelona is already pulling away in the Spanish league, and it's favored to win the Champions League. If the club can raise both trophies again, there will be no doubt: Barça is the team of our time.

LIONEL ANDRÉS MESSI has inspired millions of words in a babel of tongues, but perhaps the best way to summarize him is this: When he is in the game, even hard-core fans might witness something they have never seen before. Take Barcelona's 2–0 victory over Granada on September 22. Late in the game Messi dribbled from the left side into the penalty area, where two defenders sandwiched him, briefly dislodging the ball. In a split second, at full speed, Messi flicked his foot behind him to tap the ball, ran around the defender to meet the ball again, and pinballed a low cross off Granada defender Borja Gómez and into the net.

The stat sheet would list it as an own goal, but the rest of us could only watch in disbelief. *A backheel to himself. In the box.* Even Hudson, calling the game on TV, was at a loss for words: "Just another out-of-body experience for Lionel Messi." Indeed, it's hard not to get spiritual watching Messi. Just as the Bulls' triangle offense needed a sporting genius for it to enter the pantheon, so too does Barcelona's triangle offense. "It's a special group of players with obvious talent," says Fàbregas, "and the best player that there has ever been."

The résumé Messi has already produced at age twenty-five only begins to make the case: a world-record 73 goals in all club competitions last season, including an unprecedented 5 in one Champions League game; 252 goals and 89 assists in 331 Barça appearances at week's end; three Champions League and five Spanish league titles; and three straight world player of the year awards, also unprecedented. Already he has joined Pelé and Diego Maradona in the debate over the greatest player of all time, and while detractors note that Messi has yet to win a World Cup (Pelé won three, Maradona one), it's also true that the sport has changed since the days of those older stars. The Champions League is now viewed in many precincts as a superior competition to the World Cup because it features more top players, a bigger sample size, and a higher level of play than international soccer's marquee quadrennial event. Pelé never played club soccer in Europe, while Maradona never won the top European club crown, which was decided by a smaller-scale tournament during his career. If Messi keeps winning the most important club trophies and putting up off-the-charts numbers with Barça, he may not need the World Cup to be called the greatest.

Messi's relationship with his Barcelona teammates is strikingly symbiotic. For all of Barça's ball possession, little of it would matter if Messi were not there to finish. To understand what Barça might be like without Messi, look at Spain during much of Euro 2012, when La Roja kept other teams from scoring but had trouble doing so itself. Yet Messi needs his Barça teammates if he's to play at *his* highest level. Without them—and especially without the intuitive understanding he shares with Xavi and Iniesta—Messi can sometimes be frustrated and diminished, not least when he's playing for Argentina.

When fans from his home country want to sting Messi, they say he's more Catalan than Argentine. It's not true. Messi still consumes Argentine beef and maté tea, speaks Spanish with an Argentine accent, and is awaiting the birth of his first child with girlfriend Antonela Roccuzzo, who's from his hometown of Rosario. Then again, Messi also embodies traits more commonly associated with Catalans, who are known for dealmaking, efficiency, and a cleverness that has a softer edge than its Argentine counterpart. While Maradona's brilliance came by any means necessary—including scoring a goal with his fist in the 1986 World Cup—Messi is known for his fair play. Despite the sometimes brutal defending he faces, he does not dive. Messi's rise into the sporting stratosphere has paralleled Barcelona's. Small wonder that Barça's fans in the Camp Nou consider him one of their own.

The 5'7" Messi is a master of many things, from balance and coordination to speed and a seemingly limitless imagination on the field. Alas, describing his talents in his own words, as many have learned, is not among them. Perhaps by design, Messi is as reserved as Maradona is bombastic. Fortunately, Messi's teammates are happy to speak for him. They grow animated when asked the question "As someone who has reached the top of the sport yourself, what do you see in Messi that impresses you the most?"

On a sun-filled morning at the team's training complex, Xavi's eyes widen and he gets jazz hands as he talks about Messi. "The hardest thing in soccer is to take on the defender and dribble around him," he says. "Well, Messi dribbles around four, five, six, seven, and scores. That's practically impossible today. Everybody is physically strong, tall. In a combination play you can get there, but he does it by himself and does it in each game. In soccer there are two speeds: physical, the speed of your legs, and mental. I only have this one"—Xavi points to his head—"but he has both. That's why he's the best in the world."

Other elements are in play too. Fàbregas explains why he thinks Messi is the real thing: "When the final ball is played he's always on the end of things, but it's because he makes the really big effort to get in the nice positions. His desire is so big that he makes the other players look like they don't want it as bad."

What's more, Messi's teammates say, he's the last person you'd expect to issue an "Are we talkin' about practice?" rant in the Allen Iverson mold. "[He] could say, 'OK, I'm the best, but in training I don't care, I can be lazy,'" says Piqué, "but he's working at the same level in training as well. It's unbelievable."

Xavi thinks Messi will spend his entire career at Barcelona. "He's happy, and he was raised here," Xavi says. "I don't think he can leave for another club." That's not to say Messi will stand still. In the face of new challenges, remaining at the top requires reinvention. Barcelona lost enough of its edge last season to finish second in the Spanish league behind Real Madrid and go out in the Champions League semifinals to the eventual surprise winner, Chelsea. Pep Guardiola, the Barça coach and mastermind who also developed as a player at La Masia, left his job at age forty-one after a remarkable four-year run. (He's taking a year's sabbatical with his family in New York City.)

Can Barcelona return to dominance under Guardiola's former assistant, Tito Vilanova? And can Messi and Barça find ways to beat teams that follow Chelsea's playbook and pack as many players as possible in the defensive end? "That's the key about Messi: As a player he's reinventing himself each season, improving year after year," says Carles Folguera, the director of Barcelona's youth academy. "He's not only a top scorer but an assist leader as well. He can play on the wings and up the middle. That's his own ability to grow and improve and take a hard look at himself."

With all the changes, there's a sense that Messi is entering a new phase of his career, like Picasso making the transition from his Blue Period to Cubism. In that case, Messi has chosen the right place, a city in which soccer and art are one and the same.

THE PROCESSION NEVER stops. In the shadow of the Camp Nou, Barcelona's 98,000-seat stadium, the FC Barcelona museum attracts an endless stream of visitors. Foreign tourists are among the pilgrims, of course, but so are waves of Catalans: schoolkids on field trips, old-timers reliving childhood memories, teenage girls tittering over giant photographs of Piqué and Messi and Fàbregas. The shrine to Barça's past and present is the most visited museum in the city, more than those devoted to Picasso and Miró, more than the museum at La Sagrada Família.

The FC Barcelona motto—*Més que un club*, Catalan for "More than a club"—is deliberately open-ended. In one sense it refers to Barça's social mission as a 113-year-old organization with 118,000 dues-paying members who vote in elections for the club's leaders. For years Barça was the only major soccer team that refused to sell space on its jersey to a corporate sponsor, before making the novel decision in 2006 to donate about $2 million a year and put UNICEF's logo there. (The big-spending Qatar Foundation replaced it last season in a $225 million sponsorship deal as Barça addressed a $430 million net debt amassed largely through bank loans to pay for transfers; but UNICEF remains on the back.)

In another sense the motto highlights Barcelona's place as a touchstone for Catalan identity. "It's the people's club," says Rosell, a former Nike executive who once served as a ball boy at the Camp Nou. "It's a club that understands what it means to be from Barcelona and Catalonia, what it means to be a club that had run-ins with a dictatorship for forty years and survived with values opposed to what the dictatorship stood for."

FC Barcelona first became a political force in 1918, when it joined a campaign for the autonomy of Catalonia from Castilian Spain. After Barça fans booed the Spanish national anthem in 1925, the military regime of Miguel Primo de Rivera shut down the club for six months and forced its founder, Joan Gamper, and his family to leave the country. During the Spanish Civil War police supporting General Francisco Franco arrested and executed Barça's president, Josep Sunyol, after he tried to visit Republican troops protecting Madrid against a right-wing siege. Catalonia bitterly resisted Franco's coup, and when Barcelona finally fell, the general's troops bombed the building that held Barça's trophies. Problems between the club and the Spanish state only continued during Franco's thirty-six-year rule. The dictatorship forced the club to change its name to the Spanish Club de Fútbol Barcelona and ended its direct elections. Yet Barça's stadium remained the only place where 100,000 Catalans could voice their fury at Franco, who refrained from crushing their protests.

Franco was a soccer fan. His favorite team was Real Madrid, which met Barcelona in the semifinals of the General's Cup in 1943, four years after the end of the Spanish Civil War. Barça won the first leg 3–0, but Franco's director of state security entered the locker room before the return leg in Madrid and warned Barcelona's players that the regime had graciously allowed them to return to Spain from wartime exile. During a time of violent reprisals against dissidents, the menace in his hint was unmistakable; Barcelona took the field and lost 11–1.

Barça won two Spanish titles over Real Madrid in the early 1950s, but in '53 the Franco-controlled national soccer federation settled a dispute between the two rivals over the signing of Argentine star Alfredo Di Stéfano that resulted in his joining Madrid. He would lead Real to an unprecedented five straight European Cup titles from 1956 through 1960 and help turn Real into the world's preeminent team.

"When I talk to Real Madrid historians, they always ask me, 'Was Real Madrid manipulating the military or was the military manipulating Real Madrid?'" says Carles Santacana, a historian at the University of Barcelona. The Marshall Plan had given nothing to Spain, a neutral Axis ally that was isolated internationally after World War II. But relations between Franco and the former Allies began thawing in the 1950s, leading to Spain's admission to the United Nations in 1955. Real Madrid became a face of that change. "Starting with the European Cup, it was a way for the Spanish authorities to say, 'We're something in the world, in Europe,'" says Santacana. "A foreign minister said Real Madrid was Spain's best ambassador."

The turning point for Barça came during Franco's final years, in the early 1970s, when more backroom intrigue sent the visionary Dutch player Johan Cruyff to Barcelona. After the Di Stéfano controversy, the Spanish federation forbade new signings of foreigners for two decades, unless those players were the sons of Spaniards who had emigrated to Latin America. In 1971, the federation allowed thirty-eight of those so-called *oriundos* to join Spanish teams but nixed Barça's signings of two of them. Suspecting it was being singled out, Barcelona sent a lawyer to South America to check the documentation of the thirty-eight, according to Santacana. "Only one had legitimate paperwork," the historian says. "The rest falsified theirs. Barça put the report on the table and came to an agreement with the federation not to release it in exchange for the lifting of the ban on foreigners. And that's how they signed Cruyff in 1973."

One of the greatest players of all time, Cruyff had the attitude to match his stature, and he wasn't afraid to voice his political views: He said he would never have joined Real Madrid because of its association with Franco. In his debut season with Barcelona, the twenty-six-year-old Cruyff led the club to the Spanish league title, its first in fourteen years, including a historic 5–0 victory at Real. "You can still get older people to start crying about that day," says Sam Lardner, a former Barça ice hockey player who has lived in Barcelona since 1997 and served on the board of Cruyff's foundation. "Catalan culture is wrapped up in pact making. Catalans are not an aggressive people. They have never had a decisive strategic military victory in their history. So Johan was walking into a cultural feeling of never quite being able to win that goes way back. When he did that, it was like: wow."

Yet Cruyff's legacy at Barça has come less as a player than as the embodiment of a philosophy, one that now seeps through every level of the club down to the youth teams. Based on the Dutch school of soccer, it values skill over brawn, ball possession over quick-hit counterattacks, entertainment over pragmatism. Cruyff instilled the idea as Barça's coach from 1988 to '96, winning four Spanish league titles and a European Cup, and the style is constantly being refined. "Cruyff's first rule or idea was to defend through ball possession," says Xavi, thirty-two. "If there's only one ball in play and you have control of it, you don't need to defend. And then the idea of attacking soccer: triangles, long possessions. We've had this philosophy since Cruyff came, and now we've had the good fortune of having a fantastic generation of players."

How that generation arrived at the top of the soccer world is the story of La Masia.

CESC FÀBREGAS CAN remember the exhaustion he felt as a ten-year-old. Every weekday at 5:00 P.M., a taxi would pick him up at his house in Arenys de Mar, twenty-five miles outside Barcelona. In the next two hours the taxi would make five other stops before delivering the half-dozen boys to practice at the Barça youth academy, which in those days was next to the Camp Nou. A ninety-minute practice would follow, and then another two-hour cab ride home, followed by dinner, homework, a few hours of sleep, and back to school the next morning at seven. "I was too tired as a young boy, and I couldn't sleep very well, but this is what I loved," he says. "So after three years I moved to La Masia."

They all have their sacrifice stories, from Fàbregas to Messi (who moved from Argentina to Barcelona with his family in early adolescence) to hundreds of other prospects who didn't make the grade.

Founded in 1979 as the brainchild of Cruyff, Barcelona's youth academy is based on the one run by Ajax, the Amsterdam club that gave the Dutchman his start. The guiding principle is to instill the same skill-based philosophy that guides the senior team. "It's like getting a master's in soccer," Xavi says. "In each session they teach you objectives. Why do we do this exercise? Many teams train just to get physically fit, but the key is to understand the game, to choose the moment you play the ball short in order to then play it long. To know how to decide on the field is the most important thing they teach at La Masia. But it's also a school of life because it teaches you the values of respect, humility, and camaraderie. It's a way to live soccer and life."

The emphasis is on quality over quantity of practice time. Training sessions take place from 7:00 to 8:30 P.M.—three times a week for academy members under thirteen, four times for older ones—with a game on the weekend. For boarders, the typical day involves attending school from 8:00 A.M. to 2:00 P.M., returning for lunch and then homework until six, followed by practice. Of the eighty current residents at La Masia, fifty-eight are there for soccer, the rest for basketball, handball, and ice hockey. Merely by being admitted to the academy, youngsters have survived a competitive winnowing process. "You always seek talent," says Guillermo Amor, a former academy graduate and Barcelona player and now La Masia's sporting director. "That's fundamental, to have very good players at a young age. Before, you sought out fourteen- and fifteen-year-old kids. Now you have to go younger. That makes us work hard to get the best players in our seventh soccer division, who are the smallest and start with seven-year-olds."

The way Amor sees it, La Masia's success comes from having the confidence to place faith in young players and train them to excel on the global stage. When in doubt, most top teams choose to spend millions to bring in a proven star. While most major European clubs have youth academies, few are as committed to inculcating in their young players an entire philosophy. Barça has selectively tabbed established players, such as David Villa and Ronaldinho, but its preference is to dip into the prospect pool. It helps that everyone can see the results of the process every time Barcelona's senior team takes the field. But unlike the first team, the youth academy isn't about the unceasing pursuit of trophies. "We never tell kids, 'Go out and win, win, win; we want titles,'" says

Amor. "We're forming players—people—and there will be time to win the day they play on the first team. But not to win at any price. We want to win by controlling the ball, bringing it up from the back, taking the initiative, dominating. That's our style."

There's a human side to the academy, of course. Only a handful of chosen ones will reach the senior team. At the end of every spring the academy directors make their cuts—"the hardest moment," Amor says, in part because the emotional bonds are so tight.

"When we talk about La Masia, we do so as if it were a family for these kids," says Folguera, the academy director. "We know about their grades, their nutrition, the problems they have, how they get along with their families, if they have girlfriends. We're always with them." For the same reasons, those who do make it feel as if the club is part of their fundamental identity. For them, the Barcelona shirt is never just laundry.

Nor for Barça is producing players the same as making widgets. "We're not going to clone Xavi, Messi, or Iniesta just because in X number of years they're not going to be around anymore," says Andoni Zubizarreta, Barça's football director, "but the idea behind our style will be."

Who will be La Masia's gems of the next generation? Perhaps Gerard Deulofeu, eighteen, a forward from nearby Girona who has already debuted with the senior team. Or Jean Marie Dongou, seventeen, a marvelously talented Cameroonian striker. Or Alejandro Grimaldo, seventeen, a gifted left back from Valencia. Who knows? For the first time there's even an American at La Masia: Ben Lederman, a midfielder from the Los Angeles area. After being chosen in a tryout, Lederman moved to Barcelona with his family last year so that he could join the academy.

He's twelve.

———

MORE THAN A club. The reminders of Barça's transcendence are large and small, global and domestic. During a Champions League game at the Camp Nou last month, large sections of the stadium dusted off the old chants for Catalan independence, amid Catalan political leader Artur Mas's calls for fiscal sovereignty from the rest of Spain and a subsequent march of 1.5 million Catalans in the streets of Barcelona on September 11.

What's more, at a time when the unemployment rate in Spain is hovering at 25 percent, at least one player is acutely aware of the role Barça plays in society. Messi may be Barcelona's resident genius, but the keeper of Cruyff's flame is Xavi, the figure who most clearly embodies the club's philosophy, now and in the future. Cruyff himself rarely visits anymore, the result of disagreements with Rosell, the club's president. But Xavi has lived the apotheosis of Cruyff's Barcelona, winning three Champions League titles—and, playing a similar style, a World Cup and the last two Euros with Spain. Xavi thinks the game more than any other Barça player. In the past two seasons he has nine of the top fifteen Champions League performances in terms of completed passes in a match. He will almost surely coach Barcelona someday.

In an era in which athleticism, defense, and brawn have threatened to take over the world's game, Xavi feels in his core that Barcelona is fighting for the soul of soccer. "I believe in this philosophy of ours," he says, "but years ago, because we weren't winning, people had doubts. Italy had won the World Cup; Greece had won the Euro. The Champions League was won by physical teams. And I thought, No, it can't be. Soccer is talent, you know. For the good of the fans, for the good of the game, talented players should always play the sport. But I'm a soccer romantic, and there are others who only want to win, win, compete, defend. Hell no. Soccer can be very beautiful."

If that sounds romantic, then so be it. Barcelona has taken the game to places it has never been, exceeding what we thought was possible, creating new fans in the process. "They've raised people's appreciation of what they do beyond simple sport, as all greats do," says Graham Hunter, author of *Barça: The Making of the Greatest Team in the World*. "I don't think it's false to say that in times of economic crisis, when a lot of people around the world are fearful for their daily existence, it's as if God sent this era at Barcelona."

In a sometimes ugly world the team of our time brings a simple joy. When Xavi ventures out into the city, older fans, the ones who know the history, stop him on the street, pulling him close. "They tell me, 'Thanks for playing soccer like that. You make me enjoy it,'" he says. "You can't top that for me."

He smiles. History matters. Beauty, too.

A Team Is Born

FROM *Sports Illustrated*, JUNE 3, 2019

By 2019, the Women's World Cup had become the most significant event on the year's international sports calendar. The tournament in France generated tens of millions of dollars in sponsorships and broadcast fees, FIFA issued some 1,300 media credentials, and the games were broadcast to record audiences around the globe. In the United States, Fox and Telemundo televised and streamed every match live, with onsite studios and extensive pre- and postgame shows. The U.S. women were bona fide stars, with personal endorsement deals, magazine cover shoots, and national television appearances, and their demand for pay equity with the U.S. men had become a hot-button political issue leading into the tournament.

Such a landscape would have been unrecognizable to the pioneers of the U.S. women's national team, who participated in the first such competition, in China in 1991, telecast in the United States on an obscure subscription cable channel, on tape delay with commercial breaks during the action, and not even officially called a World Cup. Even Wahl, the preeminent chronicler of the women's game in the United States, admitted he had known little of the USWNT's origin story and had been surprised by what he found when he began digging: athletes playing in hand-me-down men's uniforms, subsisting on $10 per diems supplemented by sponsors' candy bars, and traveling on shared charters that would make stops to pick up other women's teams along the way. Through interviews with dozens of figures—including stars Michelle Akers, Mia Hamm, and Julie Foudy; intense, charismatic coach Anson Dorrance; and even scandal-tainted former FIFA president Sepp Blatter, with whom he jousted over the years—Wahl captured the rise of America's women's sports juggernaut. This piece, which appeared in the run-up to the 2019 tournament, was a companion to *Throwback*, a six-part podcast series Wahl did for *SI*. *Throwback* remains available on major podcast platforms.

H OW DO YOU START A NATIONAL TEAM? IN THE CASE OF THE U.S. women's soccer team, it began with a letter sent to seventeen players in 1985. The U.S. Soccer Federation had been invited to send a squad to an international women's tournament in Italy known as the Mundialito (the "little World Cup," even though it had nothing to do with FIFA, which wouldn't stage an official Women's World Cup for years). Michelle Akers, a hard-ass midfielder who'd played collegiately at Central Florida, was one of the seventeen who received the letter asking her to attend a three-day training camp on Long Island with the chance to go to Italy. "At first I had no idea what the national team was," Akers says, "but I said yes right away because I was going to be playing soccer somewhere with a lot of people and thought it would be great fun."

Thanks to Title IX, the landmark 1972 legislation that created equal university scholarship opportunities for women, soccer programs had sprung up on campuses around the country. But a U.S. national team for women? That was new in '85. Mike Ryan, a gruff college coach who lived in the Seattle area, was the first U.S. women's manager. Born in Ireland, he knew the significance of representing one's country in the world's most popular sport, and during his team's initial training sessions at Long Island University's Post campus—which took place right next to a cheerleading camp—he quickly grew frustrated by his players' lack of seriousness. Finally, he stopped practice and issued an unusual demand. "He made us stand there," Akers says, "and sing the national anthem." And so they did.

Everything about the USWNT's first tournament was unusual. For example: the uniforms. They were hand-me-downs made for men, not women. On the night before the team left for Italy, players and staff members stayed up late doing emergency cutting and sewing to make them wearable. And when the U.S. took the field? They played four games against vastly more experienced teams like Denmark, Italy, and England. The results: three losses, one tie, zero wins.

The Americans were naive in the international game, and their opponents took advantage of it. "It was like they were playing against little kids in a way," Akers says now, "because we were like 'Wait a minute. That's so unfair. You're grabbing my shirt or grabbing my crotch' or 'You're kicking me' or 'You just fouled the crap out of me,' and the referees just kept saying 'Play on.' We got our asses kicked."

There's a misconception—even in the American soccer community—that the U.S. had a head start on the rest of the world in the women's game and dominated as a result. But that's not really true. The USWNT played in four international tournaments in the late 1980s and didn't win any of them. But Title IX did have a major impact on the U.S.'s rise. As Caitlin Murray, the author of a book called *The National Team*, notes, in 1974, right after Title IX was passed, there were around 100,000 girls registered to play soccer with the U.S. Youth Soccer Association. Today that number is in the millions, not least because so much scholarship money is available to female athletes.

Title IX also changed cultural attitudes toward women playing sports, but it was a slow process in some areas. When national team forward Carin Jennings (later Gabarra) competed in high school soccer in California in the early 1980s, she had to deal with a societal stigma. "It was not accepted to be a female athlete at all," she says. "And every day I'd go to school, someone would ask me about sports, and I'd say, 'Oh, I don't play sports.' I denied it all the way through high school because it wasn't the cool thing to do."

Women's sports may not have been fashionable everywhere, but Jennings had still been playing soccer most of her life, which meant that by the mid-1980s she and women like her were part of a rapidly growing U.S. talent pool. But beyond college there had been no women's national team program to hone that talent. Now, finally, there was.

———

How DO YOU start a Women's World Cup? First, a quick history lesson. Women have been playing soccer since at least the nineteenth century. Jean Williams, the author of several books on the subject, points out that an 1869 issue of *Harper's Bazaar* included an image of women playing. Matches between England and Scotland began in 1881, and much like the baseball games in *A League of Their Own,* there were women's soccer games in England that drew more than 50,000 paying fans during and after World War I. But soon after, English soccer's governing body, the

Football Association, banned the women's game, arguing that it was unsuitable for the participants and could possibly threaten their ability to bear children.

Similar bans on women's soccer were also imposed by the all-male-led federations of Germany, Brazil, and other countries. But by the late 1960s, as women's rights movements gained steam, unsanctioned teams were starting to spread, especially in Europe. With FIFA and its member nations staying out of women's soccer, an unofficial world championship backed by the Italian beverage company Martini & Rossi took place in Italy in 1970 and again in Mexico in '71. More than 100,000 people filled Estadio Azteca to see Denmark win its second straight title by beating the host country. National federations in England, France, Germany, and elsewhere ended their bans in the early '70s, which brought about official recognition from FIFA. But that actually made things worse. For two decades after the first official international women's game in 1971, FIFA couldn't be bothered to organize a women's world championship.

By 1986, a Norwegian federation member named Ellen Wille had seen enough. So at the FIFA Congress in Mexico City she addressed the nearly 100 percent male gathering. Wille says she was nervous. The only other women were translators. And that's the way it had always been. "It was the first time a woman spoke at a FIFA Congress," Wille says.

The men Wille was addressing weren't exactly known as feminists. The FIFA president was João Havelange, a Brazilian who'd been in charge since 1974 but had never pushed for a women's global tournament. His right-hand man, FIFA's secretary general, was a middle-aged Swiss man named Sepp Blatter—the same Blatter who would go on to be FIFA president from 1998 until 2015, when he resigned in the wake of a U.S. investigation into global corruption that would produce dozens of indictments and convictions of officials across seven countries. Blatter is now eighty-three years old, and when he was growing up in Switzerland, the idea of women's soccer was foreign to him. "Football was the macho game, and it was definitely not a game for girls," he says now.

Blatter had plenty of cringe-inducing moments over the years speaking about the women's game. As FIFA president in 2004, he said in an interview that women's players should wear "tighter shorts" to increase their appeal. When asked if he regrets that statement today, he says, "No. I said they should be feminine, but then the good people from the press, they said I said they should be sexy. I would never say that. The future is feminine. So please look like a woman. Easy."

And yet Blatter, as crazy as it sounds, is one of the most important figures in the history of women's soccer. He's also one of its biggest disappointments. Which is to say: It's complicated. At the 1986 FIFA Congress, when the president opened up the floor for questions and comments, Wille stepped to the microphone and made herself heard. She spent ten minutes addressing the room, saying that FIFA needed to organize a Women's World Cup. Havelange's response, rather than answering her directly, was to refer the issue to his top deputy. So all eyes turned to Blatter.

"First of all, I was a little surprised by the reaction of the president," Blatter says. "This was the moment when I had been challenged by a lady for women's football. But then I was a very happy man, because I said, 'OK, madame, I will accept the challenge. You will see. We will go for the organization of a Women's World Cup.'" Without Wille, who knows how long it would have taken FIFA to act? But it was a reckoning that came far later in soccer than in other sports. Women's volleyball and women's basketball, for instance, had official world championships in the early 1950s. Why did it take FIFA twenty years after the first official women's soccer game to organize a World Cup? "Because FIFA was sleeping, that's all," Blatter says. "Let's say you can blame me because I was technical director of FIFA [in the '70s], but I had other problems."

But even the first Women's World Cup was complicated. For starters, FIFA didn't use the term World Cup because it was concerned the event wouldn't be a success. So the official name was the First World Championship for Women's Football for the M&M's Cup. The indignities didn't end there. FIFA nearly decided to use a smaller ball before reconsidering. But the organizers did change one of the fundamental aspects of the sport, making games eighty minutes long instead of ninety. Says Blatter, "It was the impression at that time, from the physical point of view, that ladies maybe are not as much prepared as men, and could play only forty minutes [per half]." Yet to save money, FIFA forced teams to play their group-stage games every other day. (Men's teams at the 1990 World Cup had at least four days between games, as remains the standard today for both genders.)

Blatter takes pride in his role helping to create the Women's World

Cup and in the slogan he first used in 1995: "The future of football is feminine." For her part, former USWNT captain Julie Foudy feels conflicted about his role in the women's game. "He was such an easy target for us with the things he would say," Foudy says. "Maybe behind the scenes he did more than we've given him credit for, but . . ."

For Foudy, beyond Blatter's *Mad Men*–era comments, there was a deeper problem with FIFA. Under his seventeen-year presidency it didn't invest in women's soccer and grow the game the way it could have. "How can you not turn to your people at FIFA and say, 'We are totally missing this market. We are not tapping into it'?" Foudy says. "If you put millions of dollars into women's soccer, you're going to reap the rewards of that because it's a totally untapped market, as we're now seeing finally, which to me is inexcusable. If you're Sepp Blatter, you wield the power."

⸺

How do you build a powerhouse? The U.S. women's national team went from embarrassing in 1985 to contenders to win the first Women's World Cup in 1991. The transformation started in '86 with the coaching hire of Anson Dorrance, who had led North Carolina to four of the first five women's collegiate titles and took on the U.S. gig as a second job. When he was hired, his bosses told him the aim was just to be better than Canada. But by the '86 Mundialito he had already surpassed that goal. "All of the sudden we discovered we could probably compete with a lot of these European teams," Dorrance says. "Now, were we overwhelming and dominant? Well, not really, but we were certainly competitive."

A year after getting zero wins in four games at the first Mundialito, the U.S. team under Dorrance beat China, Brazil, and Japan to make it to the final, where the Americans fell 1–0 to host Italy. Dorrance brought a tougher mentality, an obsession with fitness, and a high-pressing style that he had used at Carolina. And perhaps most important, he tapped into the Title IX talent pool. It started with a fearsome front three led by his captain, the freakishly competitive April Heinrichs, who had played for him at UNC. More than any other player, Heinrichs was a culture changer. She made no apologies about doing everything possible to gain an advantage and just win, baby. "She was like a shark with blood in the water," Dorrance says. "One of the biggest adjustments for a woman coming into a competitive environment is she comes with a cultural expectation of genuflecting to everyone around her. And this was not Heinrichs. She competed from the first second of practice until the end."

Says Heinrichs, "He really gave me permission to be me. He tells stories about how players would come into his office and say, 'How are you going to manage April?' And he jokes, 'We're going to clone her.'"

Also on Dorrance's front line was a towering figure with a flowing mane of hair: Michelle Akers. She was one of only two players from the 1985 debacle whom Dorrance kept on the national team long term. "Akers set the bar," Dorrance says. "She was a player without a weakness." Her U.S. teammate Shannon Higgins (now Higgins-Cirovski) recalls a collegiate game when her UNC team played against Akers's Central Florida: "Michelle went up and headed a ball, and she basically came down with her teeth right on top of Lori Henry's head and lost her two front teeth right in Lori's head. She just kept playing the game."

Early on, Dorrance added another force to his front three with Jennings. She was a pigeon-toed dribbling master who had starred at UC Santa Barbara. "Jennings would basically run through teams," says Foudy. "We called her Crazy Legs because she was like a Gumby, like her legs would turn in ways that you never knew they should go."

Dorrance was also fearless when it came to giving chances to young players. In 1986 he got a call from a friend who said he needed to fly halfway across the country to see a special player. "I said, 'What's her name?'" Dorrance recalls. "He says, 'Mia Hamm.' And I said, 'How old is she?' And he said, 'She's fourteen.' I just started laughing on the phone and said, 'John, you mean you want me to fly to Dallas, Texas, to look at a fourteen-year-old for the full national team?' And he said, 'Yes.'" It's a story that's a classic in the annals of sports. Dorrance didn't want to be told which player was Hamm. He wanted to see if he could pick her out on his own. "It took me three seconds," he says, "because on the kickoff this short-haired brunette is shot out of a cannon, just like on a rocket ship. I could see her raw athleticism."

A year later, in the summer of 1987, an unusual set of circumstances meant Dorrance's U.S. senior team played in the same tournament as the U.S. under-19 team, which had Hamm, Foudy, Kristine Lilly, Joy Biefeld (later Fawcett), and Linda Hamilton. The teens held their own against the veterans. "That gave me a reason to make the decision to completely revamp the U.S. senior national team," Dorrance says. Out went several experienced players. In came the five youngsters, all of whom would end up being starters at the '91 World Cup.

Dorrance's national team was coming together. He had assembled most of its core, and the culture it was creating was unstoppable. The U.S. beat powerhouse Norway for the first time in 1987 and defeated West Germany in '88. But progress wasn't a straight line upward. In '88, when FIFA organized a World Cup dress rehearsal in China, the U.S. tied Sweden and Czechoslovakia and went out in the quarterfinals to eventual champion Norway.

The travel and the competitions were special. Yet for the players it was a huge financial and personal sacrifice. U.S. Soccer didn't give them any money other than a meager $10 a day while traveling. Jennings took a series of nine-to-five jobs that she had to quit whenever she left for a new trip. And Higgins, who was making just $7,000 a year as a collegiate assistant coach, would end up retiring from the sport at age twenty-three after the 1991 World Cup final to make ends meet.

In those days the women's team would see U.S. Soccer's boys' youth national teams receiving better travel accommodations. And the federation rarely issued any gear that looked official. When Foudy finally did get something, she was not only grateful but also thrilled. "We had these windbreakers, and amazingly they happened to be the colors of the United States, because usually they were like white or purple or something random," Foudy says. "And this one was a navy blue windbreaker with red stripes on the sleeves, and it said 'USA' on it. And they're like 'You get to keep it.' I was like 'What? I get to keep this!? Are you kidding me?'"

At the regional World Cup qualifying tournament in early 1991, the U.S. outscored its opponents 49–0, and by the time the Americans headed to China, their confidence was peaking. No player had a stronger mentality than Akers. "It's just like the sun was coming up tomorrow, the sky is blue, and we would win," she says. "It just was that simple." Yet there remained skeptics. Dorrance still remembers a column in *Soccer America* that said the U.S. team was headed for trouble.

"You know, if we had any thoughts of winning the World Cup, we should just lay them aside because this was different," he says. "This was going to be something completely different than we would ever experience, and the American team was never going to be prepared for this event because our culture doesn't understand how to win these events, and blah blah blah."

The U.S. went on to win the first world championship by an American soccer team with a 2–1 victory in the final against Norway. Akers scored both goals, giving her ten for the tournament. After FIFA determined that the event had been a success, it decided to stage the Women's World Cup every four years thereafter—and it retroactively dubbed the 1991 edition a "World Cup." The USWNT players would continue fighting for better treatment from U.S. Soccer in the years ahead, both before and after their cultural-breakthrough victory at the '99 World Cup.

This March, the current U.S. women's players filed a gender discrimination suit against U.S. Soccer, citing inequality with the men's team on issues such as pay and training conditions. Their battle wouldn't be possible without their predecessors. "Our fight was for 'equitable,' their fight is for 'equal,'" says Foudy. "It's the logical progression. Players around the world have to stand up to enact change, and unless they stand up, change isn't happening."

7

ROYALTY

THOUGH EUROPEAN MEDIA OUTLETS MIGHT OPEN THEIR WAL-
lets to secure an interview, Wahl wasn't able to do that. International
soccer stars didn't move magazines off U.S. newsstands the way pro
football or basketball players did. Besides, *Sports Illustrated* had a
long-standing policy of neither paying for interviews nor promising
a spot on the cover. But when he kited off on some overseas story,
Wahl had a trump card to play: The U.S. remained the game's last
frontier, and every segment of the global soccerverse was eager to
make inroads there. Superclubs wanted to sell jerseys as well as tickets to their summer exhibition tours; superstars, having maxed out
their exposure in Europe, Africa, Asia, and the rest of the Americas,
drooled over the game's biggest untapped market. To international
press officers and agents, Wahl would make the case explicitly: Work
with me, and your club or client will reach the full range of American fans, from the small but growing coterie of passionate soccer
followers to the everyday sports nut who had maybe heard of Lionel
Messi, perhaps seen a Cristiano Ronaldo highlight clip, and might
be soccer curious. That was how Wahl secured cooperation from
Champions League regulars such as FC Barcelona and Bayern
Munich and landed sit-downs with such personalities as Didier
Drogba and Mario Balotelli. And when U.S. soccer eventually pro-
duced its own royalty, homegrown icons such as Clint Dempsey and
Abby Wambach? Wahl had covered them from the beginning.

Big Bend

From *Sports Illustrated,* June 23, 2003

This 2003 piece introduced American readers to the global icon, England captain, and Spice Girl spouse that was David Beckham. And it launched a relationship between writer and subject that would affect the lives of both. Four years later, after Beckham signed a $50 million annual deal with the Los Angeles Galaxy of Major League Soccer, Wahl interviewed him for a second story, whose publication led Crown to approach Wahl with the idea of writing a book. For his cooperation, Beckham wanted a million dollars plus editorial control. Wahl chose the alternative: no one-on-ones with Beckham, but the same access to Galaxy games and press conferences as any reporter, with the final word ultimately Wahl's. Reflecting sixteen months of covering the team and its megastar, *The Beckham Experiment: How the World's Most Famous Athlete Tried to Conquer America* was "neither 'authorized' nor 'unauthorized,'" as Wahl put it. As much as he flinched at the idea of being Beckham's stenographer, he also recoiled at the tawdry descriptive "unauthorized." Playing it straight, documenting the commercial success of the signing as well as the messes that Beckham had left behind on the pitch and in the locker room, the book became a *New York Times* bestseller.

DAVID BECKHAM CRIES. ALWAYS HAS. "I GET IT FROM MY MUM," he says. "My dad's sort of a man's man, but I've got more of my mum's personality. She's a lot softer, a lot more affectionate. We both get really emotional."

Beckham cried when his wife, Victoria, the former Posh Spice, gave birth to their sons, first Brooklyn and then Romeo. He cried that awful night in 1998 when he was red-carded at the World Cup and became the Most Hated Man in England. He cried a year later when he won back his nation's affection. "I'll even watch films and cry," he says.

Ask Beckham to pick the most significant moment of his childhood, and he doesn't hesitate. He was eleven, a working-class kid from East London who'd just finished playing a game for Ridgeway Rovers, his Sunday League team: "My mum came up and said, 'It's good that you've played well today, because Manchester United were watching you, and they want you to come down and have a trial.' I just stood there and cried."

Stood there and cried.

In international soccer, if you survive the Darwinian winnowing process, if you come up through the youth ranks and stay with your team, the attachments run deep. Beckham began training with Man United at fourteen, signed a contract at sixteen, and joined the starting lineup for good at twenty, in 1995. For the past fourteen years Man U—the world's most popular sports franchise, the team he grew up supporting—has been the only professional home Beckham has ever known. With more than two hundred official fan clubs and an estimated fan base of 50 million, Man U has helped turn Beckham into a global phenomenon. "There's no doubt that he's the biggest sports star in the world now," says Nick Hornby, the British writer (*Fever Pitch, About a Boy*) and devout soccer fan. "One of my friends at *The New Yorker* thinks Shaq is the world's biggest sports star, but you can't be if you play a game that several continents have only a passing interest in."

Beckham is not the planet's highest-paid athlete. (That would be Tiger Woods.) Nor is he its finest soccer player. (That would be France's Zinedine Zidane.) Yet he is undoubtedly Earth's most talked about sportsman, more Madonna than Maradona, a (mostly) silent oracle whose all-purpose celebrity transcends race, gender, nationality, sexual orientation and sports itself. From Cardiff to Kuala Lumpur, every new Beckham haircut—a Mohawk, a shaved head, even cornrows—sends acolytes scurrying to their salons. "Whereas Tiger Woods and Michael Jordan are respected, Beckham is loved, adored, *worshipped* in some parts of the world," says Ellis Cashmore, a Staffordshire University professor who has written a book, *Beckham,* on the effect. "He has an almost godlike status."

Almost? At a Thai monastery, Buddhist monks kneel before a gold-plated Beckham. In Japan nightclubbers don plaster casts in homage to their idol's recently broken right wrist. When Nelson Mandela met

Becks in Johannesburg last month, you'd have judged by the coverage that the privilege was entirely Mandela's. Like Kim Jong Il's mug in North Korea, Beckham's face is everywhere in the U.K. Depending on your reading preferences, he "sets the nation's emotional agenda" (*The Observer* of London) or inhabits "the sentimental terrain once occupied by Diana, Princess of Wales" (royal biographer Andrew Morton). It's a lot to ask of a soccer player.

Let's make one thing clear, though: Beckham, for all his beauty and all his endorsements, is not the male Anna Kournikova, a winless wonder. Not when he has started on six championship teams in eight English Premier League seasons. Not when the world's national team coaches have twice voted him the second best soccer player on the planet (behind Rivaldo in 1999 and Luís Figo in 2001). Not when he possesses a physical genius for spinning an inert ball into a remote corner of the goal, a skill that inspired a movie to be made in his name.

Yet talent and looks can't explain everything. How do we account for Beckham's unique appeal, his transformation into the icon of Cool Britannia? Is it because of his remarkable resurrection from his costly gaffe in '98? His pop-star wife? His peacock-dandy fashion sense? Is it his rejection of Europe's macho soccer culture? Or his decade of success with Manchester United?

What's all the fuss about? And if Beckham is so worthy of our attention, then why is Man United's knighted manager, Sir Alex Ferguson, trying to get rid of him?

To UNDERSTAND BRITAIN'S hysteria over Beckham is to realize how closely it's tied to the fanatical hatred of him in 1998. When Beckham was ejected from a second-round World Cup match for kicking Argentina's Diego Simeone, contributing to England's elimination, the public onslaught that followed went beyond your ordinary media lynching. Rallied by the tabloids, punters hanged Beckham in effigy outside a London pub. An Islington butcher put two pig's heads in his front window, one labeled DAVID and the other VICTORIA. For months Beckham was subjected to death threats, chants wishing cancer upon his son, even a piece of "fan mail" bearing a bullet with his name inscribed on it.

Though Beckham returned to Manchester United later that summer, ending speculation that he might have to join a team on the Continent, he kept his head down, his mouth shut. "It was hard concentrating on football," he recalls. "It was like '*I'm a soccer star*. Nobody was killed. This isn't right.'"

Truth be told, he wasn't just another gifted midfielder. From the moment Beckham began dating Victoria Adams, at the height of the Spice Girls craze in 1997, they had been daily gossip fodder. After the period of national grieving over Diana's death in August 1997, the royal family appeared drab next to the new pop couple. (The tabs dubbed their twenty-four-acre spread outside London "Beckingham Palace.") Introduced by Posh to the fashion world, Beckham embraced its trappings; he was photographed wearing a sarong while staying at Elton John's vacation house in France. "Kids love each change of hairstyle, and I think he has taste," says Hornby. "Maybe not your taste or my taste, but a real instinct for keeping himself looking cool in the eyes of five- to twenty-year-olds. And he's actually pretty sweet and likable."

Beckham's detractors tried hard to spin the hype machine into reverse after the World Cup debacle, seizing on anything at hand: his wife, his fashion forays, his high-pitched Essex patois. "But they were flailing about a bit, to be honest," says Hornby. "That's why the hatred of him was so inflated. People wanted to loathe him, but they couldn't get a handle on anything. A brief moment of indiscipline against Argentina, and people are hanging effigies? If it had been any other English player, all the focus would have been on Simeone. Kicking Argentines is generally approved of, but not in this specific case."

Then something odd happened. Through a combination of PR savvy, quiet dignity, and, above all, unimpeachable play, Beckham turned the media coverage on its head. Running tirelessly, serving exquisite crosses into the penalty box, scoring timely goals, he helped lead Man United to an unprecedented Treble in 1999, winning the English Premier League, FA Cup, and European Champions League trophies. Within two years he'd be named captain of England—forcing fans to suspend all hostilities in the name of national pride—and would preside over a stunning 5–1 win against Germany in a World Cup qualifier. When Beckham buried a penalty kick to beat Argentina at last year's World Cup, his transformation from pariah to paragon was complete.

Redemption has proved lucrative. Beckham's annual income of close to $30 million ($8.8 million from his Man U salary and upwards of $20 million from such endorsers as Adidas, Pepsi, and Brylcreem) makes him the world's highest-paid soccer player. The key to his popularity is his ability to function as a one-size-fits-all vessel for his fans' hopes and dreams. It's revealing that he doesn't say a word in the film *Bend It Like Beckham,* serving instead as a listening post—in the form of bedroom wall posters—for the deepest secrets of a teenaged Anglo-Indian girl. "He's this phantom of the imagination," Cashmore explains. "Because he doesn't actually come out and say anything, he gives the people carte blanche to construct their own David Beckham." To claim that Beckham doesn't say *anything* is a bit uncharitable. Granted, like Woods and Michael Jordan, he's not Muhammad Ali refusing induction into the Army. "I try to stay away from as much politics as possible," says Beckham, who admits he doesn't vote in elections. Yet his open-mindedness often features a candor you'd never expect to hear from Tiger or Michael.

Consider his stance on homosexuality. Beckham happily speaks out against the raging taboo of male locker rooms worldwide. "Being a gay icon is a great honor for me," says Beckham, who posed suggestively for the cover of the British gay magazine *Attitude* last year. "I'm quite sure of my feminine side, and I've not got a problem with that at all. These days it's the norm, and it should be. Everyone's different, everyone's got their thing."

And Beckham's thing is, well, everyone. Race? One British TV show, citing his cornrows and chunky jewelry, recently dubbed him "an honorary black man." Religion? He's one-fourth Jewish. Women's soccer? "Someday I'd like to have soccer schools for girls and boys," Beckham says. "People always say to me, 'Why girls?' And I say it's important that girls get involved in sports."

The person who has the biggest influence on Beckham is his wife, whose own fallen star has caused U.K. pundits to suggest she's using her husband as a prop to boost her career. (Or, as *The Guardian*'s Julie Burchill none too delicately put it last week, "Beckham has been grotesquely, massively p——whipped by his talentless ambition-hound of a wife.") Ask Victoria how she has changed David's life, and she steers clear of such trivial matters as love, family, and maturity. "I've changed his dress sense," she says, munching on a strand of grapes. "Drastically." Her face is blank. Is she in on the joke? Or is that really all there is to it? It's impossible to tell.

By all accounts, though, theirs is a strong, stable marriage, which makes Beckham a welcome contrast to such previous U.K. soccer stars as Paul Gascoigne (who beat his wife and spent his free time getting hopelessly drunk with a sidekick named Five Bellies) and George Best (the Man United playboy star of the late 1960s who once famously quipped, "I spent a lot of money on booze, birds, and fast cars. The rest I just squandered"). Their travel schedules be damned, the Beckhams have chosen not to hire nannies for Brooklyn (age four) and Romeo (nine months), relying on their parents when necessary. "David is a model dad," Victoria says. "If I leave him with the children, he'll look after them just as well as I can."

Naturally, Beckham's New Age family-man side appeals to housewives and grandmothers. Yet by pursuing so many nontraditional sports demographics, he has long run the risk of alienating hard-core soccer fans, to say nothing of Ferguson, his no-nonsense Man U coach. For no matter how gorgeous he may be, the sportsman must constantly prove his superiority in the arena. Beckham certainly has his flaws: ordinary speed, weak heading skills, not much of a left foot. But for someone regarded as a pretty boy, his capacity for work is breathtaking. Simply put, he runs his butt off. Nor can any other player on the globe serve a bending, thirty-yard cross on the run better than Becks. And don't forget those free kicks. Oh, those glorious free kicks.

TIME FOR A set piece: Manchester, England. April 23, 2003. Champions League quarterfinal. Real Madrid versus Manchester United.

This is David Beckham's signature moment, when it becomes instantaneously clear why his free kicks inspire such singular awe (and, for that matter, why there are no films called *Bend It Like Blyleven*). His teammate Ruud van Nistelrooy has been fouled just outside the penalty box, to the right of the Real goal. A hush falls over the 67,000 fans in Old Trafford, then morphs into a pulsating, expectant thrum. "As soon as a free kick is given and it's anywhere near the box, I get excited," Beckham says, his eyes closed as he recalls the scene. "The crowd lifts theirself, and there's a buzz around the stadium. I know it's my turn for everyone to watch me. I practice this thirty, forty, fifty times a day in training, and when I do get the chance, I like to hit the target."

The charged tableau packs even more drama than usual. This is Europe's game of the year, an elimination match pitting its two most popular soccer teams, and Man U is desperate, needing four goals in the final twenty minutes to survive. All week the tabloids have been filled with rumors that Beckham will move to Real Madrid, which already boasts three former world players of the year (Ronaldo, Zidane, and Figo). Yet when the opening whistle blew at this match, Beckham was not on the field. Ferguson had benched him. Benched him! "When you're not in the starting lineup of any games, especially the big games, you're disappointed," Beckham says. "I just have to prove that I *should* be playing."

Here's his chance. Eight minutes earlier Beckham had trotted onto the field, the world's highest-paid sub. Now this. Beckham places the ball gently, as if he's laying a wreath on a loved one's grave, then takes six steps backward and to his left. He sucks in two quick, deep breaths. A pair of human barriers loom before him. The Real goalkeeper, Iker Casillas, crouches twenty-two yards away, his 6'2" frame coiled in the goalmouth's left-hand side. Lined up ten yards away is a five-man Madrid wall, its purpose to block the goal's right-hand side.

"I don't really concentrate much on what side the keeper is on," Beckham says, "because I always think that if I catch it as well as I can, then I can beat him whichever way he goes." And the wall? "I do see them. Some walls, they jump, so some players hit it under the wall. But that's sort of lazy. I like doing it the hard way."

He springs forward. At the moment before impact Beckham is a picture of serenity and balance, his legs splayed, his right arm pointing straight down, his left arm extended like a traffic cop's. All angles and energy, he looks like a Keith Haring drawing come to life. Physicists from Europe to Japan have spent hundreds of hours studying his free kicks, the perfectly calibrated mix of forces—angle, speed, spin, and direction—that conspire, as one researcher puts it, to achieve "optimal turbulent-laminar transition trajectory." Or, as Beckham says, he knows precisely how "to get as much whip on it as possible," to strike the side of the ball with his right instep, sending it screaming over the wall, then dipping, improbably, thrillingly, under the crossbar, past the helpless keeper's outstretched hands.

A million little things can go wrong, of course. "If you don't catch it right, it can end up in Row Zed," Beckham says. "It's happened to me a couple of times, when my boots or my standing foot give way. That's pretty embarrassing."

This is not one of those times. "As soon as I hit the ball, *I know it's in,*" Beckham says, a smile cleaving his face. "I know it's in. Even before it reaches the wall." Roberto Carlos, Real's gnomic Brazilian defender, jumps skyward, only for his bald dome to get buzzed by a Becks flyby. Poor Casillas is doomed. In a flash the ball is droppingdroppingdropping . . . *in.* With a kiss off the crossbar for good measure.

Fourteen minutes later Beckham scores again on a tap-in. It's not enough for Man United to win the two-game series, not when Ronaldo has scored three searing goals of his own, but here at Old Trafford, on soccer's most memorable night of 2003, it does make you wonder. *What about that benching, Sir Alex?*

FOR SIR ALEX Ferguson, a sixty-one-year-old taskmaster raised in the shipyards of Glasgow, old school isn't a marketing catchphrase. It's standard operating procedure. Not long ago he read *When Pride Still Mattered,* David Maraniss's biography of Vince Lombardi. "I saw myself," says Ferguson, taking a break after an April practice at Man United's Carrington training compound. "Obsession. Commitment. Fanaticism. It was all there."

Like Lombardi, he is ruthless, maintaining iron-fisted control of his team despite his players' rising salaries. "I never have a problem with egos," says Ferguson, who has been the Man U coach for seventeen seasons. "You know why? Because you have to win. You can't escape the field. And if the money has affected them, they have to go. Easiest decision ever made." Imagine a hybrid of Joe Torre and George Steinbrenner. No wonder everyone calls Ferguson the Boss.

When Man United announced last week, after months of speculation, that it had conditionally agreed to sell Beckham to Barcelona of the Spanish league for $50 million, it sent the expected convulsions through the English media. By now Britons are so Beckham-addled that they can think about him only in hysterical terms. But the real news wasn't that he was headed to Barcelona. (Beckham's handlers indicated he'd veto the move, as is his right.) The real news was this: The Boss doesn't want David Beckham anymore.

Why on earth would Man U consider selling its most valuable asset? And why now, just as the club is set to embark on a highly anticipated U.S. tour meant to boost its image in the States? Four reasons:

- **Money.** Because Beckham has two years left on his contract, Man U can sell his rights to the highest bidder so long as Beckham is willing to join the new team and agrees to salary terms. Beckham's market value is as high as it will ever be, and Man United can use the money from his sale to fill needs at several positions, such as goalkeeper, defense, and the central midfield.
- **Tactics.** In the one-forward alignment the Red Devils introduced last year, they rely far less on crossing the ball—Beckham's forte— than they did when two forwards were roaming the penalty box. The system values dribblers who can beat defenders one-on-one, hardly Beckham's strong suit. As if to prove Beckham was dispensable, Ferguson kept him out of the starting lineup for last season's two most important games, against Real Madrid and Premier League archrival Arsenal.
- **European struggles.** Though Manchester United won the Premier League title for the sixth time in eight years, the club has floundered in the Champions League, failing to appear in the final—Ferguson's Holy Grail—since the Treble four years ago. Changes must be made.
- **Fergie versus Becks.** In the end, though, Beckham's likely departure can be attributed to the bitter unraveling of what Beckham calls "a father-son relationship." The tabloids feasted on a locker room accident in February in which Ferguson, livid after a loss, kicked a boot in anger, dinging his star in the forehead and opening a gash above Beckham's left eye. But there's more to it than that. To hear Ferguson discuss the teenage Beckham is to hear a tale of youthful innocence and talent corrupted—or at the very least distracted—by fame. "He was blessed with great stamina, the best of all the players we've had here," Ferguson says. "After train-

ing he'd always be practicing, practicing, practicing. So there's a foundation there that never deserted him. And then . . ."

It's a long pause, one of those times when silence communicates more than words ever could. Suddenly you realize, in this fleeting moment, how deeply Ferguson longs for the schoolboy Beckham, for a simpler era, for a time when his star wasn't spending his free hours with Jean Paul Gaultier and the Naked Chef.

". . . his life changed when he met his wife, really," Ferguson finally continues. "She's in pop, and David got another image. And he's developed this *fashion thing*." (He says "fashion thing" in the bewildered way you'd expect to hear from, say, Vince Lombardi.) "I saw his transition to a different person. So long as it doesn't affect his football side, it doesn't bother me at all." Clearly, in the past three months Ferguson has decided: The glitz has indeed affected Beckham's football side. *You can't escape the field.*

For his part, the boy who cried with joy for Man U as an eleven-year-old wants to stay. "At the moment I'm contracted to Manchester United, and as far as I'm concerned, I'm happy with that," Beckham says. Yet he is keenly aware of one thing: If and when he leaves Man United this summer, it will be up to one man, a cranky but altogether charming Scotsman whose other kindred spirit, Yank Division, is John Wayne. "I've got all the Duke's movies," Ferguson says proudly. "I always pictured John Wayne as a man you could bring on if you needed a last-minute goal. Know what I mean? He's a battler. Always winning every fight, every shoot-out."

Beckham won't win this gunfight. But someday soon, when he's wearing the jersey of Real Madrid or AC Milan or some other fancy European team, he'll meet Ferguson again on the soccer field.

Sounds like the basis for another epic redemption story.

Soccer Savior

FROM *Sports Illustrated*, MAY 24, 2010

During a decade in charge of *Sports Illustrated,* managing editor Terry McDonell often asked the staff for ideas he called "mix makers," stories that would contrast with others in the table of contents or somehow confound readers' expectations. For an issue in late May 2010, already clogged with obligatory coverage of the NBA and NHL playoffs, McDonell did something unheard of: He ordered up three soccer stories from Wahl, whom he had just charged with full-time soccer duty, and collected them under a cover with the billing THE BEAUTIFUL GAME: WHAT SOCCER MEANS TO THE WORLD. One piece was devoted to the death of the free-spirited samba style of play in Brazil. Another featured U.S. star Clint Dempsey and his sandlot origins in rural Texas (page 206). Leading the package was this portrait of Didier Drogba, the star striker for Chelsea and the Ivory Coast. Wahl was a master at engaging the senses. Here, right in the first sentence, he conjures up a scent: the "peaty tang" of the soil in Drogba's homeland during the rainy season. Throughout the rest of the piece he goes beyond how soccer explains the world to show how the game might actually be able to change it.

DIDIER DROGBA CAN CLOSE HIS EYES AND RECALL THE SMELL OF the earth during the rainy season in Ivory Coast, the peaty tang that filled the air during warm afternoon cloudbursts. The childhood memory, a touchstone of his Ivorian identity, is part of what draws Drogba back to Africa. To Abidjan, the city of his birth, where he has acquired the land to build a hospital. To South Africa, home of this summer's World Cup, where his three-hundred-foot-high likeness graces Johannesburg's tallest building. And even to this remote place: a dusty compound in Cabinda, Angola, where he is guarded by more assault weapons than a Mexican drug lord.

It's January. Angola is hosting the Africa Cup of Nations, the continent's biennial soccer championship, and Drogba has journeyed to Cabinda, a tiny exclave separated from the rest of Angola by a strip of the Democratic Republic of Congo. Drogba, the captain of his national team, known as Les Éléphants, will go wherever Ivory Coast plays, even if it means leaving London and his club team, Premier League giant Chelsea, for games in Sudan or Libya or Angola, which ended its twenty-seven-year civil war only in 2002. But Drogba's beloved African soil is again tinged with blood. A few days earlier Cabindan separatists machine-gunned a bus carrying the Togo team, killing two delegation members and the driver and casting the shadow of tragedy on an African soccer celebration.

Black-suited Angolan soldiers with AK-47s patrol outside as Drogba—6'2" and a sculpted two hundred pounds—leans back on an orange couch in his living quarters and exhales deeply. "We felt really sad, really scared," he says. "Our families and our clubs wanted us to go back home [because of the attack], and we wanted to go as well. After that we spoke together as a team and decided to stay. When the crisis started in Ivory Coast [in 2002], one of the first countries to come and help us was Angola. To leave wouldn't look good for the relations between the two countries." He pauses, fully aware of the forces at work. "This was more than football. A lot more than football."

Few twenty-first-century athletes are as familiar with the transcendent power of soccer as Didier Yves Drogba Tébily, thirty-two, United Nations goodwill ambassador, reigning African Player of the Year, three-time Premier League champion. It isn't just that the feared striker has turned Ivory Coast into a fashionable dark horse for the 2010 World Cup, the first to be held in Africa. How many sportsmen have helped end their nation's civil war? "When you're a leader like Didier, people think maybe he can be a politician someday," says his Chelsea and Ivory Coast teammate Salomon Kalou. "If he decides to, he will be a great one. People listen when he's talking."

And singing.

We salute you, O land of hope,
Country of hospitality.

Thy gallant legions
Have restored thy dignity.

—from "L'Abidjanaise," the Ivory Coast national anthem

"When I hear the national anthem, I feel something in my stomach," says Drogba, whose deep singing voice is better than most players'. "There's something strong coming from there." To hear him talk about Ivory Coast is to detect an expatriate's lament. Drogba left Africa at age five when his parents, Albert and Clotilde, sent him to France to live under the roof of his uncle Michel Goba, a professional soccer player. By Drogba's count, he moved eight times as Goba bounced around various French teams and leagues. Drogba has dual citizenship in France and Ivory Coast, but if you ask him why he feels such a deep connection to his native land, he doesn't have to think long. "Maybe because from the day I left I was missing my country so much—my parents, everything," he says. "I felt like part of me was left there. Even if I was in France, I always felt part of Ivory Coast."

From the moment Drogba first donned the sherbet orange jersey of Les Éléphants on September 8, 2002, in a friendly against South Africa, his national-team career acquired a symbolism that far exceeded the boundaries of a soccer field. It was the first time Drogba had played a competitive game on African soil, and he felt a rush of national pride. But change was afoot outside Abidjan's Félix Houphouët-Boigny Stadium. Days later came an attempted coup against Ivorian president Laurent Gbagbo, touching off a bloody struggle that divided the nation between the rebel-held north and the government-held south, between Muslims and Christians, immigrants and native-born Ivorians.

Even as the fighting intensified, Les Éléphants kept winning, aided by a golden generation of players from all over the country: from the south (Drogba and Kalou) to the north (brothers Kolo and Yaya Touré) to the east (Emmanuel Eboué). When teammates prayed together on the field, they alternated between Muslim and Christian verses. "In the national team we are all brothers," Drogba says. "After games people would call and say, 'We are so happy. Everybody was in the streets dancing.' And we'd say, 'There's war in Ivory Coast, but people are outside when we win? Is football that powerful? Wow." That's how we started. We were playing for the country, trying to show a different image from what the news was showing."

Drogba's credibility only grew as he scaled new heights for an Ivorian player in Europe. A late bloomer who says he didn't take soccer seriously until he met his wife, Lalla, Drogba spent four years with Le Mans of the French second division before his breakthrough with Guingamp at twenty-three; then came a nineteen-goal season at Marseille and a move to Chelsea in 2004. Three league trophies, three FA Cups, and eighty-four Premiership goals later, Drogba is a phenomenon in Abidjan, a city of nearly 3.6 million where his blue Chelsea shirt is ubiquitous. One-liter bottles of Bock, an Ivorian beer, are known as Drogbas owing to their robust size and strength. Musicians write songs in his name. If you visit a nightclub in Yopougon Sicogi, Drogba's home neighborhood, chances are you'll see Drogbacité—an homage in which acolytes copy his soccer moves on the dance floor.

In turn, Drogba has used his popularity—and his influential stature outside politics—to spread a message of peace after three years of bloodshed that left four thousand dead in a nation of 20.6 million. In October 2005, after Ivory Coast had beaten Sudan 3–1 to qualify for its first World Cup, Drogba called on his teammates and a cameraman from Radiodiffusion Télévision Ivoirienne to gather around him for an impromptu national address. "Ivorians, men and women, from the north and the south, the center and the west, you've seen this," Drogba announced, his words halting at first but then quickly gathering strength. "We've proved to you that the people of Ivory Coast can live together side by side, play together toward the same goal: qualifying for the World Cup. We promised you this celebration would bring the people together. Now we're asking you to make this a reality. Please, let's all kneel."

In their finest hour a nation's favorite sons dropped to their knees, and so did that nation itself. "The only country in Africa with such wealth cannot sink into war like this!" Drogba concluded. "Please, put down your weapons, organize the elections, and things will get better." Drogba's speech was replayed for months on Ivorian television, and tensions eased throughout the country.

There was more to come. When Drogba won the African Player of the Year award in 2007, he flew to Abidjan for a photo op with President

Gbagbo and made a nervy request: that Ivory Coast's next game be moved to Bouaké, the northern stronghold of the rebels fighting Gbagbo's government troops. The president accepted, and that June Les Éléphants met Madagascar in a historic Africa Cup of Nations qualifier. Before the game Drogba presented Guillaume Soro, the onetime rebel leader, with a pair of soccer cleats that bore Soro's name and the slogan TOGETHER FOR PEACE. A sold-out crowd of 25,000 roared when Drogba scored the final goal of a 5–0 victory. The headline in one newspaper the next day read FIVE GOALS ERASE FIVE YEARS OF WAR.

Ending the fighting required more than soccer, of course. The Ivorian government and rebel leaders had reached an agreement in March 2007 that installed Soro as prime minister under President Gbagbo. Nor has life returned completely to normal: Long-awaited elections have yet to take place. But that hardly diminishes the impact of Drogba and Les Éléphants, whose arrival in Bouaké announced to Ivorians who had fled the fighting that it was safe to return to their homes. "I believe only this team could do that," says Lassiné Koné, a journalist for the newspaper *Le Patriote*. "Drogba's message got the attention of the people. Football permitted this."

Drogba still marvels at the scene in the stadium that day, especially the moment when the crowd in the rebel stronghold sang a full-throated rendition of the national anthem. "What I saw there were Ivorians," says Drogba. "Not people from the north. Ivorians. Believe me, football matters." For the first time since the start of the war, members of the government army had entered the rebel capital. In the stands two hundred government troops joined in singing "L'Abidjanaise" with the rebel soldiers they had been fighting for the past five years.

> Beloved Ivory Coast, thy sons,
> Proud builders of thy greatness,
> All mustered together for thy glory,
> In joy will construct thee.

On March 29, 2009, the same Éléphants who had brought so much joy to Ivory Coast bore witness to a scene of horror. An overflow crowd at a World Cup qualifier in Abidjan turned into a stampede, killing 22 fans and injuring more than 130. The next day Drogba visited patients—

the injured and the sick—at a local hospital. The conditions there shocked him. "There were six kids in the same small room, and some were on the floor," Drogba says. "It's crazy. If you go there your chances to survive and get better are reduced, not because of the doctors but because of the environment."

Drogba hatched a plan with his sponsors from Pepsi and his club, Chelsea: The entirety of his reported $4.4 million endorsement fee would go toward the construction of a hospital in Abidjan through the Didier Drogba Foundation. With services in pediatrics, oncology, and gynecology, the hospital plans to offer inexpensive consultations to ordinary Ivorians while training Ivorian doctors and treating 250 to 500 patients a day. After acquiring donated land, Drogba raised an additional $675,000 at a charity ball in London last November that featured appearances by his Chelsea teammates and the Senegalese American singer Akon. "Now is the time to show people in Europe and around the world that we are going to rebuild our country," Drogba says. "It's a big fight, so that's why I started to raise money. It's not enough. We need more, not only to build the hospital but to run it afterward." More charity events are in the works, and Drogba's foundation is accepting donations on its website.

For now Drogba has no plans to enter the political arena as did his friend George Weah, the 1995 FIFA World Player of the Year, who lost the 2005 election for the presidency of Liberia. Drogba is on good terms with Gbagbo and Soro and keeps his political leanings to himself. "That's why people respect me in the country, because they don't know who I am supporting," Drogba says. "And they will never know. I love my position because when I have something to say I can come and say it. When I speak, I only speak for the people in the country, not for the politicians."

Perhaps it's no surprise that Drogba refrains from using the widespread term Group of Death to describe Ivory Coast's first-round draw for the World Cup, which includes world number one Brazil, number three–ranked Portugal, and an unknown quantity in North Korea. "We are the unluckiest team," says Drogba, laughing, as he recalls drawing powerhouses Argentina and the Netherlands in '06 and losing to both, 2–1, to end Les Éléphants' World Cup run. "But let's see what we can do. Let's play!"

This time there will be a big difference. The World Cup will be played on African soil. Sacred soil. "Our soil," Drogba says. On June 15 in Port Elizabeth, South Africa, eleven men in orange will line up shoulder to shoulder, and the Ivorian national anthem will ring out louder than ever:

> *Proud citizens of the Ivory Coast, the country calls us.*
> *If we have brought back liberty peacefully,*
> *It will be our duty to be an example*
> *Of the hope promised to humanity,*
> *Forging together in new faith*
> *The Fatherland of true brotherhood.*

A Gringo's Game

From *Sports Illustrated*, May 24, 2010

Sports Illustrated's broadening soccer coverage made for a manic travel schedule for Wahl during 2010, a men's World Cup year: In just the first four months, his reporting took him to South Africa, Angola, the Netherlands, Greece, and Brazil and twice to England, one of those latter trips for this piece on the pugnacious American striker Clint Dempsey. Given the intense workload—in one eight-day stretch in April he calculated that he had traveled 19,030 miles and touched down on four continents—he couldn't be everywhere, so as he was meeting Dempsey in London, *SI*'s Melissa Segura flew to Texas to do additional reporting for the story. She recalls "sitting in LaGuardia with ten minutes until boarding and getting a call from Grant to walk through what he needed. I was a baseball reporter who didn't even know what stoppage time was at that point, but in ten minutes Grant taught me what made Clint exceptional and the key differences between traditional Latino, British, and American styles of play. In less time than it took me to order a sandwich, he'd imparted all he needed with the clarity and specificity that made Grant, well, *Grant*." Segura gathered far more material than Wahl could use in his piece, so, she says, "He kindly did the *other* thing he did best: encouraged a young reporter. He helped me spin off my own story for the website about Dempsey's connection with a former high school teammate. Then he made sure to forward me Clint's response to it." Stories like these were countless throughout Wahl's career and made him as admired for his mentorship and support of young colleagues as he was for his writing.

THE MAN WORE CROCODILE BOOTS, A WHITE COWBOY HAT, AND a belt buckle the size of a license plate. Clint Dempsey doesn't remember his full name—hell, nobody in Nacogdoches, Texas, does—but you couldn't miss him on the sidelines of Nac-town's Mexican League games, amid the cigar smoke and the fajita carts and the horchata peddlers. He was the guy betting cash money on the cocky fifteen-year-old gringo to beat men more than twice his age, proud men from Mexico and El Salvador who'd throw you to the East Texas dirt for trying a fancy move on them. *Sixty, eighty, one hundred dollars!* The man kept wagering, and Dempsey's team, Zamora, kept winning. "He called me," says Dempsey, "his Little Rooster."

Years before he would score in the World Cup for the U.S., the Little Rooster swallowed his fear, unleashing all the tricks he'd seen in his Diego Maradona highlight videos, and noodled on in his grandma's backyard with his older brother, Ryan. Stepovers, nutmegs, dipsy-dos: The Little Rooster had everything, even moves without names, moves nobody had seen before. Childhood friend Frankie Rivera recalls one Mexican League game when Dempsey "did some kind of weird trick—it was so awesome—and the guy got mad and spit in his face. Clint just went at him. He had three guys trying to fight him, but he did good. He did good."

And when the Little Rooster scored goals, he wouldn't hold back on his foes. "He'd run around to the faces of all of them," says Dempsey's mother, Debbie.

"They'd be so mad," says his father, Aubrey. "They'd scream and holler."

Says Dempsey, "I'm surprised I didn't get stabbed out there."

———

WHEN CLINTON DREW Dempsey, the U.S.'s most inventive and unpredictable soccer player, joined the national team in 2004, then coach Bruce Arena summarized his primary asset in three words: "He tries s——." It's an approach common in Latin America, where kids often learn the game on the streets, and rare among U.S. players, who are channeled into organized soccer from an early age. Dempsey's style is self-taught, intuitive, like a jazzman's.

"It's a little bit of Pete Maravich," says U.S. coach Bob Bradley. "Clint's capable of making an attacking play that's a little different, that can create an advantage, that can lead to a goal. To have a player who can come up with something different at the right time, that's still such a special part of soccer."

As it happened, Bradley was in the stands at London's Craven Cottage on March 18 when Dempsey delivered his version of Thelonious Monk's "Straight, No Chaser." In the final minutes of a Europa League Round of 16 game against Italy's mighty Juventus, Dempsey's Fulham needed a goal to complete a remarkable four-goal comeback and advance. Stationed just outside the penalty box, Dempsey received a pass with his back to the goal and took two touches while moving to the right, creating a pocket of space. Still, it wasn't a dangerous position. Dempsey was facing the sideline, with the Juventus goal twenty yards away over his left shoulder. His defender was closing, and his momentum—like that of a quarterback scrambling to his right—would prevent him from putting much force behind a shot.

"Something told me just to go for it. What do you have to lose?" says Dempsey. "When you come on as a substitute, you have to take shots. Otherwise why are you playing in the game?"

Ruling out a near-post attempt, Dempsey hit an audaciously delicate, no-look chip to the far post.

"I knew where the goal was, because when I'm looking at the ball you can see the side of the goal," Dempsey says. "I didn't know the keeper was out. I just hoped he was off his line. Lucky for me, he was."

With his right foot Dempsey clipped the ball like a Phil Mickelson lob wedge. "If you know Clint, you know what he's trying," says Bradley, who rose from his seat, "and now the ball is sort of sitting up there for a second." Time froze. Dempsey compares the feeling to the one you get when you've released a bowling ball and think you can still control it with your body language before it hits the pins. Goalkeeper Antonio Chimenti could only look skyward and hope the ball sailed over the crossbar. But slowly, slowly, slowly, it fell into the net, with the softness of a baby's breath.

Bedlam.

"There's no better feeling than getting crunk after scoring an important goal," says Dempsey, whose celebration with his teammates and fans practically tore the roof off the old barn. Fulham would advance to the Europa League final, the biggest accomplishment in the club's 131-

year history, but the goose-bump moment will always be Dempsey's strike—the finest big-game goal ever scored by an American in European club soccer.

"It's not just that not many American players would have tried to do that," says Sunil Gulati, the president of U.S. Soccer. "Not many players outside of South America would have even thought about it."

And therein lies a riddle: As the U.S. develops as a soccer nation, where do skills like Dempsey's fit into the big picture of a country known less for its soccer technique than for athleticism, effort and speed?

IF A COUNTRY'S soccer style embodies the nation's aspirations, its strengths and its component groups, then the U.S. "hasn't found yet its real identity," says Jürgen Klinsmann, the former German star who has lived in California for most of the past decade and nearly took the U.S. coaching job in 2006. "I'm talking about a philosophy, a style of play, that marks every nation." For Klinsmann, the question is simple: What style should represent American soccer?

Yet others don't think the questions—or the answers—are so easy. For one thing, the U.S. is still a young soccer country compared with the giants of the footballing world. Major League Soccer is in just its fifteenth season, and the U.S. returned to the World Cup only in 1990, after a forty-year absence. What's more, U.S. demographics are changing rapidly, not least in the skyrocketing growth of the largely soccer-loving Hispanic community. One-third or more of MLS's fans are Latinos, and it should come as no surprise that the U.S. television rights for World Cups 2010 and '14 sold for far more to Spanish-language Univision ($325 million) than to English-language ESPN/ABC ($100 million).

For years the U.S. Soccer Federation drew criticism for failing to cultivate the Hispanic community or to include more Mexican American players in its national teams and development initiatives. But the landscape appears to be changing. One prominent example is José "El Gringo" Torres, a twenty-two-year-old creative midfielder who grew up in Longview, Texas, just an hour away from Dempsey. Torres, who plays professionally for Mexican power Pachuca, chose to compete internationally for the United States (his mother's country) rather than Mexico (his father's). He's among the thirty players in the U.S. World Cup camp this week and is a good bet to make the final twenty-three-man squad. More such players are in the pipeline.

For Gulati, a Columbia economics professor who was recently elected to his second term as USSF president, U.S. style won't be a choice so much as an evolution. "We've got elements of European soccer in our teaching and elements of Latin soccer in our playing, primarily at youth levels," says Gulati. "That's all still being shaped, and I don't think that's a decision that gets made by an individual. That comes over time."

Gulati himself prefers the attractive Latin style, which values technique, short passing, and creativity. He has hired Wilmer Cabrera, a former Colombian international, as the men's under-17 coach, and last month he tapped former U.S. star Claudio Reyna as the federation's new youth technical director. Reyna, who speaks English, Spanish, and German, will be in charge of producing a sort of national education policy for the coaches of millions of young American soccer players.

The 2010 World Cup offers the U.S. a rare chance to show how far it has come as a soccer nation, including in the sophistication of its playing style. Still, winning is what matters most. The U.S. isn't Brazil or Spain, after all, and Bradley knows his team's performance will be measured not by style points but by how far it advances. In fact, Bradley's definition of style has little to do with notions of national identity. What he calls "the modern game" is about tactics and matchups, whether you're the U.S. or Brazil or Spain.

"A style anywhere takes into account the qualities of the players—the strengths and the weaknesses—and on any given day what the game will be like," says Bradley. "For us to play at the highest level, there has to be a collective idea of how the ball can be moved around, how you can make sure that your more talented and creative players are getting the ball in situations that allow them to make the plays that make a difference. When the ball turns over on the international level, what's necessary as a team is to stop the other team and win the ball back. You're trying to build on all of those qualities and put them to the test of playing against the best teams."

That may not sound sexy, but it's intended to produce results. And if in South Africa next month the U.S. can repeat performances like last year's 2–0 upset of Spain, neither Bradley nor his boss will complain. "In the end, we need a style that is conducive to winning," says Gulati. "I don't want to play brilliantly, look good, and come up short every time. That doesn't do us any good."

CLINT DEMPSEY DEFINES himself as a risk taker. An avid bass fisherman, he'll happily cast into a tree-shaded shoreline if he thinks it gives him a better chance of landing a fish. "Sometimes I get my line stuck in the tree and have to break it," he says. "But sometimes those casts pay off and you catch a fish." He plays soccer much the same way. That goal he scored against Juventus? "If I went for it eighteen times, it would only go in once," Dempsey admits. Indeed, when his risky moves don't come off, it can look ugly. That's part of the package that comes with Dempsey's capacity for brilliance.

Finding the right balance between risk and safety has been an ongoing process. The push and pull between Dempsey and Bradley is among the most fascinating relationships in U.S. soccer, not least because it combines mutual respect and occasional open disagreement. After Dempsey and the U.S. struggled in losses to Italy and Brazil at last summer's Confederations Cup, Bradley arranged a private meeting with Dempsey and the coaching staff. "What's going on?" Dempsey says Bradley asked. "Why are we not able to get the best out of the team and the best out of you?"

"I just feel in the attacking third we lose ideas and aren't playing with confidence," Dempsey replied. "You have to take risks."

It was a long talk. "There were some things we threw at him, and he throws just as much back," says Bradley. "It's not so much about the specifics as about putting it all on the table. You could tell by the next day he had a good frame of mind." Dempsey showed it on the field, too. In the next game he scored the decisive goal against Egypt that sent the U.S. to the semifinals, and he followed that up with a goal each against Spain and Brazil, the world's top two teams. Ultimately Dempsey would be named the third best player in the tournament.

The lesson was a useful one: Dempsey's unpredictable style can fit on this U.S. team. He tries s——. Sometimes it works. Sometimes it doesn't. But if the Americans are going to make an impact in South Africa next month—and beyond that, to climb into the ranks of true soccer nations—they'll need a healthy dose of the Little Rooster's style.

Abby's Road

FROM *Sports Illustrated*, JUNE 8, 2015

Wahl covered Abby Wambach for her entire career and considered
her one of the most honest subjects he'd interviewed—"sometimes
too honest for her own good," he once said, as her candor and
penchant for speaking out ruffled plenty of feathers among soccer's power brokers. Wambach's penetrating self-awareness shone
through in this 2015 World Cup preview piece. Though she hedged
about the significance of finally winning a World Cup as her career
wound down, other evidence points to what it meant to her. After
the United States' 5–2 win over Japan in the 2015 final in Vancouver,
Sports Illustrated managing editor Chris Stone made the unprecedented decision to give every player on the team her own individual
cover, with issues sent randomly to newsstands around the country.
For their shoots, the other twenty-two players beamed joyously or
goofed around with the trophy. Wambach's cover is a stark contrast:
She is the only one not looking at the camera; rather, she cradles
the trophy gently, her head bowed in contemplation, reverence,
satisfaction—and, maybe, relief.

IN APRIL, SIX WEEKS BEFORE THE START OF HER FOURTH AND
final Women's World Cup, Abby Wambach parachuted into New York
City for twelve hours, donned a tieless tuxedo, and walked the red carpet at Lincoln Center with her wife of two years, Sarah Huffman. The
occasion: the annual Time 100 Gala honoring the most influential people on the planet. When Wambach learned she was among the hundred,
she thought she was being punked. Then she was simply overwhelmed.
"The most humbling thing ever," she says of being named in the same
group as Pope Francis, Angela Merkel, and Hillary Clinton.

The night unfolded like a supercharged version of Wambach's dinner parties back home in Portland. She fangirled with tablemate Sarah Koenig, creator of her beloved *Serial* podcast. She spoke at length with Dr. Pardis Sabeti, who'd led a team that sequenced the Ebola virus in real time. And she traded laughs with John Oliver, the British comedian who has been as pointed in his (hilarious) criticism of FIFA's rampant corruption as Wambach has been of the organization's decision to stage the upcoming World Cup on artificial turf.

Time's choice of thirty-five-year-old Mary Abigail Wambach made perfect sense. The 2015 Women's World Cup, with twenty-four teams competing across six Canadian cities over the next month, will be the biggest women's sporting event of all time. In her fifteen-year U.S. career Wambach, an aerial threat like no other, has scored 182 international goals, 24 more than the next closest man or woman in history. She has won two Olympic gold medals and the 2012 World Player of the Year award, and her miraculous last-second goal against Brazil in the 2011 World Cup quarterfinals—a forty-yard Hail Mary—has entered the pantheon of dramatic sports finishes. What's more, Wambach has been fearless in speaking truth to power, publicly chiding FIFA and its seventy-nine-year-old president, Sepp Blatter, for an institutional sexism that's straight out of *Mad Men*.

Wambach likes to say that as a Gemini she has a twin personality disorder. Wambach the Person is aware of her accomplishments, and proud of them. But Wambach the Competitor told herself a few other things that night in Gotham as Kanye West performed and all these extraordinary figures approached her to take selfies: Don't they know I may not be a first-choice starter in Canada? Don't they know I'm sometimes the U.S.'s worst player on the field? And most of all, don't they know Ms. Fancy 100 Most Influential People in the World has never actually won a World Cup?

"I'm much more motivated by my failures than my successes," the 5'11", 179-pound Wambach says one afternoon in the living room of her four-bedroom house, sprawled out on the couch next to the family dogs: Kingston, a bone-chomping English bulldog, and a pug named Tex. Ask her to look back at her previous three World Cups, and she says, "You mean the devastating losses? And the serious heartbreak?"

Well, if you put it that way . . .

"OK, 2003," she starts. "My mark scored in the semifinal loss against

Germany. Garefrekes. I'll never forget the moment." The Americans, tied at 0–0 in the fifteenth minute, were defending a corner kick, and their scouting report said that towering Kerstin Garefrekes always ran to the back post. This time she went near post, lost Wambach, and scored on a header. "So I feel like we lost the World Cup because of me," Wambach says of the eventual 3–0 defeat. "And at the time I knew it was going to be the last World Cup for Mia [Hamm] and her generation. So that hit me extra hard."

In 2007, the U.S. imploded during (and after) its 4–0 semifinal loss to Brazil in China, the lowest point in the team's proud history. "One of the most embarrassing times of my life," Wambach says. "I remember wishing I could vanish into thin air and feeling so deeply that I embarrassed my country and my family."

As for 2011, well, Wambach says she still meets people who remember her goal against Brazil and think that the U.S. ended up winning that World Cup instead of coughing up two leads to Japan in the final and losing on penalties. (Of the Americans' four penalty takers, only Wambach scored.) "It still baffles me—*baffles me*—that we didn't win that game," she says. "It was going to be the perfect way to go out. I'm still not right with it."

Three World Cups, three excruciating exits—three failures, to use Wambach's term. "The failures are really what make people adjust and make different decisions," she says. "On July 17, 2011, we didn't win that game. And so we have to do something different that causes a different outcome."

This is her last chance to win the trophy that matters most.

⸻

IN THE SUMMER of 2004, not long after scoring the extra-time winner in the Olympic gold medal game against Brazil, Wambach loaded up her Jeep with a sturdy bike, a tent, and a knapsack, and she disappeared by herself into the mountains. If she wasn't exactly Cheryl Strayed in *Wild*, there was at least a kinship. Both were trips of self-discovery. She went mountain biking in Moab and Sedona and Four Corners National Park. She camped alone under the stars, stopping just twice at motels to shower. And she rescued something that she feared she might be losing.

"I was so afraid of letting soccer and that life take hold of me in some way," she says. "In a spiritual way, I was trying to protect my soul from crossing over into being money driven or fame driven rather than knowing who I am and trying to continually evolve as a person. I happen to be really good at something that's kind of cool to people, and marketable, and you can sell yourself in that way. But I didn't want to lose sight of the fact that it's still just something I do. It's not who I am."

Wambach's pursuit of her curiosity is relentless. Swerving from one fascination to the next like an X-wing fighter in *Star Wars,* she's all-in one moment and—*vrooooosh!*—disengaged the next. Some pursuits have been short lived: yoga, fad diets, remote control helicopters. Others have lasted longer. When she and Huffman, herself a retired midfielder, bought their gorgeous house three years ago after having seen it only in internet photos, Wambach took charge of the remodeling, doing research online and working with the architect. Her latest fixation is golf. Huffman says Wambach came home one day recently and announced that they were joining a club. Using top-of-the-line gear, Wambach has become a fixture on the driving range and on the course. "She can absolutely crush the ball," golf buddy Scott Dougherty says of Wambach's three-hundred-yard drives. "Maybe I'll join the LPGA if I get really good," says Wambach, her straight face suggesting that she might be serious.

Growing up as the youngest of her family's seven children in Rochester, New York, and later attending the University of Florida, Wambach says she'd challenge herself by not studying, just to see if she could still pass her tests. "It's the same with soccer," she explains. "I've always toyed with being unfit and then getting really fit just at the end. That's kind of been my rebel nature." Due in part to women's soccer's unbalanced calendar—the World Cup and Olympics are played in consecutive years, followed by two years without any major events—Wambach went into something close to hibernation in late 2012, promising to reemerge and peak just in time for this World Cup. "I know she'll do what she needs to do to be ready," says U.S. coach Jill Ellis.

It's a tricky balance, though, especially as Wambach has gotten older and her goal production against top teams has declined. How much should Ellis trust Wambach's promise that she can summon one last superhuman effort? Has the rise of skilled passing teams like France and Japan neutralized the athleticism and brute force that Wambach embodies? When she's on the field, the U.S. has to play a certain style of soccer: in the air with plenty of crosses. Is this the best way to win a World Cup in 2015?

Wambach herself notes that her principal strength—heading the ball—makes her different from speedsters like Alex Morgan or creators like Megan Rapinoe. "With the skill set I have, I need my teammates in order to be good," Wambach argues. "And if something is off just a little bit, whether it's my speed or my timing going into a header, then my average is below average. When I'm good, I'm the best in the world. But when I'm average, I'm the worst player on the team."

You can call it a special strain of twin personality disorder—but when she's on, man, she's on. Like the Rivera cutter and Kareem's skyhook, Wambach's thundering header goal has become one of the sporting world's signature moves. With an eye for ball trajectory that she honed as a rebounder in basketball, Wambach added the timing, the strength, and the vicious snap before impact that have scared defenders the world over. She has fond memories of practicing diving headers in the mud in high school and hurtling her body after loose balls on the basketball court; it was the physical nature of it all that she loved the most. Only later did she realize that she could turn that into a career. "It's just a mathematical equation," she says. "I'm taller. I can jump. And when you're shooting with your head, it's impossible for goalkeepers to know where the ball is going."

But Wambach really does need her teammates, and not just to serve her crosses. As the major link between Hamm's generation and the current roster, she has tried to pass along the all-for-one culture that has defined the U.S. since the 1990s. Not everyone buys in completely. "We've got kids with healthy egos who all think they should be starting and deserving endorsements," Wambach says.

Yet no player has listened more than Morgan, the heir apparent to Mia Hamm in performance and popularity, who marvels at the way Wambach not only refused to resent her emergence but welcomed it. In fact, Wambach says she wants Morgan to break all her scoring records. "I have complete trust in Abby," Morgan, twenty-five, says. "It's hard to have absolute trust in someone, especially someone you're possibly competing against for a spot on the team. Abby is incredibly selfless, and she understands the idea behind team sports. The more selfless you are, the more it comes back to you."

The question now is simple enough: Is Wambach a starter in a must-win game? There's no doubt she'll make starts at the World Cup, where the U.S. could play seven matches in twenty-eight days. But Wambach has been used more often as a second-half substitute recently, including in the Algarve Cup final in March, a 2–0 win over France. "Do I feel like I can and want to be starting every game? One hundred percent, absolutely," says Wambach. "Am I disappointed when I'm not starting? Yes. But that's the competitor in me. All our forwards have different strengths and weaknesses. It's going to be about who's playing the best together."

A few weeks ago Ellis sent each of the twenty-three U.S. players a handwritten note card. On Wambach's card the coach wrote that she was sure her role in this Cup would be a defining one. "I've never said she's going to be a bench player," Ellis says of speculation about Wambach's role. "Historically, the closer Abby gets to an event, the more she fine-tunes and the more she gets into her zone. I have the utmost confidence in what she can give us—whether that's starting a game and playing ninety minutes or coming in for the last thirty. What I do know is we need Abby Wambach to win a World Cup."

"Opponents have to play a different way when she's on the field," adds Morgan. "To have to alter the way you play? That's crazy."

IF THE U.S. were to win the final on July 5 in Vancouver, Wambach would earn a face-to-face meeting with Blatter at the postgame awards ceremony. They have a history. Wambach tells a story from the time that she and Huffman were backstage in a VIP room in January 2013 before the World Player of the Year awards gala in Zurich, Switzerland. "Blatter came into our little area, and he walked straight up to Sarah and thought she was [Brazilian star] Marta," says Wambach, who recalls Blatter exclaiming, "Marta! You are the best! The very best!" as he hugged a bewildered Huffman, who doesn't look much like Marta at all.

"He had no idea who Marta was, and she's won the award five times," says Wambach. "For me, that's just a slap in the face because it shows he doesn't really care about the women's game."

Blatter recently called himself the "godfather" of women's soccer, a comment that made Wambach want to retch, but in her eyes FIFA's paternalistic attitude toward the women's game extends beyond Blatter. When it was announced that this Women's World Cup would be played exclusively on artificial turf fields—marking the first time that any senior World Cup match, men's or women's, would not be played on grass—Wambach, along with players around the world, organized a legal challenge in Canada, trying to force a switch. The men's World Cup would never be played on fake turf, they argued. Their challenge failed. There just wasn't enough time to change the plan, she says.

In January, Wambach met in Switzerland with Blatter's number two, FIFA general secretary Jérôme Valcke. In a conversation that she calls "a big waste of time," she says that Valcke opened by insisting that there was no way this tournament would have grass fields. "I said it's a real shame, because women's soccer has come so far," Wambach recalls. "And this isn't two steps backward—this is fifteen steps backward. You can sit here and give me all the reasons in the world, that Canada was the only country that bid, that their bid only included turf fields. . . . But you can't tell me the World Cup is going to be better because of it. There isn't one player in the world that would prefer playing on an artificial surface."

Wambach takes one consolation from the mess: FIFA promised that the next Women's World Cup, in France, would be played on grass. As for Blatter, will she shake his hand if he presents her with a World Cup winner's medal in July? "I mean, if I'm winning a World Cup, I'm happy, and I'm not too worried about Sepp Blatter," she says with a laugh. "I don't hold ill will to the man because I don't think he's the one making all these decisions. I don't think he cares enough, truthfully."

HIGH ON A ridge overlooking a pine-filled valley near Portland, the house owned by Wambach and Huffman is bathed in warm wood interiors. There's barely a suggestion of soccer inside, other than the World Player of the Year award hanging out near the bar. Portland is an ideal fit. The couple chose to move here from Los Angeles for a number of reasons: Huffman works in product testing at Nike, and they have several friends in the area who lobbied hard for the Rose City, where signs instruct the populace to KEEP PORTLAND WEIRD.

"Good food is important to me," says Wambach. "Food, beer, and coffee. Portland has my three favorite things. And it's an authentic town. I appreciate people owning themselves and their weirdness. Because we all are weird."

Wambach remains unsure about exactly what she'll do when she's done playing soccer. She knows that she wants to keep going through the 2016 Olympics, if possible, and after that she wants to get pregnant and have a baby. "I could probably genetically engineer a professional athlete on some level," she says. "Maybe get somebody else's stuff who plays a sport, like American football. I just need to find somebody who would be willing to do it."

Real life, a life outside of soccer, is pulling at her harder than ever, and the battle between Wambach the Person and Wambach the Competitor rages on. Time and again she has said that her career won't be complete unless she wins a World Cup. "It's something that motivates me," says Wambach the Competitor. But Wambach the Person allows that it's not really true. "I wouldn't define myself or my career on not winning a World Cup," she says. "I will define myself on 'Did my character shine through in a way that I'm proud of?'"

Did we mention that she's a Gemini?

"At the End of Mourning,
You're Supposed to Disengage"

FROM SI.COM, AUGUST 17, 2021

Wahl first visited Argentina in 1994 on a Princeton undergraduate research fellowship and made a second, longer trip there a year later to work on a senior thesis about the role of *fútbol* in the nation's social, cultural, and political life. From that early exposure, he fell in love with Argentina and came to consider it his adopted second country, returning regularly with his wife, Céline, for vacations, especially after long reporting trips or tournaments. (Wahl even had his shoes custom made by Buenos Aires designer Sylvie Geronimi.) More than anything, he learned of *el sentimiento*, the bond between supporters and teams, and how, amid the country's pervasive *machismo*, connectedness among men is "sublimated to an object that represents them all . . . the team," as he wrote as an undergraduate. So when Diego Maradona, the troubled superstar and iconic figure of Argentinian culture for four decades, died in November 2020 at age sixty, no American journalist was better positioned to convey his stature and significance to the U.S. reader. Much more than an obituary, Wahl's reflection on Maradona—built on a quarter century of immersion in a culture, drawing on contacts cultivated over that time, and reflecting his own formative journalistic experiences—is a profound examination of how a single individual can come to embody the spirit of a nation.

IN THE HEART OF BUENOS AIRES, THE OBELISK—A WHITE CONcrete cousin of the Washington Monument—is a place to celebrate greatness. The greatness of one of the world's key port cities. The greatness of any number of soccer outfits, whether it be an Argentine club or the national team, whose fans flock here to toast triumphs in major competitions. Or, say, the greatness of an individual. On March 10, three and a half months after Argentina's most beloved public figure died of congestive heart failure, the Obelisk is where thousands of angry acolytes joined the ex-wife and two daughters of Diego Maradona to celebrate the soccer legend—and to demand justice following reports of negligent medical care surrounding his death at age sixty.

They sang. They blew horns. They waved sky-blue-and-white flags.

They cried. They chanted. They fired off flare guns.

"It was a demonstration that he was alive, that justice needed to be done," says José María De Andrea, who was part of the throng that southern summer day at the Obelisk. De Andrea, forty-seven and a father of four, is a member of the Church of Maradona, a group of spiritually hard-core devotees that was founded in 1998. "As a soccer player, he's a god," De Andrea says. "I have seen extraordinary things over the years. I have shed tears."

De Andrea can speak in endless detail about the church's lodestar, including his first memories of the man, watching at his grandmother's house in 1981 as Maradona and Boca Juniors won the Argentine league. Five years later, when Maradona led his country to the World Cup title in Mexico, De Andrea was twelve. And he was hooked. "I celebrated in a Fiat 600, a very small car. There were like twelve people inside of it," he says. "The magic I saw in that World Cup! We touched the sky with our hands."

De Andrea demonstrated last November, too, joining thousands of mourners at the Casa Rosada, Argentina's version of the White House, where Maradona's casket lay in state. That scene turned violent when authorities threatened to remove Maradona's casket before the entirety of the gathered crowd had been able to see and mourn him. Angry citizens confronted police, threw barricades, and scaled walls. Police fired tear gas and rubber bullets into the masses. "These people hugged and cried. We were there solely for him," De Andrea says. "But here in Argentina, things get out of hand."

If there's any comparison to be found to the ongoing fervor over Maradona's death, it's in the public outpourings, recriminations and eventual court cases following Michael Jackson's death in 2009: Weeping masses. National and global mourning. The greatest hits running on constant loop. And the parallel makes sense. Maradona's mythology in his home country always resonated far beyond the sporting sphere. He was Argentina's most prominent celebrity of any kind.

Outrage, naturally, ensued April 30, when a special board that had been appointed to investigate Maradona's death concluded that his own medical team acted in an "inappropriate, deficient, and reckless manner" following his brain surgery for a subdural hematoma last November. Seven members of that team, including neurosurgeon Leopoldo Luque and psychiatrist Agustina Cosachov, were indicted on charges of "simple homicide with eventual intent." (All seven have denied any wrongdoing.) Court hearings began in June and are expected to continue into the fall, with a judge deciding at some indeterminate point whether the case will go to trial.

Fans, frustrated and furious, marched on the Obelisk in the spring.

What's indisputable, though, is that the mix of worship and outrage—a soccer player's posthumous grip on Argentine society—remains just as strong nine months after his death. Maradona-themed graffiti and artwork are everywhere in Buenos Aires. Billboards of the teenaged, mop-haired player with his parents, Don Diego and Doña Tota, are plastered across the city, reminders of a time with infinite possibilities. The words DIEGO ETERNO ("Diego forever") appear on signs and on flags.

"I imagine that if they had scheduled a monthlong funeral," says De Andrea, "it would have been full the whole month."

So: Why has the reaction been this . . . *extreme*? And what can that reaction tell us about the man, the country, and his place in it? For years I have been fascinated by a particularly Argentine phenomenon: the elevation of Maradona to a godlike status on par with Eva Perón, who also grew up in poverty and became a global icon as the first lady of Argentina. Today, Maradona's stature here is far above that of any other soccer player, including Lionel Messi or anyone on the country's *other* World Cup–winning team, in 1978. And, for that matter, far above the cultural position of his longtime rival, Pelé, in neighboring Brazil. Argentina is my adopted second country; in '95 I lived there for three months, researching my college thesis (on the nation's politics and soccer), and I have since visited more than a dozen times, including for Maradona's testimonial match in 2001.

I know my stuff. But I am not Argentine. And so I sought to learn from those who might know better than me.

———

ANDRÉS CANTOR CAN'T read the news stories anymore. Last January the legendary soccer broadcaster, known largely for his trademark *Gooooal!* calls, stopped consuming the coverage of Maradona's final agonizing days. His decision came soon after the Argentine news site Infobae first published an exposé revealing callous and seemingly damning WhatsApp messages between Maradona's caregivers, suggesting that they had been negligent in his medical supervision and had left him alone in his room for the last twelve hours before his death.

Those messages, says Cantor, are "so sad to hear. So I made myself a promise just to read the headlines—but nothing more than that. It's like salt in the wound every time."

Born in Argentina and now living in Miami, Cantor can't escape the notion that the sport he grew up worshipping died along with Maradona, who dominated a World Cup (in 1986) like no other player ever has; who won two Italian league titles with Napoli; and who possessed a swashbuckling verve and genius with the ball that were uniquely his own. Yes, there were drug and alcohol addictions, children born out of wedlock in multiple countries, conflicts, and an air gun incident with reporters. But Maradona remains a deified figure among his supporters.

Cantor can still remember clearly the first times he watched the teenaged Maradona play the sport. "That was when the love affair started, and I wasn't the only one," Cantor says. "He played football like nobody else. I enjoy Lionel Messi. I enjoy Kylian Mbappé. I enjoy Cristiano Ronaldo. All the great players of today. But I haven't seen one close to Maradona. So I'd say that, symbolically, football died with him."

For Cantor, it's all deeply personal. In 1979, while reporting a story for the Argentine magazine *El Gráfico,* Cantor sat in the back of a Chevy Camaro, laughing, as the eighteen-year-old Maradona screeched through the streets of Los Angeles on a test drive. In '83, Cantor took the budding hero to a hot New York City club, only to flee from their front-row table when they experienced firsthand that the crowd threw bottles at unfavored bands. And in '87, after Maradona won his first Italian league title, Cantor witnessed the fan fervor in full: He was in a line of fifteen cars on the way to a celebratory party when the sight of Maradona speaking to a tollbooth operator caused havoc among the vehicles moving in *both* directions. The two men continued to connect over the years, usually at World Cups, always meeting with a hug.

Like so many people who knew Maradona personally, Cantor disapproved of the full-time hangers-on who surrounded the superstar and indulged his worst vices over the years. But Cantor never suspected that this group would ever include Maradona's doctors, lawyers, and caregivers.

"I still don't believe he's gone," Cantor says. "He's the person who gave me the most joy in the world of soccer. For the life of me, I cannot understand how the biggest idol in Argentina was left to die this way."

Argentines detest the mediocre and fear to be thought mediocre. It was one of Eva Perón's words of abuse. For her the Argentine aristocracy was always mediocre. And she was right. In a few years she shattered the myth of Argentina as an aristocratic colonial land. And no other myth . . . has been found to take its place.
—V. S. Naipaul, *The Return of Eva Perón*, 1980

NAIPAUL, A NOBEL Prize–winning author, was a few years too early. Maradona would create his myth at the 1986 World Cup. But other soccer players have delivered international glory to Argentina, have risen to Maradona's heights in the club game. So why do Argentines view him as if he exists on a wholly different plane?

You can find reasonable soccer enthusiasts around the world who will argue that Messi is the greatest men's player of all time, even better than Maradona or Pelé. Usually that argument rests on the notion that in the modern game the annual UEFA Champions League, which Messi has dominated individually, is a better measure of greatness (with a larger sample size, all the best players, and a higher standard of play) than the quadrennial FIFA World Cup. But the people making that argument are rarely Argentine. Messi's compatriots have at times been merciless about his not winning a World Cup—or, until this summer, *any* major senior title—with his national team. They have even characterized Messi, who moved to Barcelona at age thirteen, as being more Spanish than Argentine.

But if Argentines use World Cup victories as the standard for greatness, then why is Maradona's status not shared by Mario Kempes, who scored six goals (one more than Maradona netted in Mexico) as La Albiceleste won the 1978 World Cup on home soil? Kempes is respected and admired, of course; he has a stadium named after him in his hometown of Córdoba. But he holds no mythology in Argentina. And so I asked Alejandro Gardella, an old friend of mine who has lived in Argentina, the United States, Brazil, and Great Britain and who has always been interested in seeking out Argentine and non-Argentine perspectives. (He has even spent time reporting in the Falkland Islands, which few Argentines have visited since the end of their country's ten-week war with Great Britain in 1982.)

Gardella, a fifty-year-old HR exec, lives with his three children in Tigre, the Buenos Aires suburb where Maradona spent his final days, and my friend puts Argentina's soccer conquests in the context of what the nation was experiencing at the time. The 1978 World Cup, he argues, "was mixed with the dictatorship in the Argentine psyche. We won, but the junta"—the right-wing military group that in '76 overthrew president Isabel Perón—"was involved [in organizing the tournament]. We had 'the Disappeared' "—the state-led killing of thousands of citizens— "and people were being tortured near the stadium. It was like a dirty World Cup. Then we lost the [Falklands] war in '82. But in '83 democracy came back, and free elections were won by a moderate guy, [president Raúl] Alfonsín. When we won the '86 World Cup, that was the real thing. And at the helm of '86 was Diego."

By winning under those circumstances, Gardella says, Maradona evoked a better time, a century earlier, when Argentina had one of the world's most prosperous economies. He represented an "avenger hero for the country." Never was that more the case than in the quarterfinal against England, four years after the Falklands fiasco. In that game, Maradona scored two of the most famous goals of all time, just four minutes apart: the so-called Hand of God goal, in which he got away with punching the ball into the net; and the greatest goal in World Cup history, a seventy-yard slalom run through six England players, in which Maradona touched the ball with only his majestic left foot.

"I would dare say that [Maradona's mythology] was more about that game with England than winning the World Cup itself," Gardella says. "It was a revenge. We had lost the [Falklands] war, and that was a deeply rooted thing in the pride of the nation. The first goal"—the Hand of God—"was part of the local psyche. Cleverness with an edge is like an asset here. It was like 'We screwed you in a way that you're going to regret for years and years.' By winning, we recovered something that had been lost, and we did it during our political renewal." (My old friend laughs remembering how he eventually moved to London for a few years and there discovered that the sense of enmity over the Falklands wasn't the same as back home. "I thought I would be looked at badly in London for being an Argentine, and actually they didn't give a f—— at all," he says. "I told myself: I need to reformat my head about these guys.")

The myth of Maradona was just as much about what he represented to Argentines as it was about what he accomplished on the field. He became the national apotheosis of the so-called *pibe* archetype, the kid from the streets with a dusty face and a thatch of black hair whose cunning and instincts give him an edge over those born into privilege. Maradona grew up in a Buenos Aires shantytown, and though he eventually became fabulously wealthy, he never lost the qualities of improvisation and misdirection that served him so well against bigger and stronger opponents.

There's another paradigm that applies to Maradona and that is celebrated in Argentina, notes Carlos Forment, a professor at the New School for Social Research (and my college thesis adviser) who lives for part of the year in Buenos Aires. "The picaresque hero is a classic part of Spanish literature, and Maradona has some of that," says Forment, the author of *Democracy in Latin America*. "It harks back to his plebeian origins. This is really central for Argentine political culture: [It's valued] to be from the bottom and rise to the top—and once you're at the top to scorn the elite."

Evita had that. Maradona had that. It's a characteristic, moreover, that tends to separate Argentina from Brazil.

WHY DO ARGENTINES revere Maradona in a way that Brazilians don't hold Pelé? These two are, with little global debate, the two premier men's soccer players of the twentieth century. Pelé, now eighty, won three World Cups, two more than Maradona, and performed more consistently at the club level for a longer period of time. . . . Maradona, unlike Pelé, played in the European club game, winning Napoli's first league trophies at a time when Italy's Serie A was at the height of its powers. . . . As breathtaking as Pelé was during his career, Maradona's ceiling from 1986 to '90 was even higher. . . .

One can argue forever over which player was better, but there's no denying that Maradona's place in Argentina's cultural firmament is on a higher level than Pelé's in Brazil. Pelé has plenty of admirers; he's a beloved figure around the world. But you don't need to spend much time around Brazilian soccer to find contrarians who contend that the dribbling maestro Garrincha was a better player, or that Pelé has been too corporate in his pursuit of endorsement riches. It's a measure of Maradona's status within Argentina that he's idolized just as much by fans of River Plate—the archrival of his former club, Boca Juniors—as he is by everyone else in the soccer sphere. Yet Pelé, who played near São Paulo for Santos, has never totally won over fans in Rio de Janeiro, where public backlash recently led government officials to scrap a proposal to rename the Maracanã Stadium after him.

Of course, there's context to consider. Maradona, for starters, was twenty years younger than Pelé, which means that millions more people in today's Argentina lived through the visceral experience of watching their star's finest moments in real time. There are also historical and cultural differences between Argentina and Brazil, Forment points out, that create better conditions in Argentina for the deification of a larger-than-life figure.

"Brazil is a very hierarchical and structured society, and that produces very stable institutions—even when they had a dictatorship, it was a stable dictatorship," says Forment. But "in Argentina, because it's not institutionally stable, they don't function well, and everything's kind of chaotic. That opens the space for the rise of a heroic figure, because that person becomes more powerful than the institutions.

"The dark side of this is that there's no authority. That's why institutions crumble, why people don't pay taxes, why traffic is [terrible] in Argentina. Maradona, in many ways, symbolizes all of this. There's a kind of improvisational quality, very creative, in Argentina. You see this in art, in music. . . . But when you translate that into running a society, you need to have a little order as well. And that's what's lacking here." In other words, the instability in Forment's and Maradona's Argentina helped create not just the myth of the superstar *pibe* soccer player but also the chaos in the aftermath of his death.

The word *order* appears on the national flag of Brazil but not on Argentina's. That Maradona is bigger in his country than Pelé is in his should come as no surprise.

———

LAST NOVEMBER, WHEN *The New York Times* headlined its Maradona obituary THE MOST HUMAN OF IMMORTALS, "human" was meant to suggest—not inaccurately—that the man was flawed in a deep and abiding way. But the word *human* has other connotations, too. Maradona was transcendent because he was not some untouchable figure among the gods.

"Maradona is, for two or three generations, part of our family," says the Argentine sports journalist Verónica Brunati. "He's the person who gave us the most important happiness in football. And you know what football means for Argentines—it's our passion, our identity. When a woman is pregnant, the first thing we think of is the name. And if it's a boy, the first name we think of is Diego."

Brunati did not, in the end, name her own son after Maradona, but she did have a closer perspective of the man than most. In 2007, she helped arrange the first joint newspaper interview with Maradona and Messi, and she remembers being touched when Maradona took Messi's arms and prayed to him like a son, saying, "You are going to be better than me." Later, while Maradona was managing the Argentine national team, he earned a laugh from Brunati, who was pregnant, by placing his hand on her stomach and "blessing" her child. (She recalls her husband saying, "My son is going to be a football player because Maradona did this!") Maradona eventually met that son, Agustín, at an art exhibition that Brunati organized. The boy was nearly two, and Maradona made a ball out of crumpled-up paper, playing with him in the museum. "He was so friendly, so lovely," Brunati says. "I couldn't believe I was watching my son play with Maradona."

In July 2014, on the night before Argentina won its World Cup semifinal, Brunati's husband, Jorge "El Topo" López, died in a traffic accident in São Paulo when his taxi was struck by a car fleeing police in a high-speed chase. During the days and weeks after the tragedy, as calls grew for accountability from Brazilian police, some of soccer's most prominent figures—including Messi, Pep Guardiola, and Diego Simeone—took part in a campaign seeking justice. But Brunati remembers above all the man who reached out to her with a personal message. "When my husband died, Maradona was the first person in the world who sent me the message 'Justice for Topo,'" she says. "He was the first."

EARLIER THIS SUMMER, during the Copa América soccer tournament, the Argentine beer company Quilmes ran a television ad that could easily have been scripted by the writer Jorge Luis Borges, the Argentine master of magical realism. In the spot, Argentina and Brazil are tied in the dying moments of an imagined final at the Maracanã when an unseen mystical force, symbolized by tango music, redirects a Brazilian free kick off of Argentina's crossbar and sends the ball on a long, mazy path back toward the opposite end of the field. Eventually the ball reaches and then teeters on Brazil's goal line before *finally* rolling in for the deciding score. As overjoyed Argentines at home celebrate a miraculous triumph over their archrivals, the ad delivers a final message: *It's the first Cup with God in the sky. If he did what he did on the field, imagine it from the heavens.* (No imagining was necessary: On July 10, Argentina beat Brazil 1–0 in the Copa América final at the Maracanã, marking the country's first major title since 1993.)

Nine months have passed since Maradona's death, and in these parts it all still feels inescapable. The first thing Carlos Forment sees when he leaves his home in Buenos Aires every morning is a billboard. The same billboard is all over the city, capturing a teenage Maradona and his parents, frozen in time, an epic life's journey still to come. The sign reads AMOR ETERNO. Eternal love.

"One morning we wake up, I go outside, and it's there," Forment says.

Argentina, it is widely known, has more psychologists per capita than any other nation. Perhaps it's not surprising that those who live there view the ongoing legal battles surrounding and the continued public bereavement over Maradona's death through a psychological lens.

"There was a long period of mourning," Forment says. "Normally, when you go into mourning, what you're doing psychologically is you mourn the loss, and gradually you're able to remove the person from your life. But in Argentina the mourning [for Maradona] became melancholia—when the object has disappeared but you remain attached to it. Which is strange. It's not supposed to happen that way. At the end of mourning, you're supposed to disengage.

"Argentines remain attached to this object, Maradona. And he's not there anymore."

8

FAR AFIELD

A GLANCE AT WAHL'S DATELINES OVER THE YEARS SHOWS HOW thoroughly a midwestern kid with emergent wanderlust took to the global game. World Cups delivered him to Paris, Tokyo, Seoul, Berlin, Shanghai, Johannesburg, Rio, Moscow, and Doha; Summer Olympics found him in Sydney, Athens, Beijing, and London. Tournaments, U.S. team coverage, and feature assignments sent him to a wide scattering of other great cities across six continents. Yet there were roads less traveled, and less salubrious: an armed compound in the Angolan enclave of Cabinda for a piece on Ivorian star Didier Drogba earlier in this volume; Transnistria, the Russian-controlled mafia state inside Moldova, for a story collected in this chapter; Torreón, in Mexico, a front line in the drug war, deemed "the seventh most dangerous city in the world," where he and U.S. striker Hérculez Gómez drove through darkened streets, on the alert for carjackers or worse.

The travel wasn't always underwritten by a corporate conglomerate, either: In 2003, Wahl flew on his own dime to Finland to watch the young Freddy Adu tear up the under-17 World Cup. When he went full-time on soccer in 2009, though, he insisted that he be sent to every U.S. game, as well as every major European and international tournament. And the journeys didn't stop after he left *SI* and set out as an independent journalist. While the archetypal Substack writer files observations from the comfort of a home office, Wahl was constantly on the road, providing the same on-the-scene reporting for subscribers as when he had been backed by legacy media.

Most significantly, he wanted to share his experiences. Whether on assignment for *Sports Illustrated* or traveling for his Substack site, Wahl used his web columns to provide glimpses of his adventures—people, landscapes, food, music, traffic, danger. Chris Stone, his former boss at *SI,* compared Wahl to Anthony Bourdain for how he had taken readers along on a life of "globetrotting freedom, adventure, and pleasure."

Personal Recollections of USA's 1995 Copa América Semifinal Run

From SI.com, June 20, 2016

On several occasions over the years, the United States has been invited to play in the Copa América, the South American football championship. At the 1995 tournament in Uruguay, the Americans were expected only to fill out the draw but instead stormed to the semifinals, defeating powerhouse Argentina in the process. Here, on the eve of the 2016 Copa semis, in which the United States—hosting a special centennial edition of the event—was again to face Argentina, Wahl recalled his madcap experiences at that '95 tournament, which had kindled his passion for both the game and what would become his adopted second country. A familiar image takes center stage in the piece: The Obelisk in downtown Buenos Aires, where he and an American friend danced after the U.S. victory, is the same monument Wahl described in his essay earlier in this collection as the focal point for swarms of mourners after the death of Diego Maradona a quarter century later. And it is the landmark that drew millions of fans in riotous celebration after Argentina's World Cup victory in 2022, a scene Wahl would have relished.

HOUSTON—IN THE BASEMENT OF MY NEW YORK CITY APARTment building, at the bottom of a plastic storage container, I keep an old ugly T-shirt. I bought it for $5 from a street vendor in Montevideo in July 1995, the last time I attended a Copa América semifinal, when I was twenty-one years old, exactly half the age I am today.

When I say it's an ugly T-shirt, I mean it. There's a crude soccer ball superimposed over the light blue stripes of the Uruguayan flag, surrounded by COPA AMÉRICA '95 URUGUAY in black lettering. For some reason there are yellow sun rays coming out of the shirt's neck hole—

another ode to the Uruguayan flag—that make the wearer look like he's dressed up as a giant sunflower.

Yet this clothing abomination might be the favorite T-shirt I own, because it brings back a flood of memories from a special time and a special place. Memories of attending my first U.S. national team game. Memories of living alone for the first time and setting off with the guys on an unplanned road-trip adventure. Memories of eating spaghetti every night on a tight budget while seeking out experiences worth more than anything money could buy.

In 1995, I was a college student living in Buenos Aires for three months and doing research for my senior thesis on politics and soccer in Argentina. For my thesis, I interviewed all kinds of people: club directors, historians, social scientists, and journalists like Ezequiel Fernández Moores and Sergio Levinsky, guys I still know today. One day I met with a man named Mauricio Macri, who was running for the Boca Juniors presidency and would become the president of Argentina in 2015.

Argentina was where I truly fell for the sport. I traveled overnight with Boca fans to a game in Rosario. I stood in the cheap seats with my buddies at a Boca Juniors–River Plate Superclásico. I attended a Copa Libertadores game at River where Colombian legend René Higuita did his famous scorpion kicks in the goal. Argentines are the most passionate soccer fans in the world, I'd argue, and I was full-on smitten with everything about the culture there.

We had a solid group of people to hang out with, too, a mix of expat Americans and cool Argentines: Channing and Matt, Alejandro and Lynn, Maribel and Ricardo, Holden and Scott, and two terrific guys we called Diego El Negro and Diego El Blanco. (Neither one was particularly "darker or lighter" than the other, so their nicknames were always a bit of a mystery.) We couldn't afford to go out to clubs, but I'd host parties at the apartment I was renting on Calle Aráoz near Avenida Las Heras. We'd buy big bottles of cheap Quilmes beer and play Los Fabulosos Cadillacs, and when the Argentines stayed until 7:00 A.M. on Sunday mornings (as is their custom) I'd sprawl out on my bed as a way of saying "This was great, but could we please, please call it a night?"

I learned a lot that summer, including some embarrassingly basic stuff. When I invited my thesis adviser and his wife over for dinner, she had to show me how to use a corkscrew and how to cook a chicken the right way. My friend Channing taught me how to make coffee with her French press. I had no TV, no internet, and plenty of time on my hands. So I read a lot: Bill Buford's *Among the Thugs*, Tocqueville's *Democracy in America*, copies of *The New Yorker* that my parents sent in a CARE package.

In July, the 1995 Copa América started. It was the year after the U.S. had hosted the World Cup, and the U.S. team was playing in the tournament. I watched its opening game at a neighborhood pizza place and pumped my fist when Eric Wynalda scored twice in a 2–1 win over Chile. A loss to Bolivia followed, setting up the group finale against a stacked Argentina team with Gabriel Batistuta, Diego Simeone, and Javier Zanetti.

My friend Matt and I bought U.S. jerseys (vertical red wavy stripes) at a sports store on Calle Florida, and we watched USA-Argentina at Diego El Negro's house. Argentine coach Daniel Passarella decided to rest a bunch of his starters, and we stood in disbelief as the U.S. blew the doors off the Argentines! By the time the 3–0 upset was complete, with goals from Alexi Lalas, Frank Klopas, and Wynalda, the U.S. had clinched first place in the group.

We celebrated by doing what every Argentine soccer fan does when their team wins a huge game: going to the Obelisk, the centerpiece of the Avenida 9 de Julio, and jumping around like idiots waving an American flag. Bad idea. The next day my apartment got robbed, which didn't seem like a coincidence.

But something special was happening for Steve Sampson's U.S. team. The U.S. dispatched Mexico on penalty kicks in the quarterfinals thanks to a huge performance by Brad Friedel, setting up a Copa América semifinal against reigning World Cup champion Brazil. And so Holden and Scott and I decided to go. We got tickets on the Buquebus slow ferry across the Rio de la Plata from Buenos Aires to Montevideo. And when we learned to our surprise that the game was actually in Maldonado, we hopped a *micro* bus down the coast.

What do I remember about the game? Well, I remember being so cold beforehand—this was the Uruguayan winter, after all—that we did a couple rounds of shots in a bar outside the stadium. I remember getting my picture taken in my U.S. jersey with a bunch of male Brazilian fans in drag. (They never really explained why they were dressed that way, but they were clearly having a great time.) And I remember Brazil scoring a first-half goal and the U.S. never getting too close to an equalizer.

There's no shame in losing 1–0 to the world champion in the Copa América semifinals, though. We made friends with the Brazilian fans—I'd give anything to find our photograph from that night—and I knew I had the bug. My first U.S. national team game would not be my last, and sure enough, there have been 119 USMNT "caps" for me since that game twenty-one years ago.

We took the bus back to Montevideo that night and stayed at a $12-a-night hotel. I bought my Copa América '95 T-shirt the next day and finished up my three-month stay in Buenos Aires. Through the magic of the internet, I'm still in touch with several of my friends from that glorious summer.

I'll probably engage in some spirited trash talk with Diego El Negro before the USA-Argentina game on Tuesday. It's the Copa América semifinals, after all, my first since that fateful trip two decades ago, and the two teams are my birth country and my adopted country, the one that gave me a deep and abiding love for this game.

I might have to buy another ugly T-shirt.

On Safari for 7-Footers

FROM *Sports Illustrated*, JUNE 28, 2004

When commissioner David Stern wanted to spread the gospel of the NBA overseas during the early '80s, he shipped game tapes to TV networks in Europe. Two decades later, Stern's move would be hailed as prescient as leagues the world over tried to build borderless fan bases by staging events and peddling merch on multiple continents. But this tactic became obsolete with the emergence of the internet, which allowed anyone anywhere to easily access highlight clips and accelerated the globalization of sports. To explore this phenomenon, *Sports Illustrated* editors in 2004 sent a query to staff asking for story ideas. Within two hours Wahl had written a two-thousand-word memo proposing pieces on the status of soccer in the United States, the place of American football in Samoa, and basketball in Africa. The four-part series that ultimately ran included this story about a camp in Zaria, Nigeria, where NBA scouts searched for seven-foot diamonds in the rough. Wahl focused on Kenechukwu "Kene" Obi, a sweet-natured sixteen-year-old of enticing talent who, to realize his dream, would have to beat a double team of middlemen and immigration barriers. Throughout Wahl's stay, players desperate to break into the U.S. or European systems would press their email addresses into his hands. "So many players want to get out," he said, "and it's pretty poignant because the vast majority won't." Obi did, sort of: He wound up attending prep school in Connecticut, then sat on the bench for most of two seasons at DePaul before stopovers at Division II schools in Canada and Oklahoma and a brief European club career.

To FIND THE MOST PRIZED BIG MAN AT THE WORLD'S MOST remote big-man camp, you have to take four flights, hop on a pothole-weary bus, and light out through the desert of northern Nigeria, past bright-red flame trees and mud-brick huts, past giant anthills and emaciated cattle, past Muslim villages where women in multihued boubous draw water from the community well, until you come upon an astonishing sight: a *Hoosiers*-style gymnasium, rising from the scrub in the town of Zaria. Inside, as daylight fades on an April afternoon, former Michigan coach Brian Ellerbe is running sixteen-year-old Kenechukwu "Kene" Obi, an impossibly long 7'1", 240-pound Nigerian, through the Mikan drill. "*Left* leg up!" Ellerbe bellows.

The drill, a series of alternating left- and right-handed layups, is a staple of most junior high practices. But for Kene, who picked up a basketball for the first time just over a year ago, Ellerbe might as well be teaching him the tango. Before long, though, Kene masters the footwork. His eagerness to learn, to make full use of a frame that has earned him the nickname "Agwo" ("snake" in Igbo, his native tongue), is palpable. "*Right* leg up!" Ellerbe says. "There you go. Put it right up on the square. *There!*"

Surveying Kene and the twenty-seven other gangly teens in identical powder blue jerseys, all at least 6'8", you can understand why American coaches view Africa—particularly Nigeria, the continent's most populous nation—as the next step in the sport's manifest destiny. "There's a lot of physical talent here, but we lack coaching and facilities," says Masai Ujiri, a U.S.-based Denver Nuggets scout from Nigeria who helped organize the camp. "I want more people to come here and develop the continent because it's the next big thing in world basketball, just like Europe was fifteen years ago."

It's starting to happen. Last September, Kene spent six life-changing days in Johannesburg, South Africa, at the NBA's inaugural Africa 100 Camp, the league's first effort at player development on the continent. Despite Kene's rough edges, he drew the attention of Bill Duffy, the superagent whose international clientele includes Yao Ming, Steve Nash, and Rasho Nesterović. Already established in Europe and China, Duffy is setting his sights on Africa, which he views as the most fertile new ground on the planet for basketball players.

"Obi was by far the best prospect there," Duffy says. "He can touch the rim on his tiptoes, he can shoot jump hooks, he's got nice hands, and he can run. I think there are a couple of hundred guys in Africa who could be NBA stars, kids twelve or thirteen years old right now, and he's a case study: Can we take somebody from scratch and develop him? If we do that for four years, by the time he's nineteen or twenty, he could be the first pick in the NBA draft."

Nigeria is at the leading edge of a changing world in which the NBA and its top agents are investing more time and money in more places searching for precious resources (read: seven-footers). These prospects are gradually becoming more accessible—every player in Nigeria will offer you his email address—and are more readily cultivated than they were just a decade ago, thanks to the rising number of options they have worldwide. Should Kene and his fellow campers try the American school system, which offers a free education to go with his basketball training (but limits their practice time)? Or should they opt for the European apprentice system, which places no bounds on the hours players can spend with their coach (but often binds them to brutally long contracts)?

For Kene the speed and scope of the process have been mind-blowing. Suddenly a shy schoolboy from dusty Enugu had American friends in very high places. UConn assistant coach Clyde Vaughan had identified Kene as a potential Huskies recruit and helped broker his admission, including a full-ride scholarship, to the prestigious South Kent (Conn.) Prep School, a rising hoops powerhouse. When it came time to apply for a U.S. visa in May 2003, his supporting documents included a letter from Connecticut's senator Joseph Lieberman—written as a favor to Huskies coach Jim Calhoun. Kenechukwu Obi was on the verge of realizing every Nigerian hoopster's dream: to get out of his country.

But the forces of globalization aren't always in sync. Post-9/11 security concerns have made immigration more difficult, and not even Lieberman's support was sufficient to secure Kene's visa. Throw in a host of other obstacles—a transatlantic turf war, a Nigerian Svengali, and prowling street agents whose aggressive tactics drove Kene from the courts in Lagos—and Kene barely played basketball in the seven months between the camps in South Africa and Zaria. "I just don't know how much the kid has worked," says Ujiri, shaking his head. "Physically he's gifted, and he went to South Africa and progressed by the day. Then he comes back here and there's no progress."

NOONTIME IN ENUGU, eastern Nigeria. The dirt streets of the Achara neighborhood are clogged with kids, animals, sanitation trucks. In a small apartment overlooking a rusting Peugeot on blocks, Godwin Sunday Obi, a sixty-four-year-old retired school principal, welcomes his visitors in the Igbo tradition: with cola fruit, peanut paste, and a prayer. "Come here," he says, walking past family portraits and a wall covered with religious slogans: TO KNEEL IS TO WIN. JESUS CAN SET YOU FREE. GOD WORKS WONDERS. Next to the doorway is a winding trail of hash marks that stops seven feet, one inch above the floor. "When Kenechukwu was little, I started measuring him," says Godwin. "After three months I did it again, and then again. Finally I had to stand on a chair. Now he may be the tallest man in Enugu State!"

Kene smiles sheepishly. "People are always making fun of me because I'm too tall."

"But you've been blessed," his father says. "People have come from all over the world to *nowhere* to see you. Use it proudly!"

Kene, the oldest of Godwin's five children with his second wife, Catherine, inherited his height not from his father and mother—who stand 5'10" and 5'8", respectively—but from his maternal grandfather, Okomkwo Ngwu, a seven-footer. Like many Nigerian kids, Kene is a fan of R. Kelly and Kevin Garnett, and he likes studying economics, the subject his dad once taught. He is also meticulous to an extreme, using his schoolmarm penmanship to log the address of everyone he meets and hand washing his white NBA socks, AFRICA 100 T-shirt and ATLANTA HAWKS sweatpants after every use. (He hangs them to dry only in places where he knows they won't be stolen.)

It's hard to say how Kene will handle the shock of moving abroad; the big-man camp in Zaria was his first trip to northern Nigeria. He can be too gentle, too trusting, and his confidence wavers. In one breath Kene embraces the chance to leave Nigeria ("I know it will be hard, but basketball is my future"), while in the next he disses his game ("To me I'm not good. But they say I'm good"). Shy with strangers, he flashes a sly sense of humor around those who've spent time with him. Asked one day if there are any fat people in Nigeria, he says, "No. Ugo is the only one."

Ugo Udezue, an affable twenty-six-year-old Nigerian who played at Wyoming, is the African basketball director for Duffy's BDA Sports and

Kene's informal adviser. When their relationship began, Udezue knew that college basketball would be an option for Kene only if he did not sign with an agent. "I could have Kene under contract right now, and I don't," Udezue says. Still, he's performing agentlike tasks, keeping tabs on Kene from his Laurel, Maryland, base, seeking to place him in the right situation abroad, and steering him clear of crooked Nigerian suitors: There's a reason, after all, why Colin Powell once called Nigeria "a nation of scammers." Last year Udezue warned Kene not to play at the National Stadium courts in Lagos after one street agent there offered him a plane ticket, a fake visa, and a contract with a team in Lithuania— but only if Kene left for the airport that moment without telling his parents.

Udezue could arrange an eight-year deal for Kene with a European pro team tomorrow, or he could place him in a forward-thinking basketball academy in Spain's Canary Islands. Primarily, though, Udezue has been seeking a midlevel European club willing to exchange the publicity Kene would bring for a year or two of free instruction while he finishes high school. Clearly, such thinking flies in the face of the European system: What incentive does a team have to develop a player if it can't sign him and profit from a buyout if he eventually reaches the NBA?

It certainly would have been easier had Kene been granted a U.S. visa last year. Though the State Department refuses to comment, South Kent Prep coach Raphael Chillious says a consulate official told him the consulate believed Kene was older than his stated age. Indeed, fraud is so pervasive in Nigeria that deceit is often assumed. "If a player goes to the embassy with a fake birth certificate and gets found out, the interviewer is going to have a grudge against any player who comes in," says Udezue. "We have to find a way to make them trust us, because a lot of kids are being left behind."

TOYIN SONOIKI LEANS forward, eyes wide, and jabs his index finger into the table. "Ugo is living in a dream world!" he bellows. A former national-team coach, lawyer, and owner-coach of the Lagos Islanders semipro team, the forty-five-year-old Sonoiki—everyone calls him Noik—is the prime mover in Nigerian basketball. With his round face and abbreviated mustache, he looks like a cross between Nolan Richardson and der Führer. "Ugo is looking for a situation where Kenechukwu goes to Europe without a contract? And somebody should want to develop him?" Sonoiki asks. "Ugo should jump in a coffin! It won't happen. Kenechukwu is a late starter. On an athletic scholarship in America, kids can play only twenty hours a week, four months a year. In Europe the kids are practicing with coaches twice a day, 365 days a year. That's what he needs! Yes, you sign contracts that are not very palatable. But that's the system."

There was a time when Udezue and Noik were the closest of friends. In the mid-1990s, when Udezue decided to pursue a basketball career, he moved into Noik's spacious Lagos house, starred on his Islanders team, and (through Noik's connections) secured a visa to attend high school in the U.S. "He is the best basketball mind here, and he is a good coach," says Udezue, one of four dozen players Noik has helped send to the U.S. over the past decade. "If Kene had been with him for the past year, he would be something else right now. But Noik comes with a price we can't afford."

Sonoiki has a reputation as a scheming Svengali who profits from Nigerian players when they sign lengthy deals with his sketchy Eastern European contacts. Though Kene's family says Noik never had permission to pursue any opportunities for their son, that didn't keep him from negotiating a deal for Kene with a Greek pro team last year. (The Obis declined the offer.) Likewise, the parent of a player at Admiral Farragut Academy in St. Petersburg, Florida, says he gave Noik $2,500 for "transportation and visa costs" in June 2003 after Noik claimed to be Kene's guardian and promised to deliver him to the school. "He described him as this 7'1" wonder kid," says Tommy Lampley, an AAU coach whose son, also named Tommy, was the captain of Farragut's state champion team last spring. "I'm salivating. So I ask, 'What would it take to get him to Farragut?' Without hesitation he said '$2,500.'"

According to Lampley, Sonoiki was certified as reputable by a coaching contact, so he wired him the money. Soon afterward, Lampley says, all communication with Noik stopped. (Sonoiki claims the money went toward a nonrefundable plane ticket for Kene to Florida that was never used.)

Of course, Kene claims he didn't know then that Sonoiki was passing

himself off to American schools as his guardian, never knew he was taking money in his name. Mention Noik around Kene these days, and his
fear is obvious. Whatever happened with Kene, independent observers
acknowledge that Noik's decision to wheel and deal in the largely un-
regulated global marketplace has tarnished his reputation as a builder of
talent. "I wish I could go back to the days when I'd come to the National
Stadium and Noik would be sitting in a chair and all the kids would be
working their asses off," Ujiri says. "Noik then was not so aware of the
dealing world. It was more in the best interests of the kids. Kene would
be perfect in that situation. Unfortunately, I don't think it can be like
that again."

Nor should it be, Noik says. "Why should I work with kids and watch
other people who have done nothing with them come and take them
into situations for their own benefit?" he says, his voice rising. In other
words, it comes down to turf. Noik's message is simple: Duffy can send
his minions to Nigeria, but I'll be damned if I give up my stake without
a fight.

Suddenly, the power at the Lagos Sheraton goes out. Nigeria is the
world's sixth biggest oil producer, a resource-rich West African giant
with 150 million people, and yet every night the electricity fails with
head-scratching regularity.

In the pitch black, Noik keeps talking as if nothing has happened.

⸺⸺

ON KENE'S LAST day at the big-man camp in Zaria, the coaches separate the top ten players and have them play short games of three-on-
three. Kene is the youngest camper chosen, and it shows. He doesn't
demand the ball or initiate any moves—it takes a leap of imagination to
envision him on the same court with Shaq—but he blocks a few shots,
grabs some rebounds, and sticks a putback.

It's nothing special, but the mere fact that Obi is competing after his
seven-month layoff is a major victory. Nobody thinks it's too late for
Kene to develop into an NBA prospect—not Ellerbe, not Ujiri, not even
Noik. The lingering question is where that growth will take place. Will it
be the Canary Islands, where former U.S. college coach Rob Orellana
has agreed to admit Kene, scholarship included? Or will it be Norway,
where big-man camp attendee Will Voigt, the American coach of the

professional Ulriken Eagles, has consented to work with Kene and even found him an Igbo-speaking host family? If the right visa were to come through, either place would meet Udezue's goal of not tying Kene down to a long-term pro contract, and the Canary Islands option would allow Kene to retain his college eligibility. (Duffy would have to cover Kene's living expenses in Norway, thus foreclosing the college route.)

As of Sunday, Kene was still in limbo, staying with a friend of Udezue in Senegal and waiting to interview for a Spanish visa. If it isn't granted, he'll spend the summer in Lagos living with his aunt and uncle and suiting up in the Nigerian league for Dodan Warriors, the archrival of Noik's Islanders. "He needs to play," says Warriors coach Alex Owoicho. "In Enugu they don't play a lot of games, but in Lagos we play a lot. He's going to have a chance to play for three months nonstop."

A chance. It's all that Kene wants. That's why he keeps working with Udezue despite all the setbacks, why he's out here on the basketball court at Ugo's hotel in Enugu on a hot Saturday afternoon in April. Surrounded by a grove of cashew and mango trees, Udezue runs Kene through jump hooks, free throws, spin moves, and the Mikan drill before going over one last thing. "Now you're going to take a dribble and do a jump stop," he says. "Most big guys on the break go to the rack, but if you just stop, you can do this." Udezue demonstrates, stopping and leaning to his right as he jumps to get off the shot. To his surprise, Kene gets it right the first time.

"Good job, Kene! Now do one more . . ."

Meet the President, Get Robbed: Just Another Day in Honduras

From SI.com, October 10, 2009

Tales of hostility when the U.S. national team ventures to play in Central America are legendary: fireworks and raucous bands outside the U.S. hotel in the wee hours to disrupt sleep; stale beer, batteries, and bags of urine hurled at Americans in the stadiums; heat, altitude, humidity, unconscionable traffic. Wahl had seen so much during his many reporting trips to Latin America that he used an all-purpose modifier, "CONCACAF-fy," to describe it. But nothing prepared him for what happened in October 2009 while on assignment in Honduras for a critical World Cup qualifier staged in the midst of a constitutional crisis following a de facto coup d'état. In the end, Wahl's lifeline in Honduras was every traveling sportswriter's best friend: Recalling the incident in a post on his Substack in 2022, he noted, "Since my wallet and credit cards had been taken, [I] was able to get a hotel room at the Tegucigalpa Marriott using my points. Marriott points: Saving my rear for more than two decades."

The Honduran postscript to this piece: Roberto Micheletti, who had been the country's president for only a few months when Wahl met him, ceded the role following free elections in November 2009. (His rival, Manuel Zelaya, became first gentleman of Honduras in January 2022, when Zelaya's wife, Xiomara Castro, was elected president.) As for the soccer, which had been the point of the journey, Honduras fell to the United States 3–2 in the match that night in 2009. But the next week Los Catrachos advanced to the 2010 World Cup with a victory in El Salvador, the country with which Honduras fought the infamous 1969 Guerra del Fútbol, in which a soccer match touched off a hundred-hour-long war that killed three thousand people.

Tegucigalpa, honduras—For a few minutes on Friday night, Honduran interim president Roberto Micheletti sounded happy to be talking with a reporter about something other than the political crisis that has engulfed his country.

Micheletti is a soccer fan, and tonight in San Pedro Sula, the Honduran national team plays its most important game in twenty-seven years, a World Cup qualifier against the United States. If Honduras wins, it will almost certainly clinch a World Cup berth for the first time since 1982. And Micheletti, for his part, thinks his Catrachos will do more than just win.

"Honduras four, United States zero!" Micheletti told me in Spanish. "The heart of the Hondurans is bigger than ever!"

Micheletti has a lot on his plate these days. With mediation from the Organization of American States, his aides met this week with representatives of Manuel Zelaya, who was deposed as president on June 28. Zelaya sneaked back into Honduras on September 21 and has been holed up in the Brazilian Embassy here ever since. No other countries, including the U.S., have recognized Micheletti's regime.

Even though no resolution to the standoff has been reached, Honduras will put aside politics for ninety minutes tonight to support their national team. "Soccer unites all Hondurans," Micheletti explained during our ten-minute conversation, "without distinction among classes, political parties, religion, or race. Soccer brings everyone together.

"We still remember our national team from 1982, and we Hondurans all live with the dream of returning to the World Cup. Let's hope that God gives us the opportunity to achieve this goal, which we'd do by beating the Gringos and the Salvadorans [on Wednesday]."

A fan of two Honduran clubs (Real España and Motagua) who says he still plays soccer once or twice a year, Micheletti won't be at the stadium tonight, but he did say that he would be watching the game in his living room at home. "I have to watch at home because I scream a lot at the TV," he said.

The de facto president is no dummy: He knows that a Honduras win tonight will be good for him politically. But he also seemed to be a genuine fan, naming off several of his favorite Honduran players, including

Carlos Pavón, Carlos Costly, David Suazo, and Ramón Núñez, and he seemed more than a little bullish about tonight's game.

"We have players from international clubs on our team, and therefore we have a lot of confidence, hope, and faith that we will achieve this victory," he told me. "But I want to wish both teams luck, that they play a clean game, and that for a moment we can forget any sadness [in the country] and enjoy a great soccer game."

And if Honduras qualifies for the World Cup? "I'll call a national holiday," said Micheletti. "We are going to celebrate!"

FRIDAY WAS AN odd day for me. One moment I was speaking with the man who runs Honduras, and another moment I was being robbed at gunpoint in Tegucigalpa.

My idea had been to drive from San Pedro Sula about 150 miles southeast to the capital, stopping to interview people along the way about the significance of the Honduran soccer team's success during a time of deep divisions within the country.

And that's exactly what I did. I spoke to businessmen in San Pedro Sula, gas station workers in Comayagua, and even a clown that I encountered on the side of the road in a dusty town outside Tegucigalpa. (The man, whose nom de clown is "Chiquitón," said he'd be watching the game. He also said that he clowns at birthday parties, Christmas celebrations, and even funerals.)

Along the way I discovered that Honduras is a beautiful country, with forest green mountains, gorgeous lakes, and friendly people.

Except, perhaps, for one. On Friday afternoon, I ventured to the embassy district of Tegucigalpa, where hundreds of gun-toting police have surrounded the Brazilian Embassy (and its occupant Zelaya). The police chief gave me the clearance to interview some soccer-loving police officers, whose scowls melted into smiles as they talked of getting a few hours off from work to watch USA-Honduras.

After we finished, I started walking back to my car, which I had parked a few blocks away in what appeared to be a safe part of town a stone's throw from the U.S. Embassy. And then, in broad daylight, with hundreds of police officers only a couple hundred yards away, a twenty-something male ran up behind me, pulled out a gun, and threatened to kill me if I didn't give him my things.

I've had experience working in some hairy situations—from a week in Nigeria to a drive across Mexico, from a story near the Israeli-Lebanese border to a road trip with hard-core soccer fans in Argentina—but I had never been threatened with a gun before.

I gave him my wallet and iPhone, and thankfully he disappeared down the aptly named Avenida de Paz (Peace).

But I did survive, chastened and a bit embarrassed. Interim president Micheletti apologized for the robbery and said that it no doubt was a Zelaya supporter.

The Craziest Sports Story of the Year Is FC Sheriff

FROM FÚTBOL WITH GRANT WAHL, NOVEMBER 10, 2021

For the bulk of his career, Wahl could draw on the resources and count on the support of a legacy media company such as Time Inc. or Fox when he traveled to distant or dangerous locales. Once he went independent in 2021, however, he was on his own. For this excerpted piece on FC Sheriff—the unknown underdog that had shocked Real Madrid in the 2021 Champions League group stage—Wahl traveled to the team's home in Transnistria, the Russian-dominated enclave within Moldova in eastern Europe. The piece exemplifies Wahl's fearlessness and fierce curiosity, as well as the enterprise with which he approached unfamiliar stories and places, laying the pretravel groundwork by chatting up experts and cultivating sources, and then taking chances on the ground, following the story where it led. Only now he would do it with no global network of news bureaus or corporate security to fall back on if trouble arose. Three months after this piece appeared on Wahl's Substack, Russia invaded Ukraine, and Transnistria—sitting forebodingly on Ukraine's western border—would become a potential flash point in that conflict.

TIRASPOL, MOLDOVA—HOW DO YOU BEGIN TO UNDERSTAND THE strangest upset in the history of the Champions League? Maybe a souvenir, I thought, would be the place to start.

So earlier this year I flew from New York through Istanbul to Chișinău, the capital of Moldova, Europe's poorest country, hired a driver for a ninety-minute trip east on bumpy roads, and showed my passport at a grim customs station for a nation that doesn't exist.

Continuing onward, I crossed the Dniester River, where the language switches from Romanian to Russian, the alphabet from Latin to Cyrillic, passing still-honored statues of Lenin fronting brutalist Soviet-style buildings topped by the flags of Russia and unrecognized Transnistria (green and red; hammer and sickle)—or Pridnestrovie, as the locals call it.

Eventually I passed a Russian military base, which minds one of the world's largest weapons dump, in a twenty-five-mile-wide disputed territory known for porous borders and spectacular amounts of smuggling (arms, cigarettes, anything else you could imagine) until I reached a dilapidated nine-floor apartment building on October 25th Street, Tiraspol's main drag.

There, Keston Julien, a twenty-three-year-old left back from Trinidad and Tobago who plays for Tiraspol's FC Sheriff, welcomed me into his third-floor apartment, which is nicer on the inside than on the outside. And there, hanging like a hunting trophy on the living-room wall, is the game-worn Real Madrid shirt of David Alaba, which the star defender traded with Julien after Sheriff had done the unthinkable, beating the thirteen-time European champions 2–1 in a UEFA Champions League group-stage match at Madrid's Santiago Bernabéu Stadium on September 28.

Julien never thought he'd live in a place like this, where Western credit cards don't work, cellphone service for visitors is spotty at best, and an unrecognized country has its own currency, the Transnistrian ruble, that's worthless everywhere else. "If you see any Black people here," he says, "they're football players."

Then again, he never thought he'd be part of the craziest global sports story of 2021.

Run by a former KGB agent turned oligarch, Viktor Gushan, who named it after the heroes of the movie Westerns he favors, Sheriff is more than a soccer team. It's a business entity that owns everything that matters in Transnistria: the grocery stores, the gas stations, a casino, a TV channel, a telephone company, a winery, a reportedly vast smuggling network, and Transnistria's most opulent structures: a $200 million soccer stadium and fourteen-field training facility complex.

But despite that wealth and power, Sheriff, the first team from the Moldovan league to reach the Champions League group stage, doesn't spend nearly as much on players as the elite teams it's playing against. And while the club saves money by forbidding its players from trading away their uniform jerseys in domestic games, it makes an exception for high-profile Champions League matches. Julien, the first Trinidadian in ten years to play in the Champions League, took full advantage of that with Alaba, one of his idols. "I still haven't washed it yet," Julien says with a smile.

In twenty-five years as a journalist, I had never encountered a sports team whose star players are infinitely easier to reach than the club press officer whose job is to connect with the media. Sheriff is the first. And so, within an hour of arriving in Tiraspol, five days before the November 3 Champions League game against Italian champion Inter, I find myself meeting with a procession of Sheriff's top players from a Champions League roster that represents fifteen nations, including Brazil, Colombia, Ghana, Greece, Guinea, Luxembourg, Mali, Peru, and Uzbekistan. (Yes, there are even a couple of players from Moldova.)

Rugged center back Gustavo Dulanto, Sheriff's twenty-six-year-old Peruvian captain, meets me at the restaurant Kasta with his wife, Daniela, and their daughter, Rafaela, four. "Thank you for coming to, as I tell my friends from Peru, the end of the world," he says in Spanish with a laugh. Dulanto joined Sheriff in February from Portugal's Boavista, but his strong play and outsized personality earned him the captaincy within months.

"Not all of us handle English that well, but there's good vibes in the dressing room, so we make ourselves understand each other in any way we can," he explains. "It's really funny, because we try to communicate in signs. The truth is that this is a large group with so many nationalities, so you end up learning their cultures. We also have different religions, so you'll learn about that too. This is the beauty of soccer."

Sheriff's path through the 2021–22 Champions League has bordered on the miraculous. It had to play eight qualifying games, dispatching the champions of Serbia (Red Star Belgrade) and Croatia (Dinamo Zagreb) along the way just to reach the group stage. Then Sheriff beat Ukraine's Shakhtar Donetsk 2–0 in the group-stage opener and pulled off the upset of the decade at Real Madrid. Sheriff has come back to earth with consecutive losses to Inter, but it's still just one point behind Inter and three behind Real Madrid with two match days left.

After the game in Madrid, a wiseguy reporter from *El Chiringuito*, Spain's popular telenovela-style soccer TV show, cornered Dulanto and asked him if Sheriff's players were all fully professional or had other jobs outside of soccer. "It was a pretty silly question," Dulanto says. "It seemed disrespectful. The truth is we're a team nobody knew, and we're making a name for ourselves with all the performances we've had."

But *El Chiringuito*'s question wasn't far off base. That becomes clear when I meet Sheriff's breakout star, twenty-seven-year-old midfielder Sébastien Thill of Luxembourg, for lunch at Love Café, a cute French bistro on Lenin Street that serves delicious omelettes and macarons for dessert. Thill scored a *golazo* for the ninetieth-minute game winner at Real Madrid and added a brilliant thirty-five-yard equalizing free kick at Inter on October 19 before Sheriff ended up losing 3–1.

A relentless runner who idolizes former German star Bastian Schweinsteiger, Thill wears Schweini's number 31 and has devoted one of the tattoos telling his career story on his left leg to the 2014 World Cup winner. But while Thill comes from a soccer family—his parents, Serge and Nathalie, and two younger brothers, Olivier and Vincent, have all played for the Luxembourg national team—it was only just more than a year ago that Sébastien wasn't a fully professional player himself.

In fact, his side gig in Luxembourg was mowing the same playing field at Progrès Niederkorn's Jos Haupert Stadium that he would compete on when the weekend arrived. "I worked in the morning, and then in the afternoon I'd go to training," Thill explains. "I worked on the pitch, so I'd know where to run, where the pitch is good and where it's not."

But when Thill saw his two brothers having success as full professionals playing outside Luxembourg, he decided to give it a go himself. "I didn't want to finish my career and say, 'I have some regrets,'" he says. "And so I had this chance to sign in Russia, and I decided to use my chance."

After a successful half season on loan at Russia's Tambov, Thill joined Sheriff on a one-and-a-half-year loan in January. Not only has he scored massive goals in the soccer cathedrals of the Bernabéu and San Siro, but he has run more in this season's Champions League than any other player (49.1 kilometers)—not bad for a guy who quit smoking only fifteen months ago.

No matter what you may think about the people who own FC Sheriff, the story of its players in the Champions League is one of the most compelling underdog tales in sports.

"My teammates' personalities are spectacular," says Dulanto. "They have a courage that I had not seen much before, they're hungry for glory, and that makes me improve every day. It's like family, right? You always try to be with someone who makes you better every day. In my case, it's my wife and daughter. And my teammates do the same. I would kill for them. That's the truth."

BEFORE I LEFT for Europe, I contacted a few people who had experience in Tiraspol. One of them was Slava Malamud, a Baltimore-based teacher and freelance sportswriter. Until his teenage years, Malamud lived in Soviet Moldova (in what is now Transnistria) in the city of Bender, a ten-minute drive from Tiraspol, where he spent much of his time in small, crumbling stadiums watching desultory lower-league soccer games.

As the Soviet Union was breaking up, he says, Bender was where most of the fighting took place in 1991 and '92 between Romanian- and Russian-speaking Moldovans. "It was a war being fought, but for the stupidest of reasons: Should we or should we not learn the Romanian language?" Malamud says. "Basically that was the whole thing." Malamud was sixteen, and when fighting factions started trying to recruit him, he decided to leave the country as a refugee.

Eventually, after twenty months of fighting, the sides reached a truce. Transnistria was technically still part of Moldova according to the international community, but it was separate in virtually every other way, with military forces tightly guarding the so-called borders.

"Transnistria was never recognized," Malamud explains. "They received military help from Russia. In the '90s, the Russians came in as quote-unquote peacekeepers, but in reality they just established this buffer state in order to keep Moldova from running too far away from the Russian sphere of influence. They wanted to keep Moldova from joining Romania. So Russia set up shop in Transnistria, and if Moldova tries anything, we're going to just annex this—like a trial run for what they did with Crimea and eastern Ukraine. And because Transnistria was never recognized by anyone, including by Russia, they were basically left to their own devices, meaning you survive every which way you can."

More than anything, that meant smuggling. Transnistria's lightly monitored eastern border with Ukraine allowed for easy and furtive access to and from the Black Sea port of Odessa, sixty miles away, which opened up supply lines of contraband to Asia, Africa, and the rest of Europe. And Transnistria was already home to an enormous weapons depot for the former Soviet Army. Much of the arms cache had been phased out by the Russians but later found its way to crisis zones in regions around the world.

"Sheriff is just an organized crime group. That's it," says someone I spoke to who has spent significant time in Transnistria and studied the area. "And they own the soccer team for some reason. And now these guys are doing well in western Europe, and nobody there has any clue that these guys are owned by monsters."

So Sheriff is just a giant money-laundering front? "Oh yeah, everybody knows this," Malamud says. "The number one business in Transnistria, which finances most of their budget, is gun trafficking. A lot of illegal guns get trafficked between Europe and Asia through Transnistria, because with a large enough bribe you can accomplish pretty much anything. So this is how they get their money. And this is how the [Sheriff] supermarket chain exists, and this is how the stadium was built— because there's not enough money in all of Transnistria, except in Swiss bank accounts, to finance a four-star UEFA stadium. That's like the one claim to fame they've got.

"You should expect to see a very nicely preserved slice of the Soviet Union," Malamud tells me. "And they're very proud of it, too. Everything is in different shades of gray. You've got lots of Lenin statues and random statues of tanks and red banners with the hammer and sickle everywhere. And this stadium is the one splash of color anywhere around, this beautiful blue, yellow, and black arena in the middle of nothing, just pastures everywhere. It's an extremely surreal sight."

Everyone I talked to was excited that I was getting to visit Tiraspol. "It's going to be something else, I'm telling you, Grant," said Octavio Zambrano, an Ecuadorian who had coached in Major League Soccer before taking a two-year stint with a team in Tiraspol and who offered to connect me with a friend there. "Be ready for it. I could start describing it, but it would not do justice to what you're about to see."

Malamud, for his part, signed off with a piece of advice. "If they offer you what they call local cognac in Tiraspol, you may sip it, but I mean, it knocks out a horse," he said.

"What's it called?"

"It's called Kvint. Most Russians are able to withstand it. But it's strong stuff."

"GRANT! GRANT! GET in the car!"

This is concerning. I have been in Tiraspol for only half an hour, just long enough to check into the Hotel Russia. It's the lone decent hotel in town, the one where Inter and Real Madrid will stay when they visit, the one with the Sheriff Casino.

My driver has already left to return to Chişinău. I am by myself, standing on a corner of October 25th Street and staring at my phone as I try to connect with Keston Julien on a maddeningly poor signal to meet him for an interview at his apartment somewhere in this area.

I haven't met anybody in Tiraspol yet. But for some reason a guy in a car is yelling my name (how would he know my name?) and telling me in English to get inside.

I flash back to the U.S. State Department's website, which on October 12 posted its most severe travel advisory warning in bright red about Moldova: Level 4, Do Not Travel:

Do not travel to Moldova due to COVID-19 and unresolved conflict. Exercise increased caution in:

• Transnistria due to the **unresolved conflict** between this breakaway region and the central government.

Transnistria Region: A separatist regime controls the region and access to U.S. citizens is difficult. The U.S. Embassy may not be able to help if you encounter difficulties there. There are many checkpoints along roads leading into and out of Transnistria. Taking photographs of checkpoints, military facilities, and security forces is prohibited.

A thousand things are racing through my head: *Am I being picked up for taking photographs of the customs checkpoint for Transnistria? Those military guys in fatigues took my name and passport info, after all. Is something bad about to happen? I already got mugged at gunpoint in*

Honduras in 2009 while reporting a story. I'd prefer not to be abducted in Transnistria.

The car stops. It's a black BMW. I look inside. The driver informs me that he is Illia Kraskovski, Octavio Zambrano's friend. He smiles. "I thought it was you!" he says. "Welcome to Tiraspol!" Releasing a giant sigh of relief, even though I'm still weirded out that the one person who'd know me in a city of 135,000 would just happen to drive by, I climb into the passenger seat and explain that I'm trying to locate my interview subject. Illia nods, lets me out of the car, and says he'll pick me up at the Hotel Russia at seven and take me to dinner.

Aside from my player interviews, my first day in Tiraspol is a series of fish-out-of-water vignettes. I love to do what I call "Benjamins trips," which is to say reporting trips in which Western credit cards aren't accepted and I have to bring U.S. hundred-dollar bills in an old-fashioned money belt. It means I'm getting off the beaten track. Instructed by the woman at the Hotel Russia front desk to prepay for my room in Transnistrian rubles (i.e., cash), I walk across the street and enter what I think she told me was the bank.

But I'm terrible at reading Cyrillic letters, and it turns out not to be a bank at all. Too late. The woman inside doesn't speak English, and I have the idiotic habit of getting flustered and trying to speak the one foreign language I do know (Spanish) to a person who still has no idea what I'm saying. After listening to my gibberish, she points me upstairs to a room where a man in his twenties is giving a lecture on Transnistria (in English!) to a group of three visitors.

With the help of the lecturer, I find the bank—the word "bank" in Cyrillic letters actually does look a lot like "bank"—and convert a few of those Benjamins to Transnistrian rubles to pay for my hotel. After that, I spend the afternoon checking out the Sheriff supermarket (which operates like any other grocery store, except with more alcohol) and walking down October 25th Street, taking pictures of the Transnistrian Supreme Soviet, with its Lenin statue and more hammer-and-sickle flags.

When Illia meets me at the Hotel Russia that night, a fleet of black-windowed SUVs is outside the front entrance. "The Sheriff bosses must be having a meeting at the hotel," he tells me as we pull away.

I perk up. "Do you think Viktor Gushan is here?" I ask. I have become borderline obsessed with the Sheriff kingpin, by far the most powerful person in Transnistria. Gushan doesn't give interviews with anyone these days, and the only one with an English-language outlet that anyone can remember took place for a 2005 *Vanity Fair* story. "Bring any businessman from France or the United States here, and he'll hang himself in six months," Gushan told the story's writer, Brett Forrest. "The [Transnistria] stamp is not recognized internationally. Nothing is allowed. We have had to operate . . . between things."

My Viktor Gushan pursuit continues all week.

"You can try your chance to have an interview with him, but I think it will be hard," Sébastien Thill says.

At one point I get Gushan's phone number from a source who says it's legit. I send texts and call him but receive no responses. Then, on Champions League match night against Inter, I stake out the stadium's VIP entrance in the hours before the game. Gushan never appears.

GAME DAY IN the Moldovan league: On the Sunday night before the Sheriff-Inter Champions League game, I've come to Hîncești, a town of 12,000 an hour's drive southwest of Chișinău. It's a top-of-the-table clash between host Petrocub and Sheriff, and the vibe is a lot like a high school soccer game in the U.S. Tickets are free. There are maybe three hundred fans and just one table selling hot coffee and tea, which hit the spot on a chilly evening.

The scene is a charming one, and the soccer isn't bad—Sheriff, which has claimed nineteen of the past twenty-one Moldovan titles, wins 2–0—but it's hard to wrap my mind around the fact that one of these teams just won a Champions League game at Real Madrid.

More important, while the contrast between the Champions League and the Moldovan league may seem quaint on the surface, teams in the Moldovan league are dying in a system everyone here says is corrupt, and Sheriff isn't doing anything to help matters. I ask Ion Testemițanu, one of Moldova's greatest players and a former national team assistant coach: Does FC Sheriff's success have anything to do with the Moldovan league?

"No, never," he says. "That is absolute. We have a lot of problems in the Moldovan league, like fixing matches. Our national teams are regressing every year. In Moldovan football, every year clubs disappear. There are problems with finances, with sponsors, with everything. So we don't really have any professional football in Moldova. Before, fifteen years ago, we had something. Now, nothing. Only fixing games. I saw it yesterday, fixing games."

Seriously?

"Sfîntul Gheorghe beat Dinamo-Auto," Testemiţanu says. "So I see the goals and I understand what happened there. I see the games. FC Floreşti–Zimbru, 3–0. I see the goals. I understand how they won. I know everything that has happened." He shows me the highlights on his phone. They're certainly soft goals, marked mainly by goalkeeper blunders.

Compared to the rest of Moldova's teams, Sheriff is swimming in money. But while Sheriff is technically in the Moldovan league, the requirements for a team based in Transnistria are different from those for the other clubs.

"Sheriff Tiraspol pays not one single lei [the national currency] to the Moldovan economy. Not one," says Octavian Ţîcu, the former national minister for sport. "And I put this question in parliament because Petrocub, for example, which is from Hîncești, a small regional center, the owner paid [to] the Republic of Moldova taxes for salary, taxes for international transfers, taxes for participation in the Europa League. Sheriff pays nothing.

"They simply destroyed our football," he continues. "They use our football for their own interest. They have football success, and Moldova is a kind of sparring partner, using the boxing terminology. They have almost no Moldovans in their team and no benefits for the national team or the future of Moldovan football. Because we know they don't invest in Moldovan football properly. They invest in Sheriff."

FIVE DAYS AFTER my arrival in Tiraspol, the big night finally arrives: Sheriff is hosting Inter on UEFA Champions League match day four. If Sheriff wins, it will stay top of the group, ahead of Real Madrid and Inter, with just two games left. A Sheriff loss will likely leave it in third place, behind the two favorites. Before the game I attempt to find some Sheriff merch and locate a tiny tent outside the stadium. There are no jerseys for sale, only half-Sheriff, half-Inter scarves commemorating the game. I buy three for people back home.

After my fruitless Viktor Gushan stakeout, I venture thirty minutes before kickoff into the Ultras Sheriff section of the stands. It's like any other supporters group anywhere in the world: They raise their Sheriff scarves in unison, belt out chants, and raise an elaborate tifo right before the game. Not many of the ultras are comfortable speaking English to me, but I have a fun conversation with Alex Sazonov, the friendly lead drummer.

Is this the most important game in Sheriff history?

"Yes. Now this is the biggest game, because Inter is the biggest club who come here. But Real Madrid will be even bigger!"

And what do you want people in my country to know about FC Sheriff and Tiraspol?

"That Sheriff will win the Champions League!"

When I speak to Sheriff's players, one thing becomes clear to me: The contrast between the Moldovan league and the UEFA Champions League is huge, but the one between Sheriff's shady ownership and its thoroughly likable players may be even bigger. These guys uprooted their lives and their families to come to "the end of the world," as Gustavo Dulanto says. They have pulled off miraculous Champions League upsets and put themselves into a position to be bought by richer teams in more established soccer countries that can offer a better standard of living. You can't help but root for them.

Keston Julien left Trinidad and Tobago at age nineteen, spent three years with a club in Slovakia and came to Tiraspol with dreams of playing in the English Premier League. He checks the Transfermarkt website and sees the value of Sheriff players increasing by the month. "A lot of clubs are interested in our players," he says. "I have a friend, [midfielder Edmund] Addo, the number 21. He's from Ghana. I think before the Champions League his value was maybe $300,000. Now his value is $1.2 million."

Dulanto may not be able to get Disney+ in Tiraspol, but he appreciates the opportunity that Sheriff's European run has afforded him. "My life has changed a lot since we qualified for the Champions League," he says. "Good performances, both individually and at a group level, help finding another team in a better league and help financially speaking. That's why I came here."

Only one year into his life as a fully professional soccer player, Sébastien Thill is still discovering what he can achieve. He went to Russia to find out, and now Tiraspol, and having scored at the Bernabéu and San Siro, he'd love to continue his path upward in the European game and lead Luxembourg to a major tournament.

Thill says he has more tattoos on the way. Maybe he'll get one on his left leg with the date of his goal at Real Madrid. "I need to finish [covering] my back, so this will be a big project," he says. "For the rest, there's not that much space. Maybe my neck? But I wait for my marriage. I want to look normal on photos, and then afterward, maybe."

The Champions League game against Inter goes well—for the first half. Inter dominates, but Sheriff holds firm and the teams are scoreless at the break. The Italian champion's quality takes over in the second half, however. Goals by Marcelo Brozović, Milan Škriniar, and Alexis Sánchez give Inter a 3–0 lead. A late goal by Sheriff's Adama Traoré isn't enough. Inter wins 3–1, leaving the group standings like this: Real Madrid 9 points, Inter 7, Sheriff 6, Shakhtar 1.

As I leave Tiraspol for the long journey home, I can't help but think back to something Slava Malamud told me in our conversation. "If you've ever read Russian literature of any kind," he said, "there's no clear border between happy, sad, depressing, uplifting, horrifying, and wonderful."

The story of FC Sheriff has all those elements. There's no clear border on the page. There's no clear border between countries. Seeking clarity is a lot like pursuing Viktor Gushan. You'll probably never find it.

A Love Letter to Korea

FROM SI.COM, JUNE 24, 2002

While magazine stories typically called for strict objectivity and the third-person voice, by the early 2000s the internet was becoming a looser place where journalists could get personal, tell behind-the-scenes tales, and open up to their audience. Wahl saw the value of the platform in its promise of connection between writer and reader, and he loved to provide glimpses into what he was experiencing beyond the pitch as he chased stories around the world. This short column written during the 2002 World Cup, for which the United States was based in Seoul (Japan served as cohost), became a sensation in Korea and made Wahl an instant celebrity there. So pleased were his Korean hosts with his kind words about their country that he eventually landed a spot on the Seoul equivalent of *Oprah*. For the last two decades of his life, Wahl and his wife admired a vase that enjoyed pride of place in their home—a gift from a grateful Korean monk.

SEOUL—WELL, THAT SETTLES IT. FROM HERE ON OUT, YOU CAN call me an honorary Korean American. This is my thirty-second straight day in this country, and it's still providing no end of amazements. Not just on the soccer field, either—though South Korea's miraculous run to Tuesday's semifinal against Germany is an irresistible story—but in everyday life.

Today, for example, I was waiting in the rain at a crosswalk here. Suddenly a middle-aged Korean man walked over, smiled, and held his umbrella above my head. Last week a colleague told me a story about how she had collapsed into a subway seat one night after a game. Exhausted, she closed her eyes, only to feel a sensation on her right shoulder. The elderly Korean woman sitting next to her was giving her a massage. After that, she softly sang a lullaby in her ear.

Understand, back in December I was disappointed when I learned the U.S. team would be based in this country instead of in Japan. I'm not sure why. Maybe it was the food. Maybe Seoul somehow seemed less intriguing than Tokyo. Maybe I was just a little ignorant.

The fact is, I couldn't have been more wrong—or more lucky. I always tell my Argentine friends that I wish I had been there in 1978 when the streets filled with joy after the home side won the World Cup. Before this year's tournament, I felt a loss knowing that I wouldn't experience the festive atmosphere that reigned in France when Les Bleus hoisted the Cup four years ago.

Wrong again. While taking the night off from work last Tuesday, I caught the South Korea–Italy match with an *SI* editor (and fellow soccer nut) at the 3 Alleys pub in Itaewon, Seoul's Yank-friendly entertainment district. The place was full. Half of the denizens were Koreans, and half were Anglos rooting for Korea. When Ahn Jung-Hwan's overtime header sent the Italians packing, this city erupted. Streets filled. Fireworks lit up the night. At Gecko's tavern afterward, Koreans and non-Koreans alike danced on chairs to the music of Bryan Adams and Bon Jovi. It was even more memorable than the night on the Champs-Élysées when I waded through 2 million victorious Gauls—and this was after a second-round win.

(I'm still bitter that I was on deadline for the magazine this past weekend and missed the festivities after South Korea eliminated Spain in the quarters. Must have been off the hook again.)

I'm leaving the peninsula in two days, and you know what? If South Korea makes the World Cup final, I'll be watching the game at a stadium in Japan, wishing all the while that I were back in Seoul with the most fervent, good-hearted fans you'll ever see. Who knows? It may be Argentina '78 all over again.

What do I love about Korea? I love . . .

. . . the way sweat starts beading on my scalp the second I swallow a bite of kimchi (which tastes way better than you'd think).

. . . the style of the South Korean team. Not only are they relentless, but they're also skilled and tough, and they know how to come back. (Ask the U.S. and Italy.) Have they gotten some breaks from the referees? Maybe, but guess what that's called? Home-field advantage, folks. The Koreans deserve to be in the semis, and all the whining Europeans should sit down and shut up.

(Does anyone think Duke doesn't deserve to win so much just because the Blue Devils get a lot of calls? No. I rest my case.)

. . . the soccer commentators for Korea's SBS network, who turn a game, any game, into high theater. In Korean, *ne* (sounds like "nay") means "yes." This still confuses the heck out of me, but it leads to a hilarious description of the action that goes like this:

> Commentator 1: Blah-blah-blah-blah-blah. Commentator 2: *Ne!*
> Commentator 1: Blah-blah-blah-blah-blah. Commentator 2: *Ne!*
> Commentator 1: Blah-blah-blah-blah-blah. Commentator 2: *Ne!*

And so on. The SBS guys groan whenever a player, whatever his nationality, screws up, and scream over each other when the South Koreans score a goal. They even started to cry on the air after their quarterfinal victory. It's blatant homerism, of course, and yet here it's somehow endearing.

. . . how the masses of Koreans watching games in public squares pick up their own litter afterwards.

. . . the Korean fans' BE THE REDS T-shirts and KOREA TEAM FIGHTING scarves. (And while we're at it, the USA TEAM FIGHTING T-shirts I saw on Yank fans.)

. . . Ahn's speed-skating celebration following his goal against the U.S. (Wait: Sorry, that was bush league, pal. A question to ponder: What if Clint Mathis had done the same after his goal?)

. . . how the Korean organizers stocked the media center with fluorescent "happy lights" and free sports massages. (Let's just say this didn't happen in France.)

. . . Park Ji-sung. The guy whose jaw-dropping goal against Portugal opened the door for the U.S. to reach the second round should have his own little spot at the U.S. Soccer Hall of Fame. Most Korean fans have Ahn Jung-Hwan on the backs of their jerseys. (He's their pinup version of David Beckham.) Me, I'm going to get a Park Ji-sung shirt.

. . . the scene outside my hotel. Since the South Korean team moved in the other day, masses of fans and media have been gathering outside around the clock. As I carried my bag full of dirty laundry outside today, I got an ovation. Why? Who knows? Just realize, my new Korean friends, that I return that ovation to you.

9
TAKING A STAND

"Most journalists nail together the boards of the fence," Wahl's college mentor Gloria Emerson liked to say. "I prefer to paint them." Of course the best reporters are general contractors, able to do both. Yet for even the finest journalists, to keep a hammer in one hand and a paintbrush in the other is a constant struggle, particularly on the two beats where Wahl distinguished himself. Big-time college sports through the first decade of the twenty-first century, when Wahl followed college basketball, were tainted by unprecedented amounts of cash flowing into athletic departments. And Wahl swung onto soccer full-time just as the rot from decades of corruption had become too pungent to ignore. Yet the gemstone events of both sports—the Final Four and the World Cup—rarely fail to activate a sense of wonder in those who watch them, even journalists. It takes enormous discipline not to suspend your inner skeptic when you find yourself courtside in a domed stadium on that first Monday night in April or when billions of people around the world must watch on TV a match that you're privileged to see in person. Each of the following pieces is an example of Wahl, if you'll indulge a sports metaphor, keeping his eye on the ball. That kind of discipline was learned—taught to him by Emerson, whose voice abided inside his head to the end.

Rethinking the Legacy of "Legendary" Pete Carril

FROM *The Daily Princetonian*, MAY 13, 1996

During four years of covering the Princeton men's basketball team, Wahl had heard whispers that coach Pete Carril abused his players verbally and emotionally. Early in the 1995–96 season, Carril's last, Wahl and his *Daily Princetonian* co–sports editor, Nate Ewell, met with much of the team in a dorm room on the edge of campus to hear the players out. It was all on background. But that spring, after Carril announced his retirement and the team had scored its historic NCAA tournament upset of defending champion UCLA, Wahl circled back, securing the players' permission to write this column. It's a stark departure from the consensus of the national press corps, which had sent Carril off with a chorus of unreserved tributes. "Grant's reaction after the first meeting was 'We've got to be alert and aware, but we've given them our word,'" remembers Ewell. "My hunch is that, with Carril retiring, more players were willing to go on the record." Wahl's last story for the *Prince* is an opinion column, to be sure, but one marked by deep reporting, impeccable timing, and scrupulous even-handedness. "It was remarkably disciplined for a student journalist," Ewell says. "How many journalists even forty-five or fifty would have approached it that way?"

LAST WEEK, AMONG THE INTERMINABLE TASKS OF SENIOR CHECK-out, the Class of 1996 voted for its honorary members. As far as I could tell, one choice was particularly easy for my classmates, for there, near the middle of the candidates' page, was the name Pete Carril.

Automatic vote, right? After all he's done for the university and, especially, all he's done for his players, Princeton's only living legend deserved one last acknowledgment. Evidently, this was the thinking of most seniors—nearly everyone I spoke with said they had used one of their two selections for the now-retired basketball coach whom the national media adore.

Yet I did not vote for Pete Carril, and I want to explain why.

It has nothing to do with his knowledge of basketball, which is plainly apparent. Only two months ago I called him a genius in these pages, and I still believe that. What's more, it has nothing to do with his treatment of the media, which has been impeccable, despite my share of inane questions at press conferences over the past three years. (My favorite: "So, Coach, why did Princeton lose this game?")

Instead, Carril's failing—at least in recent years—has been a chronic lack of respect for the most important part of the basketball program: his players. With a few notable exceptions, even the most obstreperous coaches in collegiate sports, the ones who enforce a high degree of discipline, have boundaries that they do not cross. Carril crossed them.

Publicly, you have seen it in flashes, heard it in whispers, read it between the lines of comments from a player so scared to tell the truth he suffered nightmares. Privately, in practice or in the locker room, what you haven't seen is the daily hell promulgated by "Princeton's professor of basketball," whose vicious assaults on the characters of his "students" would have gotten any real professor fired on the spot.

───

BECAUSE CARRIL COACHED at Princeton, his legend has been weaved by many of our country's best writers and thinkers, as well as a long line of luminaries from the Princeton family. Among them are writing professor John McPhee '53, *Sports Illustrated*'s Alexander Wolff '79, emeritus professor Marvin Bressler, former university president William Bowen, graduate school, '58, athletic director Gary Walters '67, Carril's predecessor, Butch van Breda Kolff '45, and his biographer, alumni council director Dan White '65, all of whom wrote paeans to Carril in the most recent *Princeton Alumni Weekly*.

Much of it rings true and is indeed worthy of praise: the determination of an undersized Carril to excel in the game at the collegiate level, his deeply principled views on the values of education, his emphasis on character encompassing and yet transcending the game.

But one anecdote struck me as especially ironic, because Carril's recent actions have totally contradicted it. White tells the story of a former team captain, Bill Sickler '71, who was playing in his last game at Princeton. Just before the final buzzer, Carril substituted for Sickler, as White notes,

> so he could receive the ovation customarily given senior athletes at their last performance. . . . As Sickler came to the sidelines, Carril took his arm and raised it in the traditional gesture of a champion boxer. Then he hugged him. Surprised, the modest Sickler tried to step away, but Carril clung to him with one arm while encouraging the crowd with the other.

Where was that respect, or even a fraction of it, on the night of March 8, 1995? That evening, during the final throes of Princeton's season-ending loss to Penn, Carril's captain—Rick Hielscher '95, the finest Tiger basketball player of the last five years—languished on the bench. Although the game was out of reach, Carril did not insert Hielscher into the contest, remove him, and raise his arm for the fans to give him one last, deserved ovation. Even senior *benchwarmers* usually get to take one final bow in college basketball, but not Hielscher. As the seconds ticked away, Carril sat, schizophrenic, in his chair, ignored the catcalls from the crowd, and refused to look even once at his captain.

And where was Carril's respect for another player during a pregame speech some years back? On that occasion, Carril told the player to stop playing for his mother and think of the team. She had died; the player was still grieving. Carril knew that, and yet he did not hesitate to broach the subject, in front of the rest of the team members assembled. The remark stung the normally mild-mannered athlete especially hard, and it brought him to tears.

The details of Carril's insensitivity largely remain unspoken. Even privately, his players will speak only in suggestive but vague terms— "You wouldn't believe the things he gets away with" . . . "He's worse than the worst of yelling coaches" . . . "I could give you a long list of offenses" . . . and, resignedly, "That part of my life is finally behind me," as if playing for Carril were a drug addiction or a bad marriage. One player, now graduated, went so far as to keep a catalog of Carril's most uniquely savage attacks.

But publicly they are conspicuously quiet or, at times, even supportive of Carril, although they don't believe a word they are saying. And why *should* they talk? In many cases, future playing time or even real jobs are on the line. Carril's alumni support is strong; what player wants to take on the Princeton establishment and risk his prospective liveli- hood for one sweet, fleeting revelation of truth?

———

IN RECENT YEARS, the relationship between player and coach in the Carril system was never love-hate, as many have suggested, but rather accommodate-hate or, just as common, hate-hate.

Those who chose to accommodate Carril's abuses stuck with the pro- gram and endured. But only a very few of them came to love him, even after they graduated. They are the ones, countable on two hands, who propagate the Carril legend to its eager scribes and talking heads.

Others, however, elected not to accommodate Carril—they left the squad. A glance at the ever-changing team rosters of the last three years shows that this list is much longer than most schools', and it is populated not just by several members of the varsity's supporting cast (including a bevy of gifted athletes who were recruited but cast aside like empty soda cans, not having fit the Carril "system") but by players who saw signifi- cant playing time or even started for Princeton at some point in their careers. Peter LaMantia '95, Jason Osier '97, David Weaver '97 (now at Harvard), and Chris Long '97 were all regular contributors who decided to leave the team. "Coach Carril didn't seem to have any respect for the players, and that bothered me," Weaver later told the *San Francisco Chronicle.*

The process has been called "Darwinism" by some, as if losing one smart, talented player after another were a natural event or the fault of the players. It was neither. "Attrition" and "Darwinism" are charitable euphemisms for a coach whose erratic, boundless temper caused him to give up on capable performers. Carril's doghouse, it seems, had a one- way entrance.

The current case study of the Carril Effect—a virus which tears down formerly confident athletes until they are nothing but a frazzled mass of nerves—is Brian Earl '99, another former starter who said that he had never encountered Carril's level of maliciousness before last season. Earl, who is considering a transfer to another school, still might return to Princeton next year, but if he does it will be primarily because Carril has retired.

Ultimately, due to the culture of fear he created for Earl and others, it was Carril himself who most explicitly addressed his excessive tirades. "I'm a little too rough, too severe for the kind of kid who comes to Princeton today," he said upon announcing his retirement. "These kids are getting me at a time when I have less understanding."

That kind of self-recognition, however understated it may be, is worth applauding, as are Carril's longevity, determination, and prodigious understanding of basketball. Moreover, we will never forget the euphoria of watching the old coach's final trip to the NCAA Tournament.

But those successes don't erase the unceasing, often inhuman torments Carril hurled at his players. Which is why, despite his positive attributes, when Pete Carril is awarded an honorary membership in the Class of '96, I may stand with the crowd, but I will not clap.

Unwilling Participants

From SI.com, August 19, 2004

The best stories sometimes start with a simple question. "President Bush has included the Iraqi Olympic team in his latest campaign advertisements," Wahl said to members of the Iraqi soccer team in the midst of a surprising run at the 2004 Olympics in Athens. "How do you feel about that?" Wahl sensed that Iraq's success, a year after the United States had invaded the country and deposed Saddam Hussein, was being turned into an *American* feel-good story, without anyone asking the Iraqis themselves about it. The resulting piece sparked an international furor, which Wahl had anticipated, as well as questions about his reporting and journalistic ethics, which he hadn't. Two former members of the Coalition Provisional Authority, the U.S.-dominated interim government of Iraq, tried to discredit the story, suggesting it had been "engineered" or that "something was lost in translation." Wahl responded forcefully in a follow-up piece five days later, talking directly to one of those doubting ex-CPA bureaucrats, who backtracked from his original assertions. Wahl also replayed the tape of the interviews and their translations for a second interpreter, who confirmed that the originals were precise and accurate. As committed as he was to his craft and as reluctant as he was to become the story, he knew that sometimes he needed to speak up not just for his subjects, but for himself.

PATRAS, GREECE—IRAQI MIDFIELDER SALIH SADIR SCORED A goal here on Wednesday night, setting off a rousing celebration among the 1,500 Iraqi soccer supporters at Pampeloponnisiako Stadium. Though Iraq—the surprise team of the Olympics—would lose to Morocco 2–1, it hardly mattered as the Iraqis won Group D with a 2–1 record and now face Australia in the quarterfinals on Sunday.

Afterward, Sadir had a message for U.S. president George W. Bush, who is using the Iraqi Olympic team in his latest reelection campaign advertisements.

In those spots, the flags of Iraq and Afghanistan appear as a narrator says, "At this Olympics there will be two more free nations—and two fewer terrorist regimes."

"Iraq as a team does not want Mr. Bush to use us for the presidential campaign," Sadir told SI.com through a translator, speaking calmly and directly. "He can find another way to advertise himself."

Ahmed Manajid, who played as a midfielder on Wednesday, had an even stronger response when asked about Bush's TV advertisement. "How will he meet his god having slaughtered so many men and women?" Manajid asked me. "He has committed so many crimes."

"The ad simply talks about President Bush's optimism and how democracy has triumphed over terror," said Scott Stanzel, a spokesperson for Bush's campaign. "Twenty-five million people in Iraq are free as a result of the actions of the coalition."

To a man, members of the Iraqi Olympic delegation say they are glad that former Olympic committee head Uday Hussein, who was responsible for the serial torture of Iraqi athletes and was killed four months after the U.S.-led coalition invaded Iraq in March 2003, is no longer in power.

But they also find it offensive that Bush is using Iraq for his own gain when they do not support his administration's actions. "My problems are not with the American people," says Iraqi soccer coach Adnan Hamad. "They are with what America has done in Iraq: destroy everything. The American army has killed so many people in Iraq. What is freedom when I go to the [national] stadium and there are shootings on the road?"

At a speech in Beaverton, Oregon, last Friday, Bush attached himself to the Iraqi soccer team after its opening-game upset of Portugal. "The image of the Iraqi soccer team playing in this Olympics, it's fantastic, isn't it?" Bush said. "It wouldn't have been free if the United States had not acted."

Sadir, Wednesday's goal scorer, used to be the star player for the professional soccer team in Najaf. In the city in which 20,000 fans used to fill the stadium and chant Sadir's name, U.S. and Iraqi forces have battled loyalists to rebel cleric Moktada al-Sadr for the past two weeks. Najaf lies in ruins.

"I want the violence and the war to go away from the city," says Sadir, twenty-one. "We don't wish for the presence of Americans in our country. We want them to go away."

Manajid, twenty-two, who nearly scored a goal of his own with a driven header on Wednesday, hails from the city of Fallujah. He says coalition forces killed Manajid's cousin, Omar Jabbar al-Aziz, who was fighting as an insurgent, and several of his friends. In fact, Manajid says, if he were not playing soccer, he would "for sure" be fighting as part of the resistance.

"I want to defend my home. If a stranger invades America and the people resist, does that mean they are terrorists?" Manajid says. "Everyone [in Fallujah] has been labeled a terrorist. These are all lies. Fallujah people are some of the best people in Iraq."

Everyone agrees that Iraq's soccer team is one of the Olympics' most remarkable stories. If the Iraqis beat Australia on Saturday—which is entirely possible, given their performance so far—they would reach the semifinals. Three of the four semifinalists will earn medals, a prospect that seemed unthinkable for Iraq before this tournament.

When the Games are over, though, Coach Hamad says, they will have to return home to a place where they fear walking the streets. "The war is not secure," says Hamad, forty-three. "Many people hate America now. The Americans have lost many people around the world—and that is what is happening in America also."

Setting the Record Straight

FROM SI.COM, AUGUST 24, 2004

ATHENS, GREECE—I had a feeling SI.com might ruffle some feathers in Washington with my story last week about Iraqi soccer players' displeasure with President Bush after he used the Iraqi Olympic team in his latest reelection campaign ad.

But I can't say I expected former Coalition Provisional Authority (CPA) officials to publicly question the accuracy of the story, so let's set the record straight.

When asked about the SI.com piece on Monday's ESPN2 broadcast of *Cold Pizza*, former senior CPA official Don Eberly reiterated a quote from a Reuters interview of Mark Clark, a British consultant for the Iraqi Olympic Committee and himself a former CPA official. Clark's statement, which was passed along by Eberly, was this: "It seems the story was engineered."

I don't know about you, but I take "engineered" to mean anything from "not on the level" (at best) to "fabricated" (at worst). Curious about Mark Clark's definition of the word, I called him on Monday.

Clark told me two interesting things: (1) When he commented on the SI.com story to Reuters, he hadn't yet read it, and (2) he "didn't recall" using the word "engineered" in the Reuters interview. When I asked Reuters reporter Alastair Himmer, who quoted Clark, Himmer said, "He [Clark] told me straight up, 'Mate. I'm not in the business of making up quotes.'"

If Clark did use the term "engineered," then he's simply wrong. The two Iraqi players I interviewed, Salih Sadir and Ahmed Manajid, were asked simple questions. (The interview is on audiotape.) One of them was: "President Bush has included the Iraqi Olympic team in his latest campaign advertisements. How do you feel about that?"

The players answered the question—no more, no less.

Clark also told Reuters, "It is possible something was lost in translation" in the SI.com story.

Well, no, it isn't. On Tuesday, I played the tape of my original interviews (and the accompanying translations) for Chawki Rayess, an Arabic/English interpreter working for Olympics organizers in Athens. Rayess, a member of the respected International Association of Conference Interpreters, confirmed as accurate the following:

From Sadir: "Iraq as a team does not want Mr. Bush to use us for the presidential campaign. He can find another way to advertise himself."

And from Manajid: "How will [Bush] meet his god having slaughtered so many men and women? He has committed so many crimes."

Then again, I already knew that the original translations were made in precise language, hardly a sign of confusion. If Clark and Eberly wish, I would be happy to provide them a copy of the tape. Until then, let's keep following the Iraqi soccer team's march to a possible bronze medal—in my mind the best story of these Olympics.

What Happened When I Tried to Run for FIFA President

FROM SI.COM, APRIL 1, 2011

Wahl flew to Zurich in late 2011 to cover the votes to award the 2018 and 2022 FIFA World Cups to Russia and Qatar, respectively. He inhaled the stench that rose from the lobby of the Hotel Baur au Lac that day and knew that two members of FIFA's executive committee had recently been caught trying to sell their World Cup votes. "It was the ultimate in shadiness," Wahl would say of the betrayals and grifting that had taken place virtually in the open. "I felt like I needed to take a shower." After plotting with his friend and fellow journalist Gabriele Marcotti, who helped him scour the fine print of the FIFA rule book, Wahl launched a bid to supplant incumbent Sepp Blatter of Switzerland as president of soccer's global governing body. On February 17, 2011, he announced his campaign, with its platform of reform and radical transparency. And so the clock began ticking. Here Wahl recalls the forty-three-day window for securing a formal nomination from one of FIFA's 208 member federations. In the end, only two candidates succeeded in doing so: Blatter and Qatar's Mohamed bin Hammam. But Wahl enjoyed a kind of last laugh. FIFA ultimately adopted goal-line technology, a major plank in his platform. And Wahl's calls for a female general secretary and increased representation of women on the FIFA executive committee (soon rebranded as the FIFA council) both came to pass after the weight of scandal became too much and Blatter was forced out.

I F I'M BEING HONEST, THE HIGH POINT AND THE LOW POINT OF MY campaign for FIFA president took place minutes apart in the lobby of the Hilton Arc de Triomphe hotel in Paris on March 21. The Hilton was the official hotel for the UEFA Congress, the annual gathering of the people who run the fifty-three European soccer nations, and I had crossed the Atlantic to do two things:

1. Show I was serious about my campaign
2. Meet with officials from various FAs to see if they would nominate me by the April 1 deadline

At 9:30 that morning, there were only a half-dozen people in the plush lobby of the Hilton. One of them was Mohamed bin Hammam, the Qatari who'd just announced his FIFA presidential candidacy three days earlier. But I was there to see someone else, a top official from a World Cup–winning FA who had (to my delight) agreed to meet face-to-face to discuss my campaign. I had long ago realized that my best chance for landing a nomination was a mid- or large-sized FA, mainly because the small nations are so indebted to the development money train of FIFA's GOAL program that they would never risk losing it by nominating an outsider.

But if I could persuade one of the world's most respected, successful FAs to nominate me? Now that would make history. It got off to a perfect start. I shook the official's hand, and as we walked over to a quiet booth in the corner, he stopped and said a quick hello to bin Hammam, who now saw that I had landed a meeting with a very big fish. That couldn't have gone any better if I'd planned it, I thought to myself. (Sure enough, a few minutes later I got a long-awaited email from bin Hammam's assistant confirming a meeting between me and bin Hammam later that day.)

After some initial pleasantries, my conversation with the World Cup–winning FA man started off straightforward enough. "Why won't the U.S. federation nominate you?" he asked.

"They're like everyone else," I said. "They fear the negative reaction down the road from Blatter and FIFA."

Then he explained his FA's position, one that was influenced not just by Blatter but also by UEFA president Michel Platini of France. "Tomorrow at the UEFA Congress, Blatter will announce that he will not run in 2015," he said. "Platini wants to run in 2015, so Platini will ask all the big European nations to support Blatter this year. We don't like Blatter that much, but now we will owe Platini as well."

The problem, he explained, was that nominating a candidate for FIFA president would be a public declaration—subject to negative blowback from Blatter and Platini—while the actual vote on June 1 is a secret ballot. "We would be more likely to vote for you in the election than to nominate you," he told me. "Nominating you is impossible."

I didn't know whether to pump my fist or hang my head in despair. On the one hand, a top official from a World Cup–winning FA had taken me seriously enough to schedule a meeting, had even gone so far as to tell me he'd consider voting for me if I was able to gain a nomination. On the other hand, it was possible (likely?) that he was just being nice about his vote consideration and the news he delivered showed exactly how difficult it would be to crack the inner circle and persuade an FA to nominate me.

I kept trying to secure that nomination right up until the last day before the deadline. I owed that to the thousands of soccer fans around the world who had put their trust in me as the People's Candidate, who had expressed their support on Twitter and Facebook over the past six weeks. They came from dozens of countries, making clear that the simple message of cleaning up FIFA resonated around the globe. It was a rollicking adventure, one that I'll never forget. By the time it was over, I had contacted some 150 national federations and had received responses from around thirty FAs, from countries big (Australia, the U.S.) and small (Iceland, Dominica, FYR Macedonia) and somewhere in between (Sweden, Chile, Ireland, Israel).

Many of them voiced the same message I heard in that Paris hotel lobby: We don't really like the status quo, but nominating you is impossible. Nobody had the courage to do it. The prevailing mood was fear.

Did anyone think you were joking or that you were a madman?
—Interview question from the *Shanghai Morning Post*

I DECIDED TO run for FIFA president one night in January. Wherever I go around the world covering soccer, the fans complain about Blatter and FIFA, saying the organization isn't clean, that the two FIFA executive committee members suspended for trying to sell their World Cup votes last year might well be the tip of a rotten iceberg. If that was the case, I found it strange that Blatter had no challenger in the 2007 FIFA election and none as of January 2011, either. It's one thing to complain about FIFA, but it's another to actually do something. So one night the idea came: Can anyone run for FIFA president? Could I?

I bolted out of bed, turned on my laptop and spent the next three hours doing research. On FIFA's website, I learned that anyone can announce their candidacy for FIFA president; you just have to be nominated by one of the world's federations. I studied the writer Norman Mailer's campaign for mayor of New York City in 1969, noting his efforts to show that he was unconventional and somewhat satirical but still serious about enacting major reforms. (Mailer ended up getting 41,000 votes.) And I read up on the history of FIFA's eight presidents, three of whom had worked at one point as sports journalists. I brought up the idea with my editors at *Sports Illustrated,* and they told me to go for it.

After showing them the column announcing my candidacy, I visited *SI*'s main office in New York, where we spent most of a day filming my campaign video with *SI*'s video maestro, Ian Orefice. The production values were disarmingly high (HD video, quality background score and voiceover), and Ian came up with the idea to have me go out on the streets to shake hands with the masses across from Radio City Music Hall.

I had to take a deep breath on that one, but you'd be surprised how many people will stop and talk to you if they see a guy with a video camera. We had a blast, and Ian edited the video to strike a good balance between humor (a powerful tool) and the real changes I was proposing for FIFA.

We launched the campaign announcement and video publicly on February 17 in the magazine, on SI.com, and on my Twitter and Facebook pages. I expected it would be noticed, but I had no idea it would spread globally with such speed and volume. Social media is a remarkable thing. On the first day, the campaign was endorsed on Twitter by NBA star Steve Nash, NFL receiver Chad Ochocinco, comedian Drew Carey and *Saturday Night Live*'s Seth Meyers. Spanish soccer player Xabi Alonso sent a message of good luck. Media from around the world contacted *SI* to set up interviews, and I did video hits for CNN, Bloomberg TV, and Reuters, among others.

The message found an audience. My main campaign promises were simple enough: As president I would do a WikiLeaks on FIFA, releasing every internal document to the public so we could find out how clean or unclean FIFA really is. I would push for term limits to prevent any FIFA president from serving more than two four-year terms. I would support (with the approval of IFAB, the sport's international rules-governing body) the introduction of video replay technology for all close calls on the goal line. And I would name a woman as FIFA's general secretary, the organization's most powerful appointed position, to change the old-boy network culture that will continue to thrive as long as all twenty-four members of the FIFA executive committee are men.

The response was overwhelmingly positive. Some three thousand people started following my Facebook campaign page, while another three thousand signed a Twitter petition started by a college student in Minnesota. Over the next six weeks I did more than sixty interviews with media outlets in Brazil, Argentina, Russia, Malaysia, Canada, the United States, England, Ireland, the Netherlands, Norway, Portugal, Chile, Nigeria, South Africa, France, Germany, Switzerland, China, Australia, and New Zealand.

Nearly all the interviews started the same way, by asking if the campaign was a joke. (Only the Chinese asked if people thought I was a madman, which was an inspired question.) I reminded them that I wrote in the second sentence of my campaign announcement that I wasn't kidding, but I also knew I would have to reinforce that with my actions by doing everything I could (including traveling to Paris) to seek an official nomination.

I was also well aware that cynics might view my candidacy as an effort simply to draw publicity for myself, so I made sure to steer interviews as much as possible toward my message and limited my Twitter posts on the campaign to no more than two per day.

At one point my wife asked me: "Do I have to think about moving to Switzerland?" (FIFA's headquarters are in Zürich.) I told her to come back to me in a few weeks, but I wasn't naive. My chances of beating Blatter were minuscule, but I thought it might just be possible to land a nomination. With all the countries and all the fans who were dissatisfied with Blatter, there had to be one FA out of 208 that would have the guts to nominate me, right?

If FIFA were truly a representative democracy, I'm convinced that not only would I have been nominated, but I also would have beaten Blatter and bin Hammam in a landslide on election day. In a survey of readers, SI.com asked who they would vote for if given the chance. I got 95 percent of the vote, bin Hammam had 3 percent, and Blatter had 2 percent. FIFA and the world's FAs talk a good game about the importance of the fans, but when it comes to the politics of the sport, the fans just don't matter. Not one bit.

And that's a shame. Interacting with the world's supporters was my favorite part of running for FIFA president, and they did some amazing things. On the opening night of MLS, a D.C. United fan hung a banner that read WAHL 4 FIFA PRES. And in early March I had no idea what was awaiting me when I spoke at the Las Vegas rally of the American Outlaws, the U.S. national team's largest supporters' group. One of the event's sponsors, an energy drink called Golazo, made dozens of campaign signs and buttons that read WAHL FIFA PRESIDENT. I was floored. After I gave my speech, the Outlaws and I taped a video message for Blatter out on the Strip.

Still, it was one thing to win support from the fans. Persuading the world's stuffy old soccer politicians to nominate me was another matter entirely, one that brought all sorts of people—and, let's be honest, some unusual characters—out of the woodwork.

———

THE EMAIL ARRIVED in my general SI.com mailbox on March 2:

> *Dear Mr. G. Wahl,*
>   *We want to contact you with a FA!*
>   *2 smaller countries.*
>   *Want to back you up.*
>   *xxxxxxxxxxxxx Phone*
>
>   *Regards,*
>   *F. T. García*

I have a healthy skepticism when it comes to people on the internet who claim they can "hook you up," but as a journalist I was also curious about this F. T. García. (I have changed the name he gave me.) Even if he was a hoax, the mere fact that someone was contacting me in such a manner revealed something about the murkiness of FIFA politics.

So I called him on the European cell number he gave me. "FTG," as he came to call himself, became a constant correspondent on email and the phone, contacting me several times on some days. No matter how often I asked him to explain who he was and what he did, he said he didn't want to do so. But he claimed to have ties to various figures who themselves had ties to the powerful men in FAs who (supposedly) would nominate me. A typical email from FTG was this one:

> *Hello Mr. Grant,*
>
> *1) I have contacted the Danish Lawyer who will call his friend at FA Denmark for meeting.*
>
> *2) I contacted a personal friend who has close ties to Luxembourg FA. He will call me back or e-mail about meeting.*
>
> *3) I contacted Dutch/Suriname Agent Mr. Xxxx Xxxxx. He has ties to Suriname FA.*
>
> *4) Contacted Danish agent Mr. Xxxxx Xxxxx also for Danish FA.*
>
> *When do you want to come to Paris, France?*
>
> *Meetings at Embassy?*
>
> *You have a Lawyer, etc.?*
>
> *Morocco FA?*
>
> > *Warm regards,*
> > *F. T. García*

I played along with FTG (to an extent), but I made sure to keep plenty of my own irons in the fire. By then, I knew I would have to persuade a federation other than U.S. Soccer to nominate me. The USSF, which along with other CONCACAF nations has supported Blatter over the years, was bitterly disappointed by losing out to Qatar in the bid to host World Cup 2022—Blatter is thought to have voted for the U.S. over Qatar, for what it's worth—but USSF president Sunil Gulati told me from the start that he had decided not to nominate anyone.

That left me using the means at my disposal to try to hustle some contacts inside the world's FAs. If I knew journalists in a particular country, I would email them and ask if they had any contact information for their FA president. In some cases, I already knew members of various FAs' PR staffs and contacted them. And for others I simply went onto the country pages on the FIFA website, which included general email addresses for all of the world's federations.

You could learn some intriguing things on these pages. Burundi, for example, has a female FA president, Lydia Nsekera. (I promised to consider her for FIFA general secretary in my letter, but she still failed to reply.) Gambia's FA president may or may not be a seedy character, but he is most certainly Seedy: a guy named Seedy Kinteh, to be exact. He didn't answer, either.

Indeed, most of my 120 or so emails to these general FA addresses disappeared into the abyss. For days I kept getting "failure notice" bounce-back messages from the official FIFA mailbox of the Bermuda FA. ("Failure notice" now seems like a good title for the state of my campaign.) The Seychelles FA mailbox was full, but the automatic reply message ("Undeliverable") was probably an accurate description of its nomination. The general secretary of the Mauritania FA, Massa Diarra, replied to my letter, even if he just wanted it in French. Dominica FA head Patrick John responded to let me know his nation would be supporting Blatter. And Iceland FA president Geir Thorsteinsson called and asked for more information before eventually telling me his board had decided against nominating me. At least he denied me in an extremely polite way.

Another FA that replied was Finland, but on that one I screwed up royally. In most letters, I would write a sentence or two unique to that country before launching into the stump speech about my candidacy. But with Finland I accidentally forgot to take out this line from my letter to Denmark: "I think it would be great for Denmark—the least corrupt country in the world according to Transparency International—to nominate me after Blatter was nominated by the FA of Somalia (the most corrupt country in the world)." After a friendly executive assistant forwarded the email to the Finnish FA heads, I discovered my error and apologized profusely. "No worries," she wrote back. "These things happen, and I want to think myself that Finland is on the same level as Denmark when it comes to corruption, despite the latest betting fraud case here." The Finns are nice people, but they still didn't want to nominate me.

Scandinavia in general was a harder sell than I expected. While I was hoping the region's reputation for transparent government might attract nomination interest, my unconventional candidacy seemed to be frowned upon by the humorless in some quarters. Lennart Johansson, eighty-one, the Swedish former UEFA president, told Fotbollskanalen.se I was "totally unknown," "not a serious candidate" and that "the U.S. is not a superpower in football," as if that mattered. He then presumably growled, "Get off of my lawn."

England, for its part, never engaged me seriously, despite its lingering anger over receiving only two votes in an embarrassing first-round exit in the balloting to host World Cup 2018. I had contact with a few England officials who said they forwarded my information to FA chairman David Bernstein and general secretary Alex Horne, but I never heard from either of the two men directly.

All the same, I did enjoy meeting some good people over the past six weeks. Early on, I had a productive hourlong Skype conversation with Oliver Fowler, a Barcelona-based British journalist who started ChangeFIFA, an organization dedicated to reforming world soccer governance. Fowler connected me to David Larkin, a Washington, D.C.–based lawyer who is also part of ChangeFIFA. In late February they informed me they were in discussions with Chilean Elías Figueroa, the former three-time South American player of the year, about potentially running for FIFA president on a reform platform. Figueroa was interested. Would I be interested in working with him? I said I'd be happy to talk to Figueroa, and if our ideas were similar and he was able to get a nomination, I would endorse him and drop out of the race.

Unfortunately, though, Figueroa was never able to land his own nomination. If you're wondering how impenetrable and fear-inducing FIFA's ruling hierarchy is, imagine this: The Chilean FA refused to nominate the greatest player in its nation's history. Think about that for a second. If Figueroa couldn't do it, it shouldn't be surprising that I couldn't, either.

Yet I kept trying until the deadline. Most of it was done on my own. But the mystery man F. T. García was contacting me nearly every day, sending emails like this one:

Sir,

Georgia? It's an Obscure Country . . . anti Russia!
Their ex FA president is current owner of Dutch club Vitesse.
My contact can approach him easy.
Your thoughts please?

Warm regards,
F. T. García

FTG was even loopier over the phone. In one conversation on March 11, he "informed" me that:

- The Morocco FA wanted to meet me at their embassy in Paris. (This never happened, and I never got any indication it was true.)
- He was setting up meetings with the Georgia FA. (This never happened, either.)
- Pro-Blatter forces thought I was a threat using social media and were starting a "campaign" against me in Europe. (FTG's credibility was really starting to erode here.)
- I might have to cast a wider net. "You have to understand the countries, the culture of paranoia," FTG said. "Maybe a smaller country can nominate you, like Brunei or Tonga. But maybe they ask for money. That's the name of the game."

On March 14, tiring of FTG's conspiracy theories, I laid it on the line to him: For a week he had been promising contacts with several FAs, but I had yet to hear from anyone other than him, and he was still refusing to explain anything about who he was. He was wasting my time, I told him, and I was done talking to him unless he provided some evidence to back up his claims—like, say, real people. "You keep telling me about hooking me up with FAs," I said, "but I do a better job of that on my own than you do!"

That probably wasn't very nice, but it was true. At that point he had about as much credibility with me as a Nigerian email scammer. I thought it would probably be our last conversation, but two days later FTG rang me in the morning. "You will start getting calls from FAs in the next thirty minutes," he said. Rolling my eyes, I said: "OK. I'll keep an eye out for them!"

And then the craziest thing happened. I started getting calls. One of them came from the former Yugoslav republic of Macedonia. The secretary on the line (she had a Macedonia country code) gave me her name and the cell number for general secretary Igor Klimper, who she said wanted to meet me the following Monday in Paris. A few minutes later, I got a call from a top official with a World Cup–winning European FA. He, too, wanted to meet me in Paris and asked me to send him an email. He replied a few minutes later from a legitimate email account from his FA. And if I needed any further confirmation that he was the real thing, I got it when I checked the caller ID number on my phone. It matched perfectly with the number that FIFA's website listed for his nation's FA headquarters.

Suddenly, amazingly, F. T. García had some credibility, even if he still wouldn't tell me who he was.

<hr />

Grant Wahl, an American journalist, has some good ideas but no chance at all.

—*The Economist*

My cellphone rang in Paris on the afternoon of March 21. The voice on the other end was a familiar one: FTG, the mystery man. "You're wearing a nice striped suit today, Mr. Grant," he said.

My brow furrowed. I had yet to see the man in the flesh. This was starting to feel like a poor man's Jason Bourne movie. "Are you here at the UEFA hotel in Paris?" I asked.

"I'm in Paris. We can meet."

"Today or tomorrow?"

"Today is better. Call me in ten minutes."

FTG didn't want to meet in the lobby of the UEFA hotel—that paranoia again—so he asked to rendezvous at a pharmacy down the street. When I finally saw the guy, he looked a lot like your typical middle manager from Syracuse. Wearing a navy blazer and a shiny black tie, FTG carried a blue backpack that made him appear as though he had just left school for the day. He was in his forties, slightly overweight, and nervous in his mannerisms. His eyes were bloodshot. FTG thought we were being watched and asked to duck into a brasserie next to the pharmacy.

I won't bore you with the details of our conversation, not that one or the one the next day that took place—*cliché alert!*—on a park bench near the Champs-Élysées. Suffice it to say, F. T. García never explained who he was or why he was spending his time and money to speak to me. He never brought much to the table, really, but just enough to keep me intrigued. Ultimately, FTG wasn't fascinating for what he accomplished. He was fascinating because someone like him existed—a peripheral figure in the sprawling FIFA demimonde who knew a guy who knew a guy (or maybe not). Even the ties that he did have weren't close. The Macedonian general secretary, Igor Klimper? He answered my calls just once in Paris, said he'd ring me in an hour and never did. As for the ex-president of the Georgia FA, his secretary told me he was now busy—for the next month.

That said, my trip to Paris wasn't a complete waste of time. I had my meeting with the official from the World Cup–winning FA. I interviewed bin Hammam for a story. I got interviewed by *Le Monde* and by the investigative reporter Andrew Jennings for an upcoming BBC special on FIFA.

And I learned an important truth: No matter how much support you may have from the world's fans, an outsider candidate is doomed to fail in the world of FIFA politics, where the old men in the navy suits have all the power. That outsider candidate could be Kofi Annan or Bill Clinton or George Weah, but even if they ran they could not win, nor might they even be nominated. Remember, public opinion does not matter in FIFA election campaigns. The greatest player in Chile's history, a man with political experience and popular acclaim, could not get nominated by the Chilean federation.

And so we're left today with two nominated candidates: Sepp Blatter and Mohamed bin Hammam, two longtime FIFA insiders, two men who may disagree on small points but are in perfect lockstep on the most important topic of the day. Is FIFA corrupt? Both Blatter and bin Hammam say they are certain that it is not. How can anyone be certain of that? And if they are certain, they should welcome a full and independent investigation of FIFA from top to bottom, one that would address the tarnished reputation that the organization has acquired.

Even though I failed to secure a nomination, the message I wanted to send got out. Ordinary fans in countries around the world talked a little bit more about the absurdities of FIFA's electoral process. They asked why their voices don't matter, why so few people challenge the unpopular status quo, and why an organization that purports to be a great democracy has so many one-candidate elections at its various levels. They asked why the leaders of FIFA don't make commonsense reforms that would give the world's greatest sport the clean and respected administration it deserves.

As for me, I'm done with being a candidate in soccer elections, at least for the next few decades. Running for office closer to home would conflict too much with my journalism and book writing, and those are the things I do best. But I'll never forget the positive response from the sport's fans, near and far, who wanted to see real change in FIFA. Thank you for everything, and I'll see you at the games.

The Qatar Chronicles, Part I

FROM FÚTBOL WITH GRANT WAHL, SEPTEMBER 15, 2022

In August 2021, Wahl launched his Substack site, Fútbol with Grant Wahl, with a commitment to continue the deeply reported magazine-quality journalism he had done over the course of his career at *Sports Illustrated*. But now he would do it on his own: conceiving stories, setting the publishing schedule, monitoring the budget, and producing each piece using Substack's turnkey content management system. On the road, he was also his own photographer, videographer, and sound technician. His lone assistance came from former *SI* colleague Mark Mravic, whom he hired to review feature stories before posting, and Ireland-based illustrator Dan Leydon, who created lead artwork.

But while much of the process was new to Wahl, one element was familiar: For stories written off of big games, he wanted the pieces to hit readers' inboxes by 9:00 A.M. Eastern time the next day. So, harking back to his NCAA tournament days, he would profile sections of the story to Mravic before kickoff, and after the final whistle add a top and bottom, some match detail, context and color from postgame interviews, and file the final story to Mravic by 7:00 A.M. for a one-hour turnaround. Operating on little, if any, sleep, Wahl would then post the story himself by that 9:00 A.M. deadline.

His style evolved on the new platform. Writing for his own subscribers rather than the nebulous "*Sports Illustrated* reader," he adopted a more direct approach, employing first person extensively, detailing the reporting process, and providing transparency about difficulties he might have encountered. His most challenging, and rewarding, Substack story was this piece, for which he pounded the pavement alone in Qatar, approaching migrant workers to talk about the conditions under which they toiled, and whether promises of improvements were being fulfilled as the 2022 World Cup loomed. Wahl knew the story would have an impact, but his overriding concern was to protect the identities of the "invisible" subjects who had trusted him enough to open up to a Western journalist and risk retribution from their employers or Qatari authorities. The first of a two-part series, "The Qatar Chronicles, Part I" was nominated for the Dan Jenkins Medal for Excellence in Sportswriting, awarded by the University of Texas for the year's best sports story. You can read Part II on the Fútbol with Grant Wahl site.

D OHA, QATAR—THEY'RE EVERYWHERE HERE IN QATAR, EVEN IF nobody acts like they see them.

The authoritarian Persian Gulf nation that will host World Cup 2022 has 2.1 million migrant workers, who make up 95 percent of Qatar's workforce and 73 percent of its population. If you spend any time at all in Qatar, you'll see sprawling groups of blue-clad, neon-vested laborers, largely from the Indian subcontinent, toiling in the sun on construction sites and roadsides. If you stay at a gleaming new hotel, chances are the valets, the security guards, and the staff cleaning your rooms and serving your food are from somewhere in East or West Africa.

In my experience, which has included weeklong trips to Doha in 2013 for *Sports Illustrated* and in 2022 for this story, migrant workers are treated by Qataris as though they are invisible—unless locals in the planet's wealthiest nation per capita are unhappy with, say, their service at a restaurant or private hotel cabana, when they can be bracingly cruel to the waitstaff.

Looming over everything are Qatar's migrant worker death toll (often related to long hours in the infernal heat) and its apathy toward investigating the cause of those deaths. Last year, *The Guardian*'s Pete Pattisson cited government sources to report that more than 6,500 migrant workers had died in Qatar in the decade since the country was awarded the World Cup in 2010. (A total of 38 deaths have been directly tied to World Cup stadium construction, though nearly all of Qatar's infrastructure growth has some connection to the World Cup.)

Amnesty International cited data from Qatar's Planning and Statistics Authority that an even higher number—15,021 non-Qataris of all ages, occupations, and causes—had died in Qatar in the past decade. (Qatari officials claim the migrant mortality rate is within the expected range given the workforce size.) Just as troubling, Amnesty says Qatar has failed to properly investigate up to 70 percent of its migrant worker deaths, noting that "in a well-resourced health system, it should be possible to identify the exact cause of death in all but 1% of cases."

When the World Cup starts on November 20, the primary focus for billions of fans around the globe will be the soccer on the field. The same will be true for thousands of visiting sports media, including me. But I didn't feel right about covering the soccer in Qatar without first visiting and doing independent reporting, speaking to migrant workers about their experience there. And I thought my readers would want to know: What is life like on the ground for these workers? What has Qatar actually done to improve conditions for its workforce since it got the World Cup twelve years ago?

By the time I arrived earlier this year, World Cup stadium construction was basically complete. And so for Part I of "The Qatar Chronicles," I traveled to Qatar in late February and trained my energy on migrant workers in the hotel sector. In Part II, I'll detail what U.S. Soccer has been doing behind the scenes to prepare for the nonsoccer aspects of a World Cup in Qatar, including educating its players and doing due diligence on its hotel and vendors, as well as addressing LGBTQ+ rights in a country that represses them.

My plan for Part I: to visit all fourteen of the FIFA-affiliated hotels in the main sections of Doha in the West Bay and the Pearl (including where the USMNT will be staying), and speak to at least one migrant worker at each one.

Promising them anonymity for their protection, I wanted to hear their thoughts: How were they being treated by their employers? And was the new set of worker protection laws announced by the Qatari government to its own great fanfare in 2019 actually being followed on the ground?

There was a reason I didn't publicize my Qatar visit on social media and didn't say anything publicly about it until I had left the country. The fact is that journalists can get detained in Qatar—including two reporters for the Norwegian TV World Cup rights holder last November—and I wasn't hoping for a repeat of that during my time there.

More important, risk is ever-present for workers, too. Malcolm Bidali, a Kenyan who worked as a security guard in Qatar and wrote a human rights blog under a pseudonym, was detained for five months last year (often in solitary confinement) by the Qatari authorities and eventually deported for spreading "fake news," creating a chilling effect across the migrant worker community.

But independent reporting on Qatar is important. In early September, the Qatari government spent a large sum of money to provide first-rate travel and accommodations to journalists from around the world who visited Doha, with the expectation that they would report favorably on Qatar's readiness to host the World Cup. Not surprisingly, many did. Accepting thousands of dollars in free travel from the people you're covering is a violation of ethics for reputable media organizations. Nor is it independent reporting when Qatar's Supreme Committee for Delivery & Legacy organizing the World Cup handpicks migrant workers to speak to the media.

For me, the only way to do truly independent reporting was to use GrantWahl.com's money and travel to Qatar, spend two days in a state-mandated Covid hotel quarantine, deal with a government-required Covid phone app that doubled as a surveillance tracker, and then introduce myself to random migrant workers at those fourteen FIFA hotels. I had to earn their trust in ninety seconds, explain who I was, give them my business card, and ask them questions about their experience.

I was also well aware that I shouldn't arrange any interviews in Qatar with government- or World Cup–affiliated groups. When I did that during my trip in 2013 for a *Sports Illustrated* story, the Qataris made sure to fill my schedule with so many meetings that they knew I wouldn't have time to do any reporting on my own. This time, I waited until *after* I returned from my visit to contact Qatari authorities and FIFA for their perspectives.

In the end, the only thing I wanted to do on this trip was to interview migrant workers. And that's all I did. Several of them have stayed in touch since then via WhatsApp. For their honesty and trust I am grateful.

WHICH LAWS HAVE changed for migrant workers in Qatar since December 2010, when it won the right to host the World Cup? In 2019, after years of pressure from human rights organizations and global trade unions, Qatar announced sweeping labor reforms that it said marked the end to the kafala system, common in the Gulf states, which required migrants to have sponsors who controlled their exit visas and could thus prevent them from leaving the country.

"For the first eight, nine years, there had been no progress, and the ongoing abuses and exploitation of migrant workers continued because there was a bit of a denial from both Qatar and FIFA about the need to do any reforms," May Romanos, a lawyer and Amnesty International Gulf researcher on human rights who has worked in Qatar since 2017, told me. "Qatar finally agreed [to reforms], I think, because of the ongoing pressure and the spotlight it came under because of this World Cup. They signed an agreement with the International Labor Organization [ILO] committing to a reform program and started to introduce some important legal reforms.

"Three years after the start of this program, we have seen some important legal reforms being introduced," Romanos went on. "Now migrant workers can leave the country and can change jobs without the permission of their employer. There is a new minimum wage"—1,000 Qatari riyals a month, or $3,296 a year—"and new labor committees that are supposed to expedite the access for justice for migrant workers. So the legal framework is better, but the implementation and enforcement are weak. And there have been also ongoing loopholes in the system that allow abusive employers to continue exploiting migrant workers."

According to the new laws, it is now illegal in Qatar:

- for employers to keep the passports of their workers,
- for employers to prevent their workers from changing jobs inside Qatar if they so desire, and
- for workers to pay a "recruitment fee" (sometimes $2,500 or more) to agents in their home country or in Qatar to secure employment in the country.

But are those new Qatari laws being enforced on the ground? The only way to find out for yourself is to go to Qatar, walk around Doha, and talk to the workers themselves.

At first, I was really, really bad at that! Because I was staying at one of the fourteen FIFA hotels in Doha's West Bay—all of which are high-end international brands—I was able to station myself on a relatively quiet beach chair near the outdoor swimming pool. Over at the bar, hotel guests were ordering beers and cocktails, which are a lot easier to find in Doha today than they were when I visited nine years ago.

When a worker from the pool staff walked by, I stopped him, introduced myself, gave him my business card, and explained my story, adding that I would look forward to interviewing him when he wasn't on the clock if he wanted to send me a message. (I wanted to respect that he was busy doing his job and would probably prefer a more discreet location.) He smiled and took my card, and quite reasonably I never heard from him again.

By the time I recorded my second audio track the next morning, you could hear some anxiety in my voice. Time was running out on my stay in Doha, and I needed to start getting some interviews done. I resolved to continue being discreet (it helped not to have TV cameras with me), but from now on I would try to strike up a conversation the moment I met someone.

IN THE END, I spoke to a total of twenty workers at all fourteen FIFA hotels in Doha's West Bay and the Pearl, and I did interviews at all but one hotel, which happened to be the one I was staying at. Long story short: The vast majority of the migrant hotel workers in Doha are men, so I wanted to interview at least one woman. When I introduced myself to a woman working in the lobby of my hotel, she asked if she could bring me to their corporate communications head. I explained I was speaking to workers themselves. She asked for my name, and I gave her my first name before racing upstairs, packing my bags, and checking out immediately. By that time, thankfully, I was well on my way to completing my interviews.

By the time I was done, I had a mixed bag of responses in a few areas, but some clear patterns emerged about which new laws were being enforced and which weren't.

Passport confiscation. The majority of the workers I spoke to at FIFA hotels said they had possession of their passports. But multiple respondents told me their employers had control of their passports, in clear violation of the new Qatari law. "It has now been three years without my passport," an East African security guard who said he works seven days a week, twelve hours a day, told me. "I'm supposed to ask the company for my passport when I finish."

At another FIFA hotel, an East African bellman who works six days a week, twelve hours a day, told me his employer "kept my passport for three months. When I finished three months, I was qualified. They returned my passport to me and gave me a Qatari ID."

The workers I spoke to who didn't have their passports did not work directly for their hotels but rather for subcontractors who have agreements to provide laborers for the hotels. I quickly learned from speaking to workers that subcontractors are far more often in violation of Qatari laws than the hotels themselves are with their direct employees. But that doesn't absolve the hotels of responsibility; the subcontracted employees are still working at their properties.

"Passport confiscation is illegal, but it's still happening," Amnesty's Romanos told me. "You will find it with many migrant workers, including domestic workers. You rarely find a domestic worker in possession of her passport."

Sharan Burrow, the general secretary of the International Trade Union Confederation (ITUC), was one of Qatar's most vocal critics before the legal reforms were announced in 2019. When I interviewed her in 2014, she told me, "Qatar is a country without a conscience," as the ITUC demanded that FIFA take a revote for the host of World Cup 2022.

But when I interviewed Burrow eight years later for this story, the global trade union leader had done a near 180 on the Qatari government's stance toward migrant workers. What happened? Well, these days she and the ITUC, as well as the ILO and several other global trade unions, are working *with* the Qatari state, following their negotiated agreement in 2019.

"We got to the point [in 2014] where I was totally frustrated with [Qatar's] lack of interest in the issues, in talking to us or indeed the International Labor Organization in dialogue, to look at how to fix the problems," Burrow explained to me. "So as the workers, the union, took a complaint to the ILO, the highest form of complaints is called an Article 26. And it's basically heard before the governing body of the ILO. Its ultimate end could be in sanctions, but we were determined to continue to offer the route of negotiations, because we wanted to change the laws and change the country, not to actually just see the country punished. And at a certain point [Qatar] decided to negotiate, and so the ILO and the ITUC, represented by myself and my legal team, sat down, and we negotiated an agreement for legal changes that would be effected over three years. And they were. And so those changes are in place."

You can't help but notice the tensions these days over Qatar between the global trade unions (which have joined forces with Qatar following the settlement) and human rights organizations like Amnesty International (which continue to release reports about the new laws not being enforced on the ground). Perhaps that's not surprising given the structural differences between unions and human rights groups.

"Unions were probably one of the main critical voices when it came to Qatar in 2014," Amnesty's Romanos told me. "They brought a complaint accusing Qatar of forced labor, which eventually pushed the country to agree to this reform process. Since then, many of the unions backed the reform process, supporting Qatar and the ILO to deliver on these reforms. They considered the progress that has been made as one that should be celebrated for improving workers' rights and conditions in the country. Whereas for us, we see our role as a human rights organization that should continue to monitor the situation and acknowledge progress, but also point to the gaps and continue to push the government to reform the system. As long as we continue to document human rights abuses, we will continue to speak up and ask for more."

As for the ongoing confiscation of workers' passports inside Qatar, Burrow spoke like someone who's now a Qatari government insider. "If you're still in touch with those people and they don't have a passport, suggest they ask for it back," Burrow told me in an interview. "And if they don't, then I'd love to help them, because one phone call and I could fix that."

Recruitment fees for agents. About half the workers I spoke to at the fourteen FIFA hotels, including several who had moved from their countries to Qatar *after* the new laws had been announced, said they'd had to pay recruitment fees to agents, which is illegal.

"In our country we paid agents," an East African security guard who works six days a week, twelve hours a day, told me. "They told us we are supposed to pay, so we paid. It was around five thousand riyals [$1,373]." That put the worker in a hole of debt that he had to start digging out of from the moment he arrived in Qatar.

"The payment of recruitment fees is just a rampant issue," Amnesty's Romanos says, even after the new Qatari laws were announced. "Over seventy percent of low-skilled migrant workers in the country would have paid recruitment fees to come to work in Qatar."

The ITUC's Burrow, who's working with the Qatari government, says, "The recruiting fees remain a problem. And you can't actually blame the Qatari government for this one, because they're deregistering any recruitment agency in Qatar where they have the power. They did like twenty in the last couple months which are not indeed heeding the laws. But it's the countries of origin that we have a problem with. And even though in some of those countries the Qataris set up their own visa center, there are still agents that are charging to get people through the door. So it remains a real problem. It's not just limited to recruits to Qatar. It's recruits to almost every Gulf state."

The ability for migrant workers to choose to change jobs inside Qatar. One of the watershed aspects of the new Qatari laws was supposed to be workers' ability to choose to leave their job for another one inside Qatar without needing permission from their employer. But a clear majority of the workers I spoke to said that was not possible with their employers, which is illegal.

Here's a selection of what workers told me: "You can't change your job. If you need to, they send you home and you come back with a new visa for a new company." . . . "It's very difficult to change jobs. For our company, they don't allow it." . . . "The transfer from one company to another company is the main issue. It's almost not possible, because they require permission from your employer, which most of the companies aren't giving." . . . "I would change my job if I could, but it's not possible." . . . "I got another [job] offer, but my company doesn't allow changing."

When I informed the trade union's Burrow how many workers in Qatar told me they couldn't change their jobs, she said, "Well, they can. And 242,000 workers did change jobs from October 2020 to October 2021. The problem is no longer with the laws."

Yet clearly there is a major problem if so many workers told me it wasn't possible. Amnesty's Romanos said, "On paper, you can change jobs because you don't need the permission of your employer. But then your employer can retaliate by filing absconding cases against you and canceling your Qatari ID to block your job transfer, meaning that you are then at risk of being forced to leave the country or be deported because you ran away from your job, which is still considered an offense."

Wages. One new law that appeared as though it was being followed was Qatar's new minimum-wage law of 1,000 riyals a month (or $3,296 a year). None of the workers I spoke to said they were being paid below the minimum wage, and none said they were failing to be paid on time.

That's not to say that it doesn't still happen. "The issue of unpaid salaries remains rampant, with thousands of cases being heard in court," Amnesty's Romanos told me.

On wages, the ITUC's Burrow, who works with the Qatari government, said, "There's a minimum wage that is evidence based, and it has a capacity to be reviewed regularly. It includes not just a wage base but an allowance for food and accommodation. And the minimum wage not only raised wages for about three hundred thousand workers, it ended the apartheid system of wages where some nations, like Nepalis, were paid less than Indians. It is also applicable to domestic workers and [Qatar is] probably the only country in the world where domestic workers are guaranteed the minimum-wage equivalent to any other worker."

What do you see when you look at Qatar's minimum wage? Progress or outrage? Qatar is the richest country on the planet measured by GDP per capita. The new minimum wage works out to about $1.25 an hour. That's shockingly low by Western standards. But it's also an improvement over what used to be the case.

At the end of every interview I did with a migrant worker, I asked a question: Do you regret coming to Qatar? I heard plenty of criticism about living conditions and work hours and day-to-day aspects of their jobs. But it was admittedly striking that nobody I spoke to said they regretted coming to Qatar. A lot goes into that answer, obviously, especially the conditions in the countries where those migrant workers come from.

"From the job side, it's cool," a West African security guard told me. "I work twelve hours a day, seven days a week. They say all work and no play make Jack a dull boy. So I'm dull. For real."

"Do you like it here?" I asked.

"Not really," he said. "But you know, I don't have a choice. The reason is I'm saying if you compare it to my country, here I've got a job. So it's OK, but not really. I mean, I don't like it here like I want to stay here forever. But because of the job, that's why I'm here."

When I told Amnesty's Romanos none of the workers I interviewed said they had regrets about coming to Qatar, she said she wasn't surprised.

"That's exactly what I was expecting the answer to be," she told me. "I think this stems from why they come to Qatar in the first place. They just come in search of better job opportunities. They tell you, 'I'm here to work so I can send my kids to a good school so that my kids don't have to go through what I'm going through.' That's why migrant workers migrate in the first place. They want to make a better future for themselves, for their families back home and their kids. And I think this remains the ultimate reason that pushed them to leave their home countries.

"For many it's not necessarily the harsh working conditions that push them to complain," Romanos went on. "It's just the way they are treated. All they ask for is: 'Treat us humanely and pay us our money, because that's why we're here.' They're not asking for much, right? They understand that they're not in Qatar on a vacation. It's not a job where you're going to have fun and enjoy it. But it will be enough to pay your recruitment loan back home and support your family somehow. That's why we say 'Don't use people's vulnerability to allow for your system to exploit them.' It's not OK to say 'They come from different or less privileged backgrounds, so whatever we offer them here is better than what they get back in their home countries.' Qatar, like any other government, has an obligation to ensure that every person on its territory is enjoying their human rights, including being treated fairly and paid on time and not suffering any labor abuses."

The message came from David (not his real name) in Qatar on WhatsApp in May, in reference to FIFA inspections and the subcontractor he works for:

DAVID: *Hey brother*
I'm David in Qatar one day you did for us interview
ME: *Hi David, it's good to hear from you. How are you?*
DAVID: *I'm good brother you are still in qatar*
ME: *Good to hear. I am at home in New York now. I'll be in Qatar for the World Cup in November and December.*
DAVID: *OK I want you to come in our company yu see how we live cause this people are lies they brought other people to interview in accommodation and they lock us inside another accommodation for us to not talk with fifa people*
ME: *I'm so sorry to hear that. Are you OK?*
DAVID: *My company is called —— it is very bad we pass alot off staff but people are afraid to say that why I look for your number*
ME: *Thanks for contacting me. I'm writing a story soon on worker treatment in Qatar. Would you be OK speaking to me again? I wouldn't use your name.*
DAVID: *This is how we live six people per room*

[embedded video showing cramped, cluttered conditions, with three bunk beds in a room about twelve by twelve feet]

People working in hotel are living good two people per room but us supply company we pass alot of staff and your fifa people are hide alot of things. If you work in hotel they will give you good place to live most people are suffering from this contract company they treat us like animals

I still get regular WhatsApp messages from some of the workers I interviewed in Qatar. Most of them are questions about whether I can help them obtain work visas for the United States. It's difficult. There's almost nothing I can do in that area.

When I visited Qatar in February, it did not appear that FIFA was doing due diligence on hotels and subcontractors supplying those hotels with laborers. A FIFA statement says it has since conducted an audit of Qatari hotels. Based on the WhatsApp message I received, it's fair to ask if those FIFA audits are being corrupted by some of those being audited.

───────

IN MAY, AMNESTY International issued a new report and a public call for FIFA and the Qatari government to create a fund for Qatar's migrant workers of $440 million—an amount equal to the prize money FIFA will give for World Cup 2022.

So far, FIFA and Qatar have not responded. Amnesty's Romanos hopes the players from the thirty-two World Cup teams will speak up on behalf of Qatar's migrant workers.

"When FIFA awarded Qatar the right to host this World Cup, it knew or should have known about the labor abuses that would happen as a result of the labor system in place in the country," Romanos told me. "It wasn't a secret. It was well documented that there is the kafala system, exploitation will happen. Migrant workers will be the ones building this World Cup and preparing Qatar to host it. Yet FIFA chose to give Qatar this right without imposing on the country any labor conditions to protect migrant workers.

"So fast-forward ten years," she went on, "and we've seen lots of abuses. While acknowledging some reforms are being put in place, we shouldn't forget the past abuses. A lot of people suffered: those who died, those who lost their salaries, those who paid recruitment fees. That's why we call on FIFA to work with the Qatari government to set up a remedy program to compensate workers who suffered to make this World Cup."

The migrant workers I spoke to on my visit to Qatar were, to a person, extremely thoughtful. Several had educations that in the U.S. would have targeted them for much higher-paying jobs. Their dignity and honor give them powerful voices.

"Some people might have come through some bad things here by not going through proper channels," one worker told me. "If you go through the proper channels, your government knows you're here, the government of Qatar knows you're here. But if you step out of channels, you won't be treated good. Because they know you're different. The law is not on your side."

Another told me, "We appreciate the improvement made by the [Qatari] government. I don't think they will go back [to previous laws after the World Cup]. But the issues are on ground level. The laws are OK, but implementation at the ground level, there's some improvement needed. The people in management in companies—that's the challenge in implementing the rules."

An Unexpected Detention by World Cup Security

FROM FÚTBOL WITH GRANT WAHL, NOVEMBER 21, 2022

In a February 2022 audio clip embedded in Part I of "The Qatar Chronicles," Wahl talked about the precautions he was taking to avoid the attention of Qatari authorities. "I don't want to be detained," he noted. "At all." He would suffer just that fate nine months later—not for his reporting, but for the rainbow T-shirt he wore to the United States' opening match, against Wales. Both FIFA and Qatar had issued assurances before the tournament that expressions of LGBTQ+ pride and support would be permitted, and in Part II of "The Qatar Chronicles," a U.S. Soccer official who had lived in Qatar for six years and led the American Chamber of Commerce there told Wahl, "Nothing's going to happen if people are walking around in rainbow flags."

Wahl's detention made international news, as did the confiscation of rainbow hats from Wales supporters trying to enter the same ground. Wahl eventually made it into the stadium that night; Doug Zimmerman of ISI Photos snapped a shot of him at his pressroom workstation, decked out in the shirt—a picture that led numerous news reports after Wahl's death. In late December 2022, the apparel company Olive and York created a limited-edition Grant Wahl memorial soccer jersey inspired by that tee: black with rainbow sleeves, Wahl's profile as the crest, and a lyric from his favorite band, the National, on the inside collar. It sold out within days, with proceeds going to the International Women's Media Foundation. After Wahl's belongings were repatriated, his wife, Céline, gave the original shirt to his brother, Eric, who is gay. "You understood me," Eric says to his late brother in a June 2023 video tribute in which Eric wears the shirt to an MLS match in Kansas City. "You understood that queer people were part of a world that wasn't always welcoming. . . . Wearing that shirt was courageous. It put you in a line of fire that I knew you could handle. Because you weren't doing it just for me. You were doing it for all of us."

DOHA, QATAR—WHEN I ARRIVED AT THE STADIUM MEDIA EN-
trance to cover the United States–Wales World Cup game today
wearing a rainbow soccer ball T-shirt supporting the LGBTQ community, the security guards refused to let me in, detained me for twenty-
five minutes, and angrily demanded that I remove my T-shirt.

"You have to change your shirt," one guard told me. "It's not allowed."

Same-sex relationships are illegal in Qatar. But FIFA has been clear in
saying that the rainbow flag would be welcomed at the World Cup. The
Qatari regime, however, has said very little on the topic, raising concerns that things would be different on the ground.

I sent out a hasty tweet:

> Just now: Security guard refusing to let me into the stadium for USA-
> Wales. "You have to change your shirt. It's not allowed."

A moment after tweeting that, one guard forcibly ripped my phone
from my hands.

Nearly half an hour passed. One security guard told me that my shirt
was "political" and not allowed. Another continually refused to give me
back my phone. Another guard yelled at me as he stood above me—
I was sitting on a chair by now—that I had to remove my shirt.

I told him no.

"You can make this easy. Take off your shirt," one said.

I told him no, adding that my shirt wasn't political at all.

My friend Andrew Das, a reporter for *The New York Times,* walked
past, and I informed him what was going on. They detained him, too.

Eventually, the guards made me stand up, turn around, and face the
CCTV camera above us.

"Are you from the U.K.?" one guard asked.

"New York," I said. This was getting annoying. I arrived when I did so
I'd have enough time to watch the Netherlands-Senegal game, and now
I was missing it.

Finally, they let Andy go. And then a security commander approached
me. He said they were letting me through and apologized. We shook
hands.

One of the security guards told me they were just trying to protect me from fans inside who could harm me for wearing the shirt.

(A FIFA rep later apologized to me as well.)

But the entire episode left me wondering: What's it like for ordinary Qataris who might wear a rainbow shirt when the world isn't watching here? What's that like?

They Just Don't Care

FROM FÚTBOL WITH GRANT WAHL, DECEMBER 8, 2022

As with his first feature for *Sports Illustrated,* on the Howard University soccer team (page 146), so Wahl's penultimate published piece spotlights injustice and holds the powerful to account, as he torches Qatari and FIFA officials for their appalling indifference to the death of a migrant worker during the World Cup. Wahl himself died the following day of an aortic aneurysm while covering the quarterfinal match between Argentina and the Netherlands.

Though the circle on his professional career was closed, much of Wahl's work remains available through the *Sports Illustrated* Vault, SI.com, YouTube, podcast platforms, and his Substack site, whose paywall was removed after his death. Fútbol with Grant Wahl had been thriving, its paid subscription numbers exceeding Wahl's projections for the first year—though those numbers were minuscule compared to the audience he had reached during the heyday of *SI.* "He was really excited because he'd gotten his three thousandth paid subscription to his Substack," says sportswriter Jeff Pearlman, recalling one of his last exchanges with his former *SI* and recent Substack colleague. "I think a lot of people don't know how Substack works and how hard it is to get paid subscriptions. I remember thinking at the time how cool it is that a guy who at one point was writing for a magazine that had three million subscribers was just as passionate, if not more so, about writing for three thousand." Adds longtime colleague Jon Wertheim, "He just wanted his name associated with quality. That was the driver. That's what mattered to him."

DOHA, QATAR—THEY JUST DON'T CARE.

The Supreme Committee in charge of Qatar's World Cup doesn't care that a Filipino migrant worker died at Saudi Arabia's training resort during the group stage. He suffered a fatal blow to the head during a fall in a forklift accident (information that was kept under wraps until being broken by The Athletic's Adam Crafton).

We know the Qatari Supreme Committee doesn't care because its CEO, Nasser Al-Khater, told you all you needed to hear in an interview with the BBC that was breathtaking in its crassness.

"We're in the middle of a World Cup, and we have a successful World Cup. And this is something that you want to talk about right now?" Al-Khater said when asked about the worker's death. "I mean, death is a natural part of life, whether it's at work, whether it's in your sleep. Of course, a worker died. Our condolences go to his family. However, it's strange that this is something that you wanted to focus on as your first question."

He actually said that. But Al-Khater didn't stop there.

"Everything that has been said and everything that has been re-flected about worker deaths here has been absolutely false," he said. "This theme, this negativity around the World Cup, has been some-thing that we've been faced with, unfortunately. We are a bit disap-pointed that the journalists have been exacerbating this false narrative, and honestly I think a lot of the journalists have to question themselves and reflect on why they've been trying to bang on about the subject for so long."

Just think of the context in which Al-Khater said this. A migrant worker died here during the World Cup. If I were a family member of the worker who died, I can't imagine how I would feel.

Al-Khater and the Qataris really do see themselves as the victims here and not what they really are: the rich and powerful petrobarons who have built an empire in the desert on the backs of far too many migrant workers who have been treated poorly and, yes, have died.

How many have died? We'll never know for sure, in part because Qatar hasn't cared enough to document the losses.

Last year, The Guardian's Pete Pattisson cited government sources to report that more than 6,500 migrant workers had died in Qatar in the decade since the country was awarded the World Cup in 2010. (A total of forty deaths have been tied to World Cup stadium construction, though nearly all of Qatar's infrastructure growth has some connection to the World Cup.)

Qatari officials claim the migrant mortality rate is within the expected range given the workforce size, but experts Amnesty International spoke to were skeptical of that claim because the data on migrant deaths is of such low quality.

Meanwhile, Amnesty says Qatar has failed to properly investigate up to 70 percent of its migrant worker deaths, noting that "in a well-resourced health system, it should be possible to identify the exact cause of death in all but 1% of cases."

When a country fails to take the time to properly investigate up to 70 percent of its migrant worker deaths, that's a sign: They just don't care.

Last week, the general secretary of the Supreme Committee, Hassan Al-Thawadi, told Piers Morgan on his TV show that "between four hundred and five hundred" migrant workers have died on World Cup–related projects. A Supreme Committee spokesperson later said those numbers referred to national statistics for all work-related deaths in Qatar from 2014 to 2020.

On Friday, FIFA general secretary Fatma Samoura didn't look good, either, evading questions on the Filipino worker's death at the Saudi camp. Entering a FIFA meeting, she was asked by a Reuters reporter about the fatality. "If you want [an update on] the conference, I'm ready," she said. "If it is about anything else, I'm sorry. We've already elaborated long, long interventions and messages on what we are doing with Qatar. So I don't think that [question] is appropriate when people are coming here to learn things, that we are talking about things we have already discussed, months and months and months, time and time again. Sorry. Thank you. Bye."

Let me be clear here: Covering a worker's death, covering issues of human rights and this World Cup, isn't a sign of being anti-Islamic. The Middle East deserved to host a World Cup at some point. And Western countries have all sorts of their own problems. But this World Cup has been a human rights disaster. My friend Musa Okwonga got it right more than a month ago, when he tweeted:

The World Cup in Qatar has already failed, and its organizers know it. The goal of each World Cup is to get the bulk of its viewers to suspend their disbelief and focus on nothing but the football: that won't happen. The only question now is as to the degree of that fail-ure.

Today we saw the evidence right in front of us from the CEO of the Qatari Supreme Committee organizing the World Cup. A worker died, and they just don't care.

Acknowledgments

FRIENDS AND ADMIRERS FROM AROUND THE WORLD HAVE COME together to affirm Grant Wahl's memory and legacy since his death in December 2022. In much the same way, a constellation of people rallied to help make this tribute to his life and work a reality.

Grant got his start at *The Daily Princetonian,* and among former *Prince* staffers and current trustees who assisted in this project are David Baumgarten, Nate Ewell, David Landes, and Tom Weber. Rosalba Varallo Recchia, a special collections archivist at Princeton University, helped unearth copies of Grant's early work for a since-discontinued student publication, *The Vigil.* Grant could trace back to college two of his original mentors in soccer, Bob Bradley and Jesse Marsch; both abided as friends and sources as Grant made his way as a journalist, and each answered our questions promptly and thoughtfully.

Grant's uncle Robert Wahl helped shed light on the earliest chapters of the Wahl family story.

An array of Grant's colleagues during nearly a quarter century at *Sports Illustrated* suggested pieces for inclusion and provided rich material for the introduction and headnotes. Many of these coworkers are quoted in the text, sometimes from podcast or print interviews. They include Bill Colson, Avi Creditor, Richard Deitsch, Adam Duerson, Lee Feiner, Hank Hersch, Greg Kelly, Jeff Pearlman, Melissa Segura, Chris Stone, Jenny Vrentas, and Jon Wertheim. We're particularly grateful to Prem Kalliat and Authentic Brands Group, without whose cooperation this book would have never found its way into print. We're likewise in debt to Bryan Curtis, Gabriele Marcotti, and Musa Okwonga, as well as the team that pulled together the extraordinary celebration of Grant's life on December 21, 2022: Blythe Adamson, Stephanie Gounder, Ingrid Herrera, Carolyn Jasik, Jon-Claude Nix, Joel Samuels, and Sabine Wallis.

A couple of stalwarts in Grant's life as an author of books—his agent,

Chris Parris-Lamb, and his editor, Mary Reynics—left that December 2022 celebration struck by much the same thought we had: that this begs for a book. We're grateful for the mind meld between Chris and Mary and in turn with us, as well as for the contributions of Aru Menon at the Gernert Company and many members of the Ballantine publishing team at Penguin Random House: Wendy Wong, Ivanka Perez, Kara Welsh, Kim Hovey, Jennifer Hershey, Kathleen Quinlan, Megan Whalen, Jennifer Garza, Steven Boriack, Mark Maguire, Craig Adams, and Simon Sullivan, and copy editor Lynn Anderson.

Finally, we wish to thank Grant's widow, Céline Gounder, and his brother, Eric Wahl, for their support, forbearance, and grace. They helped set the general contours of this collection and signed off on its particulars. Without their willingness to do at least some of their grieving in public and to pay conscientious attention to this project during an excruciatingly hard time in their lives, this book would never have come to be.

—MARK MRAVIC and ALEXANDER WOLFF, editors

Grant Wahl spent the bulk of his career at *Sports Illustrated*, writing for the magazine and the website, and much of his work can be found online in *SI*'s print and digital archives.

Sports Illustrated

Every issue of *Sports Illustrated* from the magazine's launch in August 1954 through September 2019 is available on the *SI* Vault at si.com/vault. The archive includes PDF versions of each magazine issue and digitized versions of most stories. Here you will find Wahl's magazine features and columns from 1997 on, ranging from the college basketball beat— including his NCAA tournament finals pieces—to soccer, including coverage of the men's and women's World Cups, Olympics, European championships, and the U.S. domestic game. In a number of instances you'll find Wahl dipping back into his past for the germs of stories, including in a couple of pieces from 2003: a feature about the spread of the Princeton Offense, for which he dusted off some of his oldest basketball contacts; and a puckish essay about his mother having been a classmate of Wilt Chamberlain's at Kansas. You'll even find a few pieces from outside his regular beats—stories on rugby, college football, and the NFL, including a 2002 cover story billed as the WAR FOR TEXAS, as the expansion Houston Texans prepared to face the Dallas Cowboys in their first game. Also available are two groundbreaking investigative pieces written with colleague Jon Wertheim: a 1998 cover story, "Where's Daddy?," about athletes fathering children out of wedlock, and a 2003 exposé on hazing in a Long Island high school, "A Rite Gone Terribly Wrong."

While digitized versions of some of the more prominent pieces in the *SI* Vault have received a reader-friendly design treatment, others are in more bare-bones condition. The search function for the site is not optimal, so it helps if readers know what they're looking for. At this time, access to the *SI* Vault requires a subscription after a set number of free articles.

The Web

Wahl's Substack site, grantwahl.com, which launched in August 2021, remains up and running, with the paywall for his premium content removed. Here readers will find the long-form stories he worked on as an independent journalist—including a delightful feature on Howard Webb and Bibi Steinhaus, two of the world's top international referees and also husband and wife; and a deep dive into the culture shift behind the rise of Barcelona's women's team—as well as weekly newsletters, interviews, game stories, reaction pieces, and his reporting on the 2022 World Cup in Qatar, including his daily posts during the tournament.

Wahl's regular Planet Fútbol columns for SI.com, as well as his Q&As, mailbags, posts from reporting trips, and other content, are available on the *Sports Illustrated* website going back to 2008, at si.com/author/grant-wahl. Many of his print magazine stories after 2010 are also posted there, as are long-form features he wrote exclusively for the website. His penultimate story for SI.com was a 2021 investigation into the possibly politically motivated murder of an Azerbaijani reporter, "A Journalist Died over a Soccer Feud. . . . or Was There a More Sinister State Plot Involved?"

Wahl's web content from before 2008 is harder to come by, as *SI* went through several server migrations and URL changes that consigned older digital content to the ether. The truly intrepid reader looking for his online reporting from, say, the 2002 World Cup or 2004 Olympics, or his regular soccer and basketball columns from the early 2000s, can take their chances with the hit-and-miss results on the internet Wayback Machine at web.archive.org, searching with the URL sportsillustrated.cnn.com.

Video

Wahl's video work for *SI* and other outlets included news hits, sideline reporting, onsite dispatches from matches and tournaments, and, beginning in the mid-2010s, a weekly show he hosted on SI.com offering analysis, opinion, and guest interviews.

He was most drawn to the opportunities for long-form video story-telling. Three projects stand out.

- Ahead of the 2018 World Cup, Wahl and producer Lee Feiner traveled to Iceland, Japan, Argentina, and Germany for a four-part series, *Exploring Planet Fútbol,* immersing themselves in the distinctive soccer cultures of each of those countries. In the Argentina episode, Wahl reunited with some of the friends he had made on his visits to the country as a college student in the 1990s, and his love of his adopted second home shone through. For the Iceland episode, he and Feiner circuited the island in a camper van, visiting remote villages and marveling at the rug-ged landscape as they explored how a tiny, isolated nation of 300,000 succeeded in qualifying for the world's most prominent and exclusive sporting event. In one outtake, Feiner suggests that they pull over for a view of the ocean. As Wahl clambers precariously up an icy, rock-strewn incline in the looming dark-ness, wind whipping off the Norwegian Sea, he takes a little poke at an *SI* friend and colleague from a more mainstream beat: "Peter King wouldn't do this, just so you know!" *Exploring Planet Fútbol* is available on YouTube.

- Drawing on his extensive experience coving the U.S.-Mexico soccer dynamic, Wahl served as coproducer for (as well as ap-pearing in) *Good Rivals,* a three-part Prime Video series from Meadowlark Media, former ESPN president John Skipper's pro-duction company. Originally titled *Good Neighbors,* the series drew on the perspectives of the major figures in American and Mexican soccer over the last three decades to go beyond sports, probing the wider cultural and political forces that influence the sporting rivalry and reflect the complex, troubled, and promis-ing relationship between the two border countries.

- In August 2022, Wahl sat down with CBS Sports for a lengthy interview that served as the foundation for the three-part series *The Billion Dollar Goal,* which recounts the tortuous history of soccer in America, from its long years in the wilderness to the climactic moment in 1989 when Paul Caligiuri's game-winner against Trinidad & Tobago sent the men's national team to the 1990 World Cup—and, as Wahl puts it, "changed the trajectory of soccer in the United States." Wahl served as supervising producer for the series, which features rare archival footage; interviews with players, analysts, and historians; and surprising stories of soccer's struggles, setbacks, and ultimate acceptance. *The Billion Dollar Goal,* which debuted on Paramount+ in December 2023, is dedicated "to Grant Wahl and his contribution to American soccer."

Podcasts

A month after leaving *SI,* Wahl launched his independent twice-weekly podcast, *Fútbol with Grant Wahl,* offering analysis, opinion, and interviews. Despite having no legacy media backing, the podcast attracted the biggest names in American and international soccer and beyond, from Landon Donovan and Alex Morgan to Jürgen Klopp and Jason Sudeikis, as well as prominent journalists and broadcasters from around the world. He also regularly welcomed young reporters and podcasters onto his show, to give them a lift up and share his reach. He did much the same at *SI* with his weekly *Planet Fútbol* podcasts from the mid-2010s to April 2020. Both are available on all major podcast platforms.

In addition to his weekly work, Wahl produced two serial podcasts:

- *Throwback,* a six-episode series for *Sports Illustrated* on the 1991 Women's World Cup and the birth of the U.S. women's team, offers a deep dive into U.S. soccer prehistory—the hazy days of the 1980s, before either the men's team or the women had made a national impression—and examines the legacy of that first U.S. team to win a World Cup. The magazine piece included in this volume is a companion to that series.

- *American Prodigy, Season 1,* an eight-episode series for Bluewire Podcasts, traces the arc of Freddy Adu from a thirteen-year-old soccer phenom billed as "the next Pelé" to a thirty-year-old "what might have been" who reflects on his experience with wistful bemusement. Through the series Wahl explores America's fascination with the concept of the sports prodigy, the pressures such a designation places on young athletes, the role of the media (himself included) in building up expectations, and what happens when those expectations run up against reality.

Throwback and *American Prodigy* are available on major podcast platforms.

Photo Credits

About the Authors

GRANT WAHL spent nearly twenty-five years on the staff at *Sports Illustrated*. While he primarily covered basketball early in his career—including a groundbreaking cover story on a high schooler named LeBron James—his true passion was soccer. Wahl emerged as the authoritative American voice on the sport and a key driver of its growth in the United States. He made an impact in podcasts and video series, through a vibrant social media presence, and in two books, *Masters of Modern Soccer: How the World's Best Play the Twenty-first-Century Game* and the *New York Times* bestseller *The Beckham Experiment: How the World's Most Famous Athlete Tried to Conquer America*. His Substack, Fútbol with Grant Wahl, burnished his reputation as one of sports journalism's most influential and distinctive voices. He was posthumously inducted into the U.S. Basketball Writers Association Hall of Fame and awarded the National Soccer Hall of Fame's Colin Jose Media Award for contributions to the American game.

grantwahl.com

DR. CÉLINE GOUNDER is an internationally renowned internist, infectious disease specialist, and epidemiologist. In addition to serving as a clinical associate professor of medicine and infectious diseases at New York University, she cares for patients at New York's Bellevue Hospital Center and works as a podcaster and as a journalist and commentator for CBS News and KFF. Her specialties include all kinds of epidemics, from Covid, Ebola, and opioid to mental health, gun violence, and disinformation. She and Grant Wahl were married in 2001.

MARK MRAVIC was an editor at *Sports Illustrated* for more than two decades. He worked closely with Grant Wahl on coverage of international and domestic soccer and in pushing for soccer's integration into the American sports mainstream, and served as editor for Wahl's Substack site from its launch in 2021. He lives in Noank, Connecticut.

ALEXANDER WOLFF spent thirty-six years on the staff of *Sports Illustrated*, overlapping with Grant Wahl for two decades. He is a former Ferris Professor of Journalism at Princeton University and the author of many books, including *Big Game, Small World: A Basketball Adventure* and *Endpapers: A Family Story of Books, War, Escape, and Home.* The editor of the Library of America collection *Basketball: Great Writing About America's Game,* he lives in the Champlain Valley of Vermont.